AND HELL
FOLLOWED
WITH HER

# AND HELL
# FOLLOWED
# WITH HER

*Crossing the Dark Side of
the American Border*

## DAVID NEIWERT

NATION
BOOKS
New York

Published by Nation Books,
A Member of the Perseus Books Group
116 East 16th Street, 8th Floor
New York, NY 10003

Nation Books is a co-publishing venture of the Nation Institute and
the Perseus Books Group

Books published by Nation Books are available at special discounts for bulk
purchases in the United States by corporations, institutions, and other organizations.
For more information, please contact the Special Markets Department at the Perseus
Books Group, 2300 Chestnut Street, Suite 200, Philadelphia, PA 19103, or call
(800) 810-4145, ext. 5000, or e-mail special.markets@perseusbooks.com.

Library of Congress Cataloging-in-Publication Data
   Neiwert, David A., 1956–
And hell followed with her : Crossing the dark side of the American border / David
Neiwert.
     p.   cm.
   Includes bibliographical references and index.
   ISBN 978-1-56858-725-7 (hardcover : alk. paper)—
ISBN 978-1-56858-970-1 (e-book)
    1. Border patrols—Mexican-American Border Region.   I. Title.
JV6483.N43 2013
363.28'509721—dc23
                                        2012036641

10 9 8 7 6 5 4 3 2 1

*To Len and Dee, Who Taught Me to Stand Up*

*Wolves cull themselves, man. What other creature could? And is the race of man not more predacious yet? The way of the world is to bloom and to flower and die but in the affairs of men there is no waning and the noon of his expression signals the onset of night. His spirit is exhausted at the peak of its achievement. His meridian is at once his darkening and the evening of his day.*

—CORMAC MCCARTHY,
*Blood Meridian: Or the Evening Redness in the West*

# CONTENTS

# 1

# "I Can't Believe They Killed My Family"

The Flores-Gonzalez home in Arivaca. DAVID NEIWERT PHOTO

Night descends like grace on the Arizona desert. It endows the landscape, and everything in it, with dark cool relief from the relentless, suffocating heat of the daytime. Things are different in the winter, when everything is colder, but by late spring in Arizona, the dusk becomes a respite and a refuge for the people and the creatures who live here.

But nightfall does not always bring peace. The daytime desert heat often boils tempers, but it is after dark that Arizona police often find themselves the busiest, as though the setting sun releases all the bad feeling and bad luck that has built up during the day, expiating it in violence.

The people who work as dispatchers in Arizona's law enforcement offices know all about this phenomenon. In the wintertime, when the days are cooler and not as oppressive—and the nights decidedly colder—they see little difference, but by late spring in Arizona, crimes become a common part of nighttime duty.

Tanya Remsburg had worked a lot of nights. In her twenties, she is tall and slender, good at her job. In the late spring of 2009, she was doing what she had done for two and a half years for the dispatchers in the Pima County Sheriff's Office in Tucson: taking emergency 911 calls. In Pima County alone, dispatchers handle about five hundred calls a day. Over the years, Remsburg had processed thousands of calls for help—so many that sometimes they all blurred together.

Except for one: the call that came after midnight in the first hour of May 30, 2009.

Mostly it had been an ordinary night. A couple of car crashes—no fatalities. A bar fight. A convenience-store robbery. It had been a long day. Tanya was ready to call it a night. She was scheduled to clock out at 1 a.m.

And then came the call at 12:49 a.m. The board indicated that it originated in Arivaca, a little desert town twelve miles north of the Mexico border and just over an hour's drive south and west from Tucson.

"911, where is your emergency?"

It was a soft, meek woman's voice.

"Ma'am," she said, in the twangy patois of local rural Arizonans, "somebody just come in and shot my daughter and my husband."

"They shot them?" Tanya Remsburg sat up straight and began typing into her computer system, alerting her coworkers and deputies. Upon seeing her messages, the office's dispatchers began scrambling.

"Yes. I need emergency right away."

"What's your address?"

The woman gave her an address on Mesquite Place in Arivaca, and Remsburg typed it into the computer and kept typing, clacking the keys loudly. The dispatchers, reading as she typed, had meanwhile contacted deputies at the sheriff's satellite station in Green Valley, about thirty miles south of Tucson. It was the closest station to Arivaca, but getting there would take time, since the town was yet another thirty miles away.

"And your phone number? Stay on the line with me—they're dispatching as we speak, OK? What's your number?"

The caller read her number aloud, and Remsburg typed that too.

"And they shot your husband and your daughter? Are they, are they—conscious?"

The woman gave a little sob. "Please, please, ma'am, please. She's bleeding out of her mouth. Please."

"How old is your daughter?"

"She's ten."

"Ten. And where, where were they shot?"

"In the head. In the head. Should I pick her up so she's not bleeding?"

"No, no, I want you to leave her where she is, OK? What I'm gonna do—"

Suddenly there were other voices in the background. Someone—a woman's voice, but not the woman's on the phone—said, "Oh, shit!" Then she shouted something else indistinguishable.

Now Remsburg was alarmed. "Are they still there? The people who were there, that shot them?"

The woman was panicked. "They're coming back in! They're coming back in!"

"Do you know who they are?"

There was no answer. Instead, the popping sound of gunfire erupted over the line. It went on for another minute or so. Somewhere amid the shots and the shouting, there was a man's voice too. Remsburg could hear the caller cursing: "Fucking assholes! Get the fuck out of here! You've done enough!" Then there were more gunshots.

Eventually, the gunfire subsided, and Remsburg could hear the woman pick the phone back up.

"Are you still there? Are you OK?"

"Ma'am, I don't know. I'm scared."

"OK." Remsburg was thinking hard, trying to collect her own wits and re-assure the woman on the other end. She had never had to handle a call like this.

"I'm scared," the woman repeated in her meek voice.

"OK. How, how many people were there?"

"I don't know, ma'am. They—I was asleep, and I can't even move. I've been shot myself. I don't even—"

"OK, where were you shot?"

"I think I'm shot in the leg. I'm not sure, ma'am."

"OK." Remsburg entered that data into her computer, and her fellow dispatchers now began alerting medical authorities. Somewhere in Green Valley, an ambulance crew was summoned.

"Please hurry," the woman pleaded.

"Are you armed?"

"Yeah."

"OK. They're coming—lights and sirens, OK? They are coming." It was getting on five minutes now.

"Ma'am, please hurry."

"And you—did you see any of them?"

"No, I didn't. I just got up, ma'am, because they told us that the—they told us that somebody was, uh, had escaped jail or something, they want to come in and look at my house. And they just shot my husband. And they shot my daughter. And they shot me."

"OK." They both grew quiet, and in the silence, the horror started to sink in.

"Oh my God, ma'am," the woman sobbed.

"OK, just—"

"I can't believe this is happening."

"Yeah, they are coming, OK? You said that they—they told your husband that they wanted to come in 'cause there was, uh, an escaped person?"

"Yes. And that the whole party was surrounded—I'm sorry, that the whole property was surrounded, with Border Patrol and everything."

On the other end, the caller moaned in pain. "Ow—fuck, my leg is killing me, ma'am," she pleaded. "How long is it gonna take them to get here?"

It seemed as if it took forever, though in truth it was only another fifteen minutes or so before law enforcement officers arrived on the scene—a pretty reasonable time, considering the distances they had to cover and the winding nature of the desert roads en route. But for Tanya Remsburg and the wounded caller, it felt like an eternity. Every second seemed important, weighty. And they added up.

Remsburg kept the woman on the phone talking. She gathered more details—what kind of gun the caller had, descriptions of the killers—and tried to help her stay calm.

"Oh my God," the caller said at one point, as it all started to sink in. "I can't believe they killed my family."

Remsburg struggled to keep her own emotions in check. She asked the woman bland questions, like where in the house she was located.

"I'm in the kitchen right here just staring at the door."

"Are you with your—are you with your husband and your daughter?"

"No. I don't even want to look at them, ma'am."

Remsburg changed the subject to the killers, trying to gather information. The woman described a total of three people she had seen and a fourth she had heard. The two who had carried out the shootings were a "super tall" male in black face paint and "a shorter fat woman." They wore camouflage. And they were both white. The other two men, she said, were "Mexicans" who spoke Spanish to each other and came in later, while her home was being ransacked.

"And I have one of their guns that they fucking left here."

"OK, don't touch that. OK, do not touch that."

"OK. I'm sorry I'm cussing."

Remsburg almost wanted to laugh: the woman was unfailingly polite. "No, no. You're fine." There was a little sob on the other end. "Hon, you're fine. Don't worry. It's fine. Just don't worry about your cussing."

The woman gave more details. The tall man, she said, had done the actual shooting of the three of them: "Yeah, he had shot me, and I pretended like I was dead. And my daughter was crying when they shot her too."

Inevitably they would fall silent as Remsburg transcribed the information, and in those moments the wait felt interminable. Remsburg tried to reassure her. "OK, they are coming—lights and sirens. They have units in the area, OK? But I want you to stay on the line with me until they have someone with you." She knew that deputies were speeding as fast as they could, but the road to Arivaca is narrow and winding, and even the fastest cars can only go so fast on it.

Remsburg realized there was important information still to gather and tried to fathom why someone might attempt a home-invasion robbery that far into the desert and in a poor little town like Arivaca, where there are very few people with any wealth. "Now, do you—I mean, was there any, like, drugs involved? Or are they just looking for money? What were they, do you know?"

"I couldn't tell. She just said hurry up and get what we need. But I mean—we don't have any drugs or anything like that in this house."

"OK. Do you think maybe it was a mistake? Do any of your neighbors have anything?"

"I don't know."

"OK."

The woman kept complaining about her pain, telling her how badly her leg hurt. Eventually she said: "I've got to lay down, ma'am. I'm sorry."

"OK. That's fine, lay down but take the phone with you, OK? Keep me on the line. So you can keep me updated on how you're doing. Is your, your daughter still crying?"

"No. She's—I think she's gone now."

"OK."

And so they talked. They talked about what happened, and again the woman described how two people, one of them in black face paint, came up to her door and demanded to be let in, and then, when her husband noticed something not right about them—there was tape on one of their guns—the "tall man" simply turned and shot him. And then shot her. She lay on the floor and pretended to be dead while their daughter cried and asked the killers why they had shot her parents and pleaded with them not to shoot her. And then they shot her, too.

About ten minutes into the call the woman's voice became low and quiet and slow; she was beginning to lose consciousness. This was dangerous: if she blacked out, they might lose her to shock from blood loss. So Remsburg kept talking to her—about anything: getting her to talk about what had just happened, trying to get her to describe the assailants. Remsburg grew concerned momentarily that the woman wanted to die with her family.

"You're not doing anything, you're not going to do anything drastic, are you?" Remsburg asked worriedly.

"Like what?"

"Like hurt yourself."

"I have another daughter."

"OK. And she's not there, right?"

"No, she actually spent the night at my mom's house, thank God."

Her words were becoming slurred and her voice heavy. Remsburg kept her talking, though, for another eight minutes, getting her to describe the property—it was out near the end of a rural road, not far from the Arivaca Community Center, so it was simple to find but distant—and the fence around it so deputies would identify it more quickly.

Finally, the woman told her: "I hear cars driving back and forth."

"Does it sound like they're speeding?"

"Yeah."

"OK, we do have units there. Keep on the line, OK, until there's someone with you."

"You sure it's them?"

"I'm sure it's them. My dispatcher just told me that someone's there now. And they have Border Patrol with them, OK?"

"OK."

Remsburg advised her to push the gun away from her, but it wasn't clear if the woman heard. But soon there were male voices from somewhere in the room, and the woman was no longer listening to her. She was talking to officers: "I'm here in the kitchen on 911, sir. I'm right here. And there's a gun."

Remsburg could hear more voices. "Is he with you?" she asked.

"Yeah, he's with me."

"OK, I'll let you go."

"OK."

"All right, bye-bye."

Tanya Remsburg wound up testifying three times in three separate trials about that night, reliving it each time. But she has refused to ever discuss it publicly. Two years afterward, she would leave the employ of Pima County, undone by that single call.

||

Brisenia Flores loved animals, which was why she was sleeping in the living room that night.

All of her friends at her elementary school in Amado, twenty-two miles away on that same winding road into Arivaca, knew Brisenia was crazy about animals. All kinds: domestic, wild, exotic animals. She did reports on them. Talked about them all the time. Drew pictures of them.

Of course, since she lived out in the Arizona desert, she was familiar with nearly all the wild creatures who made it their home: the birds, the deer, the fish who lived in the nearby lake, the javelinas and cougars and bobcats and grey foxes who lived in the nearby mountains. She even liked the small creatures like the tiny lizards who skittered across her yard and the desert landscape wherever she walked. Her teachers were impressed with her broad array of knowledge and tried to encourage it.

But she also liked domestic animals. Her dad owned a couple of horses and kept them on their property, and she liked to feed them and water them and sometimes ride them. She kept a virtual menagerie in her home, too. She had a cage with guinea pigs, a couple of cats—who liked to play on the big cat gym her parents had bought that was in the living room—some rabbits, and two dogs, including a new puppy she had gotten the month before.

There was also a terrarium with turtles in it, but those belonged to her mother, Gina, who loved animals too. Her big sister, Alexandra—two years her senior—liked animals but nothing like Brisenia, who was practically obsessive about them. She was naturally empathic: one of those rare people who could feel what animals felt and respond in kind. At times it made everyone around her a little exasperated, but that was just Brisenia, because she was the same way with people. People who love well are well loved.

School had just let out the previous Wednesday. Summers in Arizona can be painfully boring for kids, especially for those living in the rural desert, because the intense heat forces them to spend much of their days inside—making someone like Brisenia, who longed for time out of doors, restless as a caged badger.

So Gina had signed Brisenia and Alexandra up for the summer camp at the Arivaca Community Center just down at the other end of Mesquite Road from their home, a place where Brisenia spent her afternoons every day anyway and where all her Arivaca friends would be too. But that only lasted a couple of weeks, so she signed both girls up for summer school as well, which meant that in a few weeks they would resume their regular routine of riding the school bus in the morning out to school in Amado to spend the day and riding it back in the afternoon.

Alexandra was lucky: she had gotten to kick-start her vacation on Thursday, because Gina's mother, Romy, had driven down from the Green Valley area to Arivaca to visit her daughter and grandkids, and she took Alexandra back into town with her.

Brisenia was a little jealous. So Gina—who would have to drive into Tucson on Friday anyway to pick up Alexandra—consoled her by promising to take her to town and buy her some new shoes. Brisenia was growing fast, and her toes were already touching the ends of her favorite tennies, so it was something they needed to do before camp started on Monday.

Friday, May 29, turned out to be a busy day. Gina started her day by cleaning out the girls' rooms. Brisenia was fond of letting the dogs, especially her new puppy, sleep on her bed with her, and the bedding smelled of dog. She ran it all through the wash and cleaned the room, vowing not to let the dogs sleep in there any longer, beginning that night.

Gina had lost her big ring of car keys the day before, sometime around when she came back home from taking a CPR class at the community center. So she and Brisenia spent the late morning searching for them, particularly out in the front yard, around the girls' trampoline, where she had first been after getting home the day before.

She was out near their fence along Mesquite Road, and around noon, while she and Brisenia were searching, an aqua-colored Chevy Astro van with tinted windows came driving along the gravel-and-dirt road very slowly. The van had driven up from the south, on Hardscrabble Road, where hardly anyone ever went. Gina looked up at it, curious.

It was unusual to see much of anyone out here in the quiet desert in the middle of the day, especially in a vehicle she had never seen before. She thought to herself that they must be lost. It happened every now and then that tourists would take the wrong turns and wind up out here. Inside the van, it seemed to her, the two occupants she could see in the front—a man and a woman—were talking about her. She waved at them, and they waved back. She then turned back to finding her keys. The van drove on up

Mesquite Road and disappeared in a little cloud of dust. Gina didn't think about it any more.

She eventually gave up looking for her keys, and at around one p.m., Gina and her husband, Junior—his full name was Raul Flores Junior, and he had grown up in Arivaca, where everybody just called him by his nickname—packed up Brisenia in their black Suburban and drove into Tucson. Gina tried calling Romy to find out when they could pick up Alexandra, but Romy had gone with her husband and granddaughter to Madera Canyon—a scenic day-hiking area in the Coronado National Forest—and couldn't be reached.

So the three of them went shopping at a Tucson mall, and Brisenia picked out a new pair of tennies to kick around in. Gina had a bit of banking to do too: the family had driven out to Disneyland the month before, and she needed to pay off her credit card, so she withdrew about $3,000 in cash, with the intention of making it into a money order to send to her card company. She tucked the cash into a side pocket of her big cloth purse.

They finally got a hold of Romy, who was still up at Madera Canyon and would not be back in time for Gina and Junior to pick up either Alexandra or Gina's younger sister, who wanted to come out and spend the weekend in Arivaca with her sister and nieces, as originally planned. But Romy and her husband, Alex, promised to drive them all out to Arivaca in the morning. Gina agreed, and the three of them—Junior, Gina, and Brisenia—hopped back into the Suburban and headed home.

When they got home, night had fallen, and it was time for Brisenia to go to bed. Gina informed her that the dogs could not sleep with her anymore. But her new little puppy would miss her, Brisenia said. Well, Gina told her, you can sleep on the couch with your puppy tonight so he can adjust. Brisenia readily agreed, and they got out a blanket and a pillow, and she snuggled up with the dog on the little love seat in the living room.

Gina was tired and turned in shortly thereafter. Junior stayed up watching a movie on the TV in their bedroom.

## ||

Arivaca is only twelve miles from the Mexican border, and the Altar Valley in which it sits, nestled in between Baboquivari Peak and the Cerro Colorado Mountains, has been a natural corridor for immigrants, both human and animal, traveling between what is now the United States and Mexico for centuries.

This means that, for the past twenty years, it has become increasingly used as a corridor for immigrants crossing illegally into the United States from Mexico. Often traveling at night, they use natural trails through the mountainous and generally treacherous terrain, which is laced with a variety of hostilities: thorny ocotillos and acacia, capable of ripping the flesh off your body, and the usual varieties of spiny cactuses, including a brushy species of cholla whose spines seem to actually jump off the plants and into your skin. Then there are the banditos and human traffickers who are known to waylay border crossers, and most of all the Border Patrol, with their electronic sensors and helicopters and tracking dogs and horse trackers.

In more recent years, Arivaca has attracted a new kind of hostility: border-watch vigilantes, people calling themselves Minutemen, angry American citizens who see the immigrants as invading enemies and whose activities are intended to send a message to the federal government demanding "border security." Most of the Minutemen are simply angry and bellicose, and they want something done about illegal immigration, so they organize, participate, and, most of all, ceaselessly promote themselves in watches along various stretches of the border, intending to catch stray border crossers.

Most of them know their efforts are just a finger in the dike, but they see their watches above all as a way to make a statement, to send a message to bureaucrats in Washington that they want action. Some, however, take the watches even more seriously. They see vigilante action as part of a real solution. And some of these talk cryptically about "taking it to the next level."

For people who have lived in Arivaca a long time, this kind of talk seems alien. Border crossers have been part of their lives for years. The situation had become more tense in the past ten years or so, when the feds shut down former key entry points in well-known border towns like Nogales, which had offered reasonably easy passage without having to resort to crossing in unguarded rural areas; after the shutdown, those rural areas became the primary route for immigrant workers. As the crow flies, Nogales and the Altar Valley in which Arivaca sits are only a few miles distant, but in between them is a maze of "sky islands"—ranges of high mountains like the Cerro Colorado and the Mustang and Tumacácori Mountains. These obstacles have forced immigrants attempting the border crossing to traverse the desert wastes in between, all of which funnel the trekkers into the Altar Valley.

Nowadays, though, people in Arivaca say that wandering border crossers were a much more common sight a decade ago. In the past couple of years, as the Border Patrol has intensified its presence in response to the debate over illegal immigration, much of that traffic has gone away. There are probably three times as many Patrol officers in the valley now, and you cannot drive the twenty-three miles from Amado into Arivaca without encountering at least a dozen of the agency's vehicles, which not only prowl the highway but sit in pullouts and keep watch for border crossers.

It doesn't mean the border crossers have gone away; rather, they have simply become more surreptitious. Often they do their trekking at night. And it means they do a lot of their travel in dry washes—the streambeds that weave throughout the Altar Valley, providing a pathway for the waters that occasionally flood across the valley when it gets its seasonal downpours. On the drive out to Arivaca, the highway is dotted with signs warning when you're about to cross one of these washes, accompanied by a dip in the roadway: "Do Not Drive When Flooded."

A dry wash runs directly behind the Flores-Gonzalez family home, cutting a diagonal slash across its acreage. Indeed, the Border Patrol had paid a couple of late-night visits to the Flores-Gonzalez home in the past as agents pursued suspected border crossers up their wash, but the visits had entailed polite visits by agents seeking permission to access the dry streambed behind their house.

That may have been why one of the first law enforcement agents to arrive at the home in the early morning hours of May 30, and the first to administer help to Gina Gonzalez, was a Border Patrol officer named Don Williams. Sheriff's deputies had been called out first, but they were much farther from Arivaca—and perhaps just as importantly, they did not understand exactly where they were going. The Flores-Gonzalez home was located in a small rural neighborhood consisting of some forty houses on five- to ten-acre lots, spread out on a long rectangular grid about a mile northeast of the town proper. Confusion about how to get there, for those unfamiliar with the area, was common.

Williams is normally employed by the Border Patrol as a horse tracker, but he had the midnight shift that night, which meant staying off his mount and sitting inside a pickup along the roadside, keeping an eye out for border crossers wandering up the washes. The spot where he was stationed that night—at the milepost marking seven miles' distance from Arivaca—was right next to such a wash, so it was a good place to mount a watch.

Then, at about one a.m., came the alarm from the Pima County Sheriff's dispatcher: a double homicide on Mesquite Road. Williams promptly fired up the pickup and sped as fast he could down the winding country road toward Arivaca. As he approached the end of Mesquite Road, he could see a sheriff's deputy pull up from the other direction and park in front of the Flores-Gonzalez home with flashing lights blazing.

Gina Gonzalez's seemingly interminable wait for help was over.

When Williams and the deputy entered the home together, the first thing they saw was Junior Flores on the living room couch. He at first looked as if he were dozing—he was sitting back on the couch, and his right arm was slightly raised, as though he had fallen asleep with a beer in his hand—but the blood streaming from his chest and head from obvious gunshot wounds quickly erased that illusion. He was not breathing.

The next thing they saw was Brisenia, lying on the love seat a few feet away, and there were no illusions about her condition: Her limbs were oddly akimbo, and whoever shot her had made a bloody mess of her little face.

In the kitchen, just out of view, Gina was talking to them, telling them she was there. Williams went in to help her, cautiously at first, while the sheriff's deputy worked his way down the hallway to the bedrooms to see whether anyone else was still in the house. Gina had kicked her husband's .40-caliber handgun away from her body, and Williams pushed it further away, into the entrance to the dining area, and then knelt down to see what he could do.

Gina was bleeding profusely from the wound in her leg, and part of her femur was protruding from the wound. She had another wound in her chest, but it was not draining out as badly. Williams was not trained in emergency first aid, however, and knew he might harm the woman if he tried to do too much, so he gave her a towel, attempted to help her slow the bleeding, and talked to her to try to comfort her. She tried telling him what had happened, but none of it made a lot of sense.

In a little while—Williams said it seemed as if it "was not too long," though time, or at least the memory of it, is always distorted in events like this—emergency medical technicians from Green Valley arrived on the scene and began giving Gina proper care. Williams backed out of the room and began doing what he could to help the deputies with securing the crime scene. Someone said that there was supposed to be another daughter in the house, so he and another deputy went out the back door to see if they could find her. They didn't, of course—but they did find a set of fresh footprints from an adult, and so Williams did what he's best at: tracking. He followed the prints down into the wash behind the house and then down the streambed until it intersected with the road a little further away. The prints disappeared where they intersected with a fresh set of tire tracks.

In the house's front yard and in the roadway, detectives had made an even more significant discovery: fresh blood spots, trailing out of the house and then ending at the road. Deputies placed orange markers next to them so that arriving reinforcements would be aware there was evidence. They also found a silver revolver, fully loaded and unfired, next to the fence.

Deputies found Gina's purse in the master bedroom, its contents dumped across the bed. Whoever had searched it had not been very thorough: Gina's $3,000 in cash was still tucked in the side pocket. If these killers were thieves, they were not competent.

The EMTs patched Gina Gonzalez up as well as they could, hauled her out to the ambulance, and whisked her away into Arivaca. From there a helicopter airlifted her in about thirty minutes to the regional hospital in Tucson.

||

Pima County detectives had spent the whole night and all of Saturday combing through the Flores-Gonzalez home and gathering evidence. They had heard from local sources that Junior Flores was involved in the drug-smuggling business, but there was no sign of that in the home. It soon became clear that Gina Gonzalez held the most important clues to the mystery of who had invaded their home and killed Brisenia and Junior. So a team of detectives, led by Charles Garcia, went to her room at University Medical Center to see what they could find out.

Doctors were still busy treating her, but she was conscious enough to talk. Piling atop the massive trauma Gina Gonzalez had suffered the night before—losing her husband and daughter and being badly wounded herself—doctors had informed her that she might lose her right leg too. They were going to operate and try to save it, but the gunshot had shattered her femur, and they warned her there was a chance they would have to amputate.

At first only Detective Garcia talked to her, and he collected a few simple facts that basically reiterated what she had told Tanya Remsburg. The only thing they cleared up, really, was the matter of Brisenia's age: Gina had mistakenly told the dispatcher her daughter was ten years old because she was only a few months away from that momentous birthday, but in truth she was still nine when she was killed.

Garcia also tried to probe into possible motives for the killers and wondered if Junior was involved in anything local that might get him in trouble—hinting, perhaps, at the marijuana trade that was common in Arivaca. Gina denied it. She explained: "My husband smokes pot. But that's probably all you'll find. I think he had, like, a little sack of weed that he just had for personal use."

The doctors interrupted: they were still busy working on her, and the interview became necessarily short. The detective left, and the doctors went back to their work, but they promised he could come back and interview her when they were done.

When Garcia returned, he brought with him the rest of the team: detectives Jill Murphy and Robert Svec. When Gina saw the guns on the hips of the two Caucasian detectives who came into her room accompanying Garcia, she froze. The two white people who had invaded her home and shot them had pretended to be law enforcement officers, too, and she feared—not altogether irrationally—that it was about to happen again.

Murphy and Svec saw the terrified look on her face, and it was clear something was wrong. The ensuing interview was terse, tense, and ultimately quite brief. Mostly what Gina could tell them was what she had already told the dispatcher.

But there was one new detail: As she was curled up on the floor in a fetal position, pretending to be dead, she had heard someone—two men, actually—speaking Spanish in the kitchen. And after the man who had come in the house the second time and tried to shoot her, while she was on the phone with the county dispatcher, had fled, she had seen a "Mexican" man poke his head around the corner of the front door to peek in.

"And he looked at me," she told them, "and he said, 'Oh shit.' And he ran back out. I didn't get a good look at him. But I know he was dressed all in green."

This caught the detective's attention: "He was dressed how?"

"All in green. Like a Border Patrol officer."

This was the man, she told them, at whom she had cursed, telling him to "get the fuck out of here." She told them she had fired shots in his direction, too.

"Am I gonna get in trouble for that?" she fretted.

"No. No. No. No," Garcia reassured her.

Doctors shortly cleared them all out of the room and took Gina in for surgery.

Fortunately, the hospital's skilled surgeons were able to save Gina's leg. They replaced her femur with a titanium rod, sewed her up, and prepared her for what would be the long process of recovery. She remained mostly unconscious for the rest of the day, and doctors ordered rest for her on Sunday as well. The detectives would have to wait.

On Monday morning, Garcia returned without his two colleagues. Gina was more alert and feeling somewhat better. And she wound up giving him the clues that would indeed crack the case wide open.

Garcia began with a photo lineup of potential suspects, focusing on the "short fat white woman" Gina had described several times as the apparent leader of the home-invasion operation. He showed her photos of six different women. Gina was unsure whether any of them were right—one of them was a friend she recognized, and she was certain it wasn't her—and ultimately she narrowed it down to three possible suspects. The problem, she said, was that the hair color wasn't right for any of them.

They went through a number of possibilities—a few people Junior might have had a conflict with; the "weirdo" neighbor who hated Latinos and was fond of pointing a gun at them when they were near his property; the woman Gina had gotten into a fight with at the Arivaca Mercantile, where she had worked for a number of years. All these appeared to be dead ends.

Then she mentioned the teal-colored Chevy Astro van that had driven by slowly on Friday. This caught Garcia's attention. Gina described it in some detail and told Garcia that the people inside seemed to be talking about her.

Garcia wrapped it all up around twelve thirty, and began putting away his recorder and notebook to walk out of the room, when Gina stopped him: she had remembered something else.

"The only person my husband had been arguing with was Albert," she said. "I'm not completely sure of his last name." She told them she thought it might be Sanchez.

Albert, she explained, was related to her own godmother and had been a friend of theirs for a while. Junior and Albert had been close, and the two girls adored him and treated him like an uncle. Sometimes he would pick up the girls at the community center and bring them home if Gina and Junior were busy. They all got a beer together at the tavern in Arivaca once in a while. Albert would come to their home and hang out and eat dinner with them.

But Albert had begun getting on Gina's nerves. He would come in the house and open the fridge and help himself to the beers and sodas without asking or go to the cupboard and get out a new bag of chips and open them and begin munching. When she had complained to Junior about Albert's boorish behavior, her husband's demeanor had darkened. Albert, he had told her, was not the nice person they all thought he was.

Friends in town gave her the same warning: "Albert's not all there, and he's not a good person, and we kinda started hearing that he was on drugs," she told Garcia. "My husband didn't want nothing to do with that."

It all came to a head, Gina said, when Junior caught Albert stashing marijuana on the property adjacent to their acreage where they had begun building a new, nicer home. One night, she said, they had seen him drive by in his brown-and-white Chevy Blazer, and Gina had heard him picking up something down at the property and then slamming the door to the vehicle and driving off.

About three weeks earlier, she told Garcia, Junior and Albert had come to blows over it. Albert had driven by their home on his little four-wheeler, and Junior had accosted him in the road and confronted him. The argument turned hot, and Junior had decked Albert, knocking him off the motorbike. When he had gotten back up, Albert had reached inside his toolbox for a gun, so Junior walked back into his home to defuse the situation. Albert eventually just drove off. But the bad blood was bubbling. Soon everyone in town knew that Junior and Albert were feuding.

"Everyone knew," Gina said. "Junior thought that he was a piece of shit."

And she agreed. "I mean, I saw with my own eyes him doing that in the [Blazer]. You know, and I'm, like, I have kids. And you're putting that over there. And people already talk crap about Junior, you know? And if that's over there, nobody's gonna believe that's not Junior's."

||

These were substantial clues to the mystery, and the Pima County detectives wasted no time following up on them. They quickly determined that the man Gina was describing was an Arivacan named Albert Gaxiola. As it happened, they had received another tip: there had been a commotion at about two a.m., mostly involving a car that wouldn't start, outside a house in town rented by Gaxiola.

He lived in a duplex in the town proper, a couple of blocks off the highway. A team of detectives and sheriff's deputies in police cars pulled up to the place Monday afternoon.

Sitting parked in front of the home was a teal-colored Chevy Astro van.

Detective Jill Murphy went over to the van and inspected it. She saw a speck of something red on the post between the passenger door and the sliding rear door. And when she looked through the window, she could see a large red stain on the carpet below the front passenger seat that appeared to be blood.

Meanwhile, Juan Carlos Navarro—the lead detective in the case and the man overseeing the team—knocked on the door and was greeted by a clean-shaven, neatly groomed Latino man who was in fact Albert Gaxiola. He was smooth, seemingly unperturbed by the arrival of a caravan of cops at his front door, and invited them in.

Gaxiola's home was clean and neatly appointed, with a nice TV and computer and a tasteful assortment of decorations and furniture. There were also a lot of guns in the place.

In short order, the detectives uncovered an AK-47 in a closet and a shotgun, stashed inside a bureau, with one emptied shell in the chamber. There were also a few handguns and lots of ammunition.

These could have belonged to anyone living in Arivaca, since guns are a common part of the rural Arizona lifestyle. But the most telling clue—besides the teal van with blood on it and in it—was found inside a plastic laundry basket: a green, long-sleeved uniform shirt with a Border Patrol patch on the shoulder.

Even more peculiarly, while sorting through Albert's personal possessions on a bureau in his bedroom, they found some other patches, stashed inside a little drawer with jewelry and other odds and ends: a couple of patches promoting the Minutemen. One script, wrapped around an American flag, read: "Undocumented American: I Survived The Minuteman Project 2005: Border Patrol." The other depicted a Revolutionary War–era militiaman in a tricornered hat who was pointing like Uncle Sam, with a script reading: "Minutemen Saved America Once: We Can Again: Secure Our Nation's Borders."

These were not the usual possessions of Spanish-speaking Latinos in rural Arizona.

The teal van, the blood inside it, the Border Patrol shirt, and the weaponry—especially the presence of an AK-47 similar to the one found on the stove in the Flores home—probably comprised enough evidence to take Gaxiola into custody on suspicion of murder. However, Gaxiola was also a convicted felon with a record; his mere possession of the guns was enough to make an arrest on weapons charges. So the officers made the arrest and transported him to Tucson; the next day he made bail and was released. In the meantime, they confiscated his cell phone.

One of the detectives started reading a string of text messages from the early morning hours of May 30 from someone named White.

Gaxiola had texted White at 1:33 in the morning: "Cops on scene. Lay low."

He had gotten a message back in short order: "No worries. All good. Just relax. Competition gone."

The sender named "White," it soon transpired, was a woman named Shawna Forde, using a cell phone from Washington State but sending the messages from a cell station in Arivaca.

Suddenly this was no longer a case involving a simple drug-related home invasion. Because Local deputies knew about Shawna Forde: she had made something of a local splash over the last couple of years, showing up in their desert towns with her own special offshoot of the Minutemen.

They called themselves Minuteman American Defense, and they were one of the more active Minuteman organizations still running border watches in Arizona. They also were noteworthy because Forde was especially fond of vicious race-baiting and incendiary rhetoric, and she was skilled at attracting media attention. A border watch she had overseen the previous October, in a section of the Altar Valley only a few miles away from Arivaca, had attracted international documentary filmmakers and a broad array of reporters and photographers.

Detectives asked Albert Gaxiola why Forde went by the nickname White. "Because she hates every ethnicity except Caucasians," he told them.

# Vigilance on the Border

Chris Simcox and his gun, 2004. SIAN KENNEDY PHOTO

The Minuteman movement that grabbed national headlines in the first decade of the twenty-first century was not a spontaneous eruption of border nativism, as the media would often portray it. Rather, it was the direct offspring of the border militias of the 1990s, which were the stepchild of the Klan Border Watches of the 1980s, which in turn were modeled on a 1960s vigilante movement calling itself, ironically, the Minutemen.

These 1960s Minutemen of course were not the original Revolutionary War heroes, famed for their rapid responses to military action. Rather, this was another right-wing vigilante organization claiming to be a big "neighborhood watch"—watching out, then, for Communists—and it had similarly grabbed national headlines for a brief while. It had not ended well.

These earlier Minutemen were the brainchild of a Missouri biochemist named Robert DePugh, who had made a small fortune selling a popular vitamin for dogs. In 1960 he began organizing fellow archconservatives, who were fearful of a Communist takeover of America, into paramilitary watch groups that could provide on-the-ground response by ordinary Americans in the event of a revolutionary coup or invasion, monitoring events in their hometowns. "On a local basis we feel we're in a better position to know our friends and neighbors" than the FBI, DePugh explained. Like the latter-day militiamen, these Minutemen also conducted paramilitary training sessions in the woods and promoted a broad panoply of conspiracy theories. And they ultimately came apart because of the violent, unstable personalities who not only joined the movement but led it.

DePugh's Minutemen believed not only that government had been infiltrated at its highest levels by Communists but that a Communist takeover was virtually inevitable; therefore, they told their believers to arm themselves with whatever weaponry would be effective as a counterforce when the takeover occurred. DePugh, a onetime associate of John Birch Society founder Robert Welch before being dropped from the Society for his radicalism, also instructed his followers to harass "the enemy" and compiled at his headquarters a list of 1,500 people he identified as members of the "Communist hidden government," with the intent to assassinate them in the event of the Communist coup. He also made up a list of twenty congressmen he'd like to see dead.

One Minuteman—an adherent named Keith Gilbert, who years later would become a notorious fixture in the northern Idaho neo-Nazi scene—was arrested in 1965 with a load of 1,400 pounds of TNT he later explained was intended to blow up the stage at that year's Anti-Defamation League convention in Los Angeles, during the keynote speech by the Reverend Martin Luther King Jr. The Minutemen were also connected to an October 1966 plot, broken up by the FBI in New York City, to bomb three summer camps operated by liberal East Coast organizations. Illegal caches of weapons and ammunition linked to Minutemen kept popping up around the countryside.

Then DePugh himself got into trouble. In 1966, just as he was attempting to move into the political arena by forming a right-wing entity called the Patriotic Party, DePugh was arrested and then convicted on a variety of felony firearms violations and sentenced to four years in prison. DePugh fought the conviction on appeals. A year later, a group of seven Minutemen were arrested by the FBI in the small Seattle suburb of Redmond, Washington, and charged with plotting to set off a bomb at the Redmond city hall while simultaneously detonating another at the local power station, thereby creating a major distraction while they took out police communications. The plan then called for the gang to rob three Redmond banks.

DePugh was implicated in the plot and went into hiding but was caught a few months later in Truth or Consequences, New Mexico. He was arrested and charged in the Redmond plot. Five of the seven Seattle plotters were charged, and all five were convicted. DePugh, convicted in September 1970, wound up serving four years out of a ten-year sentence on the original firearms charges, but by then, his career in politics was in the ash heap. He later tried to resuscitate his ambitions by heading up an ultraconservative organization called the Committee of 10 Million, but the numbers fell well short of those suggested by the group's name. DePugh spent a few more years in prison again in the 1990s, after he was convicted on a morals charge for sexual exploitation of a minor. He died in 2009.

DePugh gave a new shape to the idea of white-citizen vigilantes that had long been part of the extremist right's approach to politics, since at least the days of the Ku Klux Klan. DePugh's idea—white-citizen militias guarding against threats to their political supremacy—became the new focus of far-right organizing. Among the people paying attention were David Duke and Tom Metzger.

||

It was a classic media circus: TV crews and newspaper photographers out on the desert borderlands, crowded around the small cluster of border watchers, vying for a chance to interview the handful of participants, dutifully recording the bellicose warnings of their leaders regarding the dangers of illegal immigration. You could count eight times as many journalists as vigilantes.

The year was 1977, and it was the first organized anti-immigrant border watch. The leaders: David Duke and his revived Knights of the Ku Klux Klan.

At the time, Duke was riding the crest of a wave of media attention. He had first made headlines in the early 1970s by protesting on Louisiana campuses dressed in Nazi garb and then declaring himself the business-suited new face of a revamped Klan, scrubbed and polished for modern consumption. He was featured in segments on *60 Minutes* and appeared on Tom Snyder's *Tomorrow* show after challenging Snyder—who had blasted Duke publicly—to let him have his say. Afterward, Duke crowed: "We bested Tom Snyder. The show gave me national exposure and made it much easier to get my ideals across to many more people. And that's what it's all about."

The idea of an anti-immigration border watch was actually hatched by Duke's Klan lieutenant in California, another neo-Nazi named Tom Metzger.

But following in the wake of other successful publicity stunts by the Klan, Duke seized on the idea and made it into another media event.

He arrived in California to great media fanfare on October 16, 1977, at the immigration offices on the US border crossing at San Ysidro, California. Surrounded by a small phalanx of Klansmen, Duke had toured the facility while outside a large crowd of antiracist protesters threw rocks and eggs.

Asked to explain his purpose, Duke said, "We believe very strongly white people are becoming second-class citizens. When I think of America, I think of a white country."

In Sacramento a few days later, he held a press conference announcing a "Klan Border Watch" that would supposedly enlist somewhere between five hundred and a thousand Klansmen in a vigilante patrol stretching from Texas to California. Again, he was met by a large crowd of protesters. The ensuing scenes attracted more press attention, so that by the day of the event, national and state media alike were flocking to cover it.

On October 25, the border-watching contingent arrived at their announced site—the border crossing near the town of Dulzura in rural San Diego County—in three sedans with hand-painted "Klan Border Watch" signs attached to the sides. When they emerged, Duke was accompanied by a small cluster of Klansmen; all told, his contingent comprised seven people—massively outnumbered by the press corps alone, not to mention the large crowd of protesters also drawn to the site.

Duke spent the day either being interviewed by reporters or talking on a citizens' band radio, supposedly relaying information about border-crosser sightings, provided by the "hundreds" of Klansmen he claimed were participating, to eagerly awaiting federal agents. Duke announced that the information had produced "thousands" of arrests. Most of the media reported his claims dutifully—even though it shortly emerged that in fact there had been no increase in border-crossing arrests that day.

Duke later mused for readers of his Klan paper, *The Crusader*, on how easy it had all been: "When a hundred reporters are gathered around hanging on every word, when they help you accomplish your objectives by their own misguided sensationalism, if indeed it was a media stunt, it was by their own presence an admission that it was a very brilliant one," he said.

The die had been cast.

||

David Duke's star quickly faded. The womanizing and mishandling of funds that had become part of his schtick soon alienated many of his fellow right-wingers, and gradually the media lost interest in him too, at least until the late 1980s and early '90s, when he briefly resurrected his career as a Louisiana legislator and gubernatorial candidate. That star, too, burned out in short order, and eventually Duke's personal foibles caught up with him in a serious way: In 2002, he was convicted of mail fraud for bilking his followers out of hundreds of thousands of dollars and spending the money to feed his gambling addiction. He served a fifteen-month prison term and now seems to spend most of his time in Europe, organizing white-supremacist groups there.

Immigration remained a staple issue for the radical right through much of the 1980s, though it was pushed to a back burner as the white-supremacist movement focused, in the early 1980s, on creating a "white homeland" in the inland Northwest, largely revolving around the Aryan Nations organization headquartered in Hayden Lake, Idaho. This reached its apotheosis in 1984, when an Aryan follower (and onetime Minuteman) named Robert Mathews formed a neo-Nazi action group called the Order, which by the end of its yearlong rampage had assassinated Denver radio talk-show host Alan Berg, committed nearly a dozen robberies of banks and armored cars, and embarked on a counterfeiting scheme. It all ended in a blaze of gunfire, tear gas, and smoke when FBI agents cornered Mathews at a hideout on Whidbey Island, Washington, and he refused to come out after a flare set it afire.

The Order turned out to be pretty much a disaster for the white-supremacist right, largely because Mathews had drawn so many leaders of the movement into his web, handing out his ill-gotten cash to fund their activities. Federal authorities charged all of these people with conspiracy, and even though the charges eventually failed, the men who had been hauled before the courts recognized that they had a problem: as long as they were going to be urging their followers to take violent action, they could not afford to have affiliations with the people who would actually carry it out.

Thus was born "leaderless resistance," a concept developed and popularized by Aryan Nations leader Louis Beam. In a couple of essays on the subject written in 1983 and 1992, Beam explained that the traditional hierarchical organization employed by the old racist right was dangerous for any kind of insurgency, especially in "technologically advanced societies where electronic surveillance can often penetrate the structure, revealing its chain of command." He proposed instead a leaderless organizational structure, wherein "individuals and groups operate independently of each other, and never report to a central headquarters or single leader for direction or instruction, as would those who belong to a typical pyramid organization." The role of leadership is not to issue directives or to pay operatives, but rather to provide the larger inspiration and agenda for small cells or "lone wolf" individuals to follow, acting independently and on their own initiative.

Always looking for ways to return to the mainstream of American politics, white nationalists by the early 1990s had begun rebranding themselves as Christian Patriots, which was shortened by 1994 into simply the Patriot movement. It was largely the same toxic brew of right-wing conspiracism, xenophobia, and scapegoating that had always been their recipe for recruitment, but scrubbed of overt racism and focused on combating a looming "New World Order" in which global government would overtake the United States and enslave the nation.

Following the leaderless resistance concept, the Patriot movement's chief strategy revolved around forming citizen militias—and indeed, as the movement gained traction and attracted media attention, it became largely known as the "militia movement." Militia cells formed in every state of the union, all of them independent entities, all of them working toward the same, anti–New World Order agenda. They often had their own regional orientation: in the Northwest, militias were typically expressions of anti-environmental backlash; in Alaska, they revolved around efforts at seceding from the Union; in places like Michigan and Florida and Alabama, the paranoia was all about gun ownership.

But the issue of illegal immigration had remained a staple of the Patriot agenda, so in border states, particularly Arizona, California, and Texas, the focus was firmly on stanching the flow of Hispanic immigrants into their states. Border militias became popular for these Patriots, along with the usual mix of conspiracy theories and ethnic fearmongering.

The most prominent of these border-militia Patriots was a retired California businessman named Glenn Spencer. Beginning in 1992, Spencer's original organization, Voices of Citizens Together, worked tirelessly to stop the flow of Hispanic immigrants into the country. VCT was a leading proponent of the 1994 California initiative to deny educational, health, and other benefits to undocumented immigrants and their children, Proposition 187 (which was approved by voters but later invalidated by the courts).

In 1995, Spencer began spreading his message through a strong Web presence, particularly his site, American Patrol. Much of its news was dedicated to reporting on crimes committed by Latinos, as evidence connecting immigration with criminal activity. But there was also a steady theme: Spencer picked up the old Klan Border Watch concept and repackaged it by promoting the idea of border militias, along with the usual panoply of New World Order conspiracy theories. American Patrol was rife with openly bigoted contempt aimed at Latinos, embodied in the cartoon that depicted a character urinating on a picture of a prominent Latino activist. Spencer also penned missives to other publications, including a 1996 letter to the *Los Angeles Times* claiming that "the Mexican culture is based on deceit. Chicanos and Mexicanos lie as a means of survival."

Besides border militias, Spencer became devoted to his own pet conspiracy theory, promoted on the American Patrol website, in his newsletter, and on his radio show: namely, that a cadre of Latino radicals, in conjunction with the Mexican government, is conspiring to take back the American Southwest by invading the region with hordes of immigrants and then reclaiming it for Mexico as part of a greater nation called Aztlan. It became known as the Reconquista theory, a name from Spanish history that Spencer requisitioned for his own purposes. The basis of the theory is a set of obscure documents written by Chicano activists in the late 1960s calling for a reimagined America. Some of these manifestoes were associated with the founding of the student Latino organization Movimiento Estudiantil Chicano de Aztlan, better known as MEChA. Moreover, the MEChA constitution's preamble calls for the "self-determination of the Chicana/Chicano people and the liberation of Aztlan."

In Spencer's retelling, an idea aimed at multicultural solidarity was transformed into a racist and exclusionist enterprise, and an organization better known for bake sales and campus socials became the equivalent of the Ku Klux Klan. MEChA, Spencer claimed, was fundamentally racist. As early as October 1996 he was running articles with titles like "MEChA calls for the Liberation of 'Aztlan,'" which warned: "Those who scoff at the idea of a Mexican takeover of the Southwestern United States don't understand history and they underestimate the Mexicans."

American Patrol continued to make a fetish out of the Reconquista theory and MEChA in subsequent years, embodied by the section devoted to what it called "The Scourge of MEChA," not to mention the running coverage to this day of anything it can attribute to the Aztlan takeover. Spencer himself became so devoted to his theory that in 2001 he had a copy of his videotape, *Bonds of Our Nations*—which lays out the Reconquista plans in graphic detail—hand-delivered to every member of Congress. The woman making the delivery was Betina McCann, the fiancée of a notorious neo-Nazi named Steven Barry.

Eventually Spencer's theory made it into mainstream media via the right-wing blogosphere. In August 2003 bloggers Michelle Malkin and Glenn "Instapundit" Reynolds, in an effort to harm the California guber-natorial candidacy of Latino politician Cruz Bustamante, picked up Spencer's claims about MEChA whole off his web postings and began run-ning them credulously, claiming that MEChA was a racist organization of scheming, America-hating radicals. Reynolds went so far as to attack MEChA members as "fascist hatemongers." On Fox News, Bill O'Reilly and his fellow hosts repeated the claim and accused Bustamante, a former MEChA member, of dallying with racists. Bustamante wound up a distant second to Arnold Schwarzenegger in the election.

By then, Spencer had moved from California to Arizona and expanded his operations, buying a large ranch not far from the border and setting up watches for crossers on his land. He had been drawn there by a number of other ranchers who were becoming angry about the volumes of immigrants crossing their properties and had decided to take matters into their own hands. And he brought with him his penchant for hateful, bigoted rhetoric.

||

Roger Barnett was an Arizona rancher who worked some twenty-two thou-sand acres—most of it leased federal land—near Sierra Vista and Douglas. He was profiled in 2000 by *Time* magazine's Tim McGirk, for whom Barnett was emblematic of how "anger against the growing flood of 1 million illegal immigrants a year is rising fast among independent-spirited, gun-toting res-idents in the borderlands of Arizona, Texas and New Mexico." McGirk de-scribed Barnett's methods of dealing with border crossers:

> With his binoculars, an M-16 automatic rifle and his sheepdog Mikey, Barnett sometimes tracks a group of illegals for miles, following their foot-prints in the sand and bits of clothing snagged on the mesquite thorns. In the summer it's harder for his dog to track them; the incandescent heat sears away their scent. "They move across the desert like a centipede, 40 or 50 people at a time," says Barnett. Once he catches them, Barnett ra-dios the border patrol to cart them off his land. "You always get one or two that are defiant," says Barnett, who chuckles, remembering an inci-dent a few weeks back. "One fellow tried to get up and walk away, saying we're not Immigration. So I slammed him back down and took his photo. 'Why'd you do that?' the illegal says, all surprised. 'Because we want you to go home with a before picture and an after picture—that is, after we beat the s___ outta you.' You can bet he started behavin' then."

This kind of violent talk and threatening demeanor became the standard mode of operation for the "citizen border watch" organizers who followed in Barnett's wake. Indeed, the border watchers' rhetoric so starkly dehumanized and demonized Latinos that their similarity to hate groups became inescapable. Perhaps that was because it was attracting white supremacists to their cause.

In May 2000, Glenn Spencer and his Proposition 187 cohort, Barbara Coe of the nativist California Coalition for Immigration Reform, cosponsored a public gathering in Sierra Vista revolving around Roger Barnett and the rising border issues. Also in attendance were two members of David Duke's organization, the National Organization For European American Rights (NOFEAR), and two members of an Arkansas Klan group—though of course Spencer and his local cosponsors all claimed they were unaware of their presence.

The rhetoric was in keeping with such an audience, however. In her speech to the gathering, Coe declared that government border policies were an abject failure that had forced ranchers to "defend our borders and defend themselves from illegal alien savages who kill their livestock, and slit their watchdogs' throats . . . burglarize their homes and threaten the physical safety of their loved ones."

The gathering inspired the formation of one of the first and most prominent border militias, an outfit called Ranch Rescue that was run by a Texas man named Torre John "Jack" Foote. It claimed chapters in all the southern border states and Colorado as well. Foote explained in a 2003 interview with the white-supremacist website Stormfront that Ranch Rescue's first "field mission" took place in October 2000 on Barnett's ranch and that it had become intensively active ever since: "We're still seeing hordes—mobs—of criminal aliens pour across this privately-owned property, and the best thing we can expect from our own government is that they will do everything possible to aid the pro-criminal alien groups."

That first operation advertised for recruits by calling for would-be border watchers to "come have fun in the sun" while volunteers hunted "hordes of criminal aliens." Men with military and weapons training were preferred. Recruits were urged to bring their RVs, guard dogs, and trained attack dogs. Once on site, volunteers were given dire instructions warning of various lethal threats to their well-being, urging them to do whatever they needed to protect themselves. On patrol, they equipped themselves with an assortment of weapons, including high-powered assault rifles, as well as night-vision devices, two-way radios, flares, machetes, and all-terrain vehicles.

When accused of harboring racist motives, Foote responded with a peculiarly vehement bigotry: "You and the vast majority of your fellow dog turds are ignorant, uneducated, and desperate for a life in a decent nation because the one you live in is nothing but a pile of dog shit made up of millions of worthless little dog turds like yourself," Foote wrote to a Mexican American who accused him of racism. "You stand around your entire lives, whining about how bad things are in your dog of a nation, waiting for the dog to stick its ass under our fence and shit each one of you into our back yards."

In March 2002, Foote and another ex-Californian, Casey Nethercott, set up a border watch on the Texas ranch of a member named Joe Sutton and dubbed it Operation Falcon. The idea was to use the Sutton ranch as a base for hunting illegal border crossers. That was when everything started to turn sideways for Ranch Rescue.

Nethercott already had quite the track record. A big blond man, he had made his living for a few years in California as a bounty hunter but had run afoul of the law when he wrongly apprehended the son of the chief of police in Riverside. He wound up serving prison time for felony assault and false imprisonment. He had therefore lost the legal right to carry a gun—but of course, he owned and used several as part of his Ranch Rescue work.

On March 18, two would-be immigrants from El Salvador named Fatima Leiva and Edwin Mancia made the mistake of crossing the Suttons' ranch in the early morning hours and found themselves confronted by Ranch Rescue members, who chased them into the brush. Joe Sutton himself reportedly fired numerous gunshots in their direction, shouting obscenities and threatening to kill them. Eventually they were sniffed out by Casey Nethercott's Rottweiler and yanked from the brush; Mancia was ordered to stand up and then was struck in the back of the head with a handgun. While he lay on the ground, Nethercott allowed the Rottweiler to attack Mancia, ripping his sweatshirt. The pair were interrogated and accused of being drug smugglers. After enduring an hour and a half of such abuse, they were handed over to authorities. They promptly filed criminal complaints against Nethercott and one of the other border watchers. Nethercott was also charged with a weapons violation for possessing a gun.

The lawsuits followed a year later. The whole gang from Joe Sutton's ranch—including Jack Foote and Casey Nethercott—was sued the next June for civil rights violations by the two Salvadoran immigrants, represented by the Southern Poverty Law Center and the Mexican American Legal Defense and Educational Fund.

But Nethercott was just getting started. In early 2003, he purchased a seventy-acre ranch not far from Roger Barnett's in Cochise County, Arizona, and he promptly began converting it into an armed compound. He called it Camp Thunderbird. His neighbors were furious and filed numerous complaints against Nethercott for violating various county land-use ordinances.

Glenn Spencer was already a neighbor, by a matter of months. In September 2002, he announced he had given up on California: "California is a lawless, lost state," he told reporters. "There's nothing I can do for California. It is finished." Spencer also recommended white flight: "White Americans should get out of California—now, before it is too late to salvage the equity they have in their homes and the value of their businesses." He bought a property in an exclusive Cochise County neighborhood and set up his revamped American Border Patrol (ABP) organization there, with an assist from Roger Barnett and his friends, who introduced Spencer around to the locals, particularly the county's law enforcement officers.

Things turned rocky in August 2003, when Spencer shot up a neighbor's garage with a .357 rifle after hearing "suspicious" noises in his backyard. He eventually pleaded guilty to reckless endangerment and was fined $2,500 and given a year's probation. In the meantime, his upscale neighbors at Pueblo del Sol slapped him with a complaint for running his business from his home—which violated several of the subdivision's covenants. So he gave up and moved his operation to another location.

Spencer's plan was different from the others: his ABP was more of a high-tech affair, in contrast to his fellow border watchers' boots-on-the-ground approach. Spencer and his volunteers operated remote-controlled airplanes equipped with cameras and other monitoring equipment, and he flew his own Cessna over border areas with similar equipment. He also sent out volunteer "hawkeyes" to monitor border crossers' movements with video cameras and other high-tech equipment.

Casey Nethercott, however, favored the border-militia approach that Spencer had advocated previously. He and his Ranch Rescue cohorts built a base of operations at Camp Thunderbird, outside of Douglas, Arizona, that was a militiaman's dream: watchtowers, bunkers, barracks, a helicopter landing pad, an indoor firing range. In November 2003, his neighbors filed two complaints about the work, alleging various zoning violations.

It was kind of a bad month for Nethercott: on the thirteenth, FBI agents came out to the Douglas ranch and arrested him as fugitive for having fled the weapons charge in Texas. Jack Foote told reporters that Nethercott's lawyer was trying to get the weapons charges dropped. In the meantime, he said, he and his volunteers were busy building a home base for Ranch Rescue.

Their activities created fears that not only might they inflict violence on hapless border crossers, but at some point they could create an international incident—especially since they had begun to threaten the Mexican military with violence should any of its soldiers wander over the border, as was known to happen from time to time. In February 2004, Foote issued a warning that the next time a Mexican soldier set foot on their ranch, he would be fired on: "Two in the chest and one in the head," he said.

Douglas's mayor, Ray Borane, worried that they would create a cross-border shootout: "This isn't a game," he said. "That's the thing that has always worried me, that these people would cause an international incident and not only hinder relations with Mexico, but that they'd make this area become a hotbed for other organizations like that."

Over the next few months, though, Foote and Nethercott had a falling-out, and by April, the Douglas ranch was no longer the home base for Ranch Rescue. Instead, in spring 2004 Nethercott announced he was starting up a border-watch group of his own called the Arizona Guard, which its website described as "an Organized Militia dedicated to the defense of American Patriotism and to help local ranchers and citizens defend property from illegal alien activity and drug running operations."

His new recruitment chief was Kalen Riddle, a twenty-two-year-old from Aberdeen, Washington. On his own website, Riddle declared himself a "National Socialist" and ran pictures of himself in Nazi uniform, embellished with swastika armbands, brandishing a rifle. Two of his favorite things, he declared, are "ethnic cleansing and weapon making." Riddle requested that "any WN [White Nationalist] volunteer is asked to keep WP [White Power] or Third Reich imagry (sic) to a minimum and not to talk to any press."

Nethercott denied that anyone in his organization was a Nazi. "When words come up like hate, white supremacy and Nazism, and genocide, those are words that are made for people to inflame people," he said in a local radio interview. "None of those apply to us."

On August 31, 2004, three Border Patrol agents tried to pull Nethercott over as part of a smuggling investigation. Instead of cooperating, he took them on a long, slow-speed chase to his ranch, where he got out at the gate and phoned inside for help. The Patrol officers claimed he threatened them with assault and attempted to intimidate them, but they drove away at the end of the tense standoff.

A couple of weeks later, Nethercott was pulled over in a Safeway parking lot in Douglas by FBI agents, intent on arresting him on charges of assaulting a federal officer. Kalen Riddle was with him, and he was armed. During the arrest, an agent said he saw Riddle make a move toward his waist, so he shot him. Riddle was critically injured and spent several weeks recovering in a hospital. Casey Nethercott was hauled off and jailed on the assault charge. He remained there for five months, but he was later acquitted of the assault charge. (Eventually Nethercott would serve nearly five years in prison for the felony weapons-possession charge in Texas.)

Jack Foote told a local TV reporter that he and Ranch Rescue had severed their ties with Nethercott back in April over his increasingly evident racial views. "We're all better off with Nethercott in a cage, welded shut," Foote sneered.

Within the year, however, Ranch Rescue was finished—especially after the courts ruled in favor of the two Salvadoran emigrants, Fatima Leiva and Edwin Mancia. With the help of their SPLC attorneys, the pair obtained judgments totaling $1 million against Foote and Nethercott. They also obtained a $100,000 out-of-court settlement from Joe Sutton. In August 2005, Casey Nethercott's Douglas ranch was seized and deeded to the Salvadorans. Camp Thunderbird became an ordinary ranch in the desert again. Jack Foote closed up the Ranch Rescue shop and shut down its website.

But by then, they had become yesterday's news. The shiny new border watch on the block—calling themselves the Minutemen—had become the latest media darling.

||

Chris Simcox liked to pose for the media with a pistol down the front of his pants. In certain video appearances, too, when he was first attracting attention, you could see him shove his handgun under the front waistband of his blue jeans. He probably thought it made him look like a devil-may-care Western outlaw type. Of course, all it really did was brand him the outsider, the clueless city dude from California he always was in his adopted Arizona hometown.

People in the rural West—especially places like Tombstone, birthplace of the Western gunfighter mythos—grow up around guns. They're not playthings here. They're tools, necessities of life, but dangerous ones you need to respect. Only a damned fool would stick a gun down the front of his pants, unless he's courting a high voice. It's the best way in the world to blow your own dick off.

So when Simcox would swagger around the Cochise County countryside

with a gun down the front of his jeans and the adoring media in tow, the locals would smirk. Now that was a hapless rube—even if he was talking about
an issue that concerned them.

Of course, it was the gunfighter mythos that attracted a guy like Simcox
to Tombstone in the first place. The little tourist town is a kind of cultural
epicenter, since the famous gunfight that broke out on a vacant lot in the
town on October 26, 1881, between two warring factions: the Yankee Wyatt
Earp and his two brothers, along with Doc Holliday, on one side, and a cluster of outlaw, ex-Confederate cowboys like Billy Clanton and Frank and
Tom McClaury, who wound up on the Other Side at the showdown's end.
The incident gave birth to one of America's most deeply cherished and fervently embraced Western myths, that of the mano a mano showdown at
high noon, with only the tumbleweeds daring to share the street.

The reality, as always, is much more mundane: the Gunfight at the OK
Corral is the only recorded such "showdown at high noon" in all of Western history. There certainly were plenty of gunfights in the Old West, but
the vast majority of them occurred over or under poker tables or at bar-
side, with the occasional armed fight spilling out into the street. Actually,
the most common form of homicide by far in those days involved being
dry-gulched in an ambush by whoever wanted to steal your possessions or
mining claim.

The myth, on the other hand, is much more exciting and crowd-pleasing,
not to mention profitable. And so now during tourist season in Tombstone—
which is pretty much all year, except for the summertime, when only Gila
monsters and rattlesnakes are out at midday—a group of paid actors dress up
every day as the Earp brothers and their erstwhile victims and meet in an OK
Corral in the middle of town, reenacting the archetypal Western shootout
for the edification and entertainment of the city slickers.

When Chris Simcox first arrived in Tombstone in 2002, he found work
as one of the actors. It was a way of staying afloat until he could get his feet
on the ground. He had been drawn by the myth, and now he was on a mission to transform it into a kind of living reality.

A few months before, he had thrown away his previous life as a school-
teacher in California, moved out to the Arizona desert, and had an epiphany,
all because of the terrorist attacks on New York and Washington, DC, on
September 11, 2001. Traumatized by repeatedly watching the collapse of
the Twin Towers, Simcox had sold off his belongings and moved out to camp
in the Sonoran desert, where he witnessed all kinds of human and drug trafficking—or so he was fond of repeatedly telling reporters in later years. Con-

cluding that the porous nature of the Mexican border posed a post–9/11 security threat to America, he had decided to pour all his efforts into doing something about it. That was his basic story, and it eventually became a kind of mythos unto itself.

In reality, Chris Simcox's life had been falling apart for awhile. Simcox grew up in rural Illinois and Kentucky; after high school, he moved briefly to New York in pursuit of a baseball career and then moved out to California with his first wife, Deborah Crews, who harbored ambitions as an actress, and their daughter. Simcox himself would later suggest he had tried his hand at acting too, but he also went to school, getting a degree in education from LA's Pacific Oaks College.

Eventually, he found work as a teacher in Los Angeles, first in a gang-infested high school in South Central LA, before he found more sedate work as a kindergarten teacher at a prestigious private school called Wildwood. He also divorced Crews and married an African American woman named Kim Dunbar, who later gave birth to their son. He was a popular teacher, but his colleagues at Wildwood recalled Simcox as something of a condescending know-it-all who prided himself on being up to date on the latest educational techniques and letting everyone else know it too: "He had this real holier-than-thou attitude, like he was so far above the other teachers they should be grateful he was even discussing his methods with them," one of them told a reporter. "He was insulting."

Some of them also witnessed a dark side to his sunny public persona. His then-teenage daughter from his first marriage came to live with him in Los Angeles in 1998, and Simcox got her a babysitting gig with one of his Wildwood colleagues. One night, she showed up suddenly at the colleague's house, visibly upset, seeking shelter: she claimed her father had tried to sexually molest her. Simcox later claimed he had just tried to give her a leg massage and she had gotten the wrong idea. No charges were filed. She returned to New York and her mother and broke off contact with her father. (The Southern Poverty Law Center reporters who obtained this information from the girl's mother, and confirmed it with two of Simcox's ex-colleagues, were stonewalled by Simcox when they confronted him with this information.)

Gradually, it all crumbled. Convinced of his own superiority, Simcox left Wildwood to start up his own tutoring business. But Dunbar said he was also displaying symptoms of a mental breakdown. According to her sworn depositions in their eventual divorce, she had to endure episodes of Simcox's violent rages, followed by numb, glass-eyed staring sessions in which he mumbled to himself. He refused professional help. And he abused and threatened their young son. After ten years of marriage, Dunbar testified, "the only thing I could do was file for divorce."

Even as his tutoring work spiraled away because of his erratic behavior, Simcox was also becoming increasingly xenophobic and paranoid. He later told a reporter that he was dismayed by the way Hispanic gangs and students who couldn't speak English were overwhelming Los Angeles schools, and at the same time he was becoming increasingly fearful of the prospect of a terrorist attack. "You could see it coming," he said. "And then Sept. 11 hit, and that was it."

The 9/11 attacks convinced Simcox that he was right in his paranoid belief that Los Angeles was primed to become a terrorism target, and he freaked out. He called Kim Dunbar two days after the attacks and left a series of voice-mail rants about the Constitution and the impending nuclear attack on LA and how he intended to give his now-teenage son weapons training: "I will begin teaching him the art of protecting himself with weapons," he said. "I purchased another gun. I have more than a few weapons, and I intend on teaching my son how to use them. . . . I will no longer trust anyone in this country. My life has changed forever, and if you don't get that, you are brainwashed like everybody else."

Simcox also called his son and ranted at him over the phone. Kim Dunbar recorded the conversations and submitted them in court proceedings as evidence of his mental instability. On the tapes, you can hear Simcox angrily challenge the boy to become "a man and a real American."

"You better stop playing baseball, buddy, and you better do something real, 'cause life will never be the same," Simcox shouted. "I'm going to go down to the Mexican border and sign up for the government for Border Patrol to protect the borders of the country that I love. You hear how serious I am."

Simcox indeed applied to join the Border Patrol but was rejected because, at age forty, he was too old. So he sold off his belongings and headed out to the Sonoran desert, camping for three months on the wild Arizona border and, he claimed later, witnessing all kinds of criminal border activity. He had his epiphany while camping at Organ Pipe National Monument and seeing drug traffickers. "At that moment, it clicked," Simcox recalls. "The borders were wide open. Terrorists could come through."

He eventually took up permanent residence in Tombstone, getting part-time work as a shootout-show actor—playing, aptly enough, one of the ex-Confederate "cowboy" gunmen who died in the showdown. ("I always got killed," he wryly observed to a reporter.) Responding to an ad for an assistant editor at the *Tombstone Tumbleweed*, he was hired on the spot.

The *Tumbleweed* was that kind of paper. It didn't really have much of a reporting staff, who covered local news only when they could get to it. It was run out of a little hole-in-the-wall office just off the town's main street. And like a lot of such papers in dusty rural locales in 2002, it was having a hard time staying afloat, and its then-owner wasn't merely desperate for an assistant editor—hell, he wanted a buyer. Sure enough, a few months after Simcox had been hired, he cashed in his personal reserves—at one time, Simcox told reporters he had liquidated his son's college fund, but in later versions it was his own retirement fund—and bought the paper for $60,000 in August 2002.

Simcox's epiphany had given him a focus for his new career: within short order, the *Tumbleweed* became all about illegal immigration à la Roger Barnett and his nativist cohort, from whom he later acknowledged he had received his inspiration. The headlines shouted: "ENOUGH IS ENOUGH! A PUBLIC CALL TO ARMS! CITIZENS BORDER PATROL MILITIA NOW FORMING!"

He initially called his outfit the Tombstone Militia but shortly changed its name to the much more broadly marketable Civil Homeland Defense Corps. At its first gathering in December, Simcox told reporters he expected about fifty people to participate, but only a handful, about five or six, actually showed.

They may have been discouraged by the official resolution opposing Simcox's plans for border militias passed by the city council of the nearest big town, Douglas. Mayor Borane authored the bill, writing: "Douglas is a bicultural and binational community, and the majority of its residents do not wish to encourage, be involved with or associate with these types of people, nor do they want our relationship with Mexico compromised by outside, xenophobic groups perpetuating hatred of humanity."

When Simcox held a border-watch training event for his militia in January 2003, all of two volunteers showed up to take part. Four reporters were there to cover them.

That was pretty much how it went for Simcox's militia for a couple of years. The actual border watches would attract a handful of volunteers, many of them of dubious background at best. But there were always journalists of various kinds to be found: TV reporters, newspaper scribes, documentary filmmakers. They became Simcox's target audience.

It's certain that he wasn't making many inroads with his neighbors in southern Arizona. The city councils in both Douglas and Tombstone, along with the Cochise County Board of Supervisors, passed resolutions condemning efforts to form citizen-militia border-watch operations.

"We want the citizens of Tombstone, Cochise County and Arizona to know that the city of Tombstone doesn't agree with the vigilante approach he's taking," said Tombstone mayor Dusty Escapule. "It can't end in a good situation. It's gonna get somebody hurt or killed."

There were pragmatic aspects to officials concern as well—like the fact that adding amateur firepower to a complex and dangerous situation was pouring gasoline on a fire. Cochise County Supervisors chair Pat Call pointed out that Simcox's armed civilians were in way over their heads: "The Border Patrol is facing fire power greater and more sophisticated than anything they carry," he said. "Right now, every evening, there are armed, nervous Border Patrol agents walking around in the dark, armed and nervous drug smugglers, people smugglers and armed and nervous residents. To add to this mix nervous, armed or poorly trained civilians, it just isn't good."

Locals in Tombstone pretty quickly adopted a view of Simcox very much like that held by his former colleagues at Wildwood. "He's got an ego problem," said Bob Krueger, himself a relatively recent transplant. "He's got some kind of psychological need to be important and be recognized. This has more to do with him than with the real problems on the border."

Borane also made his disdain for Simcox unmistakable: "That asshole is nothing but a media-publicity hound. He re-creates himself all of the time; he resurrects himself, and he will affiliate himself with anybody who can get any attention."

Joanne Young, a bartender at the Crazy Horse Saloon in Tombstone, observed: "Simcox doesn't have 10 people in this town on his side." Noting Tombstone's reliance on tourism, she said in 2003 that "visitors are down this year from last. People are calling and saying, 'I don't want to bring my children there; it isn't safe.'"

Sheriff Larry Dever tried to discourage them too: "Unfortunately, this kind of circumstance and these kinds of cries for forming posses invite fringe associations and agendas we don't need. They think it's a game or a sport."

Around the corner from the *Tumbleweed*, Pete Tiscia was watching it all develop from the vantage point of his pawnshop, which specialized in buying and selling guns. "I think it's a big accident waiting to happen," he said. "Somebody's gonna get 'cowboy crazy' and shoot somebody."

Given this bunch, it might even be themselves getting shot. Especially if the guy leading them was sticking a gun down the front of his jeans.

It probably didn't help when, out on a Civil Homeland Defense patrol on January 26, 2003, Simcox wandered onto the Coronado National Monument, which prohibits guns within its boundaries. He was ticketed by the park ranger and his gun confiscated. Police also found the following among Simcox's possessions: a document entitled "Mission Plan," a police scanner, two walkie-talkies, and a toy figure of Wyatt Earp on horseback.

||

The thing is, there really is a problem on the border.

The extremist right in America has always fed on real grievances that go either unaddressed or are mishandled by the mainstream system—by government, and in particular the federal government. In the 1980s and '90s, they channeled discontent with badly malfunctioning federal farming and land-use policies in rural America into uprisings like the Posse Comitatus and Patriot/militia movements and their various offshoots, such as the Montana Freemen. This led to armed standoffs with federal agents and varying waves of domestic terrorism, all of it emanating from the American heartland.

What these extremists always tell their audiences is that there are simple reasons for their current miseries—inevitably, it is a combination of a secret cabal of elite conspirators running society like a puppet show at the top, crushing the middle-class working man from above, while a parasitic underclass saps his strength from below. This usually plays out, in the worldview of right-wing extremists, as being part of a secret conspiracy to enslave ordinary working people and destroy America.

What gives them special traction, however, is their knack for finding unaddressed grievances and exploiting them as examples of this conspiracy, thus manipulating working-class people who have legitimate problems. Their agenda comes wrapped in an appeal telling people that they not only feel their pain but have the answers to end it. And their strategy works, time and again.

In the twenty-first century, right-wing extremists became focused on a similarly dysfunctional immigration system as a means to recruit believers, in part because nativism is part of the genetic structure of the racist American right, dating back to the heyday of the Ku Klux Klan, and in part because it was such a ripe opportunity target. After all, American immigration policy in the past forty years and more has time and again proven a colossal bureaucratic bungle that no one has been able to untangle, which presents an opening for right-wing extremists to jump in and offer their toxic solutions. Moreover, as is always the case in such vacuums, it is ordinary working-class people who wind up paying the price for the problems that ensue from such bungles, and extremists have long honed their appeals to reach those disgruntled citizens. This was nowhere more evident than in the desert landscape of Arizona in the first decade of the new millennium. It was there that these misbegotten policies came home to roost, embodied in a flood of border-crossing immigrants who defied both death and the law—sometimes not successfully—in a desperate attempt to reach work north of the border, and who in the process trampled on people's ranches and yards and inflamed not only resentment but the increasingly paranoid fears of the people already living there.

The underlying problems inherent in the American immigration system probably date as far back as the Klan's heyday, when Congress passed the Immigration Act of 1924. Also known as the Asian Exclusion Act, this was an explicitly xenophobic law whose primary purpose was to eliminate any further immigration from Japan and other Asian nations, largely because the Japanese were believed to be incapable of becoming "real Americans." It also first enshrined in law the concept of the "illegal alien" and created a system of national quotas that would permit immigration officials to regulate the racial and ethnic composition of the people coming over American borders. Most of the explicitly racial and ethnic components of the law were gradually stripped out over the ensuing years, but the xenophobic bones of the system—predicated on creating a seemingly interminable maze of hurdles and hoops for immigrants to jump through en route to citizenship—have remained firmly in place.

The deadly crisis in the Arizona desert was created by a series of policy changes begun during the administration of George H. W. Bush and then exacerbated by the Clinton administration in the 1990s. The big gorilla among these was the North American Free Trade Agreement (NAFTA), which was negotiated by Bush Sr., Canadian prime minister Brian Mulroney, and Mexican president Carlos Salinas de Gortari in 1993, and then ratified with the active support of Bush's successor, Bill Clinton. The treaty, which in creating a trilateral trade bloc opened up the ability of investment capital to cross borders freely, was sold to the American public as, among other things, an essential component in controlling immigration.

The Clinton administration followed NAFTA with a series of border operations apparently intended to ensure that, even if capital could now cross the borders freely, labor could not. The first of these was called Operation Hold the Line, begun in late 1993, and its focus was to clamp down on the steady flow of illegal immigrants who came to the United States through the border cities of Ciudad Juarez, Mexico, and El Paso, Texas. By adding manpower and enhancing patrols in weakly secure areas where people traditionally walked across the border, the Border Patrol was able to effectively close off one of the major ports through which people usually crossed on their way north to work. This was followed shortly, in October 1994, by Operation Gatekeeper at the San Diego/Tijuana crossing corridor in California.

At first, the Border Patrol boasted of the marvelous success of these operations. Apprehensions dropped precipitously in the months after they were initiated, indicating, according to analysts, "better deterrence": that is, it was believed the programs effectively discouraged people from trying to cross the border. "We can control the border, in fact," boasted Mark Krikorian of the nativist Center for Immigration Studies, which eagerly supported the operations. "But there is more to be done."

In reality, not only did these operations eventually prove the futility of an enforcement-heavy approach to securing the border, but they also became a human disaster—precisely because immigrants were no longer crossing at El Paso or San Diego. Instead, they were now fanning out into the countryside, attempting life-threatening border crossings in the middle of the desert. Like a river when a boulder falls into its path, the immigrants simply flowed out into the outlying areas.

Hardly anyone observed this phenomenon at first, because they were so enamored with the results of their El Paso experiment. Two more Clinton-administration campaigns followed: Operation Safeguard, in Nogales, Arizona, in 1996, and Operation Rio Grande on the southern Texas border in 1998. The administration also sponsored and passed the Illegal Immigration Reform and Immigration Act of 1996, which massively expanded funding for the Border Patrol, called for construction of border fences in key areas, and toughened penalties for human smuggling. All for naught: by the end of the 1990s, studies demonstrated clearly that the flow of immigrants over the southern border had been anything but stanched. Estimates showed that by the end of 1999, some 5.5 million illegal immigrants lived in the United States, reflecting an annual increase of at least 275,000.

The numbers kept growing because the tide of immigrants had swollen to a tsunami—in large part because of NAFTA and its effects on the Mexican and American economies. When Mexico approved NAFTA in 1992, President Salinas abolished a provision in the Mexican constitution that protected the traditional small Mexican farmers from competition with corporate agribusiness, particularly American corporations. This proved disastrous for those farmers, whose chief staple was corn—a crop with deep historic roots in Mexico. For centuries even before the arrival of the Spanish conquistadors, Mayan farmers had cultivated corn in their milpas, the small acreages that farmers cleared out of the local landscapes so they could cultivate corn, beans, and squash. Over the ensuing centuries, small farms had remained one of the staples of the Mexican economy. Now, thanks to the arrival of American agribusiness under the banner of NAFTA, that way of life was being rubbed out.

Cheap American corn put over a million Mexican farmers out of business, and that was just the beginning. With the economy collapsing around them, scores of manufacturers who specialized in clothing, toys, footwear, and leather goods all went out of business. The only upside to NAFTA for Mexico—the arrival of new manufacturing jobs, including auto-building plants, as they departed the United States for cheaper shores, and of a fresh wave of maquiladora, the plants where various manufacturers would outsource their labor to Mexico—proved illusory. By 2000, many of those jobs had been taken to even cheaper labor sources in Asia, and the bleeding only grew worse from there.

In the meantime, the American economy—riding along first on a technology bubble and then on a housing bubble—was bustling, creating in the process in excess of five hundred thousand unskilled-labor jobs every year, the vast majority of which American workers either would not or could not perform. Yet the antiquated American immigration system only issued five thousand green cards annually to cover them.

The result was a massive demand for immigrant labor in the United States and an eager supply in Mexico seeking work. At the border, where a rational transaction should have been taking place, there was instead a xenophobic crackdown aimed at keeping Mexican labor in Mexico, with predictably limited success.

All that really happened as a result of the various border crackdowns was that increasingly desperate people were being forced into longer and more death-defying treks across the desert, and there were more and more of them coming. Typically they would travel to one of the old border-crossing towns—Nogales or Ciudad Juarez—and there contract the services of a coyote, or guide, who would take them out into the countryside and across the border and hook them up with transit to wherever their destination might be. As the tide rose and the crackdown increased, the prices for these services started to rise as crossing the border became harder and harder work.

One coyote told a documentary filmmaker in 2006 that the crackdowns had continually made his work more hazardous and expensive: "US border security has been tough," he said, describing how he used to just take border crossers to a spot a little outside of town and help them get over, but those days were long gone. "I used to work two hours. Then four, then six, then eight, then twelve, then fifteen, then twenty. And up to forty hours. Now it's at forty hours."

What a typical border crosser encounters depends entirely on his or her luck in selecting a coyote, and their luck in choosing a crossing time and place where they can elude the Border Patrol. Some coyotes are known for simply heading straight into the desert and marching endlessly and swiftly, and anyone who falls behind is left to their own devices. Others are part of drug-cartel smuggling operations that are de facto kidnapping operations in which the immigrants are taken to "safe houses" in places like Phoenix and held for ransom. Then there are the banditos who hide out in the desert and wait for prime opportunities to rob, possibly murder, and/or rape the border crossers.

Those are just the human hazards. Then there is the desert itself. In Arizona, the landscape—dotted with saguaros and raging with color at certain times of the year—is inviting from a distance, but it is difficult to envision an environment more hostile to humans close up: spiny cacti, thorny ocotillos, rattlesnakes, Gila monsters, scorpions, and tarantulas all comprise the landscape that greets the border crossers. Finally there are the temperatures, which can range above 120 degrees Fahrenheit in the summer daytime, falling to an only somewhat more gracious 90 degrees at night.

So when the wave of immigrants began filtering out into the desert, soon enough people began dying in large numbers. The chief causes of death, unsurprisingly, were dehydration, sunstroke, hyperthermia, and exposure (coming in fifth was drowning: people often died crossing the Rio Grande in Texas). Mind you, immigrant border crossers had been dying on the US-Mexico border for years; the previous peak year was 1988, when 355 people perished while attempting desert crossings or the currents of the Rio Grande. It had declined to as few as 180 in 1994, when, suddenly, it began to rise again, beginning in 1995, breaking the old record in 2000 when 370 people died. In 2004, some 460 migrants died, and by 2005, more than 500 people were perishing in the desert.

Much of this was happening on people's private lands along the border or on federal lands leased out to ranchers who worked them. And so naturally those people were increasingly coming face to face with the brutal realities being created by American border policies—the dead and the dying and the desperate, all wandering through the desert in hopes of reaching the Promised Land. Most of these encounters were simply with people who wanted a drink of water, but some were not so benign, and these moments could be fraught with danger, at least in the minds of the ranchers if not in reality. The crossers also left trash in the desert that was a danger to livestock, and they frequently cut fences, meaning the loss of livestock, especially if they wandered into Mexico.

These frightened ranchers were the people Chris Simcox was trying to appeal to by organizing a border militia in 2003 and 2004. And even his local critics admitted that he was onto something legitimate. One of these was Pat Call, the Cochise County supervisor who sponsored the resolution condemning Simcox's plans. At the same time, he told local reporters that he shared Simcox's view that the federal government has been derelict in its responsibilities along the border. The county's resolution "demands that the federal government recognize and take responsibility, fiscal and otherwise, for problems associated with illegal immigration."

Call admitted that there was at least a germ of good in the attention Simcox attracted to the problem, but he wanted the world to know that the average resident of Cochise County did not favor taking the law into his or her own hands. "If we're viewed that way, it'll be a lot easier for the folks back in Washington to just dismiss us," he said.

||

Chris Simcox was preoccupied with how his efforts were perceived inside the Beltway, too, but he had found a simpler solution: media time. It solved everything.

A lesser ego would have eventually foundered on the utter lack of local support his border militia attracted. Fortunately for Simcox, he had his fellow California transplants in the border-watching biz for support. And more importantly, he was even more adept than David Duke at manipulating the media to "accomplish your objectives by their own misguided sensationalism." It didn't matter to Simcox what his neighbors in Cochise County thought, as long as he could count on regular appearances with Lou Dobbs and Fox News.

Dobbs, whose *Moneyline* and *Lou Dobbs Tonight* programs were staples at CNN, had a particular fondness for Simcox. He first featured a segment on his border watches in November 2002, touting Simcox's border-militia concept as an example of "Americans taking control of their lives" and "a close parallel to the idea of school vouchers." Over the years, Simcox would be featured over twenty-five times on CNN—fifteen of those appearances as a guest on Dobbs's show.

Soon others joined in the act. Simcox found that his patrols were natural media magnets. Fox News came out in January 2003 and did a segment on his border militia, as did CNN's Jason Bellini. The latter segment featured what would become a growing theme with Simcox, who tried to rebuff claims that his patrols were xenophobic and racist by framing it all as a matter of national security. With Bellini's crew filming, Simcox enacted a scenario in which a border crosser successfully sneaked across carrying a "bag of anthrax" inside a briefcase also containing an ampule of "smallpox," all to demonstrate to the public what could happen.

"Back in August, we came across a group that we know were speaking Arabic," he told Bellini.

Soon he was expanding on the idea, suggesting that foreign troops might be massing on the Mexican border in anticipation of an invasion of the United States. In March 2003, Simcox gave a speech in California to Barbara Coe's Coalition on Immigration Reform warning of this possibility: "Take heed of our weapons because we're going to defend our borders by any means necessary," he told the audience. "There's something very fishy going on at the border. The Mexican army is driving American vehicles—but carrying Chinese weapons. I have personally seen what I can only believe to be Chinese troops."

Simcox also began sounding other radical notes. He told Nikolaj Vijborg, a Danish documentary filmmaker, "Those guys [DC politicians] need to be, you know, lynched. If we're attacked again, then we need some vigilante-ism. Then we need some going into Washington, pulling them out of their offices, kicking them out of office. We need revolution."

His attitudes about Latino immigrants were also unmistakable: "They're trashing their neighborhoods, refusing to assimilate, standing on street corners, jeering at little girls walking on their way to school," he told the CCIR gathering.

Simcox similarly remarked of Mexicans and Central American immigrants: "They have no problem slitting your throat and taking your money or selling drugs to your kids or raping your daughter and they are evil people."

He also told Vijborg: "I feel that the people that are coming across, invading this country, I think that they should be treated as enemies of the state. We need to be putting them in work camps. Anyone could walk through these borders of this country bringing bombs, chemicals, weapons of mass destruction. I think they should be shot on sight, personally."

The border watchers he attracted shared those attitudes. In Vijborg's documentary, one of them—a middle-aged man named Craig Howard—sits out in the midday sun, watching a group of cows that have been wandering over the border from Mexico, where they eventually have to be herded back to their side of the line.

Howard drawls: "No, we ought to be able to shoot the Mexicans on sight, and that would end the problem. After two or three Mexicans are shot, they'll stop crossing the border. And they'll take their cows home, too."

||

It was not at all uncommon to hear people wishing they could take potshots at border crossers as things became increasingly heated in Arizona by 2004. That same year, an organization calling itself Protect Arizona Now (PAN) organized a ballot initiative intended to prevent undocumented immigrants from availing themselves of various "public benefits," most pointedly welfare. Inspired in part by California's ill-fated Proposition 187, which attempted something similar, it opened with the declaration: "The state finds that illegal immigration is causing economic hardship to the state and that illegal immigration is encouraged by public agencies within this state that provide public benefits without verifying immigration status."

Dubbed Proposition 200, it required all state employees at agencies disbursing "public benefits" to require proof of citizenship from applicants and to report anyone who failed to do so. Clearly aimed at Latinos, it was opposed by a majority of Arizona's public officials, including both of its Republican senators, John McCain and Jon Kyl, largely because of its vague language about "public services," as well as the clauses requiring prosecution of any state employee who failed to report any untoward applications for those services. Nonetheless, it was extraordinarily popular in early polling, reflecting Arizonans' growing animus toward Latino immigrants.

The gist of the campaign was directed at the broad belief that "illegal immigrants" were soaking up billions of taxpayer dollars by obtaining social services to which, as noncitizens, they were not entitled. The PAN campaign was bolstered by a number of pseudo-academic studies from nativist organizations such as the Federation for American Immigration Reform, which claimed that undocumented immigrants "cost Arizona $1.3 billion a year."

In reality, a number of studies demonstrated that these immigrants represented a net economic gain for the state. A study published in May 2003 by the Thunderbird School of International Management demonstrated, for instance, that Arizona came out about $300 million a year ahead. While the total annual tax-burden costs of undocumented immigrants were estimated to be $250 million, and uncompensated health-care costs at $31 million, immigrants contributed heavily through taxes collected, both in paycheck deductions and in sales taxes, to the tune of $599 million annually for Arizona alone. That meant, in 2000, for example, that taxpayers came out ahead by $318 million. This study was largely ignored during the Prop 200 campaign.

Officials at PAN let slip their orientation when they hired as their chief of national operations a woman named Virginia Abernethy, who is a professor emeritus (in psychiatry and anthropology) at Vanderbilt University. As it happens, Abernethy is well known in white-supremacist circles as a reliable supporter of their agenda in academic settings. Her work is frequently about the threat posed to American culture by immigration of dark-skinned races, and she has called for a complete moratorium on immigration to the United States, claiming that immigrants devalue the work force and deplete scarce resources, and that immigration from the Third World has produced, within American borders, a rise in dangerous communicable diseases. Abernethy is best known as a propagandist for white supremacy, having worked on the editorial board of the white-supremacist Council of Conservative Citizens, as well as on the board at the *Occidental Quarterly*, a journal run by American Renaissance, an organ of academic racism.

When an Arizona reporter asked about her views on race, Abernethy replied that she was not a supremacist, just a separatist: "I'm in favor of separatism—and that's different than supremacy. Groups tend to self-segregate. I know that I'm not a supremacist. I know that ethnic groups are more comfortable with their own kind."

The campaign attracted all kinds of nativists who made the pilgrimage to the state to urge its residents to send a message to those "illegals." Among them was Terry Anderson, an African American man who hosted a radio talk show bashing Latino immigrants on Los Angeles's right-wing talk outlet, KRLA-AM.

"Just because they're poor they cannot come here," Anderson told the audience at a PAN gathering. "I don't want this country to turn into the very thing that they're running away from. I want everyone to understand that so we can work together to, as harsh as this sounds, get every one of them out of here. Deport them.

"And let me tell you how I would deport them. I would deport the kids in the grade schools, I would deport the kids in the preschools, I would go into the hospitals and take them out with the IV still stuck in their arm. I would deport them to a hospital in their own country, wherever it is. I would go into the nursing homes and I would deport old people, I would deport the mothers watching those Spanish-language soaps, and I would go on the job, kick the father right into the van and tell him to take his behind down to wherever he came from—now! That's fair!"

The audience hooted and applauded loudly.

Proposition 200 wound up winning handily in November 2004 with 56 percent of the vote. A postelection survey found that voters were primarily motivated by "negative feelings toward illegal immigrants."

||

Another KRLA-AM host, George Putnam, was also on the anti-immigration bandwagon, which made him a popular figure on the Los Angeles right-wing circuit. That fall, he hosted a number of segments on the Prop 200 fight in Arizona, and Chris Simcox was prominently featured in several of them.

Putnam's recurring theme was that the wave of Latino immigration represented an "illegal alien invasion" of America, and he had been particularly keen on promoting Glenn Spencer's work in this regard, most notably his Reconquista conspiracy theory, over the years. Simcox was right up his alley: Putnam featured an interview with Simcox as early as November 2002, and afterward the border militiaman became practically a regular fixture. On an April 2003 show, Putnam made a fundraising pitch for Simcox, claiming that his "courageous stand" had brought the *Tombstone Tumbleweed* "to the brink of bankruptcy."

Carefully listening to Putnam's show, whose primary audience was in Orange County, was a longtime fan named Jim Gilchrist. Convinced beyond doubt that America indeed was being invaded by Mexicans, Gilchrist—who had never been involved in any kind of political or other organizing in his life—decided it was time to get into action.

Gilchrist had grown up in Kansas and Texas, the third son of a World War II navy veteran. It was an unhappy childhood: both Gilchrist's father and stepmother physically and verbally abused Gilchrist and his twin older brothers. He left home at age seventeen and headed out to the East Coast, taking up residence in Providence, Rhode Island, where he completed his high school diploma while working at a car wash. Shortly thereafter he enlisted in the marines.

"I went into the recruiter's office in August 1967, six weeks after I graduated from high school. I was eighteen years old," Gilchrist recalled for Jerome Corsi, his coauthor on a book about the Minutemen. "I volunteered for the Marine Corps in Vietnam. They said they could take me in four years and put me into an air wing where I would never have to see combat."

Gilchrist turned aside the offer: "I said I wanted combat. . . . I said I wanted to fight for my country. So, the recruiter replied, 'Well, there's a two-year volunteer enlistment program. If you join that, you will be in combat in Vietnam within six months.'" Gilchrist said that appealed to him: "That's exactly what I want," he told the recruiter. He was shipped off to Parris Island for boot camp and was in Vietnam by February 10.

Gilchrist spent thirteen months, mostly on assault duty, with a unit stationed just below the demilitarized zone. "An infantry company generally had about 210 men when it was in full force. Of those 210 men, 72, as I recollect, were killed while I was there. That's about 35 percent. One out of three were killed, and everybody else was wounded at least once." Gilchrist was among them: he got "dinged" by a bullet and received a Purple Heart.

When his tour of duty was up, Gilchrist came home to Providence and went to college on the GI Fund, obtaining a degree in journalism from the University of Rhode Island. He wound up getting work at a newspaper in California in 1976, so he moved out there and settled down. After awhile the lousy pay and long hours of newspaper work got to him, so he went back to school, got a degree in business administration and an MBA in taxation, and went to work as a certified public accountant.

After building up a nice little nest egg, Gilchrist and his wife, Sandy, retired to the town of Alisa Viejo shortly after the turn of the millennium. But Gilchrist was restless, and he was particularly interested in what he saw as a looming disaster in the form of massive Latino immigration, the signs of which were everywhere in Southern California. He listened avidly to George Putnam and Terry Anderson. The idea of civilian border watches caught his imagination. And after catching Simcox on Putnam's show in September, he came up with an idea: Why not take it national? Why not draw from a national volunteer base, instead of just relying on the locals?

He sent Simcox an email with his idea, suggesting that he could send out a national call for volunteers to a couple dozen folks across the country, maybe more, depending on what publicity they could rustle up. They would hold a monthlong watch on the border and make a statement. Simcox wrote back, enthusiastic.

Gilchrist already had a name for it: The Minuteman Project.

# 3

# Aftermath

Downtown Arivaca. DAVID NEIWERT PHOTO

Chuck Stonex was just getting up at eight the morning of May 30, 2009, ready to roll to a big barbecue at Glenn Spencer's ranch, when he got the phone call from Shawna Forde.

It was a short, unpleasant, and disturbing conversation, and it went something like this:

"Do you have a medical kit?"

"Not with me."

"Gunny's been shot."

"What?!"

"It's not serious. He got nicked in the leg."

"How'd it happen?"

"We were down around Douglas, and some bandits jumped us. There was some gunfire, and he caught one in the shin."

"Is he OK?"

"He'll survive. Do you have any kind of medical supplies?"

"No, but I can run and get some."

"Can you bring them to Arivaca?"

"Aren't you going to come to the barbecue?"

"Nope. Change of plans. We need to hole up here."

"Well, I'm still going. I can bring the medical supplies afterward."

"OK. We need to get some sleep anyway."

"All right. I'll call you when I get away. It'll be sometime this afternoon."

"OK. I'll give you directions then."

He hung up and went to get some breakfast and then spent the better part of an hour chasing down medical supplies. He drove to the next town down the road, Sierra Vista, and bought what he needed at a couple of different stores: some peroxide, saline solution, bandaging material, sutures. And it gave him time to wonder what the hell was going on.

Stonex had met Forde the previous October, when she was operating her Minuteman American Defense (MAD) border watch out of an RV park south of Three Points, out in the middle of nowhere but smack in the middle of the Altar Valley, a major smuggling corridor. He and a buddy had driven out from his new home in New Mexico, where he had just moved after the better part of a lifetime spent in Iowa. They'd read about Forde's border-watch operation through Jim Gilchrist's Minuteman Project website, which promoted Forde's work in Arizona with great regularity and even greater enthusiasm.

Stonex was curious to see Forde's operation, especially because it was being run by a woman. He'd been around Minuteman operations and was perfectly aware they were dominated by men and had a distinctively testosterone-drenched flavor. He wanted to see how she did it.

He came away impressed. "It was clear she was large and in charge," he would later testify.

Shawna was running the operation out of her little copper-colored Honda Element, a boxy car with van-like capacity—Shawna could sleep in its back end, which she did—and it stood out in a milieu where SUVs and big pickup trucks were the rule.

That October day, once again, it seemed there were more media people than border watchers. Two separate film crews—one from Belgium, the other from Norway—came and shot footage and filmed interviews, mostly with Shawna. Photographers and reporters took the long, dusty jaunt out to the RV park to document the activity. Meanwhile, joining Stonex, his buddy, and Forde in patrolling the desert were only about five other people. Still, Stonex was convinced.

"She was pretty upstanding—she was a pretty upright person," he later told one of the documentarians. "She just really knew what she was doing. It was fun working with her. A woman that knows that much and is willing to go that far—you know, to take the risks she was willing to take, to go places that nobody else was willing to go."

Stonex was impressed enough that when he got back home, he maintained enthusiastic contact with Forde, who in a few short weeks, similarly impressed with his background as an E-5 army sergeant, decided to name him her second-in-command at MAD. After that, they had remained in close contact by email and phone. The May 30 barbecue at Spencer's ranch was going to be the first time they had spoken to each other in the flesh since the previous October.

In the interim, Forde had hooked up with a military veteran she would only name as "Gunny" "due to Operational Security." She described him in glowing terms: "He served 6 tours over seas, where he has several medals. He received a Purple Heart, Silver and Bronze star, Combat Infantry Badge and a Presidential citation for his actions in the Special Forces. He will be in charge of all operations on the Southern Border, assisting in command decisions Recon and Tactical training." A few weeks before, she had named Gunny her new "operations director" and announced that "we are in full operation on the border."

So Stonex was dismayed that Forde wouldn't be able to make it. Not only was he looking forward to seeing Shawna again, he was curious to meet Gunny at last and size him up. Now it turned out he was going to be helping bandage him in Arivaca.

He didn't find it all unusual that one of the Minutemen had been wounded. "Two weeks before all this happened," he later testified, "in the El Paso paper I saw it—the Los Angeles, Chicago newspaper, several different national papers carried the story—to where the cartels had told their smugglers to go to any length to get your stuff, if you've gotta fight Border Patrol, fight 'em. If you've gotta kill a cop, kill 'em. It didn't matter. So to hear that somebody was in a drug smuggling corridor and got shot, I mean, what did you think was gonna happen? It didn't surprise me at all."

What bothered Stonex was that he was going to have to drive to Arivaca. That didn't make him happy at all.

||

Arivaca is a town with a reputation. It isn't a good one.

To begin with, it's a smugglers' town, situated as it is a mere twelve miles from the border. Both varieties—drug and human smugglers—make their livings in the remote desert landscape in which it sits, and in recent years as the Mexican cartels have taken over both businesses, there is frequently little distinction between the two.

On top of that, there is no local enforcement worth mentioning. The town itself is unincorporated, so there is no mayor, no city council, no chamber of commerce, and definitely no police force. (There is, however, a volunteer fire department.) The town sits at the most distant end of Pima County from just about everywhere, so the sheriff's office only occasionally sends a deputy out to the town, usually dispatched from the Green Valley precinct, a minimum thirty-minute drive on mostly winding, narrow roads, and usually only when they're needed. Under those circumstances, the sheriff almost always sends at least two deputies. Because, well, it's known as a dangerous town.

There is a major law enforcement presence, however: the Border Patrol has checkpoints at both of the rural highways by which you can reach Arivaca, so if you want to visit, you have to pass through one of them. And then along the way it's difficult to proceed any distance at all without encountering patrol vehicles perched along the side of the road on the lookout for border crossers and drug mules. It's not a comforting presence, but rather a disquieting one: they don't bother themselves with local crime, but their presence bespeaks the constant presence of lawbreakers. Local residents, moreover, complain that their federal officiousness is a Big Brother–like element that runs directly counter to the grain in a place like Arivaca.

Whenever Arivaca was in the news, it was always something bad—there were murders sometimes, or maybe someone from Arivaca would be charged with committing a murder elsewhere; there were drug busts involving large sums of money and even larger hauls of contraband; and sometimes people from Arivaca would die of drug overdoses, often on the streets of Tucson.

A lot of it had to do with Arivaca's unfortunate location smack in the middle of what had become a major human-smuggling corridor since the days of Operation Safeguard, when Nogales had been shut down as a crossing point and the swelling tide of immigrant workers increasingly turned to coyotes who would sneak them across through the desert—often the Altar Valley. This produced a steady flow of human traffic through the once-trackless wastes, and along with it a tide of criminal behavior and horrifying incidents: coyotes in cars who, while fleeing Border Patrol officers, would intentionally injure their passengers; immigrant women being raped by bandits and coyotes; sniper shootings.

Much of the action took place in the Tumacácori Highlands Wilderness and the Pajarita Wilderness, both mountainous areas directly southeast of Arivaca and northwest of Nogales. But it crept up to Arivaca too. In one bizarre incident, the owner of a border ranch south of town encountered a large helicopter marked with Mexican military insignia that seemed to want to hijack a fuel truck that had come out to the ranch. When American authorities investigated afterward, no one could determine whether it was a real military helicopter or a cartel outfit posing as one.

Finally, there were the economics of Arivaca, which in the end came down mostly to smuggling. It had originally been a mining town and then a ranching town. But the mines all closed down after petering out. And there is still ranching being done in the area, but not much anymore: the price of cattle doesn't support grazing on the Altar Valley's grasslands anymore, so what few ranches remain manage to stay afloat by bringing in revenue from other streams, most often as dude ranches that cater to tourists and the like.

The town's image in the surrounding community was simple: it was a place you didn't want to go unless you were armed. This was pretty much Chuck Stonex's attitude: "There's no good reason to be in Arivaca, Arizona," he told the Belgian filmmaker.

The reality of Arivaca, however, is a good deal less harrowing.

Like nearly all remote and rural communities, there is a paradox to living here: people are at once extremely independent and extremely interdependent. Both are sheer matters of survival. You won't last long here if you are not able to take care of yourself and fix whatever challenges naturally arise out of the course of living. At the same time, no one lasts long here without the aid and support of their neighbors; people genuinely depend on each other, especially in a pinch, and personal generosity with each other is almost always the rule.

So despite all the incidents that keep popping up, daily life in Arivaca is largely quiet and content. Like everyone else, Arivacans appreciate peacefulness and want law and order and safe neighborhoods for their children. They also like being left alone, not required to put up with the niceties of city life, the rules and regulations and restrictions. People live here because it affords them a real freedom they can't get elsewhere, and it gets them close to the land and the natural world in a way that's meaningful.

The desert here is not like the broad, flat, alkaline desert of Phoenix and its environs. The countryside is hilly and ringed with mountains, and the desert itself is full of life—even though that life is largely suited to an arid, often waterless, and scorchingly hot climate—and like nearly all the fauna and flora here, uniformly hostile to human beings.

The hilly terrain means that driving to Arivaca is not a matter of getting onto a classic desert-strip-ribbon highway, pointing your wheel straight, and heading toward the horizon. Instead, it is a series of twists and turns, followed by occasional straightaways, succeeded by yet another series of twists and rises, over hilltops and into gullies. Periodically on the drive, the striking pyramid-like shape of Baboquivari Peak, off to the distance in the west, appears above the surrounding hills.

You can't see the town until you're about two miles out, from atop the crest of a ridge overlooking the little valley in which it is nestled. There are trees and greenery in the basin of the valley, which is where the town itself sits. Part of this is a large wildlife area with a hiking trail, administered as part of the larger Buenos Aires National Wildlife Refuge. Arivaca is situated almost entirely along the paved highway, but many of its two thousand residents live in the immediate outlying areas, particularly the "forties"—land just northeast of the main town site that had previously been the property of the massive Universal Ranch, which had some years back been parceled out into a spread-out subdivision of sorts, with individual parcels of about four to ten acres each. This is where the local community center is and where Junior Flores lived with his family.

The center of town is the Arivaca Mercantile, a classic rural store that carries a little bit of everything, from groceries and produce to fishing tackle and T-shirts. It also has the town's only gas pumps. Gina Gonzalez worked there up to the day before she was shot.

To the east of the store on the main highway are the local library and a Catholic church, while to its west are the artists' co-op, where local artists sell their wares, and the feed store. Across the street are the town's post office and its cultural center in many regards: La Gitana Cantina, a pleasant little bar with a large open patio area for smokers on the side, while inside is a dark and cozy, old horseshoe-shaped bar around which locals belly up for a cold beer and conversation on a hot afternoon.

And that's pretty much it. There is a small grid of dusty side streets to the north of the highway, about four short blocks north and five blocks west, which surrounds the town's old Western cemetery. Albert Gaxiola rented one of these homes, and it was there that police found the teal van with blood inside it. That was also, as it happened, where Shawna Forde and Gunny were hiding out on Saturday, waiting for Chuck Stonex to show up with medical supplies.

||

Oin Oakstar had gotten a couple of calls similar to Chuck Stonex's that morning. The first came from his drug-smuggling associate, Albert Gaxiola, up in Tucson, telling him to get up and run some painkillers and antibiotics over to his house. Shawna was there waiting for him with a wounded Gunny.

Oakstar had already heard about the murders just up the road, and he had his suspicions about who had done it. Gaxiola's call only confirmed it. And at first, he was reluctant to go: it was a bit of a hike from his girlfriend's house down into town, and he didn't want to go anywhere near Shawna Forde if he could help it, since he knew what she was up to. Then Shawna herself called.

He asked her about what had happened the night before. "She said things got all fucked up," he would later testify. "They had to go back to get a gun that Albert dropped, and they had gotten into a firefight with the wife."

Oakstar was an Arivaca character, one of the people who lent it a reputation as a scummy community. He had been running marijuana over the border for years, and a few years back he had assaulted a Border Patrol officer when he had been pulled over with a load. That had earned him some prison time. After he had gotten out, he had come back and returned to his old way of living.

One of the people he worked with was Albert Gaxiola. For some time, he and Gaxiola had been talking about what to do about Junior Flores. They had decided, as drug dealers are wont sometimes to do, to take their competitors out of the picture. Junior and his brother Victor were first on their list.

But their ultimate bosses, the cartels in Mexico, would not sanction violence among their dealers in the United States if it wasn't necessary. They were stuck, it seemed. So in the fall of 2008, when Shawna Forde presented them with the opportunity to outsource to her Minuteman operation any violence that might be required to deal with Junior Flores, they couldn't resist.

The previous day, Oakstar had ridden in the backseat of Gaxiola's Chevy Astro as they scouted out the Flores-Gonzalez home, with Shawna Forde riding shotgun and Gunny in the driver's seat. When he saw Gina Flores out in her front yard as they cruised past, he had ducked down in the seat so she would not see him.

But when Gaxiola had come by that night in the van to pick him up for the operation, he had found Oakstar wasted on booze and pot and saying he was incapacitated: "I had been drinking, but I was not too drunk to go with him. I didn't want to go."

So Oakstar was feeling a bit hung over when Gaxiola and Forde called him, but he finally did as they asked, grabbed the requisite pills, and headed out on foot from his girlfriend's home, where he had spent the night, over to Gaxiola's place in town. It took him about twenty minutes. Shawna let him in the door when he knocked.

Gunny was lying down in the bedroom with a bloody bandage on his leg. Oakstar poked his head in and said hello, but the whole scene made him nervous. He noticed that Gunny had something under the blanket next to him, which Oakstar assumed was a gun. It occurred to him he might not emerge alive: after all, if these people had been willing to gun down a family in cold blood, there was no telling what they might do to him to ensure his silence. He promptly headed out.

Unfortunately for Oakstar, his reputation caught up with him that morning. Someone had already figured out that he might be involved with the murders at the Flores-Gonzalez home, and had tipped police to be on the lookout for him. Police in turn had asked people around town to give them a call if they saw Oakstar.

Oin Oakstar is easy to spot. He stands about six foot three and is prone to going shirtless. On his back is a large, colorful tattoo in honor of his hometown: "Arivaca," it reads, embellished with scenery and wildlife. Sure enough, he had not gone very far up the highway back to his girlfriend's place before he had been spotted and the sheriff's department contacted. Deputies caught up with him at the highway corner near the wildlife refuge on the edge of town.

They handcuffed him and then went to his girlfriend's house with a SWAT team. When they broke in and inspected his belongings, they discovered he had several weapons in his possession: a handgun, a shotgun, and an SKS assault rifle. Since Oakstar was a convicted felon, possessing the guns was itself yet another felony.

Detectives spent the next several days interrogating Oin Oakstar. But he clammed up. He believed they were trying to pin the murders on him, and he knew they had no evidence. Knowing they had the ability to put him away for a long time anyway, they believed he would crack sooner or later and spill the beans. They were right. But it would take awhile.

||

The first reporter on the scene was Dan Shearer, the editor of the local bi-weekly *Green Valley News* in nearby Sahuarita. He had gotten the call about the crime early that morning and headed out to the scene as quickly as he could, arriving sometime mid-morning. He was interviewing people at the Arivaca Community Center when he got word that something was going down in town.

He took off in his car on the double and arrived just in time to get photos of Oin Oakstar being placed in handcuffs. "Somebody says to me, 'Oh,

I hear there were shots in town.' Recently, like in the last half hour," Shearer recalls. "I drive on into town, and I capture them taking down Oin Oakstar. Didn't know who he was, didn't know what was going on. All I knew is that he was connected to the case, and then you see him later on.

"And Oin represents the worst of Arivaca, and even the people there would say it. It's an element that's there, but then the question is, how deep is that and how pervasive is it? And I had gotten a call maybe six months ago just saying, 'Hey, look, we've seen a few people who've been out of prison lately,' and it just takes two or three to turn the whole tide of the community."

Speculation around town was rampant, and the air was thick with fear. "What caught my ear on this was I have heard for a long time that immigrants were breaking into homes, doing home invasions, pistol-whipping people, and all this type of stuff," says Shearer. He had only been at the paper for less than half a year—this was his first visit to Arivaca—and had decided early on to tackle the matter of the area's supposed violent propensities.

"I went through two years of sheriff's records and found nothing on that. Nothing whatsoever. In Green Valley or wherever," Shearer says. "You might have a break-in, but you know what? Illegal immigrants are not going to be hauling big-screen TVs through the desert. They're looking for food; they're looking for water. They might be drinking out of your hose, but for the most part, that's all."

Reputation is a creature that's inflated by its life on the urban-legend circuit: other Arizonans, particularly those with a nativist bent, will blithely claim that there are home-invasion robberies in the borderlands every week, which Shearer knows for a fact is simply false. He challenges people who make these remarks to back them up: "Take me," he tells them. "Take me right now. I'd like to talk to them."

"Not once has anybody taken me up on that," Shearer says. "I'm not saying that it's not a dangerous situation. But I'm saying that it's exaggerated. I can imagine if you lived in a somewhat rural area, you walk out, and there's an illegal immigrant drinking out of your hose—that's probably startling for you. But that's not a home invasion. That's not a guy with a gun.

"We have seen an uptick in violence among those who are carrying drugs through here. You know, shooting at people and whatever. We've written about it several times. But that's a very different ilk than the people who are just coming up to work or for whatever reason."

The Flores murders, though, revived all those clichés.

That morning, the fear in Arivaca was palpable, like a living cloud hovering over the community. The murder of a local was bad enough, but the fact that the perpetrators had coldly gunned down a little girl was a power-ful indication that they had no limits. There had been evil acts here, but nothing on the scale of the unspeakably monstrous, like this.

And there were a lot of possibilities of who might have been behind it. Hovering in that same fearful cloud were the shadows of suspicion.

"It was a real shock," says Andrew Alday, an astronomer, a longtime Ari-vacan, and a neighbor and friend of Junior Flores. "It did tear the commu-nity apart. It made people realize: Who are our friends? You know, that neighbor of mine—is he really a neighbor? It made people really realize."

That morning, he had a visit from Albert Gaxiola's aunt, Clara Godfrey. "When he [Junior] was shot, she ran over to our house," Alday says. "Came running up to the steps crying. 'Oh, isn't it terrible?' She came to see my sister.

"I came up to the door, and I just said, 'Friend or foe?' And I had my hand on my gun.

"It was like, 'Oh, what do you mean?' I said, 'Are you a friend or a foe? You know, I don't know what you're up to. At this moment, I don't trust anybody.'

"I was a Vietnam veteran. I trust animals more than I do people. So she was taken aback: 'Oh, of course I'm a friend. How could anybody think that?' But I already figured Albert was involved. So I just didn't trust her. I thought those were crocodile tears."

||

Shawna also called her mother, sixty-seven-year-old Rena Caudle, at her home in Redding, California, from Arivaca that day.

"She called me when she was in hiding," Caudle says. "She spun me a great big story. She said that she was in hiding, that they were after her.

"And I said, 'Who?'

"And she says, 'The drug cartel. They're kicking in doors and shooting people.'

"And I says, 'You're kidding.' Of course, at that time, I didn't know what had happened.

"'Oh,' she says, 'You won't believe it.' She said a plane flew over from Mexico into the United States and was shot down, and that it was loaded with drugs and that the government of this country was bringing drugs into the country, and blah blah blah.

"And she went on. She says, 'If you don't hear from me in a week, I'll be dead. But I wanted to talk to somebody sane first.' And slammed down the phone."

The bizarre call got Caudle thinking. She knew her daughter. So she got ahold of the one person she trusted in dealing with Shawna's increasingly threatening behavior: Scott North, the senior reporter at the *Herald* in Everett, Washington, Shawna's hometown and base of operations. She asked him to track down anything that had happened in Arivaca in the past couple of days, and she described the call she had just gotten from her daughter.

"So he looked it up, and he emailed me back, and he says, 'Well, there was a shooting down there, a man and his daughter was killed and the wife was shot in a home invasion.' And then I got to thinking: 'She did it.' I just knew she did it."

||

Glenn Spencer's big barbecue at his ranch outside of Hereford was scheduled to begin at one p.m., so that was about the time that Chuck Stonex pulled up and joined the festivities.

Spencer had been advertising the gathering for a couple of months, promising to have American Border Patrol's "historic" unmanned aerial vehicles on display. These were the remote-controlled planes equipped with cameras and other monitoring equipment that Spencer would send up to fly over his border ranchland and watch for illegal crossers, and they were always a hit with the Minuteman crowd. They liked to have their pictures taken in Spencer's hangar with the gadget-laden mini-planes.

Spencer also promised that "ABP will be announcing a project to expose a major smuggling corridor that is left unprotected. In conjunction with this, ABP will discuss a new technology for spotting border crossers and a 'flag raising' on the Fourth of July."

Stonex was eager to see all this and to mix with the border-watching crowd. It's a solitary sort of calling, and the critics in the media and elsewhere who wanted to depict the Minutemen as a bunch of racist yahoos helped feed their already-ample feelings of persecution. So for Stonex, gatherings of the like-minded were always fun and invigorating, even if extended exposure to some of the folks you would meet there could sometimes turn profoundly sour.

That was where he met Laine Lawless. She too had come to the barbecue, and she was deeply interested to hear that Stonex was meeting up with Shawna Forde later that day. A staunch advocate of the nativist border-watching cause, she was thinking about writing a book about Forde and her heroic efforts. So she asked if she could tag along. Stonex said sure; he was eager for the company, quite frankly.

He already knew plenty about Lawless. He knew that, like Shawna, she ran an offshoot border-watch group, which she called Border Guardians. He knew she had made headlines a couple of years before by setting a Mexican flag afire in front of the Mexican consulate in Tucson. She had been one of Simcox's original Minutemen and had previously been a big player in Simcox's Civil Homeland Defense outfit.

There were also a few things he did not know about Laine Lawless. For instance, that her real name was Roberta Dill. That she had at one time been the high priestess of the Sisterhood of the Moon, a lesbian pagan organization. That she had more recently been corresponding with neo-Nazis, advising them on how to harass Latinos. Those things he would learn in good time, however.

Spencer's "new technology," it turned out, was called a geophone: essentially a magnet inside of a coil, it is capable of detecting the most subtle vibrations, such as someone walking in the vicinity of a spot where it is buried. Spencer planned to scatter them along his borderlands and see what came up. The unanimous opinion of the barbecue goers was that it was yet another of Spencer's ingenious innovations for catching Mexicans.

Time flew by in the hot afternoon sun, and pretty soon it was five o'clock and time for Stonex to head out for his rendezvous in Arivaca. Laine Lawless followed him out of town. They made a brief stop in Sierra Vista so Lawless could pick up some notebooks for her intended interview and both of them could gas up, and then they hit the road.

Stonex relied on his GPS to get him around the unfamiliar country of Arizona, and he consulted it on how best to reach Arivaca. It offered him two route options: the shortest in terms of distance and the fastest. He chose the first, thinking his pickup would be adequate to overcome the difference in time. This, as it turned out, was a mistake.

Somewhere outside of Sierra Vista, the GPS directed him to take a dirt road, he followed it, and Laine Lawless followed him. It turned out to be an excruciatingly slow backcountry crawl over mountainous terrain, trundling interminably over hills and into valleys on roads where even the fastest vehicle could only average about ten miles an hour. Following his GPS doggedly, Stonex wandered for several more hours on these roads, Laine Lawless eating his dust the whole time. Had they followed the other route on his GPS, it would have taken them an hour and a half; by the "most direct" route, it took over three hours. Stonex had wanted to arrive in Arivaca while it was still daylight, but it was now obvious that was not happening.

Finally, with darkness descending, he called Shawna Forde, and she promptly directed him to Interstate 19. Once there, they were able to cruise up to Amado and the turnoff to Arivaca. Lawless got out and left her car there, and the two of them made the half-hour drive in the dark into the town. Lawless got directions and instructions from Forde by phone, and they found their way to Albert Gaxiola's home.

When they walked up to the door, Lawless called out a code word Forde had given her by phone. From inside the house came the expected reply, and the door opened with Shawna behind it. She ushered them into the tidy little house that Albert Gaxiola kept, a one-bedroom affair with a laundry room and a comfortable living room.

Stonex—being something of a gun aficionado himself—spotted several weapons lying about. Behind the door was an AK-47. On the kitchen table was a revolver of some kind. Under a cloth on another table was a Ruger semiautomatic 10/22 caliber rifle.

And inside the bedroom was Gunny: a big, six-foot-four man with dark hair and a receding hairline. He also had a nasty gash on his front shin.

Gunny, it emerged, was really Jason Bush, and like Shawna, he was from Washington State. He also claimed to be a veteran of three wars, an experienced sniper, an army guy with tons of combat experience. Stonex had heard all this from Shawna already, but much of it was repeated that night.

Right away there was something funny about his story, though—the fact that he used the nickname Gunny. It's typically a nickname reserved solely for gunnery sergeants in the marine corps, not the army. "He was kind of funny, he was this guy identifying himself as a marine corps rank talking about army operations," Stonex would later testify. And Bush's explanation was far from convincing: when Stonex asked him why an army guy (as Stonex was himself) would use such a nickname, Bush answered, "It just sounds better."

In fact, Bush possessed a full set of convincing-looking military papers: "He had papers that showed he was an E-8, a master sergeant in the US Army, which outranks a gunnery sergeant in the marine corps," Stonex said. "He had some interesting stories. He was gonna settle it all. He'd been to Bosnia, Serbia, Afghanistan." At other times, he claimed he'd been in Iraq, too.

In reality, Jason Bush had never seen a day of service in his life. But he talked a great game, at least as far as Chuck Stonex and Shawna Forde were concerned.

Then there was his wound. "He had an injury to his lower shin, and they had it wrapped in some kind of bandaging. I guess I cleaned it up, we took the old bandage off that he had on it, washed it with saline and peroxide, and put a fresh bandage on it," Stonex said.

Forde offered a detailed account about how he had suffered the injury.

Gunny, she said, had been working in blackface: "You ought to see how scary he is with his face blacked out." She described their evening patrol in the Douglas area, the ambush of sudden gunfire from a chance encounter with bandits, and how they beat a retreat back to the freeway and into Arivaca and the safety of Gaxiola's home. She said she was afraid the drug cartels would come hunting them, and she didn't want to go to a hospital, since they had no insurance and little money.

But Stonex, himself a real combat veteran, had seen much worse wounds than Bush's. "It was a pretty good gash in his shin," he said. "I compare it to a ten-year-old doing a crash and burn at home plate. It was a pretty good scuff. But it wasn't nothing to be really excited about." He had brought suturing material, but this wasn't a wound that could be sewn up. So he just told Bush to get himself to a hospital if he could for a proper bandage. And wondered, at least a little, why someone who had been through three wars was so easily knocked down by such a minor wound.

In the end, though, it didn't occur to Stonex that he was being had by a couple of stone-cold, highly skilled, and deeply sociopathic manipulators, who had in fact also managed to fool each other as well as everyone else with whom they came into contact. Instead, they all chatted amiably for the next hour or two about their plans for future border watches like the one at Caballo Loco.

When it was time to go, Shawna asked Laine Lawless to take her car keys to Albert Gaxiola up in Tucson so that he could drive her Element down to Arivaca and enable her to slip out of town. Forde handed her the keys and a slip of paper with Gaxiola's phone number on it.

Stonex and Lawless returned together to Amado and then split up as Lawless drove on into Tucson to deliver Shawna's keys to Gaxiola. Stonex, for his part, had had enough of back-roads driving and stuck to the open highways all the way back to his motel room in Tombstone.

||

Chuck Stonex says he did not learn about the murders in Arivaca until Sunday morning back in Tombstone, when it was on the TV news and in all the Arizona papers. It confirmed his fears about Arivaca and made him grateful he had escaped unharmed. It didn't cross his mind to connect it to Jason Bush's wound. Rather, he suspected a drug cartel. "That's the way they do it," he later told a Tucson reporter. "I thought [Junior Flores] had been messing with the wrong people. So I sent an e-mail to Shawna, and I said, 'Hey, let's send this family some flowers. You know, to let them know as Minutemen that we stand behind them, that we're here for them.'

"I never heard back from her."

Instead, Forde—having successfully crept out of Arivaca in her Honda Element, retrieved with Albert Gaxiola's help on Sunday, after which she and Jason Bush rented a room just off the freeway in Tucson—published a post at the Minuteman Project website boasting of having "boots on the ground" in Arizona, citing the deaths at the Flores home as part of a fundraising pitch, in Shawna's inimitable style: "A American family was murdered 2 days ago including a 9 year old girl. Territory issue's are now spilling over like fire on the US side and leaving Americans so afraid they will not even allow their names to be printed in any press releases."

Stonex met up with Forde and Bush again that Sunday. They went out and ate dinner that evening at a Mexican restaurant.

While they were there, Jason Bush showed him a spent bullet. It looked to Stonex like it came from a .40 caliber gun. "He said, 'This is my souvenir from the other night,'" Stonex testified.

When they got back to the room, Shawna pointed out to Stonex that they had an extra bed, since their room had two queens, and he was welcome to use the spare if he liked. "It was offered to me, but I declined," he later testified.

Stonex found himself a room elsewhere in Tucson. When they parted ways that night, they did not know that the next time they would see one another, it would be in a courtroom.

|| 

Summer camp was scheduled to begin on Monday at the Arivaca Community Center, less than a mile away from the Flores-Gonzalez home. The yellow police tape just down the road was visible as parents pulled up with their kids in the morning. Many of them hadn't heard what had happened yet.

Brisenia was supposed to be there that morning too. All the kids in the camp knew Brisenia. She was a much-loved girl: other kids would get into fights over who got to play with her.

Instead of Brisenia, there were grief counselors. They were there to explain to the children why Brisenia wasn't there. Why she would never be there again.

One of the adults at the center that day said she kept trying to explain this to the children, and they couldn't grasp it. Finally, she said, she had to simply tell them straight out that she was dead. After the shock settled in, just about everyone cried, except those who were too stunned to react.

"It was horrible," she said.

A prayer circle was formed, and then a feather was passed from child to

child. Whoever held the feather was encouraged to share their memories of
Brisenia and to ask whatever questions were on their minds. A little later in
the day, the children put together a "Get Well" banner for Gina Gonzalez.
In honor of Brisenia and her love of animals, they made animal figurines
out of clay as gifts for Gina.

Alan Wellen's daughter, Sienna, was one of Brisenia's playmates at the
center, and the girl had learned the news the day before. "She cried for
awhile," Wellen says. "She had to talk about it. My daughter has had other
people in her life that died."

Even so, this was difficult to explain to her, he said. "When kids die, it's
just horrifying. And she had questions like, 'Well, could it happen to us,
could it happen to me?' And all that stuff. That part was really hard to tell
her—that this was very unlikely to happen to us, but it still . . . It was kind
of hard to explain to her that the reputation of the family is what the whole
problem was—not the people themselves, but the way that other people in
the community viewed them."

Down the road in Amado, where Brisenia had just completed third grade
at Sopori Elementary, the news had the same effect: "This is devastating,
shocking," Sopori principal Desi Raulston told the *Green Valley News*. She
described Brisenia as a "conscientious student" who was "well-liked by teachers and other students."

"Brisenia's teacher was so upset," she said. "We are trying to reach out to
the kids and to other family members all affected by this tragedy."

Just as at the Arivaca Community Center, crisis counselors were busy at
the school. "Some of these kids still carry dolls," Raulston said. "They're
young, but they still know something terrible happened."

"We let the kids know that it's alright to feel sad—that it's not wrong to
cry or feel upset. We just encourage them to talk about their feelings."

At the community center, at least, the healing process was beginning.
"We're a very close community down here," Ellen Dursema, coordinator at
the center, told a reporter. "We love and care about each other. We're like an
extended family."

Dursema described Brisenia as "sweet, beautiful and artistic," adding that
she "loved her mother very much."

Dursema said she held a fond last memory of Brisenia, from the last day
she had seen her: Brisenia and her older sister, Alexandra, making a human
wheelbarrow on the playground, running and laughing, full of joy and life.

||

Sometime in the early evening Monday, Pima County detectives knew they were looking for a woman from Washington State named Shawna Forde. They also quickly learned that one of her chief contacts in the Tucson area was a Minuteman activist named Ken Gates, at whose home she sometimes stayed while in Arizona.

Police descended on Gates's little mobile home late that evening without any warrants, asking for Shawna's whereabouts, and saying they wanted to talk with her. Gates answered that he had no idea where she might be.

"They asked for detail on how I met her and when I had last seen her," he explained to his fellow Minutemen in an email. "They asked what she had for a firearm. They did not ask about drugs or any other contraband. My wife told me that they had dug around in the trash in my pickup after they had left.

"Before they requested that I not let her know about the search, I called Todd [Hezlitt, a friend of Shawna's who lived near Tucson] and asked if he had seen her and if he knew what was up.

"Todd said he knew nothing of it, said he had seen her at Arivaca, AZ a couple of weeks ago, and would get back with me. He hasn't done that yet."

Hezlitt in fact promptly emailed other Minutemen with the "good news" that "county sheriff and swat are looking for Shawna. Last night they raided Ken's house looking for her." The word traveled quickly on the Internet.

Meanwhile, the detectives' search was coming up empty-handed, mainly because Shawna Forde and Jason Bush—hard up for cash after their failure to retrieve much of anything of value in Arivaca—went on a road trip to California. Shawna had some easy targets in mind.

On Monday morning, they got onto Interstate 10 just a block away from their motel and kept going westward until they hit the California border. Sometime that afternoon, they stopped in the Palm Springs area long enough for Shawna to mail a letter to her most recent ex-husband, John Forde, up in Everett. Forde had been shot five times by an unknown assailant the previous December and had kept his new address a secret, or so he thought.

"Guess who?" she wrote. "Miss you babe. Call me at work so we can catch up." There was an 800 number with an extension. The letter was intended to freak John Forde out, and it worked.

She also fired off an email to a select group of associates titled "Shawna's emergency contact list," reflecting the paranoid tale she was spinning for everyone: "I'm in deep and now have targets on my head including big brother I dont know who will take me out or set me up. But operations will continue. If you dont hear from me please check the following"—listing the Tucson jails, Pima County corrections, the morgue, and the Department of Homeland Security—followed by a list of seventeen names of people to contact for more information, including Jim Gilchrist of the Minuteman Project.

As word that police were seeking Shawna spread, a number of people in Minuteman circles fired off messages to her, asking her what was happening. One of them was a border watcher named Joe Adams, who operated his own spin-off outfit called Bluelight. On Thursday, he quizzed her about Gates's report, telling her it was "serious." Her reply came the same day: "What the hell is this? are you fuckin with me Adams? I havent spoke to Gates in a year I would think they would call me if this is true and your door would be kicked in since I been around you more. So Joe I dont do hoaxes thanks anyway, someone is fuckin around."

The next day, she emailed Gates himself to reassure him:

> *Ken just to assure you I'm not even in area and I have no idea what this is about I have done nothing illegal they may be concerned that I have crews out along the border battling the cartel. So take a deep breath and know all is good.*
>
> *This is alarming but not shocking you live in a corridor that is the main vain for all dope and humane smuggling and not all law is on our side.*
>
> *copy out*
> *forde*

Gates believed her, in part because he believed "patriotic" Americans like himself were about to get rounded up by nefarious government agents: "I am very glad to hear this," he responded. "Detainments are starting across the country . . . even for the don't tread snake bumper stickers."

Forde forwarded Gates's query to other Minutemen, adding: "So just for your eyes now the po po is inquiring let them." That email in turn was forwarded to Jim Gilchrist, who began making inquiries about Forde's whereabouts.

Gilchrist phoned Forde personally to find out what was up. She dismissed the reports, saying Gates was a disgruntled ex-MAD member: "She was as calm as can be," Gilchrist later told reporter Scott North of the Everett *Herald.*

In fact, Shawna and company weren't too far from Gilchrist himself: Forde's emails in this period were sent from California. And on Saturday, June 6—a full week after the Arivaca murders—Forde and Jason Bush checked into a motel and RV park a block off of Interstate 5 in Cotton-wood, a little town just south of Redding—the city where her mother, Rena Caudle, and her half-brother, Merrill Metzger, both lived.

As well as Rena's friends Pete and Lyn Myers. Especially them.

||

On Saturday, Shawna Forde used her cell phone to call her mom, and right away Rena Caudle knew something was up. "I didn't know she was in Cottonwood, but I've talked to my kids on cell phones long distance enough to know that they sound different when they're far away," she says. "The sound is different."

She kept calling, daily, asking for this and that. The next day she needed the address of their mutual friend Lyn Myers, who lived nearby with her husband, Pete. Shawna told Rena that she wanted to send her a thank-you gift for the lovely remembrance photo Lyn had recently made for the three of them.

On Monday she called again. Shawna asked her where her brother Merrill was. Rena reported, truthfully, that he was traveling on vacation in Wyoming.

As a matter of fact, Merrill Metzger was that very day heading back home with his girlfriend, their vacation over. Shawna had first tried calling him, but she had reached his cell while he was stuck in construction traffic in Evanston, Wyoming. It put him in a foul temper, and seeing Shawna try to call him only blackened his mood further.

"I was upset with her, because when she was here, she had also stolen my pain medication from me," he recalled. "And I knew that she did it because I was telling Mom that somebody had stolen my pills, and my mother asked me, 'Well, what color are they?' And I told her, and she said, 'Oh, Shawna was counting up a bunch of them on the couch over here today.' So I knew Shawna had stolen my pills."

After escaping the traffic mess, he called Rena back.

"Hey, Shawna tried to call me," he told her. "Don't tell her where I'm at."

"It's too late. She called me after she couldn't get ahold of you, and I told her you were on vacation in Wyoming."

Metzger shrugged. "Oh, whatever."

Rena brought up her concern about Shawna's calls. "Merrill, when a person calls out of state, they usually sound different on a cell phone," she told him. "But Shawna called me, and she sounds very close. Like as if she's just right next door." Neither of them knew what to make of it.

That night the Caudles got a phone call from a neighbor of Merrill's telling them his house had been burglarized. That afternoon, a couple of men had broken in through the kitchen window in the rear, and a number of neighbors had witnessed it. Another man had been seen acting as a lookout. Merrill's son, Joshua, who had been staying with Rena, immediately went over to his dad's house to secure it.

Merrill got a call on his cell phone that same night. He and his girlfriend had rented a room in Elko, Nevada, as their stay-over on the way back to Redding. The caller was the neighbor who had been feeding his cat and keeping an eye on his place.

"Somebody broke into your house," the neighbor reported. "The kitchen window is all smashed out."

"Oh no," Metzger responded. "What did they take? Do you see anything missing?"

There was a pause. "You know, it's funny," his neighbor said. "I don't see anything out of place."

"Go in my bedroom and see if my safe is still there."

Sure enough, it was gone. Fortunately, Merrill knew, there was almost nothing of worth in the safe—some handmade jewelry that had sentimental value, and a handful of titles.

Still, it ruined Metzger's plan to get a good night's sleep. "So I said, 'Well, I'm not going to be able to sleep tonight.' We left the hotel room, even though it was paid for, and I drove on. I ended up sleeping a couple of hours in the car, and then we drove the rest of the morning."

||

Pete Myers was having trouble sleeping that night too. At about nine thirty, he was in the living room watching TV while his wife, Lyn, had retired for the night in their bedroom, and their twenty-eight-year-old son Matthew, a developmentally disabled man, was in his room asleep. There was a knock on the door of their Shasta Lake, California, home.

"These two guys are standing there in plainclothes," Myers recalls. One of them—a big guy with a beard and a receding hairline—had a badge on his belt and a blue folder in his hand. "He said, 'Hey, we're here from the marshals service. We need to ask you a few questions.' And I didn't think anything of it. I thought, 'Well, shoot, I'll help the cops out.'

"What I should have done in retrospect is to ask for picture ID, and if they didn't produce anything, I would have told them to get lost. Well, like a dummy, I just let them in the house. You know, I didn't think people were gonna do that kind of stuff—pose as cops."

No sooner were they in the house than the big guy with the badge pulled out a big handgun—Myers identified it as a Smith and Wesson .357 six-inch-barrel revolver—and looked at him coldly.

"We're not here to ask questions," he said. "This is a robbery. And we know you have a large amount of cash in the house."

The other man came up behind Myers and pulled his hands behind him and cuffed him with a long plastic zip tie. Lyn was awakened and brought into the living room. The big man with the gun ordered her to go get the money out of their safe.

"Well, she went in the bedroom, and she couldn't find the key to the lockbox I had the money in, so I had to go in and tell her where the key was," Myers recalls. "And on the way in there, the other guy that was with him—I don't know his name—told me: 'Don't worry, I'll get you out of this.' And I'm thinking, 'What do you mean, get me out of this? Not end up dead, or get my money back, or what?' Apparently it was 'not end up dead.'"

The safe duly opened, Lyn took out the two bank envelopes containing all their cash and, following the big man's instructions, placed them in the blue file folder as he held it open.

"Then we all went back out to the living room," Myers says. "They tied my wife up. They didn't tie my son up because he's developmentally disabled, and he knew that. I told him, 'You don't need to tie him up. He can't hurt you. He's disabled.' And he says, 'I know.'"

The Myerses had no idea their friend Shawna Forde might be behind the robbery. "She was apparently out in the car. Because when we went back into the living room, he called her on the phone and said, 'Open the doors and get the engine running. We'll be out in a minute.' Then he proceeded to take my cell phone from me, and he took the batteries out of our house phones." Then they headed out into the night and disappeared.

Pete Myers didn't wait long. "I had my son get a knife, and he freed me. And I went and got my gun. Because I thought, well, maybe if they're still out there, I can blow their tires out or at least put a bullet hole in the car and report it to the cops. But they were gone.

"Right after they went out the front door, Lyn ran out the back door and went over to the neighbors and banged on the door, and they called 911."

||

Rena Caudle did not hear about the home-invasion robbery at the Myers house until Wednesday morning. But she knew almost right away who had done it.

"Shawna knew that Lyn had money," Caudle says. "Lyn, her father died, and she inherited some money, and she got the first $25,000, and was happy getting things she needed for her home and that. Anyway, Shawna was friends with Lyn.

"So Shawna called one day, and she asked about Lyn, and I said, 'She's happy as a clam. She's out having a good time shopping.' You know, just general talk. And I says, 'Well, she inherited some money, and she got $25,000.' Then I said: 'But you know she's got more money coming.' And we were joking around. So Shawna knew. She knew about that money.

"So when she called a little later, she found out Lyn got another $25,000. I said, 'Well, this time she's not spending it so much. She's got $12,000 sitting in the safe at home.' And I never thought anything was going to come of it. It never dawned on me that she would do that to Lyn. It just didn't. I mean, Lyn had welcomed her into her home, was interested in what she was doing as a Minuteman, and befriended her."

Rena and Shawna were among the only people who knew Lyn had that money in the house. And now, in the days leading up to the robbery, Shawna had been asking about Lyn. Persistently. In those strange calls that sounded like they were coming from just down the block.

"Now, Shawna was calling me every day from Monday to Wednesday and saying, 'Well, how's Lyn?'," Rena recalls. "And I said, 'Well, she's fine, I guess. I haven't heard from her. She's not called me or anything, but she's fine.' And so at eight thirty that morning Shawna had called me on Wednesday.

"But about ten thirty, Lyn called me and told me that she had been robbed. And she described everything to me, and I sat there, and I says, 'Oh my God.' I says, 'Lyn, it was Shawna.' And she says, 'How do you know it was Shawna?' And I says, 'Because she was acting out of character.' She was out of character. Calling every day. And sometimes twice a day. And each time asking careful questions about Lyn. And so I just knew. Because Shawna had talked about committing home invasions. She sat here on my couch and talked about it."

||

At the Alamo Motel and RV Park, Shawna Forde asked the manager if he happened to have a crowbar. She showed him a safe and complained that she had lost the key to the damned thing. The manager declined to help out. (Merrill's safe was later found discarded in the weeds behind the motel, successfully opened after all.)

Nevertheless, Forde and Bush regaled the manager with tales of their adventures on the border. They showed off Gunny's leg wound and showed him the .40-caliber bullet that he claimed caused the wound. That impressed the manager, and he readily remembered the pair a week later when television news shows ran photos of Shawna and Jason, at which point he called police.

Shawna had also been in phone contact with a Colorado militiaman named Ron Wedow off and on throughout the week. Wedow's code name was Raven, and he was on Shawna's contact list along with another Colorado Minuteman, Robert Copley, code-named Anglo. Before the operation in Arivaca, she had talked with Wedow at length about her plan to finance the movement by hitting drug dealers and making off with their money. He and Anglo had had a meeting with her to discuss the plan. Now they wanted to know what was going on.

She had first talked to Wedow on June 2. She told Wedow that "all kinds of shit was coming down" in Arivaca. "There was a home invasion where they killed a little nine-year-old girl," she told him.

"Do you know anything about that?" Wedow asked.

"I don't know shit about that," Forde replied. "If the cops want to talk to me, they can call me."

Wedow asked Forde if she still planned the home-invasion operation they had discussed in Colorado. "Our main guy is in jail," Forde said. "We'll have to bail him out."

Forde told Wedow that deputies had arrested "all of the locals and wanted to question everybody." Wedow asked if he should come down there. "Let the heat die down for a week," Forde told him. Of course, she was already in California by then.

Wedow asked Forde: "Do you need a place to cool off?"

"I might."

"I'm here for you," he told her.

Forde told Wedow that bandits had wounded a comrade during a recent operation in a wash off of the Sasabe Highway: "I have a buddy who got two bullets in the leg" was the story now.

Wedow asked Forde how she bearing up under the strain. "I don't trust anybody," she said. "I'm the person that is willing to take it to the next level, and that scares them."

On June 9, the day after the Myers home was robbed, Shawna talked with Wedow again. He asked Forde if she had a new target.

She replied that they did. "We did a couple of operations without you," she added.

Wedow told Forde that he didn't really trust another of the informants who had met with her in Colorado on May 15. Forde answered that she did trust him, adding: "We can train him. We can start him on soft targets. Our hands are already dirty. We've got to know he can pull the trigger."

Bush got on the phone and talked about his recovery from his gunshot wound. Then he told Wedow: "We have a couple new areas; we have our eye on a couple potentials. We'll be ready to go Thursday or Friday."

Forde got back on the phone and bragged about Bush's toughness: "It's a brand-new team. They've been bled in."

Wedow offered to come to Tucson the next day. "That would be great," Forde was heard saying. They talked about finding a new base of operations in the Three Points area.

Forde then rambled on about her plans for a business, to be operated in the mold of the mercenaries at Blackwater, that would rescue people who had been kidnapped. "You can't say 'mercenary' in the US without getting arrested," she told Wedow. "A lot of people underestimate me."

Not everyone. What Forde did not know was that every word was being recorded by FBI agents, who were no longer underestimating her.

||

After talking with Ken Gates on June 1, Pima County detectives concluded that Shawna Forde was likely an interstate fugitive. That gave them all the reason they needed to call in the FBI.

As it happened, FBI agents in Colorado had received an interesting visit from Ron Wedow and Bob Copley, aka "Raven" and "Anglo," late that same day. The two men had just heard of the murders in Arivaca and had promptly gotten in touch with their handlers at the FBI: both of them, it turned out, occasionally worked as paid informants. The Denver agents then got in touch with agents in Arizona, who were already digging around for information about Shawna Forde and trying to track down her whereabouts.

Thanks to Forde's phone conversations with Wedow, they began picking up her track in California and realized that she was preparing to return to Arizona. The next question was where she would pop up.

By then, they already had a profile on the person who had dribbled blood all the way between the Flores home and the dirt road outside. They knew his name was Jason Bush. They knew he was a suspect in connection with two other murders in Washington State. And they knew he had last been living in Meadville, a little tourist town north of Kingman, near the Grand Canyon West.

Bush arrived in Meadville at his girlfriend Melinda's house early in the morning of Wednesday, June 10, a little after midnight. Shawna Forde simply dropped him off and headed down the road in her Honda Element.

Detectives, however, were monitoring Melinda's home, and on Friday, a SWAT team descended on the house and arrested Jason Bush without incident. They first took him to the regional medical center in Kingman and had his leg wound treated, and then carted him off to the Mojave County jail.

Of course, Shawna Forde knew none of this. She drove down the freeway for about seven hours, went back to the motel in Tucson she had used previously, and stayed there Wednesday and Thursday nights. That is where Pima County detectives first caught up with her: on Wednesday evening, they watched as Albert Gaxiola and his girlfriend, Gina Moraga, entered Shawna's motel room. The next day, they followed Shawna over to Moraga's home, where she and Gaxiola engaged in a conversation in the front yard. Then Shawna got in her car and drove back to her motel room.

The next morning she left bright and early and headed down to the border, south of Sierra Vista, at Hereford and Glenn Spencer's ranch. Detectives were now tracking her every move and informing the FBI of her whereabouts.

Spencer said he was working at his home when the woman who ran the office let Shawna in. "I was on my computer working on our report, and she showed up right behind me," he said.

Forde asked Spencer if she could use one of his rooms and his Wi-Fi to send an email from her laptop. Shawna told him she was organizing a program for veterans to get paid for doing border watches. He thought it sounded like bullshit, but he shrugged. No problem, he told her. Shawna went in, closed the door, and emerged a little while later with her laptop. Spencer says she just thanked him and left.

Among the people Forde emailed that day were Jim Gilchrist and his cohort, Stephen Eichler. They were discussing how to include her Minuteman American Defense outfit in their plans to create a referral system for would-be Minutemen who might want to take part in border-watch operations. Forde wrote Eichler: "The border is going to be HOT. Good things to come my brother."

FBI agents had been trailing her for some time now, following the tracks of her cell phone calls. Now the emails told them definitively where she was, and they closed in.

Forde had only pulled out onto the road from Spencer's ranch and traveled about a mile when she encountered a phalanx of squad cars containing FBI agents. They arrested her there, on the fringes of Glenn Spencer's ranch.

||

They also caught up with Albert Gaxiola that afternoon in Tucson. After Shawna was arrested, detectives took Shawna's cell phone and sent a text message to Gaxiola, pretending to be Shawna, telling him to meet up at a certain time at a McDonald's near their Tucson motel. Sure enough: Gaxiola showed up not long after detectives had set up the bust. He, too, went into handcuffs without incident.

At the press conference that afternoon announcing the arrests, Pima County sheriff Clarence Dupnik explained that Junior Flores was a suspected drug dealer, and the three people they arrested had targeted their home in Arivaca intending to steal money and drugs. Jason Bush was believed to be the shooter.

The suspects intended all along to leave no survivors, he said: "The plan was to kill everyone. To kill a 9-year-old because she might be a potential witness is one of the most despicable acts I've heard of."

Bond for each of the suspects was set at $1 million. At their booking appearances, the TV crews were waiting. One of the reporters asked Shawna if she did it.

"No, I did not do it. I had nothing to do with it," she told the cameras as she was led away.

# 4

# The Minutemen in Action

The media meet the Minutemen, April 2005. JACKIE MERCANDETTI PHOTO

In late September 2004 Jim Gilchrist and Chris Simcox sent out their initial email announcing the Minuteman Project: "Anyone interested in spending up to 30 days manning the Arizona border as a blocking force against entry into the U.S. by illegal aliens early next spring?" it asked. "I invite you to join me in Tombstone, Arizona in early spring of 2005 to protect our country from a 40-year-long invasion across our southern border with Mexico."

It was to be a monthlong convergence of volunteers from across the country on the Arizona-Mexico border near Naco and Douglas in April 2005, intended as a citizens' response to the "40-year invasion" of America by "illegal aliens." The first emails went out to several dozen people, but the list kept growing. By mid-October the announcement had gone viral and spread nationally.

By calling their new national border-watch movement the Minuteman

Project—and by extension, their participants as Minutemen—Gilchrist and Simcox were none-too-subtly tapping into their established base as an expression of the militia movement. After all, Simcox had called their operations "border militias" from the start, and both men were prone to believing Glenn Spencer's conspiracy theories about an "invasion" of America by Mexicans intent on retaking "Aztlan," not to mention their shared paranoia about border-crossing terrorists.

Many of their early appeals in late 2004 and 2005 went out to "Patriots." And it was clear that calling themselves Minutemen was a reference to the Patriot/militia movement's longstanding claim to be the heirs of the original militiamen who soldiered colonial forces to victory in the Revolutionary War. The Minutemen, after all, were the original militias' select teams— rapidly deployed, highly mobile, part of a network for early response— and they were credited with having helped pave the way to a number of military successes. Their exploits included the famed ride of Paul Revere, himself a Minuteman. That was the image these modern "Patriots" wanted for themselves.

As word spread, people in Cochise County began to realize this might turn into a circus. The three-person Cochise County Board of Supervisors split over how best to handle the vigilante army about to descend on them. At least one of the members, Supervisor Paul Newman, proposed in a February 25 press conference that participants obtain special permits under county zoning laws: "Without control, the crowd could turn into [a] mob," Newman said. If the Minutemen were gathering for a rock concert, Newman said, the county "could require permits and impose restrictions. We should provide at least as much oversight of this potentially volatile monthlong event." His two fellow board members, however, preferred a "hands off" approach and declined to require anything up front. Both indicated to reporters that they were annoyed at being pushed into taking sides.

Newman's public statements irked more folks than just his fellow supervisors. "The day after I spoke out," Newman said, "I received 250 hateful e-mails, and at least five were borderline death threats."

In the meantime, the story gained real traction on the right-wing talk circuit. Las Vegas radio talk-show host Mark Edwards of KDWN-AM was one of the first conservative pundits to pick up on the story. He began devoting entire segments to calling out volunteers for the project, and pretty soon the cable-TV talkers and Fox-style reporters came right in line, especially as the April 2005 kickoff for the monthlong mass border watch approached.

Among the first in line was CNN's Lou Dobbs, who sent out his correspondent, Casey Wian, to cover the story. Had Gilchrist and Simcox themselves scripted a promotional video, it could scarcely have been more warmly laudatory than the puff piece that Wian filed on January 25:

WIAN (voice-over): Two hours before dawn in Arizona, the office of the Tombstone Tumbleweed newspaper opens. Publisher Chris Simcox prepares to lead a group of civilian volunteers patrolling for illegal aliens.

SIMCOX: I've spent time here on the border and heard the stories of the people that live along the border, how they feel abandoned by the president and Congress.

WIAN: So he formed a group, Civil Homeland Defense.

SIMCOX: It's a direct challenge. President Bush, do your job. The people want you to spend our tax dollars securing that border. We don't need immigration reform. What we need is a secure border.

WIAN: Using thermal imaging cameras, they search the desert ravines and underbrush, popular resting spots for illegal aliens through the nation's busiest smuggling corridor.

SIMCOX: I've trained just about 400 people in the last two years.

WIAN: Some are former law-enforcement officers, and some are armed, which is legal in Arizona.

SIMCOX: We've been shot at, we've had knives pulled on us, we've had people tell us that if we didn't have that holstered firearm on our side that they'd kill us.

WIAN: When they encounter illegal aliens, they don't try to arrest or apprehend. They call the Border Patrol. Simcox says his volunteers have turned in 6,000 suspects from 26 different countries. Now they're recruiting new members willing to spend a month patrolling the border. (on camera): The Minuteman Project plans to have more than 1,200 protesters here at the border crossing at Naco, Arizona, on April 1. Then, for the rest of the month, several hundred volunteers will spread out throughout the area and try to stop illegal border crossings. (voice-over): Volunteers like Al Garza.

AL GARZA, MINUTEMAN PROJECT VOLUNTEER: I'm Hispanic, but not all Hispanics have the same concepts. We are Americans. We'll defend it 100 percent.

WIAN: The local sheriff says there's huge potential for confrontations between armed citizens, landowners and smugglers. He's warned the Minuteman Project to obey the law.

SHERIFF LARRY DEVER, TOMBSTONE, ARIZONA: Clearly, you

know, in my opinion, the cause is just. You know, securing [our] borders is an absolute necessity.

WIAN: The Minuteman Project says volunteers are being screened and
trained to avoid violence.

JIM GILCHRIST, MINUTEMAN PROJECT ORGANIZER: We will
not have a conflict with illegal immigrants. We will not confront them.
We will not engage in any combative actions whatsoever.

SIMCOX: It's not about who you are and where you come from or what
language you speak or what color your skin is. It's about you breaking
into our country.

WIAN: Casey Wian, CNN, Tombstone, Arizona.

Lou Dobbs continued to promote the Minutemen in his "Broken Borders" segments on CNN, which were uniformly reports describing how the
wave of Latino immigration was harming America, whether it was crimes
committed by "illegal aliens" (as Dobbs insisted on referring to them), or
the harm they were inflicting on American taxpayers, or the diseases they
supposedly were bringing with them—including, in one notorious segment
that aired April 14, 2005, the easily disproved claim, reported credulously by
Dobbs and his team, that thousands of immigrants were carrying leprosy.

Fears about disease-bearing immigrants had already been kicked up earlier that year, in February, by a burp of hysteria in Colorado, where health officials had been briefly swamped with inquiries regarding a rumor that
immigrants were bringing the Ebola virus—an African-sourced organism
that causes an often-fatal hemorrhagic fever in which victims bleed to
death—across the border. The calls to the Denver County coroner were inspired by Internet reports about a man's death at Montrose Memorial Hospital, suggesting that a Mexican man there might have died of an Ebola
infection. It turned out not to be even remotely accurate: the man had died
of a rare, noncontagious strep bacteria infection.

Who was behind this false and extraordinarily irresponsible rumor? Glenn
Spencer. He had posted it on his American Border Patrol website the day before, under the headline "Has Ebola Struck Colorado?"

When a reporter called him to inquire whether Spencer had checked to
see if his "reliable source" was accurate before publishing, Spencer defiantly
said he had not. "We put up rumors from people we believe to be reliable,"
Spencer said. "That's why we call them rumors."

||

Three weeks before the fraudulent leprosy report, in his March 21 segment, the Dobbs team focused on vigilante border watches like the Minutemen, propagandizing them as the efforts of noble concerned citizens out to do what government was failing to do.

News of the Minuteman Project had already caught the attention of Mexican president Vicente Fox, who happened to be on a diplomatic visit to Washington that week. And as John King reported to Dobbs early in the March 21 show, Fox was dismayed by the growth in the border-watch business. Indeed, it was one of the main topics of conversation with President George W. Bush that week.

It may have been a diplomatic mission, but Fox was in a blunt-speaking mode. Among the several unkind things Fox called the Minutemen: "border extremists" and "immigrant hunters" (*cazamigrante*). He added, "We will use the law, international law and even U.S. law to make sure that these types of groups, which are a minority, will not have any opportunity to progress."

This upset Dobbs deeply, so he invited Jim Gilchrist to come on his show and give his side:

GILCHRIST: The definition of vigilante is guardian. We're no different than the guardian angels from New York City.

As far as being migrant hunters or hunters of any kind? No, we're a giant neighborhood watch. We have a strict no-contact, no-confrontation policy. As a matter of fact, we will join our adversaries in prosecuting anyone from the Minuteman Project who attempts to harm or even so much as point a finger at an illegal alien. We're there to strictly, Lou, to observe and report that observation to law enforcement, to let law enforcement do its job. That's it.

DOBBS: As you know, there have been those who have suggested there will be hate groups that will take advantage of your organization, that will infiltrate and seek to carry out a hate agenda. What are you doing to prevent that? How concerned are you, and what assurances can you give that that simply will not happen?

GILCHRIST: Lou, there's no 100 percent ironclad insurance that you can stop anyone from doing whatever they want. I give you 9/11. There's nothing we probably could have done to stop that except not have porous borders.

We vet our volunteers as best we can. We have dismissed 1 percent of them because they had bad attitudes, mood swings, road rage. These people will present themselves in a matter of time and we will immediately extricate them from our ranks. We have a number—almost 80 members of law enforcement among us that know how to do that better than I personally would know how to do it, and they are charged with that responsibility.

Dobbs inadvertently lifted a lid on the Minutemen's paranoia, though, when he asked Gilchrist why so many of the border watchers intended to be toting guns. It turned out that what they were preparing for was an armed attack by the notorious Salvadoran street gang Mara Salvatrucha, or MS-13. Gilchrist explained that while he mostly felt safe down there on the border, there were places anyone would feel safer packing heat. For instance, the border town of Douglas, he said, is "a very dangerous community."

DOBBS: Why?
GILCHRIST: Just the message board innuendoes, the threats of, if any
    Minutemen come down there, they will be executed gangland-style.
DOBBS: By who?
GILCHRIST: It started with Mara Salvatrucha; the FBI took them out
    very swiftly. We were very impressed with their response to their death
    threats.
DOBBS: MS-13?
GILCHRIST: Yes.

That's right: dozens of armed MS-13 members were rumored to be gathering down in Douglas and Naco, ready to take out the Minutemen. The fantasy proved extremely popular with the paranoia-prone border watchers.

Likewise, Gilchrist predicted there would be over a thousand volunteers showing up on the border in April, with another "200 in reserve that we haven't activated yet."

Two days later, President Bush, saying that he would "continue to push for reasonable, common-sense immigration policy," held a joint press conference with President Fox and denounced the Minutemen: "I'm against vigilantes in the United States of America," Bush said. "I'm for enforcing the law in a rational way. It's why we've got a Border Patrol, and they ought to be in charge of enforcing the border."

That, too, outraged Lou Dobbs. As the April 1 kickoff approached, he kept referring to Bush's "insult" to the Minutemen on his show. The day of the kickoff, he hooked up by remote camera with Bay Buchanan, sister of noted nativist Patrick Buchanan and herself a right-wing pundit of some note, who was among the people gathered in Tombstone to take part. Dobbs asked her about Bush's remarks. She was similarly outraged.

"Lou, it was an outrageous response for the President of the United States to respond to a foreign leader who was saying something about Americans," Buchanan said. "We are—there's no effort here to break any laws, it's, you know, people who really feel an issue is critical and are trying to raise it to the national level.

"And for the President of the United States to chastise us, to call us names—first of all, name-calling is not a very—you know, I have three teenagers, I know it's a natural response for them, but the President of the United States should be a little above that."

"Bay, one last question," Dobbs said. "You're confident that the Minutemen will resist any violence?"

"I know that they are doing their best," she answered. "No one I met was even considering that. These people are thinking of having—you know, on lawn chairs and having binoculars and their cell phones, these are their weapons, that they'll call the Border Patrol. They have done their best to make certain. They screened people that nobody is amongst them that they haven't really checked out.

"There is no desire—we want, we are discouraging it at all points. And so if there is any, it will not be from the Minutemen, but somebody who's invaded. And I suspect that there will be none. I'm very hopeful that everybody will be safe, but that this issue will be raised to another level."

||

The project had in fact been attracting promotional help from some unusual quarters, as well as from the mainstream. News promoting the project was all over white-supremacist websites like Stormfront, where it was seen as a great example of "standing up for the white race." Likewise, at the website of the Aryan Nations, a link to the Minuteman Project was described as "a call for action on part of ALL ARYAN SOLDIERS."

Shawn Walker, a spokesman for the neo-Nazi National Alliance, told Tucson's KVOA-TV that members of his group would take part in the project. "We're not going to show up as a group and say, 'Hi, we're the National Alliance'. . . . But we have members of ours that will participate," Walker said.

Fliers from the NA—which, as Jim Gilchrist and Lou Dobbs did, described the wave of illegal immigration as an "invasion," but went the next step, claiming that it would cause white people to be "a minority within the next 50 years"—began showing up on doorsteps and bulletin boards and telephone poles in Arizona border towns like Douglas, Nogales, Bisbee, Tucson, Tombstone, and Yuma, as well as the urban centers of Phoenix and Mesa. They urged people to volunteer for the Minutemen.

National Alliance chairman Erich Gliebe told reporters that local members distributed the fliers to help the Minuteman Project. "We have found that a lot of people in the area are sympathetic to our message, but won't admit it," Gliebe said.

Chris Simcox was dismayed. "The Minuteman Project is in no way associated with these extremists," he told a KVOA reporter, insisting that his group in no way embodied racism and anti-Semitism: "In no way do we encourage or condone such anti-American hate speech."

Simcox also accused Douglas mayor Ray Borane, a frequent critic, of distributing the fliers in an attempt to smear the project.

"I wonder what he's smoking," the mayor replied. "He has no idea the kinds of people they're going to be attracting."

Jim Gilchrist had an idea of the kind of people they'd be up against, at least, expanding to reporters on the rumors he'd been hearing about MS-13. Gilchrist said he had been told that California and Texas leaders of the Salvadoran drug gang had issued orders to teach "a lesson" to the Minuteman volunteers. The Minutemen, of course, would not be intimidated.

"We're not worried because half of our recruits are retired trained combat soldiers," Gilchrist said. "And those guys are just a bunch of punks."

||

April 1 arrived, and it was April Fools all around in Tombstone.

The first day of registration for the border watch quickly devolved into a free-for-all when one of Jim Gilchrist's hard drives crapped out, wiping out the registrations of at least seventy-five of the would-be participants—over half the number who showed up. Problem was, no one knew who actually was on that list of seventy-five, which meant that everyone who showed up Saturday could claim—as many did—to be among the people whose names were in Gilchrist's dead hard drive.

So everyone wound up in a long line, waiting for their official Minuteman badges, emblazoned with the words "Undocumented Border Patrol," their official numbers, an orientation packet, and their designated patrol-station assignment. It wound up taking up to six hours, sometimes longer, even if you had signed up ahead of time.

Up till then, Gilchrist and Simcox had been claiming in their media appearances that they had been carefully vetting each and every applicant for the Minuteman Project using online databases, especially whenever they were asked about how they were going to weed out the neo-Nazis and white supremacists who had been promoting their efforts and who they claimed were banned from their project. (At one point, they even claimed to be working with the FBI to run background checks, at least until the FBI flatly denied this was the case.) After the computer crash and the resulting registration mess, however, it became obvious to everyone that there were no background checks being performed on the hundreds who showed up that day.

Although they had predicted that over a thousand would show up to volunteer, and in fact the numbers were closer to about a hundred and fifty, it was abundantly clear that the organizers were not prepared to handle even that size of a turnout.

One of the registrants was David Holthouse, who had signed up online a couple of months beforehand. Holthouse was a reporter working for the Southern Poverty Law Center's *Intelligence Report*, and the mere fact that he was simply run through the process was a pretty good indication of the quality of the Minutemen's background check. Holthouse has a long history of writing about neo-Nazi organizations, sometimes as an undercover investigative journalist, and any quick Internet search of his name would have turned this fact up quickly, because he used his own name and the SPLC's business address when he signed up.

"Their vetting process was a complete joke," Holthouse recalls. "I didn't even show them ID. They were so overwhelmed, and their computers were crashing. From the time I showed up and put my name on a list and said 'I'm David Holthouse' to the time that I actually got my badge and was told where to show up the next day was more than six hours. It was just people standing around in a horse pen. It was totally disorganized. The idea that they were in any way vetting anybody that showed up that day is ridiculous. They were just processing people as fast as they could."

When they handed him his packet and assigned him a patrol position with the other volunteers the next day down in the Naco area—rather than being shown the media tent—he knew that they hadn't checked him out at all. "It was clear they didn't even Google my name." It seemed that anyone who showed up and gave a name was issued a Minuteman Project badge and post assignment.

Other promises flew quickly out the window too, including Gilchrist's promise to the media that only volunteers with concealed-carry permits from their home states would be permitted to carry firearms at the border watch. No one was asked to produce such a permit on registration day, or at any other time for that matter. Anyone who owned a sidearm was able to carry it at will for the duration of the project.

Rifles, including assault weapons, were a different story. That afternoon at Schieffelin Hall in Tombstone, organizers held an orientation session, though only about a hundred wound up attending. There the rules were laid out: people were permitted to possess rifles, shotguns, and any kind of long gun, but they were to remain in storage unless a need for them arose.

Volunteers were to take up watch stations along a two-mile stretch of dirt road situated on the border near the Border Patrol station in Naco, about thirty-two miles south of Tombstone, with each group of between five and ten Minutemen assigned to a station. If they were to encounter any "illegal aliens," they were to simply use their cell phones to contact Minuteman HQ so that the Border Patrol could be alerted. They were not to detain any suspected border crossers by force, and they were by no means to draw a gun to detain them.

This set off a round of grumbling among a number of the volunteers. After all, most of them had spent the past year or so watching footage of Chris Simcox and his border-watching militiamen do exactly that: hunting down suspected border crossers, then drawing weapons on them and detaining them at gunpoint until the Border Patrol arrived. Most of the participants had envisioned doing just that themselves down on the border, and already they were being told they couldn't.

The grumbling dissipated for the time being, however, as nativist celebrities like Bay Buchanan and Representative Tom Tancredo, an immigrant-bashing congressman from Colorado, stepped up onstage for some rousing speeches that wrapped up the session. Tancredo was outraged about Bush's remarks, too. He got the audience roaring with laughter by telling them that Bush should be forced to write, one hundred times on a blackboard, "I'm sorry for calling you vigilantes," and then required to erase it with his tongue.

"I'm proud of every single one of you. You are heroes!" he shouted. "You are not vigilantes! You are heroes, with each one of you representing hundreds of thousands of Americans."

Buchanan joined in the Bush bashing, telling the president: "You have failed! You have failed because you allow drugs and criminals to come across our borders! You have failed America!"

||

The day after registration was primarily dedicated to a big demonstration down at the Border Patrol station in Naco—a true border town, with its incorporated municipality lying on the Mexico side, and its unincorporated neighborhoods in Arizona—where all the participants lined up along the roadside in their vehicles for about a mile and a half between the station and the actual border, many with flags waving and big signs expressing their views on immigration and border security:

"Coyotes Hide Behind a Bush"
"No Border No Order"
"Dispatch US Army Troops to the Mexico Border"
"America: Enough Is Enough"

There were lots of "Don't Tread on Me" flags and even an occasional Dixie rebel banner. The demonstration proved to be a nice bit of street theater that kept the hordes of media who had descended on the scene—nearly, once again, outnumbering the actual participants—occupied for the morning and afternoon.

Dave Holthouse was there with his Minuteman badge, walking up and down the line. Since he had gone so far undetected, he was now in full-blown undercover mode as a journalist. "I have some neo-Nazi tattoos," Holthouse explains. "I wore a shirt that displayed them—I wore a shirt and shorts so that my tattoos were obvious. And I wore a T-shirt that had a Heckler & Koch MP5 machine gun on the front, and a Celtic knot on the back. Symbols that if you know—you know, it's not as obvious as a swastika or even some of the more well-known neo-Nazi symbols, but if you know, you know.

"I just started walking up and down the line of people sitting in the chairs, and it wasn't ten minutes before I was literally called across the highway over to a group of guys who introduced themselves as being members of the National Alliance. One of them had a National Alliance tattoo, they had a sign that was a hand-drawn copy, basically, of a billboard that the National Alliance had put up just a couple of weeks before in Las Vegas, an anti-immigration billboard. So I believed them when they said they were National Alliance."

The men said they were calling their patrol group Team 14—an obvious reference to the battle cry of the neo-Nazi movement, imprisoned Order member David Lane's "Fourteen Words" ("We must secure the existence of our people and a future for white children"). Having surveyed his tats and checked him out, they invited Holthouse to join their border-watch patrol, and he did so. He was with them for the next seventy-two hours.

That afternoon, everyone at the rally scattered to their designated positions along the dirt road stretching along the border west of Naco. That was when the grumbling resumed in earnest, especially once everyone got a gander at how the whole border watch had been set up. It soon became self-evident that this was all about political theater, not about actually catching illegal border crossers.

That was at least obvious to Holthouse. "When I worked for the Phoenix *New Times* back in the '90s, I did a lot of reporting on the border and did quite a bit of work on human smuggling and the coyotes and Agua Prieta and all that, so I knew the area. I knew smuggling for tactics and techniques. And I knew enough to know that, in terms of where they were positioning the volunteers, it was purely a media stunt. They were putting them in the safest position possible.

"In other words, they were in the part of the border where they were least likely to actually encounter any coyotes bringing people across, or any immigrants in groups self-guiding themselves across the border," Holthouse recalls. "It's just a really well-traveled border road. I mean, the Border Patrol patrols it, but they more use that road where they put them on to get back and forth between smuggling corridors. They didn't put them in a smuggling corridor."

Holthouse wasn't alone in recognizing that this was the case. Most of his fellow participants, indeed, came to recognize pretty quickly, after a few hours at their posts, that they were not likely to see much action. "A lot of the people there showed up under the impression that what they were gonna be doing was actually doing vigilante stops—and I think it was important to note, of exactly the kind that Simcox had been doing for a couple of years with Civil Homeland Defense, where they would go out, find people, hold them at gunpoint and call Border Patrol," Holthouse says.

"That's what a lot of people showed up at Arizona in April 2005 thinking that they were there to do. And they were disappointed when they found out that, A, they were being positioned in a place they were not very likely they were actually going to encounter any Mexicans, and B, even if they did, they weren't supposed to draw down and play Wyatt Earp." They were in Tombstone, after all.

The Minutemen had been sold on the idea of being heroes, and this wasn't anyone's idea of the heroic. It had turned out that their jobs weren't to catch illegal immigrants but reporters.

All day long for the next week, journalists from all over—the national news and cable networks, newspapers from around the country, as well as TV reporters from Arizona and other Southwestern states—trundled up and down the dirt road in their trucks and vans and stopped at the patrol posts to interview whatever Minutemen they could find.

Even the white supremacists Holthouse had embedded himself with got it. "We understand why Gilchrist and Simcox have to talk all this P.C. crap," said one. "It's all about playing to the media. That's fine. While we're here, it's their game and we'll play by their rules. Once Minuteman's over, though, we might just have to come back and do our own thing."

Then Gilchrist himself put their tolerance to the test that first afternoon on patrol.

A documentary filmmaker came by the Team 14 post with Gilchrist along and began interviewing folks. After awhile, the director posed the Minuteman leader for an interview with the team members lined up behind him, shoulder to shoulder in front of the border fence.

Gilchrist began holding forth. "We are not racists," he told the interviewer. "We don't endorse racism, and we're not a hate group. We've told white supremacists they're not welcome here, and we've kept them out. The only hate group members here are from the ACLU.

"The ACLU are no different from white supremacists," Gilchrist said. "They're a clear and present danger. They have the same mentality that murdered Martin Luther King, and they want to kill us. Literally the ACLU wants to kill us by invoking violence. We've been vilified and castigated as ghoulish monsters, as gun-toting, baby-killing war machines.

"We are not in favor of violence, and we don't hate immigrants. We don't have any problem with Mexicans. If they come into the country legally, we want them here. We want America to be a melting pot of all different kinds of people, where every race, color and creed is blending together."

This evoked a stiff-necked but silent response from the two neo-Nazis, who exchanged looks. Gilchrist, oblivious to the men behind him, kept rattling on.

"We are a peaceful demonstration. We're doing this peacefully, the way our founding fathers wanted us to. We don't need baseball bats and tire irons and guns and flamethrowers and bulldozers to wipe people out and level villages. We can do this peacefully, same way Martin Luther King sought justice for American blacks. We're followers of Gandhi and Martin Luther King. . . ."

That was enough for the two National Alliance members, who announced abruptly: "End of interview." Then both walked off camera.

Once they were out of earshot, one of them made gorilla noises and told Holthouse that Martin Luther King was "an Alabama silverback." The other said: "I hope he doesn't believe that crap. I realize he's gotta be all PC for the media, but come on—Gandhi didn't wear a gun. We're in a race war, not a peace march."

"So that was too much for them, to actually be used as props when he was playing the media game," Holthouse recalls. Gilchrist, he said, "was in kind of a manic mode, so he was off to do the next thing. It didn't register to him what had just happened. He thought somebody had just signaled for the interview to be over or something."

||

Some of the border watchers manned their posts overnight, but no one was required to do so. In fact, after the flush of the first few days, very few actually did. They either retired to their motel rooms in Tombstone or Douglas or Sierra Vista, or went to the Minuteman Project's "command center" in the little town of Hereford, about fifteen miles away from Naco, westward on Highway 92, on the campus of the Miracle Valley Bible College.

The college had been built out in the countryside by a Pentecostal evangelist named A. A. Allen in the early 1960s, complete with classrooms, dormitories, a domed sanctuary, a large warehouse, and a residential neighborhood, all dubbed Miracle Valley by its founder. After Allen died of acute alcoholism in 1970, the property had gone through a number of hands. In 1982 Miracle Valley was briefly the center of national attention after a shootout involving a follower of Allen's named Frances Thomas, an African American evangelist from Chicago who had brought her own following out to Arizona and tried to take over the community. A series of escalating encounters with law enforcement ultimately culminated in an armed confrontation in which two church members and a sheriff's deputy were killed.

Since then, the church remained in the hands of various evangelical organizations, most recently Melvin Harter's ministries, which at the time had been trying to keep it operating as a Pentecostal theological training school but not succeeding. The property was growing dilapidated with disuse. So the opportunity to host the Minutemen was greeted with open arms: the school's website posted a press release saying it was "delighted" to host the Minutemen, to whom it offered not only RV parking, limited dormitory use, and tenting on its grounds, but regular "special revival services" in its tabernacle.

The Minutemen made the place their own for the month of April 2005. Everything underwent a military transformation: the somewhat ramshackle dorms were renamed the "barracks," the cafeteria became the "mess hall," and the campus property line the "perimeter." Guards kept watch over the "perimeter" and patrolled the security gate at the entrance, demanding Minuteman credentials from anyone entering.

The paranoia that Jim Gilchrist had been cultivating over the national airwaves—particularly the belief that the Salvadoran street gang MS-13 was planning to come through Naco and launch attacks on the Minutemen, perhaps even at their compound—came home to roost in Miracle Valley. Rumors of imminent attack swirled wildly, and campers listened to their radios in anticipation.

It finally exploded on the night of April 4, when word flew around the compound that the MS-13 attack was about to begin, based on "a credible threat" the Minutemen had received that an armed gang was at that moment leading a charge of hundreds of Mexicans "over the wire" and against the Minutemen who were camped at their posts along International Road.

Dave Holthouse was there and watching it all with bemusement. "You had all these guys scrambling, putting on their body armor and getting their assault rifles and loading them, and it was just this frenzy of men jumping into trucks, and trucks are spewing dirt and roaring down the road down to the border," he recalled. "And you know, they get there, and of course, there's nothing going on. That was the sort of paranoia that was rampant."

After several hours of roaring vehicles and shouting men, everyone figured out that it was all a "false alarm," and they returned to their beds.

||

Among the Minutemen in the compound that night were two sixtyish men from rural Washington State: Tom Williams, a sixty-four-year-old Marine veteran and clinical psychologist (specializing in post-traumatic stress disorder) who had traveled from Whatcom County to southern Arizona to join the project, and his friend Claude LeBas, a former Customs agent and burly, bearded bear of a man who had accompanied Williams to help "cover his 6" (that is, back him up). They wound up playing a role in the big MS-13 panic and its aftermath.

When they arrived in Arizona, his background in military intelligence wound up involving Williams, with LeBas tagging along, in the work of assessing the people who were joining the Minutemen.

"It was sort of interesting," Williams related later. "First night, the sheriff says, 'Well, you know, here's what we got.' Somebody stopped by and gave Bear an intelligence report that we had a bunch of pickup trucks with MS-13 guys in it in Naco, on the other side of the border, with automatic weapons, you know, ready to bust through the gate, or come in and shoot us up in this church camp we were camped in.

"We had passed on this report to Gilchrist. The chief of security comes in, and he got another confirmation—the sheriff had been by to validate it, telling him it was true, and to be careful." Williams and LeBas were asked to assess the situation and quickly realized there was nothing to the supposed MS-13 threat.

"We realized, after we assessed the place, our biggest danger is the Minutemen," Williams said. "Because everybody's armed—well not everybody, we weren't. But everybody seemed to be."

The Minutemen's security chief asked them to help get the situation under control. "So we sort of string along and he says, 'Here's the deal, in an hour and a half, we're having a meeting with all the people who are going to volunteer to be on the reaction force.' I said, 'All right, cool.'

"Then we had this meeting. And of course every gun nut shows up. So we sort of cull them out. Get rid of some of them, use some others, and keep some real close to us. Of course, everybody we throw out we give the name, rank and serial number to the sheriff so that everybody knows exactly what's happening."

When they were done and ready to return home to Washington State, Chris Simcox and Gary Cole made sure they had contact information for Williams and LeBas. The men had proven valuable and would soon prove even more so back in Washington state, with its Canadian border. LeBas, as it happened, lived only ten miles from that border.

||

The Minutemen believed lots of stories that came floating into camp. One of the more widely spread rumors was that they had successfully bottled up several hundred "illegals" and their "coyotes" in the neighboring Huachuca Mountains who were becoming desperate for the chance to make it over the border, so eventually groups of these desperate people would make their break and try to cross. One rumor had a Minuteman being nearly run over by a fleeing "load" vehicle.

During the daytime, the Minutemen mostly performed their expected duties by fielding interview requests from various media types. And for the duration of the project, no one said anything untoward or radical on camera.

But when the day was over and the cameras off and the notebooks gone and the Minutemen were on their own, with no one watching, they opened up.

The participants almost uniformly had nothing but contempt for the journalists as exemplars of "the liberal media," though they were content to participate in the media game for the sake of "delivering the message." But there was a profound mistrust: one team even dismissed a fellow Minuteman from Tucson because he kept talking to reporters. Little did this same team know that it was hosting an undercover group of journalists from Phoenix's KPHO-TV who recorded all this for their audience.

The KPHO journalists found that when the Minutemen thought the cameras were gone, they revealed more open race-baiting and ethnic xenophobia aimed at Mexicans: one reporter described the racial epithets he heard, as well as the desire of some participants to go "hunting a certain group of people." They also observed that some of the Minutemen ignored project rules about openly displaying their long guns, which made other participants nervous and underscored how little oversight was actually in place.

Over at Team 14's station, Dave Holthouse listened as his fellow Minutemen explained their border philosophy: like Simcox's old friend Craig Howard, they thought that a few well-placed rifle shots would solve the nation's border problems.

"It should be legal to kill illegals," said one of them, a sixty-nine-year old retired Special Forces veteran who fought in Vietnam. "Just shoot 'em on sight. That's my immigration policy recommendation. You break into my country, you die."

His neo-Nazi compatriots nodded in assent. "I agree completely," one of them said. "You get up there with a rifle and start shooting four or five of them a week, the other four or five thousand behind them are going to think twice about crossing that line."

In the end, the grumblers resigned themselves to the reality that they weren't going to be busting very many illegal border crossers under these circumstances. Some of them vowed to return later, maybe in weeks or months, when they might actually make a difference, and "when we can have a little more privacy," as one of the neo-Nazis put it.

||

Before the project's launch, the Minutemen's organizers were predicting over a thousand participants, but the most generous independent sources counted only three hundred or so participants over the entire month of April, with the numbers growing especially thin after about a week. That didn't prevent the Minutemen from claiming that "thousands" had come to the border to participate.

Nor, for that matter, did it prevent them from claiming victory even before the month was out: "In just 17 days, the Minuteman Project has successfully sealed the San Pedro River Valley border from illegal activity," Jim Gilchrist proclaimed on the project's website in mid-April.

Gilchrist cited a drop in Border Patrol apprehensions in the Naco area as proof: whereas officers had apprehended nearly 7,700 border crossers during the same period the year before, the numbers had dropped to about 2,500 while the Minutemen had been on the scene.

On Fox's *Hannity and Colmes*, Simcox sneered at the Border Patrol's chief of the Tucson sector: "Alan, we did in 10 days what Michael Nicely could not have done in 10 years," he said. "We've sealed this border from April 1 to April 10. The last seven days, we could have been playing cards. Thank you."

Nicely himself wasn't so sure: "They're taking credit for securing the border, and surely no one with any credibility believes that," he told a reporter, attributing the drop in apprehensions to the presence of both US agents and the increased presence of Mexican police, as well as the work of Grupo Beta, a Mexican organization that works to discourage illegal border crossings and aids people stranded in the desert.

Truthfully, the only thing the Minutemen actually shut down was a two-mile stretch of border that wasn't a significant smuggling corridor to begin with. As always, the border crossers were just flowing around the rock in the river, going around the Minutemen's lines as long as they were present.

"They are going west of Naco, but they are still trying," said Bertha de la Rosa, a coordinator with Grupo Beta.

The Minutemen may have been dreaming of nabbing hordes of border crossers when they traveled to Arizona, but for the main body of Minutemen at the Naco border crossing, there was only one actual encounter recorded: a group of five people found sleeping in a culvert one morning, only one of whom was detained initially (the other four took off into the brush), and even then it wasn't clear whether they were border crossers or just locals from the Arizona side of Naco.

However, there was a smaller, "elite" group of Minutemen (at the command center, they were referred to as "the Ninjas," and they had the mien of combat veterans, including the heavy arms they carried) who had been staked out in a chain of camps some forty miles east of Naco and thirty-five miles north of the border, and these Minutemen had been intentionally placed in actual smuggling corridors—what are known as "lay-up spots," where border crossers stop to rest and wait for their rides, usually after trekking for forty hours through the desert. These Minutemen had considerably greater success in catching border crossers, and so by the end of the Minuteman Project, its organizers claimed to have assisted in the capture of 336 undocumented immigrants from Mexico and Central America—a number that is, however, impossible to confirm, because the Border Patrol keeps the identity of citizen informants confidential.

Border Patrol officials did tell Dave Holthouse that the Minutemen, especially those along International Road, were more hindrance than help because they so frequently called in false alarms and set off ground sensors.

"The Border Patrol didn't want them, my community didn't want them here, and I didn't want them here," said Ray Borane, the Douglas mayor who frequently crossed swords with Chris Simcox and the other border watchers. "All they succeeded in doing was creating hard feelings and spreading a racist message. The amount of media attention they received has been totally out of proportion to their actual impact. The Mexicans have a saying that I think applies quite well to the Minuteman Project: 'It was all song and no opera.'"

The participants did not agree. A San Antonio man named Curtis Stewart, interviewed at the command center in Miracle Valley, was asked by a reporter what the project meant to him.

"How many demonstrations have we had in the United States for women, lesbians, blacks—minority demonstrations, right?" he asked, speaking from behind a windshield with a "Liberal Hunting Permit" sticker. "Never have you had the white, right wing say 'I've had it.' This is the first demonstration for the country since the Boston Tea Party."

||

By and large, the media seemed to agree. Aside from a few reporters who tried to get at the Minutemen's great white underbelly, coverage of the monthlong border watch was almost uniformly laudatory, and much of it was almost nakedly propagandistic. Even worse, it painted a seriously distorted portrait of what happened on the border.

As Marc Cooper observed at the *Los Angeles Times*:

> Though the Minuteman organizers vowed that 1,600 or more mad-as-hell volunteers had signed up for duty and that "potentially several thousands" would participate in the kickoff rallies during April Fools' weekend,

turnout was an unmitigated flop—less than a tenth of the promised throngs showed up at the rallies. The entire Minuteman spectacle, indeed, easily qualified for that journalistic catchall phrase, "a fizzle," but virtually none of the news media reported it as such.

"It was eye-opening to me to see how media hype really works," says Dave Holthouse. "It had been my first experience with something like that, where it had been reported so often that it just took on a life of its own, this notion that there was this huge group of people down there. And it just wasn't true. It was never true, and especially was clearly not true by the time I left, which was halfway through a monthlong operation.

"It was very uncritical reporting. The initial burst of coverage—I sort of expected Fox News to hype it, but CNN and these other stations? I was like, 'You can count, right? I mean, you can drive up and down this road in a car and count how many guys are actually out here. It doesn't match up with what Simcox and Gilchrist are telling you.' And the ACLU had observers there, and they were presenting numbers that were much closer to what I was estimating. But because it just didn't match up with the narrative, it was just disregarded.

"It was embarrassing. It was embarrassing to be a journalist, even one undercover, there. After the first three nights I started staying in a hotel in Douglas, and I would go back to my hotel and watch what the coverage looked like at night, and just go, 'Oh my God. Seriously?'"

Lou Dobbs had been among the loudest and most prominent cheerleaders. Dobbs himself had toured the border watch in Naco on April 11, visiting with various Minutemen in person, but if there was any footage of his visit, CNN never broadcast it. Instead, Casey Wian's openly promotional live reports aired almost nightly on Dobbs's show, culminating with an April 18 report that announced the launch of "the next level" for the Minuteman Project.

Dobbs opened the report by noting that "the volunteer group today said it is planning now a major expansion along our southern border, and it plans to begin monitoring our northern border as well. The Minutemen are also launching a new operation to expose U.S. companies hiring illegal aliens." Then it was over to Wian, who dropped a bit of a bombshell—namely, that Jim Gilchrist was already leaving:

What is going to happen now is, Chris Simcox, one of the founders and organizers of the Minuteman Project, when the it—when the project in Arizona ends at the end of this month, Simcox will begin consulting with organizers in California, Texas, and New Mexico to set up a Minuteman Project for the entire southern border, and they expect that to be operational by this fall—perhaps in October—and another expansion of the program, northward. They have volunteers in Michigan and Idaho who are also interested in monitoring the Canadian border and that could begin even sooner because Simcox says the volunteers don't need as much training because the Canadian border is not as violent as the Mexican border.

Also, Jim Gilchrist, one of the other co-founders of the Minuteman Project is going to be leaving active duty in Arizona to begin, as you mentioned, Lou, concentrating on employers who hire illegal aliens. He's going to be organizing protests—something he has shown with the Minuteman Project he's very good at—organizing protests against employers of illegal aliens, and he's going to be after cities who sponsor day laborer centers which, of course, are overwhelmingly populated by a majority of illegal aliens. He's going to be traveling to Washington, D.C. next week to meet with the Congressional Immigration Reform Caucus. That at the invitation of Colorado Congressman Tom Tancredo, who has sent the Minuteman Project a letter of congratulations, saying, job well done so far.

Dobbs signed off in full agreement: "You know, it's absolutely right, Casey. I had the opportunity to spend a little time down there with you along the border with the Minutemen. The success is remarkable."

Indeed, CNN had been so warmly promotional in its handling of the Minutemen that it was somewhat surprising that neither Chris Simcox nor Jim Gilchrist had appeared on their shows very often during the month the project was running. Perhaps that was because they were enjoying the warm embrace of Fox News, and especially right-wing pundit Sean Hannity.

No one broadcast more news reports on the Minutemen in April than Fox, and no talk show had more segments about the Minutemen than *Hannity and Colmes*. By the time the month was done, Simcox and Gilchrist and company had been featured on the talk show eight times. On only one of those shows (the eighth and final appearance) did the show feature anyone, besides liberal cohost Alan Colmes, who was a critic of the project. The zenith came when Hannity himself flew out to Arizona and cohosted an entire show from Hereford, with Simcox and Gilchrist at his side.

That happened to be April 18, the same day the Minutemen had announced their grand plans to expand their national presence, including border watches on the Canadian border. Colmes zeroed in on a recent report that put a different cast on the announcement that Simcox and Gilchrist would be parting their duties, if not their ways:

> COLMES: Jim, I want to ask you, Channel 13 in Tucson is reporting that the Minutemen Project on the Arizona border is expanding, but that project leader Chris Simcox, they're reporting, is—announced changes today amid rumors that he and co-founder Jim Gilchrist, that's the two of you, are not seeing eye-to-eye on the direction of the project. And that Mr. Gilchrist is leaving 10 days early.
>
> Jim, is that true, and why are you leaving 10 days early this week instead of a week and a half from now?
>
> SIMCOX: Alan, I'm not leaving. I'm here till April 30 except for two to three days where we'll be meeting with congressional representatives in Washington. I'll be coming back after that and finishing up the last three days right up through the 30th.
>
> GILCHRIST: There is no distinction between Chris and I other than we have different opinions about the media. That's all.
>
> COLMES: What are your differing opinions?
>
> GILCHRIST: We won't go there. . . . I like you and he doesn't.
>
> COLMES: Where do you—I'd say that's all about it. Now where do you differ, Chris, on the media? Where do you guys part company?
>
> SIMCOX: I don't think that's something we should be talking about, but Jim and I—there's no need for both of us to be monitoring this situation now. Civil Homeland Defense [Simcox's organization] will take over a continuous effort of monitoring the border. Jim is going to take phase two, Minutemen Project phase two and start implementing that on the interior where we're going to be—have Minutemen protesters picketing employers who are hiring illegals and see if we can't make an effort, some impact there.

Within a week, it began leaking out that in fact Simcox and Gilchrist had developed a serious dislike for each other, partly because they had difficulty sharing the spotlight. Miracle Valley, it seemed, wasn't big enough for the two of them and their egos.

Once, when Dave Holthouse was observing them at work, Simcox saw Gilchrist surrounded by reporters and said to himself, loudly: "There goes Gilchrist, holding down his own fort again."

To a group of volunteers, Simcox explained: "Listen up, I need everybody to understand that while the California people did a good job of getting you here, now that you're here, this is my show, because this is Civil Homeland Defense territory, so just understand that, okay? Thanks."

A number of Arizona participants, including organizers, said Simcox's authoritarian, control-freak style—he was known variously as the Little Prince and the Little Hitler—angered a large number of volunteers and drove them away.

Afterward, several higher-ups described the resulting fiasco and laid the bulk of it at the feet of Chris Simcox: "He just pissed everybody off," said Jim Chase, who held several leadership positions during the project, including security director. "It was ridiculous, going behind everyone's back. I'm never working with him again."

When asked whether his group was falling apart, Simcox dismissed the notion and claimed to be unaware of any criticism. He told a reporter at the end of April that he and Gilchrist still maintained frequent contact and consulted with each other on decisions. Then suddenly his tune changed.

"There are no ties," Gilchrist said a week later when asked if he and Simcox were still connected. "If we did anything else together, it would be as allies, not partners. I support his goals, but I'm weary of his management capabilities."

||

Most of the nativist border watchers in Arizona who had helped inspire the Minuteman Project in the first place—the Glenn Spencers, Casey Nethercotts, and Roger Barnetts—were basically sidelined for the month, in large part because most of them, too, had gotten crosswise of Chris Simcox's ego. None of them were particularly happy about it.

Freshly out of prison on his weapons conviction, Nethercott was particularly vindictive, maybe because Simcox—perfectly aware of Nethercott's dalliances with white supremacists and his virulent radicalism—had publicly uninvited him. In the months running up to the project, the ex–Ranch Rescue honcho had been openly critical of the Minuteman Project, predicting its failure: "The Minutemen are the civilian-bound, politically correct civilians trying to close the border," he told a reporter. "We're soldiers."

A few weeks later, he tried a different tactic, warning that the Minutemen had been infiltrated by neo-Nazis: "James Gilchrist is swinging the door open for every wacko, and wackos are the bad percentage of white supremacists, white power," Nethercott told another reporter. "They're racists he cannot control." Nethercott told that reporter that "white supremacists bother him"—an observation decidedly at odds with his previous decision to hire a self-professed neo-Nazi as "security chief" for his new "militia."

Then, as he watched the Minutemen reel in national media attention at an unprecedented rate, Nethercott changed his tune again, back to the original "we are soldiers" melody: "I applaud the Minutemen, but they are too polite and ineffective," he told a reporter from Germany. "The time of political correctness is over."

Nethercott jury-rigged a couple of SUVs with some steel plating so that he could claim he had armored vehicles for his border patrols, and told yet another reporter: "You'll get killed without them, there's been so many shootouts out here."

He announced his own border watch with the SUVs, this time beginning on the Fourth of July and extending for the whole thirty-two miles of border between Douglas and Naco.

Nethercott was planning his own contingency: "When this Minuteman thing is over, if it doesn't work, we're going to come out here and close the border with machine guns."

It didn't quite work out that way for Nethercott. On April 22, 2005, he was booked into a Texas prison to serve time for his conviction on a federal weapons violation, and he would not get out until 2009. But his contingency plan remained alive for dozens of his fellow border watchers.

# 5

# Borderline Careers

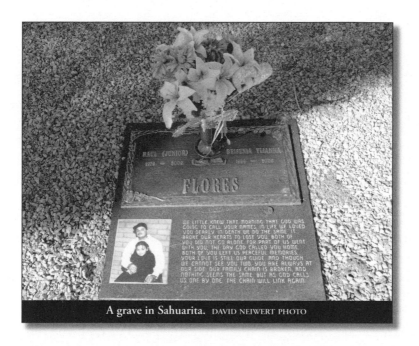

A grave in Sahuarita. DAVID NEIWERT PHOTO

Gina Gonzalez buried her husband and her daughter a week to the day after they were murdered. The funeral and wake were only open to close family members. Gina was trundled in by wheelchair. The morticians had managed to repair Brisenia's pretty little face somewhat, but Gina later told a jury that seeing the surgery, and knowing why it had to be done, was the hardest part of the funeral.

She could not bring herself to return to Arivaca, and so they were buried in Sahuarita, not far from her parents' home. She purchased a fancy memorial stone, with a laminated portrait of her husband and daughter. It was inscribed with an adaptation of the memorial poem "Broken Chain," by Ron Tranmer, which next to the image of Junior and Brisenia Flores was infused with fresh meaning:

*We little knew that morning*
*That God was going to call your names*
*In life we loved you dearly,*
*In death we do the same*
*It broke our hearts to lose you*
*Both of you did not go alone*
*For part of us went with you*
*The day God called you home*
*Both of you left us peaceful memories*
*Your love is still our guide*
*And though we cannot see you two*
*You are always at our side*
*Our family chain is broken*
*And nothing seems the same*
*But as God calls us one by one*
*The chain will link again*

Gina spent five weeks recovering at University Medical Center. Her shattered femur was replaced by a titanium rod running from her pelvic bone down to her knee. Her chest wound took an even longer time healing and would eventually require a second surgery, with more weeks spent in recovery.

A couple of months after the shootings, after the dust had settled, Gina Gonzalez made a last trip to Arivaca to participate in a fund-raiser that her friends in the Arivaca Community Center organized for her. It was intended mostly to defray her funeral, memorial, and medical costs but also to raise whatever money could be had to help out their longtime coworker with her living expenses.

Knowing this, some members of the community balked at attending. They knew that Junior Flores had been a marijuana smuggler. They also knew that Shawna Forde had emerged from the Flores home with almost no money. Many of them suspected that Gina had managed to walk away with a pile of Junior's drug money. And they were uncomfortable at the thought of just handing her more cash.

Small-town talk always runs small towns, and Arivaca is no different. Nonetheless, the fund-raiser managed to bring in over $5,000 for Gina Gonzalez, which is no small feat in an impoverished rural town. Perhaps the word had gotten around that the small-town talk was just that: Gina Gonzalez, in reality, was living nearly hand to mouth. Junior had left her only the property they owned. She was surviving by doing cleaning work at homes and businesses in the Green Valley area while staying with her parents.

In nearly any other town, being a marijuana smuggler would not be considered a normal occupation. But Arivaca—situated close to the border and in a remote, little-traveled patch of desert—has been a smuggling town for longer than anyone can remember. There have been many legitimate means of making a living here, including ranching and mining, and the grocery store has nearly always been a law-abiding operation. The people in those fields of work, however, must as a matter of course find a way to live side by side with people whose scruples about border laws are not so strong.

Shortly after the murders, Dan Shearer of the nearby *Green Valley News* penned a column contemplating how to apportion blame in the tragedy:

> Raul "Junior" Flores, Brisenia's father, has to carry a large part of it. Authorities say Flores had his head in the drug-trade toilet and wasn't shy about flashing the financial benefits of his selfishness. They also say that's what ultimately brought trouble to his doorstep and an early grave for his daughter. And for him.
>
> In the days after the shooting, residents in Arivaca heaped praise on Brisenia, her sister and mom—by all accounts they are good people who made a difference in the small town.
>
> When it came to Junior, most looked at the ground and said nothing. The few who did talk, however, showered him with praise—he was the guy who'd buy you a taco or was quick with a joke. Good guy, that Junior.
>
> But Junior Flores wasn't a good guy.
>
> And that, in part, is why the people of Arivaca have to take some responsibility for all of this. The so-called "tight-knit community" is a lot more "big city" than it cares to admit.
>
> Who in Arivaca didn't know Junior was running drugs?
>
> Who called authorities to report him, even anonymously?
>
> Who took his wife aside and begged her to get out for the sake of the children?
>
> Who had the guts to tell Junior it would all catch up with him one day?
>
> I was in Arivaca the day of the murders and several people told me it's a community that's different, built on the goodwill and genuine care of its residents. I've no doubt much of that is true—their accomplishments are notable.

But a community that cares will push its way beyond superficial relationships and into the lives of people who need to hear tough truths.

The column created an immediate uproar in Arivaca, where people believed that Shearer was smearing both the community and Junior Flores.
Two years later, Arivacans still talk about the column, often by way of explaining why they don't buy the paper any longer. Yes, they said, there
were some hard truths there, but that wasn't the whole picture by any
means either. Life is not so black and white that people like Flores are automatically bad guys and that towns like Arivaca are innately too tolerant
of lawbreaking.

"I caught hell for it for a year—people still bring it up," Shearer says now.
"The fact is, they knew what he was, but nobody, even the people who
didn't like it and understood how dangerous it was, was willing to say anything. Because that's either the culture or there was just truly fear.

"I talked to a guy when I was on this last trip who told me he talked to
Junior about three weeks before, and Junior told him, 'You know what? I'm
really thinking of getting out of this business. I want to get out of this business. I just don't know how.' Meaning, 'I don't know how to exit gracefully
without having a target on my back,' is how I understood that."

||

Arivacans like to claim that theirs is the oldest continuously occupied town
site in the state of Arizona, but that actually is not true. Local historian Mary
Noon Kasulaitis (who doubles as the city librarian) says someone with a promotional bent came up with the loose calculation some years back, based on
the fact that it was indeed an Indian village for many years before the arrival of whites. But she says there are many other older Indian town sites in
Arizona, and Arivaca can't claim continuous occupancy any more than those
other towns can.

Still, it is a very old town site, as these things go in the American West. In
the context of the desert environment, it is a natural place for human settlement, since a number of springs in the basin keep the place in a continuous supply of water. Thus the village was named La Aribac, Pima for "little
springs." It was either a Pima or a Tohono O'odham village; no one is quite
sure, because it was almost entirely abandoned after the Pima Indian Revolt
of 1751, the outcome of which forced the Indians onto reservations elsewhere. Spanish settlers then began staking out mining claims in the area.

At the time, this country was part of New Spain and subsequently became part of Mexico after 1821. In 1833, a Mexican land grant established the first official entity, La Aribac Ranch, at some 8,677 acres. After the Mexican-American War and the subsequent Gadsden Purchase of 1853, it became US territory, and so in 1856 a rancher named Charles Poston bought the massive land parcel. Poston opened up a mining operation, and by 1870, a mining boom was on. The town became a central supply depot for the men out searching the hills for one of the many veins of silver that coursed through the landscape. It was about this time that the old name of La Aribac gradually translated into its Americanized version, Arivaca.

The massive Arivaca Ranch turned the place into a company town in the 1880s, keeping the town alive, and settlement began picking up after 1902, when ownership of the contested Arivaca Land Grant was settled and parcels became available for homesteading. When Arizona became a state in 1912, the town was already fifty years old. Arivaca was one of the only precincts in the territory to vote against statehood.

The legitimate businesses in Arivaca always coexisted and commingled with the smuggling that naturally occurred in the area; indeed, they often came to depend on the economic activity of the smugglers for support. This was true from the town's earliest days.

In 1879, for instance, a fellow named E. B. Gage—who became the developer of Tempe, Arizona—arrived in Arivaca as a young man employed as a mine manager. He proposed opening a store there financed by the mining company and explained his thinking in a memorandum to his bosses:

> Now we deal mostly in miners' bits and camp supplies, but as soon as we get started we can do a big business with Sonora in all kinds of goods. There's a great deal of smuggling of goods going on in Sonora and Tucson, which would naturally be done nearer the line if it could be. In this respect, it might not be possible to have a military post too near us.

Eventually there was indeed a military presence in Arivaca, particularly during the early twentieth century and the period of the Mexican Revolution, when forces from competing armies would sometimes creep over the border. Between 1917 and 1920, Arivaca was the home base for a detachment of the famed all-black Tenth Cavalry, better known as the Buffalo Soldiers. Eventually, the town featured a parade ground, shooting range, and officers' barracks for the soldiers.

In 1918, the Buffalo Soldiers engaged a band of Yaqui Indians in what is now recognized as the last armed confrontation of the American Indian

Wars. The Yaquis had been engaged in a running guerrilla war with Mexico for a number of years, fighting to win their own independent state in northern Sonora. Many of these Yaquis had been traveling up north to Tucson to work in its orange groves and then taking their pay and purchasing guns and bullets, returning home with their lethal bounty. The military governor of Sonora pleaded for help from the United States, which was also listening to complaints from ranchers in the border area about increasing encounters with armed and hostile Yaquis. So the Buffalo Soldiers were given the task of chasing them out of American territory.

On January 9, the soldiers encountered a band of about thirty armed Yaquis in a place called Bear Valley, just southeast of Arivaca near Ruby. A short firefight ensued, with the Yaquis dodging from boulder to boulder, hiding behind brush and hills to fire back even as they retreated. The Yaqui chief, who was carrying several belts of ammunition, was hit by a marksman after stumbling. Eventually ten warriors were rounded up, including the chief, who was taken to a hospital in Nogales and died that day. The rest of the band escaped.

A handful of the Buffalo Soldiers are buried in the old Arivaca cemetery, though their identities are not known, since the graves were desecrated at one time. It's not likely that they died in action, though; the men are believed to have died in the 1918 influenza epidemic.

After 1920 and this brief period of excitement, the soldiers were returned to Fort Huachuca, outside of Sierra Vista, and things became very quiet in Arivaca for many years—as quiet as they can be, with a border nearby.

"The border is always there in terms of, it's not new," says Mary Kasulaitis. "But people who have just moved here maybe don't realize what the border, living by this border is like. Or what it means. But it's never been comfortable to live by the border. Things happen. You get waves of trouble."

The next wave didn't arrive until the late 1960s, when a band of hippies took up residence down south in the vicinity of the well-preserved ghost town of Ruby, which had been kept off-limits to the public for years, in the hands of private owners intent on preserving its historic qualities. The old town itself, located about eight miles south of Arivaca, became a kind of unofficial hippie center. The local paper of the time, the *Arivaca Briefs*, announced distastefully: "The old ghost town of Ruby is now a Hippie headquarters, where all may have their love-ins."

One of these hippies, who only identified himself as a thirty-three-year-old named Terry, attached a sign to his Ruby house dubbing it "Impossible Dream," and described it to a reporter as "a haven for anyone who had decided to take to the road, especially those refugees from the cities who seek a rural existence."

"We're a fluid community too," he said. "But we avoid the cities and the street freaks. We avoid each other also, for any long period anyway. The straights think we're all alike. That's a laugh—you can't get six of us to agree on anything."

If you keep driving south on Ruby Road after the ghost town toward the border, eventually a couple of the roads will get you to a place called California Gulch, which once upon a time was host to a number of silver-mining endeavors. By 1971, more hippies had moved there, placing themselves only a few miles away from the border itself. They took up residence in the gulch's many abandoned mines and their assorted buildings, or simply camped out in tepees. A few managed to haul in trailers. They called themselves the HIPI Corp. and told the Forest Service they were engaged in mining.

Of course, this did not fool anyone, least of all the humorless bureaucrats of the Forest Service, who instead called them squatters and "unlawful campers," and successfully prosecuted the hippies in the mid-1970s for various violations of federal forestland statutes. The hippies were given six months' probation and told to clean up the site, which they did. That was because many of them were intent on remaining in the area.

"The hippies came here in the '60s and early '70s because it was a pleasant, warm place—and isolated," Kasulaitis told the *New York Times*. "By buying up mining claims, which many of them did in California Gulch, you could get cheap private land protected by national forest land. Isolation, self-reliance, anonymity and peace—that was what they came for. Those who stayed are now the mainstays of the community."

Of course, there was an immense cultural divide between the long-haired newcomers and the hard-bitten, desert-weathered old-timers when they first met one another back then.

Clara Godfrey, one of the town's matriarchs, grew up on her uncle's Arivaca ranch and now laughs at the memory of the old cultural divide. "A lot of the people that are great people in our community now are the people that used to run barefooted through the hills," she told a film documentarian in 2008. "They were the wild hippies." Those hippies, she said, were not exactly welcomed by the old-time vaqueros who worked the local landscape.

"You know," she said, "when we talked about 'em at the ranch, it was like, 'Oh my God, don't go up to Arivaca, the heepies are there.' You know, the old cowboys would say, 'The heepies, sometimes they don't wear clothes, [groan] and there's a lot of them!'"

Allan Wellen, who grew up in Arivaca and now raises his own family there, also remembers.

"This was basically a mining-ranching town," Wellen says. "So back in the early '70s when hippies started moving in, there was this huge division. The hippies lived out there, and they were subhuman and all that, according to the people that had been here doing traditional work. And outsiders to boot."

The local drinking hole, La Gitana Cantina, was the hub of the community back then. "And the people at the bar—if anybody that was a hippie had walked into the bar in those days, they would probably get their ass kicked," Wellen recalls.

"So, there was one of the miners that just could not find any help. And so he finally broke down and he hired a couple of these damned hippies. They went out there and they worked like dogs for this guy. At the end of the week, these guys wanted to get paid, and so they walked into the bar.

"And all the guys at the bar stood up and they were gonna go over there and beat 'em up. And this miner stood up and he goes, 'You can't touch those. Those are my hippies!'" Wellen laughs at the memory. He also thinks it was a turning point.

"Ever since then, there's been this melding," he says, describing the gradual change in attitudes. "You know, OK, maybe they're not subhuman. In the mid-'70s, some of the hippies got tired of living in tents and actually bought property here. So they started moving into town."

People in Arivaca found out that these hippies were actually OK. "As a matter of fact, most of them were great neighbors," Wellen says. "Really good people, really help out with a lot of things. And brought an economy to this town—all of these things that started happening. And then of course in the late '70s, we started getting organizations that were basically founded by these hippies.

"So the community center and the fire department and the arts council and the human resources group, and the list just keeps growing on and on of all these different organizations that were basically founded by hippies or ex-hippies or whatever you wanted to call them that have made this town. This town basically would have died twenty years ago without them."

The old-timers and the newcomers found a vast area of common ground: their simple desire to be left alone to live life as they pleased. "See, the other part of it is that people come here to get away from whatever they need to get away from," one local old-timer tells me. "And it could be the law. And it could be a lot of people come here because there's not so much pollution. And people come here because they look on a map and they go,

'Oh, that's about as far away from everything as I could get,' and they go there and find that.

"So we have many, many people here who are retired or have no jobs, don't want a job, live as frugally as they can. A lot of the hippie folks are in that category. They want to get away from everything. And they want to be just hippies out here in the hills."

Indeed, Arivaca is somewhere on the low end of any real-estate developer's ideal when it comes to parading homes. Many of the dwellings in town or on its fringes are trailers or mobile homes, and their conditions vary widely. Some are neatly kept and carefully trimmed. Many more have various automobile parts scattered on them, along with personal detritus washed up on these desert shores.

A drive through Arivaca will reveal cute, neatly appointed homes decorated with lawn ornaments and fountains only a few doors down from the ruins of an old adobe tavern built in the 1800s, overshadowed by high mesquite trees. This old property is used by locals as a place to escape the sun on days when there are community gatherings in the town. A few doors down from that is a mobile home on a grassy property, decorated by the rusting hulk of a once-green dump truck, perched on blocks. Next to it, cows graze in the tall grass, their udders swaying.

There are no ordinances in Arivaca. No one to tell you to clean up your yard. And not any great social pressure to do so, either. That's the way people like it here.

Tracy Cooper is an emergency medical technician who commutes to work from Arivaca, but she wouldn't live anywhere else. "This is not a wealthy community, but it is a community of wealth, in that it has a lot of spirit and a lot of heart, and everybody helps each other," she says. "That's really appealing. The folks out here are wonderful. They give you the shirt off their back."

Adjacent to the community center is a first-class skate park, complete with bowls, ramps, roll-ins, and launches. It came about when a group of young adults, skateboarding fanatics, approached some of the town leaders about building one. The grown-ups had long been talking about ways to find constructive things for their young people to do, and this seemed like a prime opportunity. They developed a plan: find a design that was affordable and then create local fund-raisers to come up with the money. The community center would gladly donate the land.

So the kids, with a bunch of adults helping out, began selling "Team Air Vaca" shirts—complete with a logo featuring a cow on a skateboard— around town, promising that each shirt would buy a bag of cement. That

was enough to get things started with a May 2006 groundbreaking ceremony. Local businesses donated rebar and other materials, and local residents provided much of the labor, which turned out to be considerable. The
park debuted in December 2007 and now draws skateboarders from
throughout the Southwest.

It was emblematic of Arivaca's can-do ethic. "If something needs to be
taken care of, people in the community get together and do it," Andrew
Alday says. "Whether it's water problems in town, or something out in the
forties. And it's worked that way for as long as people can remember. So
why do we need a government?"

It's also a place where people shed their city skins. "People here might
look as skuzzy as they come and be really wealthy," a longtime resident tells
me. "Because they brought their money from elsewhere and they don't
want—they live here because it's not a pretentious town, they don't want to
live in a pretentious town, and they don't want people to judge them on the
basis of their money. And if they have a lot of money, you can't tell by their
dress or the car they drive.

"In fact, you're almost respected more if you have a really old but still
running car." Indeed, an informal survey on the weekend found that vintage
vehicles (though in many cases, that might be a charitable description) outnumbered newer cars almost three to one in the town.

Maybe that was part of why Junior Flores stood out.

||

Raul Flores Jr., known to everyone simply as Junior, was one of those residents
of Arivaca whose ties to the land go back not just generations but centuries.
His family history in the area went back to the days when this was New Spain,
and then Mexico, well before anyone had heard of a Gadsden Purchase.

As such, the Flores family had members on both sides of the border. And
for generations, ever since the border came to be, they had made a living by
virtue of their deep knowledge of the landscape, its hidden nooks and cran-
nies and its little-known trails, smuggling goods or people across it. Having
family members on both sides of the border was what made it work.

Junior, born in 1979, and his brother Victor inherited the smuggling
business from their father, who had inherited it from his father. The goods,
all of them illegal in America and yet in considerable demand, had changed
over the years: booze during Prohibition and even after, cigarettes made
cheaply in Mexican factories, weapons, even parrots and rare insects. In the
1960s, it became drugs, particularly marijuana, which grew plentifully and

readily in the hot Mexican sun. The Flores family had a reliable source some-where in Sonora. And as it happened, there was an eager market of both consumers and would-be dealers in Arivaca.

These were the people with whom Junior Flores made his living. He and Victor—who as boys had roamed the backcountry where they lived and knew it like the backs of their hands—had begun picking up their father's work as teenagers in the early '90s. They were prone to the rashness of teenagers back then.

"At some points, there was kind of a hierarchical thing that goes on with the different families, or different people that are doing that kind of business—that when you mess with the hierarchy, you really mess with them," says Allan Wellen. "It's kind of like the gangs of Chicago or whatever—when you go on somebody's turf, there's gonna be repercussions. And for the most part, people in Arivaca, they kind of know generally that this is the way things are, and you don't mess with that.

"Those two did. And especially as, like, teenagers and late teens. They didn't want to follow any kind of guidelines or whatever you want to call it."

Locals call it the "Arivaca Rules": a kind of ethic governing the drug-smuggling business, the bottom line of which is that all's fair in competi-tion, but you don't bring in law enforcement, and you don't bring it into people's homes and thus into the community. Junior and Victor were known for bending if not breaking those rules.

"And so it ended up pissing off a lot of people," says Wellen. "They would do weird things like send one of the local kids with a load of drugs some-where, and then call up and get them busted. So there were some serious tensions over things like that.

"But as they got older, they kind of learned, and they got better and bet-ter at doing what they did."

Junior met Gina Gonzalez at Sahuarita High School—Gina's family, like Junior's, had been in the area for generations—at age fifteen, when they were both sophomores, and they dated off and on up through their senior years. They married shortly after graduating, in the fall of 1996. Junior had a tat-too added to his right arm, reading in Gothic script: "Til Death Do Us Part—Gina."

Their daughter Alexandra was born not long afterward, in 1997, while Brisenia Yllianna was born two years later, in late 1999. Junior bought a property in the "forties," just down the Mesquite Road from the Arivaca Community Center, and put a double-wide mobile home on it, to which he added an expansion of the living-room space as well as a little shack out in the backyard. The house sat perched on a bench above a dry wash, along which immigrants and other trekkers would sometimes wander. Later, he added a barn down on the other side of the wash for keeping horses, which he would set out to graze on the property.

Junior had some close calls from time to time. On a couple of occasions, a Border Patrol tracker reportedly traced a drug mule carrying a load right into the barn, and on another, the tracker reportedly found marijuana under the house, behind coving that Junior had erected. On yet another occasion, the same tracker spotted marijuana bales in a Dumpster bin on the edge of the property, but the truck driver who was supposed to cart it off was warned away. On all these occasions, no busts resulted, largely because the tracker had also failed to obtain a search warrant.

The scares convinced him to keep his business away from the house. Gina insisted on it too. So his storage facilities and the vehicles he used were always kept at a distance, on a separate place he and Victor bought just for that purpose. He had nothing in his house beyond a little weed for his personal consumption. Thus it was that Junior Flores, despite a long career smuggling pot, had a perfectly clean criminal record.

That was probably going to come to an end soon. According to two different law enforcement sources with knowledge of the situation, Junior Flores had been under DEA surveillance for much of the spring of 2009, including a camera that had been placed near the Flores-Gonzalez home to record goings-on there. It was removed early in May, and DEA agents then began quietly assembling their case against him. At the end of May they were probably still two months away from making any arrest.

||

Junior Flores was never a major drug figure in Arivaca. Indeed, as that scene went, he was pretty small-time. Which was why they hadn't gotten around to busting him yet.

For years, there was a drug kingpin in Arivaca called Sam Romero, though that is not his real name, because he is now retired and living happily elsewhere. But at the time, everyone in town was, if not scared, decidedly respectful of him. No one messed with Romero because he was, in effect, the law in town.

"[Sam] was a businessman-type guy," a law enforcement source told me. "He had his business." Under Romero's rule, he said, there was a coterie of smugglers, including Junior and Victor Flores, as well as Eddie Valdez, Jed Lopes, and a man we will call Hernandez (again, not his real name). "They all got along; they had these little things going on with the marijuana. They used each other's gofers. Everything was fine."

Romero kept a lid on the town and kept it quiet. There was little violence, and everyone found ways to get along. When methamphetamine started making its appearance in the Altar Valley, Sam Romero was credited with running many tweakers and their toxic labs out of town. Pot smugglers could get by without harming people, but meth labs were notorious for spreading poisonous chemicals wherever they went up, and even more toxic behavior by their addicts. No one wanted them as neighbors.

There were other ways that Sam Romero kept things under control, this source told me, using an anecdote to describe it: "[Sam] had a little backhoe, and he was going to do an extra leaching field for the La Gitana Cantina. But he needed gravel." So he went to a local rancher who had some gravel in a wash on his property and asked if he could haul some of it down to the tavern. No problem, said the neighbor.

"So [Sam] brings a loader and an old truck. On the second load, ol' Don [the rancher] stopped him. He says, 'Hey [Sam], I need a favor.' Sam says, 'What do you need?'

"He says, 'You know, right across the way over there is [another rancher]. And he's got a wetback that stays there and keeps going in my barn and getting in my freezer and stealing my meat. I want it stopped.'

"'OK, we'll take care of it.'

"So [Sam] makes two more trips. And then the next morning, Sam comes up and asks for Don. He says, 'I took care of that situation for you. Thank you for the gravel.' He says: 'He's moving out.'

"We looked over there, and he had a pickup truck hauling his trailer out of there. [Sam] told him to leave. The trailer ended up over in Warsaw Canyon. And a week later it burned down."

On another occasion, a registered sex offender living in Arivaca brutally raped a local nine-year-old girl. Before anyone could make an arrest, he disappeared. It was well known around town that he was last seen being driven away into the desert by Sam Romero and his enforcer.

For awhile, everyone prospered about the same. Hernandez had a couple of gofers whom we will call Ralph and Rita. Rita was Hernandez's stepdaughter, and he set them up in a nice little house right in town in return for their smuggling services, and they had a decent life. Then Hernandez died of a heart attack, and their income dried up. Both of them wound up working as clerks at the Mercantile, until finally Rita managed to make contact with Hernandez's old supplier in Sonora, a cartel drug lord known as Fat

Boy. It took awhile and some finagling, but Rita finally managed to get back in the supply chain, and soon her smuggling business was humming along nicely again.

In the interim, a family with money and connections in Casa Grande, headed by a man named Oscar Pettis, moved into Arivaca and soon made their presence known. They set up a couple of legitimate-seeming businesses—a restaurant/bar called the Grubstake Saloon, perched next to the highway on a bench above the town site, and a tire shop in town. Somehow, that tire shop was able to report more than $800 a day in profits, though it sold maybe a couple sets of tires a week at best.

The Grubstake was a different story. It was a popular place with good food and decent drinks at a good price. The Pettis family got along with everyone, too. The restaurant became a place where everyone in town would congregate and enjoy good times. Sometimes Junior Flores would walk in and buy everyone dinner on his account.

The smugglers' relationship with the law-abiding residents of Arivaca was a complicated one. The town prospered when the smugglers did, too. And so even though more than half the town was employed in a legitimate line of work, it was impossible to do anything in the town without doing business with them or socializing with them.

It also created an ethics of judiciousness in the town. One longtime resident, a law-abiding pillar of the community, recalled the experience of an out-of-town visitor she knew: a respected member of the law enforcement establishment from Tucson who was enjoying a little vacation time deer hunting in the hills around Arivaca.

After several days in the brush and having grown a full scraggle of beard, he headed into town and bellied up to the J-shaped bar of La Gitana Cantina, looking every bit the typical hunter. After a few beers, whom should he strike up a friendly conversation with but Sam Romero.

In the course of the conversation, the man from Tucson turned to Romero and asked something most people in most towns ask in a friendly way, just by way of getting to know someone: "Well, what do you do for a living?"

The place went dead silent. You could hear a pin drop.

Sam Romero smiled and sipped his beer. "You know," he told his new friend, "in Arivaca, people don't ask people that."

The man from Tucson, sensing he had just stepped in something and really didn't want to know what it was, just shrugged and smiled and said, "OK, well." He was out there to hunt, anyway.

# 6

# Herding Cats

Chris Simcox after the makeover. DAVID NEIWERT PHOTO

While the reality of the Minuteman Project had been, in fact, pretty much as Marc Cooper described it—"a fizzle"—in the alternative reality created by media hype, it had been a smashing success. For Chris Simcox and company, that was all that mattered.

Having declared victory midway through the month of April 2005 and pretty much gone home, the Minutemen moved quickly to expand on the momentum their border-watching movement had gained in the media. The growing rift between Simcox and Jim Gilchrist had produced a plan to split the movement in half, with Gilchrist's portion focusing on organizing protests against employers who hired "illegal aliens," taking their nativist agenda to every state in the Union, and Simcox's half focused on organizing a whole raft of new border watches—not merely in other Southwestern states and their Mexico borderlands, but also in northern states that bordered Canada.

The media success did not dampen Simcox's ongoing identification of his movement with the far-right Patriot/militia movement. In his press releases over the summer announcing patrols expanding to California, New Mexico, and Texas in October, he continued describing volunteers as "Patriot-Minutemen" and concluded with the breathless proclamation that "this is truly an exciting time for Patriots!"

In one important way, the Minuteman Project was indeed a success, but not for actually doing anything substantive to stop illegal immigration. Rather, it was eminently successful in mainstreaming and legitimizing extremist vigilantism. After all, not only was it eagerly embraced by a gullible press, but in short order it was given the blessing of a wide range of public officials and politicians.

Before April was even out, Simcox and Gilchrist were both in Washington, DC, receiving a round of adulation from Tom Tancredo and the Congressional Immigration Reform Caucus on Minutemen. After meeting with them on April 29, members gushed with praise, trying to top each other in effusiveness.

Tancredo led the way: "I would like to thank the Minutemen on behalf of the millions of Americans who can't be here with you today," he said. "You have the courage to say to the government of the United States, 'Do your duty! Protect our borders! Protect our communities! Protect our families! Protect our jobs!' You are good citizens who ask only that our laws be enforced. When did that become such a radical idea?"

Congressman Phil Gingrey of Georgia chimed in: "The Minuteman Project is a shining example of how community initiative and involvement can help make America a safer, better place to live. These brave men and women are standing up for our security, defending America from the illegal immigrants who are crossing our borders by the millions."

House Majority Leader Tom DeLay voiced his disagreement with President Bush's assessment that the Minutemen were "vigilantes": "I'm not sure the president meant that. I think that they're providing an excellent service. It's no different than neighborhood-watch programs and I appreciate them doing it, as long as they can do it safely and don't get involved and do it the way they seem to be doing it, and that's just identifying people for the Border Patrol to come pick up."

Then there were the public endorsements by California's Republican governor, Arnold Schwarzenegger. Asked about the Minutemen in an interview on a Los Angeles radio station, Schwarzenegger responded: "They've done a terrific job." The governor complained: "Our federal government is not doing their job. It's a shame that the private citizen has to go in there and start patrolling our borders."

A few months later, Schwarzenegger defended the Minutemen again, comparing them to a "neighborhood watch": "It's no different than if you have a neighborhood watch person there that's watching your children at the playground," he told a reporter. "I don't see it any different."

Republican senator Wayne Allard of Colorado was so impressed with the Minutemen, he proposed deputizing them as a way to secure the American borders. "I wonder sometimes if maybe we're not looking too much to a federal solution," Allard told Homeland Security Secretary Michael Chertoff during a Senate Appropriations Committee hearing.

John Culberson, a congressman from Houston, introduced legislation that would give official sanction, for the first time, to "border militias." The Border Protection Corps Act, as Culberson titled it, would have authorized access to $6.8 billion in unused Homeland Security funds to form volunteer border militias that would report to their respective county sheriffs.

These ideas nearly started becoming a reality. Customs and Border Protection Commissioner Robert Bonner told members of the House Government Reform Committee that CBP, looking for ways to expand Border Patrol agents' presence, was evaluating the effectiveness of using citizen patrols in a "more formal" role.

"The actions of the Minutemen were, I believe, well motivated," Bonner said. "There were no incidents, there were no acts of vigilantism, and that's a tribute to the organizers and leaders of the Minuteman Project."

A couple of months later, Bonner gave outright support to the idea of actually giving the Minuteman concept official imprimatur. He told reporters that CBP was exploring ways to involve citizen volunteers in creating "something akin to a Border Patrol auxiliary."

"We value having eyes and ears of citizens, and I think that would be one of the things we are looking at is how you better organize, let's say, a citizen effort," Bonner said.

A day later, however, his superiors at the Department of Homeland Security backed away from any such proposals. "There are currently no plans by the Department of Homeland Security to use civilian volunteers to patrol the border," spokesman Brian Roehrkasse said in a tersely worded statement. "That job should continue to be done by the highly trained, professional law enforcement officials of the Border Patrol and its partner agencies."

Meanwhile, Republican legislators from Colorado—blissfully ignorant of their host's background as the leader of an organization designated a hate group by the Southern Poverty Law Center and the Anti-Defamation League—were taking fact-finding tours of Glenn Spencer's ranch while he held forth on the evils of the "illegal alien invasion." They were impressed as Spencer showed them aerial photographs and videos of immigrants crossing the border near his home. The pièce de résistance was his miniature, remote-controlled reconnaissance plane with a camera attached to it, an item he spent $40,000 building.

"We do this to expose the malfeasance of U.S. border patrol officials, who have failed us in protecting our borders," he told them. "What can U.S. citizens do to help? A lot."

The "neighborhood watch" narrative was not just a media favorite—it was the Minutemen's wide-open avenue to mainstream acceptance. What it obscured, however, was something much darker.

||

At first, Simcox and Gilchrist were reveling in the lightning flash of their media success. Then it began to dawn on them that the enthusiasm for hunting down immigrants on the borderlands would be harder to control than they ever imagined. For a control freak like Simcox, this was a serious problem.

Much of the summer of 2005 was devoted to preparing for their big nationwide border-watch expansion. "Realistically, we're looking at 10,000-plus volunteers being deployed Oct. 1st on the southern and northern borders," Simcox announced. As always, his numbers were rather optimistic.

Simcox and Gilchrist both hired attorneys to draw up the papers for their respective organizations, and they hired a Washington-based media consultancy, Diener Consulting—run by a group of conservatives headed by Philip Sheldon, son of religious-right leader Lou Sheldon, with former presidential candidate Alan Keyes as their chief figurehead—to fire up an aggressive fund-raising campaign. Suddenly, a former Keyes aide and onetime B-movie star named Connie Hair (her biggest moment of fame came in *Death Wish 4: The Crackdown*) was the Minutemen's chief spokesperson.

Simcox incorporated his old outfit, Civil Homeland Defense, into a new organization dubbed Minuteman Civil Defense Corps, or MCDC, as it came to be referred to—as distinct from Gilchrist's Minuteman Project, which retained its old name and filed for trade association status. Its new project targeting employers who hired undocumented workers was given the name Operation Spotlight.

Preparations continued apace for the fall activities. "Chris is going to Michigan in a couple of weeks to do a training session there," Hair told reporters. "But they've also got Idaho and Washington State and Vermont interested. In all they've had requests from seven states in the north," not to mention new requests "coming in every day."

The public enthusiasm was great, she said, but there was already a little problem with it: in Texas alone, for instance, there were already four groups claiming the Minuteman name. And none of them yet had the blessing of either Gilchrist or Simcox or either of their organizations. Indeed, such groups were springing up like dandelions.

"Nobody is using 'Minuteman Project.' They are using 'Minuteman' in the name of their group. You can't stop people from using the word 'Minuteman,'" Hair said, adding that Simcox would be assessing the possibility of giving some of them his official blessing.

"Endorsing an effort means we have to give them training and have assurances that they are going to stick to a no-contact policy, a reporting policy, a no-confrontation policy," Hair said.

In Texas, however, they weren't waiting for Simcox to bless them. An outfit based in Arlington, Texas, began calling itself the Texas Minutemen, earning a denunciation from Simcox, who disavowed any connection with the group and promised a press release "refuting your claims to be the official Minuteman group of Texas."

One of its cofounders, Shannon McGauley, replied that he didn't need Simcox's blessing, since he already had the approval of Jim Gilchrist, who had given his group his "blessing, endorsement and support." "I never met Mr. Simcox when I was in Arizona," McGauley said. "The Minuteman or Minutemen name doesn't belong to Mr. Simcox."

McGauley said he agreed philosophically with Simcox but objected to the national structure. He also objected to paying the fifty-dollar-per-person fee that Simcox was charging, which supposedly was being spent on "background checks," as well as "use of the national group's consultants, Web site and training."

"We wanted to keep it among Texans," he said. "And we don't charge anything."

Meanwhile, Wanda Schultz, a volunteer with Houston-based Americans for Zero Immigration, was told by Simcox's office to gear up for a month-long MCDC-sponsored mission called Operation Secure Our Borders, beginning October 1, to be held in Brownsville. But at the same time, another group of Minutemen, including McGauley's outfit, was announcing its plans for an October border watch in the El Paso area, calling it Minutemen Texas.

Simcox fretted that rogue groups like McGauley's might "step over the line" and do something that would violate the no-confrontation policy he instituted at the April border watch. "I'm pretty nervous that it will taint everything."

||

Pretty soon the disagreements turned into squabbles, which became feuds, and these eventually turned into all-out war. Rival factions fought over everything from use of the Minuteman name to email etiquette, and the verbal bombs they lobbed at each other publicly, both online and in media reports, bruised many of the oversized egos involved.

One of the more active factions started out calling itself the California Minutemen. It was led by Jim Chase, a longtime friend of Gilchrist's who had served in the same Marine Corps unit in Vietnam, though not at the same time. Wounded in combat, he eventually found work with the US Postal Service, but "what you call a post-traumatic-stress breakdown," for which he was hospitalized, forced him to retire in 1997. "Now I function pretty normal," Chase told a reporter for *LA Weekly*. "They tell me it's incurable and blah blah blah, but I function just fine in my opinion."

Chase had been a visible figure at the Minuteman command center and out on the line on International Road—he often insisted on making sure reporters knew he had been "third in command" in Arizona—up until he had taken a bad fall into a dry wash and broken his arm. He returned home to California and immediately began organizing a state Minuteman chapter, complete with a website announcing the kind of volunteers he was seeking: "all those who do not want their family murdered by Al Qaeda, illegal migrants, colonizing illegal aliens, illegal alien felons, alien barbarians, Ninja-dressed drug smugglers" and "cowardly Aztlan punks and Che Guevara pink pantied wimps lower than whale dung who should be fed to the chupacabra!"

It was also plain, from Chase's pronouncements on the site, that he didn't take kindly to disagreement: "If you are against us you are scum or just stupid beyond comprehension. Change sides fool. Lets not let OBL criminals kill the goose with the golden egg so our grandchildren suffer their foolishness. United We Stand!"

In stark contrast to the Minuteman Project—but very much like Simcox's old CHD patrols—Chase announced he would allow the California recruits to openly carry all kinds of weapons, including hunting rifles, assault rifles, and shotguns. Chase also recommended bringing "baseball bats, stun guns, and machetes."

In short order, Gilchrist and Simcox disavowed any connection to Chase's Minutemen.

"Mr. Chase has no authority to use the Minuteman Project name," Gilchrist declared in a June statement. "Neither does Mr. Chase have permission to trade upon the Arizona Minuteman Project's April record in any future border watch initiatives."

Chase didn't care. The whole brouhaha "is an internal argument," he told a reporter. "Frankly, it's taking away from the mission of watching and protecting the borders. I don't need it."

Chase said he had "verbals from about 1,000" people that they would come join his border watch, scheduled for a thirty-mile stretch along the California-Mexico border in July. "But talk is cheap," he said, "We'll just have to wait and see."

Still, he was dismissive of his former colleagues: "I keep hearing all these things: I'm a rogue. I'm a Rambo. I want to shoot the heads off people," Chase told a *San Diego Union-Tribune* reporter. "I'm a flower child compared to Gilchrist and Simcox."

Chase claimed that the root of the problem was Simcox's ego, and it dated to the Arizona project, when the two of them had developed a mutual loathing, which came to a head when Simcox decided to fire a series of volunteers whom Chase and Gilchrist considered blameless. At the time, Chase said, Gilchrist papered over their differences, but the chasm had grown.

Later that summer, Chase mucked up the Minutemen's plans further by appointing a man named Clifford Alford the leader of a group called the New Mexico Minutemen, who kicked off his campaign by claiming that members of the Minuteman Project liked to run around in paramilitary uniforms and carry assault weapons.

"They really don't give a rip about anyone's civil rights," he said. "We want our effort to be more humanitarian." Alford didn't happen to mention that Jim Chase specifically encouraged his Minutemen to carry weapons.

Of course, the Minuteman Project already had an appointed and approved figurehead for their New Mexico unit: a man named Mike Gaddy, who said Alford hadn't been part of the Arizona project: "Alford hasn't been a Minuteman for a minute," he told reporters. "He is part of a renegade organization that has absolutely nothing to do with the Minutemen whatsoever."

Gaddy said the Minutemen's own success had created a monster of sorts. "When we left Arizona in April, too many people had seen the glamour," he told another reporter. "'Gosh, I was on Sean Hannity. Gosh, I was interviewed by the *Baltimore Sun*. Gosh, I was interviewed on Spanish radio.' Egos are a terrible thing."

In California, the "official" Minuteman organizers tried to counter Chase's activities by similarly appointing their own man to head up statewide operations. Gilchrist named a conservative immigration activist named Andy Ramirez, whose Friends of the Border Patrol outfit became the officially sanctioned Minuteman unit in California. Sort of.

Ramirez, an American citizen whose grandfather emigrated to the United States, found himself in over his head quickly and soon announced that his plans for a July border watch were being pushed back to August instead. "We needed to make sure there was going to be support for all the people," Ramirez said, who had to scramble to secure everything from portable toilets to food and shelter and law enforcement cooperation.

"We're going to work with federal, state and local law enforcement. I've already met with the top ranking brass at the San Diego County Sheriff's Department," Ramirez said. He noted that some of the 775 FBP volunteers he claimed had signed up would be armed, "but only former or off-duty law enforcement persons."

However, Ramirez was shortly undercut by Chris Simcox, who had decided to withhold his endorsement. "Jim jumped the gun and endorsed [FBP] too quickly," Simcox said.

"We're not telling people we're Minuteman; we're not a variation of Minuteman. We're Friends of the Border Patrol," Ramirez explained. "That's why we're not calling ourselves 'Minuteman California' or anything like that."

||

Even though Simcox had denounced him, when Jim Chase and his California Minutemen held their first operation near the town of Campo on July 16, Chase's old friend Jim Gilchrist showed up to offer support. Not that it did a lot of good: once again, protesters and reporters outnumbered the actual volunteers who showed up to participate.

Outside Chase's headquarters, the Campo VFW Hall, a large and unruly crowd of anti-Minutemen protesters surrounded the building and twice laid siege to it. Chase and Gilchrist came outside to try to calm things and found themselves face-to-face with angry anti-Minutemen who shouted in their faces: "Go home, racists!"

Things turned even uglier that night, when a group of protesters approached a Minuteman watch post armed with a video camera. One of the Minutemen shouted at them as they neared: "Let me make this very clear to you! We are armed and we will defend ourselves! You come down here and you will be engaged in a firefight if necessary! Get the fuck out and go home!"

A protester's sarcastic comment earned an explicit threat from the shouting Minuteman: "I will shoot your motherfucking ass!"

"So are you threatening us?" asked a protester.

"Listen assholes, you wanna play? Let's play, motherfucker, let's go!"

The protesters decided to retreat rather than push their luck.

They must have deeply frightened the Minutemen, though, since two days later, Gilchrist sent out an "emergency call for reinforcements in Campo" that circulated nationally on anti-immigration and white-supremacist websites. "Be warned that roving gangs of belligerent, death-threatening, anti-American adversaries engaging the California Minutemen WILL physically attack you if they outnumber you," Gilchrist warned. "I repeat, they WILL physically attack you. Stay in groups and stay LEGALLY armed."

Gilchrist's plea for reinforcements fell on deaf ears: at their peak, the California Minutemen numbered fewer than a hundred and had only three illegal border crossers—two of whom Chase picked up hitchhiking—to show for their efforts by the time they wrapped up a couple weeks later.

Chase vowed to keep it going, with another California Minutemen event scheduled for early October—just like Chris Simcox's patrols.

"If you are not a racist and have no desire to harm the harmless migrants, come and sign up," Chase posted to his website in August. "Remember: We are harmless as doves."

||

In the meantime, Gilchrist began gearing up for Operation Spotlight. He sent out a bulletin in all caps, calling for volunteers to step forward who had experience as prosecuting attorneys, judges, and any legal professional who had a background in prosecuting immigration, tax evasion, and civil rights law. They were to be assembled into a team of legal-beagle Minutemen "for the purpose of legally providing to law enforcement agencies incriminating evidence relative to deliberate violations" of immigration, tax, or employment laws.

Among the criminals they'd be hunting down would be anyone involved in "voter fraud" or "fraudulent qualification for any type of public assistance" or "identification fraud." Of course, they also wanted to be going after human smugglers, safe-house operators, and "employers (or their agents) who have willfully exploited the illegal alien slave labor market in violation of long-standing immigration, tax and labor laws."

It also mentioned, at the end, that hunting down these criminals was to be entirely a volunteer effort, since Operation Spotlight "currently offers no subsidies or compensation for participants." Nonetheless: "The tasks at hand are not for the meek, the weak, or the selfish opportunist. It will take patience, stoic determination, integrity, an undying spirit for truth and justice . . . and a firm belief that the cornerstone of this great nation, the First Amendment of the U.S. constitution, is the lodestar to a positive and respectable resolution to the ills of a nation veering toward lawlessness, social mayhem, and a shrinking middle economic class."

Beyond the patriotic-sounding press releases, however, all was not well. The response to Gilchrist's plea was muted at best. And behind the scenes, internecine bickering was getting to Gilchrist. He issued two emails to members of his group demanding that people stop sniping at one another. When two of them responded querulously, he dismissed them both, characterizing them as "wackos."

One of his missives was signed: "An American with better things to do than baby-sit quarrelsome adults."

"It's so counterproductive. It gets people distracted," Gilchrist told a reporter. "If I were to set up some rules of conduct, it would be to stop the argumentative attitude and be pleasant."

It was enough to make one look in other directions for work—such as running for Congress.

||

The Minutemen's fractious behavior was in many ways a product of the combative personalities its core ideology attracted. The long history of nativist organizations in America is littered with the same story: gathered to fight the perceived immigrant threats of their respective times, and riding a wave of scapegoating and frequently eliminationist rhetoric, they all have in relatively short order scattered in disarray, usually amid claims of financial misfeasance and power grabbing. This was true of the Know Nothing Party of the 1850s, the Ku Klux Klan of the 1920s, and all of their many short-lived descendants since then.

"There has always been bickering among these types of organizations," observed Christian Ramirez of the American Friends Service Committee, a human rights group affiliated with the Quakers that has condemned the Minutemen and their successors. "There is always someone trying to become the leader of the anti–illegal immigration movement, because it is such a fashionable thing. People are just fighting to see who is going to get more media attention."

The Minuteman movement attracted primarily angry white men who were fearful of demographic change, which played an outsize role in the organizations' resulting volatility. Trying to rein them in was like herding cats. Big, angry cats with guns.

Simcox hired Gary Cole to ride this herd. Officially, he was named operations manager for Minuteman Civil Defense Corps, but he wound up a professional internecine peacekeeper and chief babysitter for a number of oversized, insecure egos. The splinter groups became his biggest headache.

Cole told reporters that the MCDC was trying to figure out how to bring outside groups into the organization. But the independent-minded volunteers the Minutemen attracted often bridled at the rules imposed on them. The MCDC's guidelines discouraged volunteers from pursuing or confronting undocumented immigrants, and they banned the use of rifles and shotguns in states where volunteers can freely carry firearms. This did not sit well with a number of would-be Minutemen, Cole explained.

"The different wannabes want different things," Cole said. "You have different groups that want to go out and be far more militaristic than we are. Outside listening points, sniping points . . . trip wires, all sorts of things. They feel we are way too politically correct."

The fear, Cole said, is that any mishap or violation of the law by a rogue group calling itself Minutemen could taint everyone involved.

Moreover, a number of groups were led by people who, having experienced him firsthand, wanted nothing to do with Simcox—though Cole did not mention or discuss that dimension to his problem.

Gilchrist said he had sought copyright protection for the Minuteman Project name, but he was not nearly so worried as Simcox appeared to be about the general use of Minutemen by others.

"We are in a quandary as to how do we settle this," Gilchrist said. "If they want to use Minuteman, you can't stop them. To try to stop them would be to upset them."

||

At that point, Gilchrist had other ambitions anyway. He had in fact decided to run for Congress in his Orange County home district, California's forty-eighth congressional, where the incumbent Republican, Christopher Cox, had been appointed to chair the Securities and Exchange Commission.

The special election rules created a wide-open field in the primary in which ten Republicans and four Democrats vied for their parties' respective nominations. Gilchrist ran instead as the sole candidate of the American Independent Party, which is the California affiliate of the Constitution Party. That organization, as it happens, is essentially the Patriot movement's own party: in the 1990s, it was one of the original promoters of the militia concept among mainstream conservatives, and its politics and candidates have been in that same mold ever since.

Gilchrist got a brief scare when former congressman Robert Dornan—an archconservative in the John Birch Society style, notorious in his time for inflammatory and frequently bigoted remarks (his nickname was "B-1 Bob"), who had lost his seat in the 1996 election to Loretta Sanchez—made brief waves by indicating he wanted to run for Cox's old seat under the AIP banner. But party leaders, who saw Gilchrist as a potential rising political star, rebuffed his efforts.

After the primary, only an establishment Republican named John Campbell and a Democratic attorney named Steve Young remained on the ballot—along with Gilchrist, who campaigned hard against Campbell on the basis of his supposedly "soft" stance on immigration. And when Election Day came around on December 5, it was a testament to Orange County's deep-red conservatism that Campbell still won handily with 44 percent of the vote, while Young came in second with 27 percent, and Gilchrist finished a close third with 25 percent.

Afterward, Gilchrist declared victory anyway: "The time of the modern Minuteman, the Patriot, the time of the American people is here, and America WILL return to the rule of law—whether the special interests, and the party label enforcers, and the open borders lobby—and the mainstream media—like it or not!"

||

In reality, though, Jim Gilchrist was not happy. He had actually outpolled Steve Young in the primary, and he viewed his finish behind him as a letdown. Gilchrist had handed much of his campaign over to the consultants at Diener, and at the end of the day, he felt he'd been burned. He noticed a lot of money going into Diener's coffers and not a lot of effective output in return. It seemed to him that his inside-the-Beltway consultants had become a monetary black hole.

After the campaign, he decided to end any relationship between Diener and the Minuteman Project. Chris Simcox was not happy to hear this. In a

December email exchange, the two agreed to permanently part ways. The Minutemen were now officially divorced. The final token came when the links to each other's websites disappeared from their outfits' respective home pages.

||

Some of the personalities the movement attracted were more than simply contentious, as events had borne out on the border in Arizona. And many of them had agendas well beyond the Minutemen's own stated limitations.

In California, the nativists were roaring loudly, led by an outfit called Save Our State that was focused, like Gilchrist, on calling out employers who hired undocumented workers. At a July 30, 2005, SOS rally, Gilchrist came to lend support to the group's efforts to protest a day labor center in Laguna Beach. They were met by a sizable contingent of counterprotesters. White supremacists were there in support of SOS, and after awhile they got out their flags.

Soon the Minutemen's side of the street was festooned with a large swastika banner and a Dixie rebel flag.

The neo-Nazis themselves explained their actions for readers of the Stormfront online forum, some of whom complained that they had harmed the ability of neo-Nazis to infiltrate outfits like SOS by going public:

> The flags came out in the last few moments of the protest. The commies were chanting "Nazis Go Home" for hours on end non-stop, so I and everyone present on the street in the hot sun, facing hostile commies, browns, and who-knows-what greenlighted the flag idea. We will stand behind our decision.
>
> If anyone wants to do it differently, come with us and tell us then and there.
>
> Besides, this is America and if they can fly their commie flags, burn the US flag, fly their brown flag, we can fly anything we want.

SOS leader Joe Turner pathetically tried to explain them away: "Just because one believes in white separatism, that does not make them a racist." No one asked Jim Gilchrist about it.

In Tennessee—a state with no international border—a Minuteman outfit sprang up, ready to repel the "invasion" of Latinos from elsewhere, without bothering to obtain the MCDC's official imprimatur. Leader Carl Whitaker told local reporters: "We're not a hate group. We're a concerned group. We're concerned what's happening. If people are here illegally and they want to get legal, we would be glad to try to help them follow through the process. We don't hate anybody."

His outfit, Tennessee Volunteer Minutemen, was focused on exposing companies that hired undocumented immigrants, he said, thus taking away jobs from taxpaying Americans: "We've turned in five different places of employment here that are hiring illegals."

The same TV crew, however, filmed another supporter named James Drinnon who commented: "I think they ought to get them all out. Most of them in here. That's where all the dope's coming from. Most of them's Hispanic."

Drinnon was even more explicitly racist off-camera: He complained to the reporters that there were more Mexicans than African Americans in Hamblen County, though those were not his words. He used a better-known epithet for black people.

The Minutemen and their offshoots really revealed themselves when they thought the cameras weren't rolling. In Arizona, the same Phoenix TV station that had embedded a TV crew undercover at the Minuteman Project did much the same thing with some of the splinter Minuteman groups in Arizona and came up with some deeply disturbing footage.

These Minutemen, of course, weren't avoiding contact with the border crossers they encountered. Like Simcox's old CHD patrols, these border watchers were vigilantes, hunting down immigrants in the desert, and they were drawing down on the Hispanics they encountered.

One Minuteman who called himself Pineapple 6 told reporters: "These fucking Mexicans. They will kill you. They don't give a fuck." He further declared that "Mexican immigrants are Public Enemy No. 1."

And that was the more moderate outfit the KPHO reporters covered. Another vigilante operation run by a man named Fred Puckett—who called himself a Minuteman of One—was operating nearby. Puckett had been expelled from the other group for being too radical. As Pineapple 6 explained: "They're carrying automatic weapons and they're chasing guys down and tracking them, then they tie them up."

The crew tracked down Puckett and found him as described. "We don't have no by-laws, we don't have nothin'," he told the reporters. "We go out in two-man teams and we hit them like we did 40 years ago in Vietnam."

Puckett said his outfit carried assault rifles when out on patrol and didn't hesitate to follow migrants or smugglers. They also were known to "confiscate" food, water, and whatever luggage or backpacks they came across.

"We believe our country is being destroyed from the inside," Puckett said. "Anything south of I-10 is a Third World nation."

He said he felt sorry for the immigrants but despised their coyotes: "And once you shoot a couple of these son of a bitches, they'll think twice."

While these border watchers preferred to work surreptitiously, KPHO also interviewed another Minuteman splinter group that was eager for publicity. Calling themselves Border Guardians, it was being run by a woman named Roberta Dill, better known to her adoring public as Laine Lawless.

Among the publicity stunts pulled by Lawless and her cohorts: burning a Mexican flag in front of the Mexican consulate in Tucson. As Lawless told the TV cameras: "I just don't like the idea of a group of people invading America."

One of her fellow flag burners, a bellicose nativist named Roy Warden, shouted: "And if any invader tries to take this land from us, we will wash this land with blood!"

Lawless in fact had been part of Chris Simcox's original Tombstone Militia and had remained with his Civil Homeland Defense outfit up through the Minuteman Project. Having gotten crosswise with Simcox and his ego, however, she had returned home determined to start her own border-watch operation. The Border Guardians' website explained her operating philosophy: "Disrupt and deter illegal immigration by any legal means, including psy-ops field missions, propaganda, and infiltration of organizations who are enemies of the lawful American republic and American citizenry as a whole."

When the undercover KPHO reporter first contacted her, she asked if he were interested in infiltrating local immigrant-rights groups and reporting their plans back to her.

"We always need spies, if you've got the stomach for it," she told him.

She was eager to gain recruits, she said: "What I need right now are bodies. At this point, I don't even care if they are racist."

Indeed, it turned out that Lawless had no trouble associating with radical white supremacists at all. A few months later, the Southern Poverty Law Center published secret correspondence she'd had with a group of neo-Nazi leaders from Ohio, featuring an email she'd sent them titled, "How to GET RID OF THEM!"

The message, sent to the self-styled SS commander of the Western Ohio unit of the National Socialist Movement, Mark Martin, detailed eleven ways that Martin and his thugs could terrorize Latino immigrants, including:

- Make every illegal alien feel the heat of being a person without status. I hear the rednecks in the South are beating up illegals as the textile mills have closed. Use your imagination. . . .
- Sabotage the things that they like: entertainment, food, beer, overpopulation, wife-beating, treating American women with disrespect. Bravo to the person who cut down the Spanish-language radio station towers just north of Phoenix! Now that sends a message!
- Deprive illegals of the smuggling money they pay. Steal the money from any illegal walking into a bank or check cashing place. Steal the money from smugglers. . . .
- Stand in front of public voting places and ask everyone who comes to vote if they speak English.
- Discourage Spanish-speaking children from going to school. Be creative.
- Create an anonymous propaganda campaign warning that any further illegal immigrants will be shot, maimed or seriously messed-up upon crossing the border. This should be fairly easy to do, considering the hysteria of the Spanish language press, and how they view the Minutemen as 'racists & vigilantes.' I say, if it bleed it leads, and why not work on their fears?

"Maybe some of your warriors for the race would be the kind of people willing to implement some of these ideas," Lawless wrote Martin. "I'm not ready to come out on this. . . . Please don't use my name. THANKS."

She declined to comment when the SPLC contacted her, having obtained the email through an undercover source. But when she burned a flag in front of the consulate a few days later, she proclaimed: "As always, Border Guardians remains committed to only lawful actions to combat illegal immigration. We are committed to practice only peaceful, lawful action in defense of our country."

||

One of the foremost ways of spreading information, such as it is, on the right-wing news circuit is the email forward, in which some anonymous friend of a friend forwards an anonymous piece of information, or amusingly Photoshopped picture, or amazing video or computer game, obtained from an unknown source, which is then not only consumed eagerly and credulously by conservative readers but forwarded again to a long list of like-minded friends, probably half of whom have already seen it anyway. No one is ever sure where these emails originate, but once launched into the Internet, they enjoy seemingly eternal and endless circulation.

That same April of 2006, as various Minutemen speculated on the need to start shooting border crossers, people on the nativist email-forward circuit started receiving either links to or outright copies of a computer game called "Border Patrol." The object of the game was to kill—with a roving, mouse-directed set of crosshairs as the means of aiming and shooting—as many "wetbacks" as possible as they scrambled across the American border.

The website didn't announce the game's origins, though there were some subtle clues. As you scanned the countryside for border crossers, a sign appeared on the border proclaiming "Welcome to the United States," decorated with an American flag—except that the stars in the flag had been replaced with a Jewish Star of David.

Indeed, all you had to do was strip off the remainder of the URL to see that the game was hosted by Resist.net, the home site of White Aryan Resistance. That, of course, was the same neo-Nazi organization operated by the California man who had invented the vigilante border watch: Tom Metzger.

"There is One Simple Objective to This Game," its front screen announced. "Keep Them Out—At Any Cost."

The targets: "Mexican Nationalist," "Drug Smuggler," and "Breeder," which was a pregnant woman with two small children. Hitting her scored one of the highest possible bonuses.

# 7

## Golden Crosses

Brisenia's portrait in the Arivaca Community Center. DAVID NEIWERT PHOTO

As long as everyone was getting along, the status quo among the drug-smuggling operators kept Arivaca quiet for a long time. But then Sam Romero started dating Oscar Pettis's mother. And one night he made the mistake, as macho drug lords are known to do (at least in the movies and sometimes in real life), of slapping her around. "Two days later," the law enforcement source tells me, "[Sam] was out of Arivaca living in Hawaii. He had to leave Arivaca because Oscar was going to kill him. And he knew that Oscar was a little bit tougher than he was."

Things didn't change right away, because Oscar Pettis and his organization ran Arivaca in much the same way Sam Romero had. The town was kept quiet and clean. "We had no burglaries. You could leave stuff out, and nobody would steal nothing." It was also a peaceful transition. Sam Romero's old enforcer went to work for Oscar Pettis, and no one blinked an eye.

Eventually, thanks to some assistance from alert neighbors, who reported vehicles hauling drugs out of the Pettis place, which were then pulled over in traffic stops far removed from Arivaca, the DEA was able to compile a case against Pettis and his organization. On August 10, 2006, they swooped in and closed Pettis and his entire operation down: the Grubstake Saloon, the tire shop, the house where the operations occurred.

At about five that morning, a neighbor who had been keeping law enforcement officers updated on activities at the Pettis home called one of my sources, shouting with excitement: "He says, 'Man, you can't believe this. They got a helicopter up so high you can hardly see it. There's another helicopter way off the ground; there's guys hanging out with guns. I didn't think there were so many police and unmarked cars in the world.'"

The DEA took Oscar Pettis down on criminal-enterprise charges, and within a three-month period, it did the same with Eddie Valdez and Jed Lopes. That left only the small-time operators in Arivaca: Junior and Victor Flores, and Ralph and Rita and their gang of gofers.

Not surprisingly, in the ensuing vacuum, Junior Flores began to really prosper. He was able to buy another piece of property, adjacent to his home on Mesquite Road, where he began building a big new home for Gina and the girls. They were still living in the double-wide, but work was coming along on the new property. Down in his welding shop, Junior had crafted a beautiful gate for the driveway that resembled a sunrise, with the figures of a coyote and a roadrunner in the corners. On Valentine's Day in 2008, he bought the girls matching Shetland ponies. In April 2009, he took Gina and the girls on a trip to Disneyland. It was the first vacation anyone could remember Junior ever taking.

People said he was starting to get flashy. He bought a big new black Hummer, a new diesel pickup truck, and a decent new car for Gina to drive. He dropped his money generously around the little town. In a place like Arivaca, all that stands out. And the jealous eyes of his sole remaining competitors in the pot-smuggling business were watching.

||

Over the decade preceding 2009, two previously unknown factors descended on the Altar Valley: massive immigration through the desert borderlands and the Mexican drug cartels. Together, they changed the cultural landscape there forever.

There had always been the occasional border crosser who came straggling through the Altar Valley. Before 1996 and the shutdown of the border crossing at Nogales, people in Arivaca had shrugged at the sight and, if anything, given them a hand.

"When I was about seven years old, I was out walking with my dog," recalls Alan Wellen, whose parents arrived in Arivaca in 1971 when he was a toddler, "and I came across my very first illegal. And he didn't speak any English. And I didn't really speak any Spanish. So I brought him back to the house, made him a few sandwiches.

"I called our bus driver's wife, because I knew that she spoke English and Spanish. And it was a phone number I knew. And she translated. We came to the conclusion that he was looking for a ranch that was just a few miles north of us. So I just gave him some more sandwiches and sent him on his way.

"And that's how things worked for a really long time. He would go to that ranch, and he would work, and he'd get some money, and he'd go back home, and he'd spend his money, and probably that money kept his village going for that whole year. There was a huge discrepancy between the lifestyles and the amount of money it takes to live in each country. So basically a few people in the States could make enough money for a whole village. And that's how it was for many, many years."

By 2000, that was not the case any longer. By then, local ranchers were seeing not the solo trekkers, nor even occasional packs of people being shepherded across by helpful coyotes, but long daisy chains of border crossers led by fast-moving and merciless coyotes who gave not a second's thought to leaving behind any stragglers, who would then either wander onto their ranches begging for water and help from the Border Patrol or simply die in the waterless, roasting expanse. Going out on patrol with your horse meant not only fixing regularly cut barbed-wire fences but sometimes also encountering corpses or the nearly dead. It was smart to strap a gun on your hip and an extra supply of water on your saddle.

At other times, ranchers would witness caravans of vehicles jam-packed with would-be immigrants careering along the desert roads, intent on reaching Tucson. Sometimes they would see Border Patrol in pursuit, and this was when horrible things were most likely to happen. One Arivaca rancher witnessed a pickup driver who attempted to elude Border Patrol pursuit by driving directly through a barbed-wire fence with a full load of would-be immigrants in the back end. A woman who was clutching her eight-year-old child had her scalp sheared clean off by the wire strand that flew up over the truck's front end.

Then there was the garbage. Migrant crossers dropped tons of garbage in the desert en route to their pickup spots and at those spots as well—as a matter not of slovenliness but of pure survival. Coyotes would only transport them with the clothes on their backs, but making the desert crossings entailed carrying spare clothes and shoes as well as food and water. In the Arizona desert,

canned tuna provides a compact but cheap source of protein and so is popular with border crossers, who also prefer to buy inexpensive bottles of elec-
trolytes to bottled water, since it helps them endure the roasting desert better.
So if you walked up any draw outside of town and in these hills, you were
likely to find scatterings of tuna cans and plastic electrolyte bottles.

It reached its peak in about 2006, when it was estimated by Border Patrol
officials that the 3.2 million entrants who came through the Southern Arizona desert between July 1999 and June 2005 had dumped twenty-five million tons of trash along the way. Of course, that didn't even count the trash
left by those who went uncaught. And it was piling up: the Bureau of Land
Management estimated that migrants left about four million pounds of trash
in the Arizona desert each year. Cleanup crews managed to haul in only a
fraction of all that—a meager 250,000 pounds between 2002 and 2005.

In the spring of 2006, members of the advocacy group No More Deaths—
which organizes volunteers to leave water in the desert for migrants as well
as to look for people who are injured, sick, or lost—came upon one of those
mid-desert layup points, five miles west of Arivaca in the open desert, that
occupied ten thousand square feet and was littered with hundreds and hundreds of backpacks.

"I've never seen anything that size. It's unbelievable," said Steve Johnston,
who organized the No More Deaths camp near Arivaca.

These lands also happen to be part of the Buenos Aires National Wildlife
Refuge, whose lands practically surround the Arivaca town site, the tranquil
Arivaca Cienega near the entrance to the town being its easternmost finger.
For wildlife aficionados, it's a truly special place, home to 58 species of mam-
mals, 53 species of reptiles and amphibians, and 352 bird species, including
a diverse array of raptors—eagles, hawks, vultures—whose keening cries are
often the only sound to be heard out in the open bush. There are white-
tailed deer, pronghorn antelope, tawny pumas, and desert-toughened javelinas, the boar-like animals that populate the landscape. And jaguars wander
over the border from time to time.

None of these animals get along well with the garbage, particularly the
ubiquitous plastic bags that seem to be everywhere and turn up in the stom-
achs of many a dead animal. Birds get tangled in the trash, or they pick up
foil wrappers and try to eat them.

Back in 2002, a volunteer couple went out and counted forty-five abandoned cars on the Buenos Aires refuge near Sasabe. They also collected
enough trash to fill 723 large bags with eighteen thousand pounds of garbage
over two months. Since then, the situation has not particularly improved.

These kinds of problems changed everybody's attitudes about the border crossers and their relationships with them. Nowadays, Arivacans say almost uniformly that they have lots of compassion for the migrants, but they can't afford to help out much anymore, beyond offers of free water, because the situation has grown so out of hand, so dangerous, so unhealthy.

This is especially the case because so much of the human smuggling here now occurs under the aegis of the Mexican drug cartels, whose backpack-hauling mules follow the same trails as the migrants. Indeed, many of the mules are simply migrants who have been either persuaded or coerced into carrying the loads of drugs—which sometimes are no more than a burlap sack loaded with a bale of pot and tossed over a back—while others are professional cartel mules carrying weapons. At one time it was easy—and ethically significant, in terms of how an ordinary Arivacan might treat them—to distinguish between immigrant border crossers and drug mules, but that is no longer true.

The rise of the cartels in the past decade also radically transformed the relationships among the drug smugglers in Arivaca. Most of all, it made the stakes much higher: Oscar Pettis got taken down because he was moving so much volume through the area, enough to finally attract the DEA's attention down to the Altar Valley. After the dust from the busts of 2006 settled, the remaining smugglers, like Junior and Victor Flores and Ralph and Rita, all of whom had been small-timers before, were suddenly getting opportunities to handle larger volumes. Flores did not belong to the cartels, but he did business with them as a matter of necessity. Ralph and Rita, however, were a different story: their dependence on Fat Boy down in Sonora meant their ties to the cartels were much stronger.

Word started getting around that Ralph and Rita intended to own the town of Arivaca, to force everyone's marijuana business to go through them. However, it was obvious that if they wanted to really control the smuggling business, Junior and Victor Flores—who had always been independent and neither of whom was anyone to mess with—presented a big obstacle for them, one that could only be eliminated, under the old rules, by dry-gulching them somewhere. But at the same time, it was made clear, according to law enforcement sources, that the Mexican cartels were adamant about keeping a lid on any violence north of the border. Taking out Junior and Victor on their own was out of the question. Fat Boy and the cartel bosses in Sasabe would not permit it.

So the tension simply built up. And people in Ralph and Rita's organization began wondering if there was another solution to the problem. Something outside of the traditional means—maybe even outside of the Arivaca Rules.

||

In the spring of 2008, a crew of documentary film students visited Arivaca to report about the impact of the immigration controversy on the border town. Much of the film focused on the impact of the Border Patrol's over-powering presence in the town and the way the local community insisted on asserting its own identity in the face of sometimes-overwhelming forces.

One of their chief interviewees was a Latino man identified as the man-ager of Rocking A Hardware. Ebullient and talkative, he sat in a blue fold-ing chair, his three-legged dog curled up next to him, as he held forth on a variety of subjects related to life in Arivaca.

At times, he was like a chamber of commerce chairman: "People out here are very neighborly. It's a blast," he said. "There's one store, you have a feed store, and a real cool cemetery. Some of the dates go back to the 1800s."

He touted the town's fabled generosity: "The community center helps a lot. They give free food to people who can't make it into town. They have a lot of bread, a lot of free stuff. Because, as you can tell, the poverty level here is pretty low. People are just kind of day to day."

He was proud of its quirkiness: "What makes the town so unique is the individuals. It gives it its own little flavor. Because you go to small towns in different areas of the world, and they're not all the same at all."

On the other hand, it was clear that he wasn't fond of the authorities. He also thought the border fence was a joke: "What that's going to do is hinder life and nature a lot more than it's going to hinder man," he said. He simi-larly disliked the towers erected on the outskirts of town, in the Altar Valley, with cameras to monitor movement in the desert: "The tower is Big Brother," he said. "*1984*. He's watching you."

He also had few kind words for the Border Patrol: "The trucks are always muddy, muddy, muddy, but watch them when they get out of the trucks. They're clean as a whistle. They got AC in there, they got their PlayStations, their PSPs, I don't know what all they got in there. But they are not out trekking in the dirt. What they're doing is sitting around, wasting taxpayer dollars. And oh my goodness, the new Border Patrol vehicles? Wanna talk about a pretty penny—those things are expensive.

"Me, I go down the road, I get pulled over all the time. And I tell them, 'You're profiling me.' And they laugh. I make it a joke. Because you can be mean, you can be assholes to them, but they control the roads. If you want to commute, just to commute, you have to be friendly to them."

He had a great deal of sympathy, on the other hand, for immigrant border crossers—and, seemingly, little for the people who abused them or called the Border Patrol on them: "The desert's the desert. Mother Nature. You know, in order to survive in the desert you gotta be pretty tough.

"Because me, I'm a city boy. When I come out here, I'm sweating; I look like a whore in church. People say, 'What are you doin'?' I say, 'Nothing, I'm just sweating.' The humidity. It's the dry heat. People say Arizona is cool because it's a dry heat, but 115 degrees is still 115 degrees.

"Imagine yourself, put yourself in their shoes. Look at that country. Look at those hills. Coming over, you don't know if you're going the right way because the person you gave your money to might be a fake. You might be going to get murdered; you might be going to get raped.

"And then you come to town, finally, and you're dying of thirst, and finally you ask someone, 'Please, I'm dying of thirst, could I get some water?' And they go, 'Fuck you,' and they shoot at you. Or they say, 'Fuck you,' and call the Border Patrol on you. Imagine how you'd feel.

"But would you do it again? A lot of these people do it again and again and again." He shook his head.

Then the interview took a darker turn as the man discussed the harsh realities of life in the desert.

"The law in Arivaca—I call it the Law of the West," he said. "People out here, they mind their own business; they let people do their own things, unless it gets drastic.

"And out here it's desert. Everything out here will bite you, prick you, or eat you. So you have to protect yourself. This is Arivaca, Arizona, and as long as you don't have a felony, you can carry a gun."

Did he carry a gun? the interviewer asked.

"Me, a gun? I refuse to answer that on the grounds that may incriminate me, since I am a convicted felon and proud of it. Fuck the police." He raised his arm and flipped a bird.

That man's name was Albert Gaxiola.

||

Gaxiola indeed was a convicted felon—he had served eight years in the Arizona State Penitentiary for drug trafficking, after being caught with a massive load of marijuana—and his tacit admission to owning a gun might have caught the eye of his parole officer had it crossed that person's desk. Because it took a year for the film to be edited, however, it never did.

Albert Gaxiola had been raised in California by an alcoholic mother and an abusive stepfather, and his mother, a dealer herself, had later inducted him into the drug-trafficking business as a young man. He had come out to Arivaca to go to work for his mother in the 1990s, which is what he was doing when he was busted the first time. He returned to town after getting out of prison because he had relatives there—including Rita and Ralph. He went to work for them as a gofer, while holding down a front job at the feed store.

In spite of that dark background, Albert had a sunny reputation in Arivaca. His garrulous and friendly nature made him likeable to nearly everyone, and he was known for his acts of generosity, too. The uniform description of Albert was that he was "a nice guy."

At one time, he and Junior Flores had been good friends. Junior had befriended Albert after he got out of prison, and he was a familiar sight at Junior's home, enjoying barbecues in the yard and beers with the family. If Junior and Gina were busy, Albert would swing by the community center to pick up Alexandra and Brisenia and bring them home after their regular afternoon playtimes.

The girls, especially Brisenia, adored Gaxiola. They called him Uncle Albert. He was a regular guest at their table, and the girls loved his stories.

After awhile, though, Albert started to wear on Gina Gonzalez. He was becoming too familiar with her and her home. She didn't like that he would come in their house and help himself to the beer in the fridge, or that he would open the bag of chips she had just bought at the store and plop down on the couch with it to watch TV. There was talk in town, too, that Albert had a thing for Gina, who was indeed one of the prettiest women in Arivaca.

Finally Gina mentioned to Junior one day that Albert was making her uncomfortable, and his expression had darkened. "Albert is not a good person. He's not all there" was all he would say. Around the same time, Gaxiola stopped coming around. Gina told Junior to start locking their front gate because she didn't want to be feeding the guy every day.

It's not entirely clear what had set off the feud, but it was likely the fact that Gaxiola and his cohorts in Ralph and Rita's smuggling business—including one Oin Oakstar—had taken to ripping Junior off. Oakstar later testified that in April 2009, he and Gaxiola stole a five-hundred-pound marijuana delivery from someone named Tony, who it turned out was doing a delivery for Junior Flores.

Or maybe it was the fact that Gaxiola had taken to having his mules drop bales of marijuana at Junior Flores's second property, the one where he was building a home. Junior had caught him passing by with his SUV in the middle of the night and driving down to the wash below their home; Flores could hear the thunk of someone loading cargo into the back end of the vehicle. The next day, Junior checked his property and sure enough: the barbed wire on the back end of the property had been cut, and there were tracks coming through. When Gina found out, she hit the roof. Alan Wellen explains that this was part of the native ethic in Arivaca. "If you drive by a property, and you know whose property it is, and you see a couple bales there—anyone who knows what the hell's going on would turn their head straightaway and just drive," Wellen tells me. "But if you're driving past a property that you know this stuff really should not be on, then you're gonna get out and check it out, and who knows what's gonna happen to that."

That was what Junior Flores apparently was worried about. "People would think it was his, and there's all kinds of ramifications for that." Those ramifications have to do with one's daily well-being, as well as that of your family and loved ones. As Wellen explained, "One of my not-quite-next-door neighbors was growing some pot that I could see the other day. It's like, I think I know who uses that property, and so that's something that I'm not going to mess with. I'm just going to turn my head and drive. Because you know, I have kids of my own—I'm not going to get involved in that."

Flores flatly told Gaxiola to knock it off: "He told him, you know, you better not be stashing stuff on my property because the rumors are so bad right now that, you know, they're not gonna believe that that's not mine," Gina told the detectives. But he kept doing it: the late-night vehicles kept driving past their home and loading up something from their second property.

It was enough to set off Junior Flores, who probably also suspected that his onetime friend Uncle Albert was ripping him off. In early May, he confronted Gaxiola as he drove past the Flores-Gonzalez home on his ATV.

Junior walked out to the road and stopped Gaxiola. There was a brief exchange of words, and Junior punched Albert. Gaxiola fell off his ATV. Flores turned and headed back to his house, and it looked to him like Gaxiola was trying to get to his gun on his ATV, so Junior hurried inside, since he was unarmed. When he looked outside through the front window, Gaxiola had already gotten on his rig and driven off.

As friendships went, this one had gone completely to hell. In the crucible of small-town life, this was not altogether uncommon.

||

Maybe it was the feud with Albert Gaxiola. Maybe it was the unease that came from dealing with the Mexican cartels. Or maybe it was just time. But Junior Flores wanted out of the drug trade. The problem was figuring out how.

He had his welding shop, and he was skilled at welding. He specialized in making copper fountains, the kind you see at entrances to housing developments: expensive items that could bring in several thousand dollars per job. And he was dreaming up all kinds of other schemes.

One of them involved archaeological work: not only did Junior know the backcountry like his own hand, he knew where the hidden nooks were that contained the ruins and remains of ancient Spanish settlements from the era when this land was New Spain and then early Mexico.

"The last time I talked with Junior, he was just getting back from a ride on his horse," Alan Wellen recalls. "And what he was trying to concentrate on was all of his days in the desert, looking at things.

"He was into finding archaeological artifacts, especially as they related to his family around the area. He had told me that he had found this cross from a church that was one of these nine churches from the area. And he had a golden cross off of one of these churches.

"It seemed to me like he really wanted to kind of turn over a new leaf. He would leave town for awhile to go get work in other places. Gina had actually gotten a job at the Mercantile and at the after-school program too. To try to make that jump over to the other side."

The prospect of being a respected supplier of artifacts to museums was an exciting one to Junior Flores. "When he was talking about these crosses that he was going out to find," Alan Wellen says, "he was really excited about that, and how he was going to be able to support his family by doing these archaeological things, you know—put them in a museum. He was all animated about that."

He talked with his friend Andrew Alday, the astronomer, about changing professions too. "Junior never had a real vacation," Alday recalls. "I said, 'Why don't you go to Hawaii? I can set you up with fishing, whatever you want to do.' He says, 'Wow, I never thought about it.'

"I told him, 'Get out of the business. You got family, a beautiful wife, two beautiful daughters. You got a nice spread here. You got a legitimate business with your welding and all that.'

"He said he was really thinking of getting out. But the family had been involved in that for so long, you grow up into it. And it was quite successful.

"And let me tell you, it wasn't just Mexicans. A lot of people made their money through Junior. From pot. All hippies."

Alday gladly defends Flores now, even knowing how he made his living. "The only time I raise that issue is when they say, 'Well, you know what Junior did,' and I say: 'I knew Junior very well.' He was still a good man, and I recognize that.

"Junior was a good husband, a good friend, and a good father. He happened to have dealt with marijuana smuggling.

"He wasn't dealing thousands of pounds. Over the years maybe. He wasn't the kind of guy where they'd bring a truckload in and they'd stash it in a safe house. Junior was real small-time. They never found anything in his house because he never brought it around.

"When I'd go visit, you'd never know it was anything other than a family's home. We'd have barbecues over there all the time."

Not everyone in town felt the same way. One Arivacan I meet describes Junior Flores as "a scary motherfucker," while others point out that he often adopted the style of a typical South Tucson gangster. Even Alan Wellen, who considered Junior his friend, admits, "In a lot of ways, he tried to be that." A "huge part" of that, though, was simply Flores's way of keeping potential kneecappers from fucking with him, he says. At the same time, Wellen remarks, "he didn't mess with people for no good reason."

Wellen saw both sides of Junior Flores: the "scary" drug dealer and the "great guy" who would buy people dinners. "He was both—depending on who you were, depending on whether he perceived you as a threat. There is a Hispanic machismo thing, especially in certain families where the father figure has to be this really strong, overbearing, beat-down-on-the-kids type. I think some of that rubbed off on both Victor and Junior. Both of them have this thing where they can just blow up their chest really big."

Wellen says that even as Flores regaled him with plans for making a living as an archeologist, "he would kind of slip into this whole thing where he had to protect his assets, you know. He was paranoid about other people jumping in on his deal, you know, that sort of thing."

That probably wasn't an issue when it came to recovering gold crosses in the desert. But in truth, "he was very, very right to be paranoid. Maybe he should have been more paranoid," Wellen observes. "I mean, he was—I don't want to call him naïve, because definitely, in a lot of ways, he was not naïve at all. But in other ways he seemed a bit uninformed."

Still, to people like Andrew Alday, people whom he knew and trusted, he was a friend. "A friend is somebody you know. A friend will come and help you out at three a.m. because you've called and said, 'I've got an emergency,'" Alday says.

"Junior was like that. If anything happened, he helped us with our roof; he helped with the firewood. Anytime you needed anything, any welding things, he was there. And he didn't just offer it to us—he offered it to a lot of people in the community."

Junior's chief way of being flashy, if you can really call it that, was to spread his money around town. "He made good money," Alday says. "And he didn't just spend it on himself. But instead of going to Green Valley or to a big barn to buy hay, he'd buy from the folks in town. He spent money here. I think a lot of people resented that."

Junior Flores was smart enough to sense that resentment but perhaps not enough to change. At least not just then. "I think he was trying to get out of the business," Alday says. "I really do. He just hadn't figured it out yet."

||

It didn't help that Ralph and Rita were turning up the nastiness a notch, waging a campaign of intimidation against people they saw as obstacles to their Arivacan hegemony.

One of those people was one of my law enforcement sources, a retiree who liked to go out tooling around on his all-terrain vehicle in the desert and who would sometimes come upon bales of marijuana, dropped at various prearranged spots by mules. He would call up the Border Patrol and have them come pick up the bales. Most of the time, the pot he was finding belonged to Ralph and Rita's smuggling operation.

All of a sudden, Ralph and Rita's two oldest sons started showing up on their ATVs on the dusty road leading down to his driveway and his home, throwing wheelies and making noise, trying to intimidate him. "I ignored it," he said. "I got my gun right there, and at night I would lock the gate. So I don't really worry about it."

It helped that he had an old dog, a loyal Australian shepherd, that would bark and let him know if somebody was coming down the road. One day, the retiree returned home from a trip into Tucson and found his old dog dangling in the tree outside his front door, its throat cut.

"Well, the neighbor saw me get home, so he comes over, and says, 'Hey, you know those guys that were weaving around all the time? They came in here, and they were on your property.'

"So I said, 'OK, you motherfuckers.' And I was pissed. So I grabbed my .45, and I went down there because [Ralph] and that whole bunch, when they had the feed store, would sit there in front of the feed store, chairs and a table, and play cards. So I just went flying out there, and I jumped out, and I said—there was the two oldest boys and [Ralph]—and I said, 'You motherfuckers ever come close to my house, even down the street, you're gonna die just like my dog.'"

The men just stood up and walked inside without a word. "And I drove away. And they've never come close to this place again."

||

The focus of Junior Flores's plans to get out of the drug-smuggling business was his two daughters. They represented his hopes for a brighter and cleaner future. So he tried hard to give them a good, healthy, normal family life and protected them from the realities of his business as best he could. At least, he believed he had.

Alexandra, the elder, was Daddy's girl. When she was little, they liked to play physical games, wrestling and rolling and laughing, and when she was a little older, she loved to ride with her dad on his ATV, clutching him around the belly, giggling as they bounded and careered through the desert. Watching it would sometimes freeze Gina's blood. The two of them loved to ride horses together too, which made Gina much happier.

Brisenia was more of a Mommy's girl. She loved girly things and wasn't so keen on the rough-and-tumble play her older sister loved. While Junior and Alexandra would be romping around the property, she and Gina would be puttering around the yard, tending their gardens and their animals.

They were both his *mamacitas*, his little mamas, which was how he would greet them when he arrived at the community center to pick them up at day's end. They always ran to welcome him with delight.

"In some ways, they both were Daddy's girls," says a woman who knew the family well. "As soon as they saw him, they knew they were going to the store, they were gonna go ride horses, they were gonna go on the ATVs, they were gonna go do something. Till Gina got there—then Brisenia would tag along with Gina. It was just a slower pace. Alexandra was older, and she wanted the faster pace."

Junior Flores may have been a scary guy to some people in Arivaca, but he was a doting and kindly father with his daughters. "He was great with them," says Alan Wellen. "If he had a son, he might have done the macho thing and have been tougher on them. But with his daughters, they'd come up and climb in his lap while he was talking with his friends. He was really supportive and affectionate.

"When you're talking with the parent while the kids are in the room, there's this thing that parents do that, you know, they have to divide their attention between two things. I was always interested in the way that parents react to children interjecting into an adult conversation, or wanting the parents' attention, and the way that parents handle that. He seemed like he had a real interesting way of handling that, which was to bring the child into the circle, and then the other people would stop talking and wait for the conversation between him and his kid to unfold and get done, and get back to their conversation.

"He respected his girls. He treated them well."

Brisenia had her own patch of garden, and she bought a little green turtle figurine and placed it on the patch. But what she really loved was her animals—just like her mom.

"Oh, she loved animals," says their friend. "But you know what, her mom loved animals. You would see Gina in her prime, she would have her jeans on, she would have those rubber boots, and she would be feeding and watering her animals. And just be outside."

Junior helped feed the menageries. There were the Shetland ponies he had bought as a Valentine's Day present. "They had two ponies," recalls the friend. "They had ducks. They had chickens. They had cats. They had dogs. They had turtles. They had birds. Just everything. And when you'd pass their house, if the girls weren't in school, or Gina wasn't working, she was outside. If on weekends you went over there, Junior would be barbecuing; the animals would all be running all over the yard. It was really nice to see family like that."

The girls may have had different temperaments, but they were also a unit, tightly bonded, and always had each other's backs. No doubt it was a product of spending endless days together as children at home, inventing games in the yard or playing on the swing set and the teeter-totter their dad had made them. In later years they had a trampoline, too.

"At the community center, they went their own ways," recalls an adult friend. "They weren't together much then. But when they hung out at home, or when they were here, then they were. They were good sisters, you could tell. The bond was there.

"They were pretty tight, those two. They were like most siblings in that they'd fight. But they were always looking out for each other. Because they were always together. They always stuck together."

Junior also was making enough money to spoil the girls with a vacation to Disneyland. For spring break in April 2009, the family spent a week making the trip to Anaheim and doing all the rides and seeing all the sights. Brisenia was especially thrilled: Belle, her favorite princess—the one from *Beauty and the Beast*, whose faith in the good man beneath her captor's monstrous exterior reveals her true love—had given her one of the many autographs she had collected.

While you could ask fifty different people in Arivaca their opinion of Junior Flores and get fifty different opinions, that was not the case with Brisenia Flores: she was universally loved and admired, in no small part because she was one of those people who herself loved freely and yet respectfully. Above all, she was fiercely determined to achieve things, maybe great things. Brisenia was going places. In many ways, she was the face of the town's future.

"She had so much life in her," says one adult friend. "She was an over-achiever. She had a really good attitude. You know, I talked to the coach at her school, at her memorial. He said, 'I could always count on her. Whenever you asked for volunteers, she was always in the front with her arm up. Always.'

"She was always that way. I mean, whether it was vegetables, or planning, or cleanup, or any of the chores or anything there was to do, if you asked for volunteers, Brisenia was there."

An adult who got to know Brisenia as a volunteer at the community center says the same thing. "She had no attitude at all. Everything was always light. I'd say, 'OK, if everybody picks up—especially in the summertime—if everybody picks up ten pieces of trash, I'll give you a popsicle.' She would go and do that and then ask, 'Mary, if I pick up more, can I get another popsicle?' 'Yeah, girl!'

"Even the ones that didn't, I was going to give them two. But at least we'd get the yard cleaned up, and this was their little place. Even to keep it fair to everybody else, sometimes you'd have to say to Brisenia, 'You've already volunteered, babe. Let someone else volunteer.'"

The same phrase crops up time and time again as people describe her: "So much life," says another adult who knew her from the center, whom we will call Sally. "She always got As in class. And if the little girls would get in a fight with Brisenia, it would be like, 'Brisenia's spending a lot of time with Sienna; she's not spending no time with me.' That kind of stuff. And then you'd have to either add a child or break them up some kind of way. That's the kind of complaints Brisenia got. Spending time with somebody else and ignoring another girl."

Sally recalls how, in the last week of after-school care before summer vacation that May, the afternoon project was to make earrings. "She wanted to make one for her mom, one for her Nima, one for her Nama, everybody. And she would work really hard. There would be like an hour for them to do it, and she worked twice as hard so she would get all of them."

This grown-up was a favorite friend of Brisenia's, partly because she sometimes watched the girls on weekends over at her own home and partly because she was the one adult whom Brisenia could count on to count jump rope, or hula hoops, or whatever she was working on.

"The big thing to her was, if I had any time, where I could spend just with her, where I was outside while I was watching most of them, but she would come stand by me, she would ask me if I would count for her to see how many times she could jump rope, and how many times she could go around with the hula hoop. And we'd get to twenty, twenty-one, and she'd start all over again.

"Eventually I'd have to say, 'Brisenia, you know what, I have to come back to you because I gotta go check John or Ray at the sandbox or something. But as soon as she'd see that I was standing somewhere not really doing anything: '[Sally], can you count for me?' Of course I'm gonna say, 'Yeah.'"

Sally remembers that last week in May with sharp clarity. On Tuesday, Brisenia came in bearing the fruits of her extra-credit work at Sopori Elementary, where the teachers handed out "Paws"—little paw-shaped certificates signifying each student's extra achievement levels. Students in turn could take the tokens down to the student store and trade them in for plastic trinkets of various kinds.

"She came in, and she said, 'I got my Paws for the year. And I got three bracelets and two rings.'" Sally oohed and aahed over them properly.

"And she said, '[Sally], you can pick one.'"

"And I said, 'No, girl, you worked hard for your stuff. You keep them.'"

"And she said, 'No. I only have two rings and three bracelets. You can have a bracelet.'"

"I said, 'Well, give me the one you don't want.'"

"And she said, 'No, you pick the one you want.' So I did."

The next day was going to be Sally's last at the community center for the year. And as always, she greeted each child as they arrived. "You know, I think that's our future. We need to respect them. A lot of these kids have rough lives out here. From different economic levels and stuff. So I always made sure when they came in I greeted each one by name and say, 'How's your day goin'? How was school?' If I knew they were having a test or something, I'd say, 'How'd your test go?' Whatever it was, I made sure everybody got a greeting.

"And when Brisenia came in, I asked her, 'How'd your day go?'"

"She said, 'It was a good day.' She never complained.

"She said, 'You're wearing the bracelet.'

"I said, 'I told you I liked it.' And she gave me the biggest smile.

"And whenever I want to think of her, I always think of that smile. That was the last day that I saw her."

# 8

# The Bad Girl

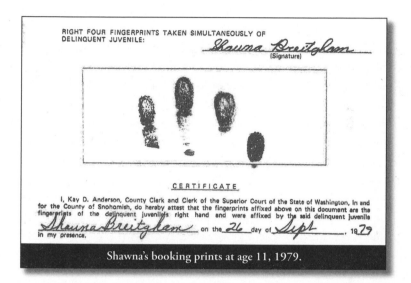

RIGHT FOUR FINGERPRINTS TAKEN SIMULTANEOUSLY OF DELINQUENT JUVENILE:

*Shawna Breitgham*
(Signature)

CERTIFICATE

I, Kay D. Anderson, County Clerk and Clerk of the Superior Court of the State of Washington, in and for the County of Snohomish, do hereby attest that the fingerprints affixed above on this document are the fingerprints of the delinquent juvenile's right hand and were affixed by the said delinquent juvenile *Shawna Breitgham* on the 26 day of *Sept*, 19 79 in my presence,

Shawna's booking prints at age 11, 1979.

In January 1972, little four-year-old Shawna Scott was given a psychiatric evaluation overseen by Washington State's Child Protective Services. The examiner asked her the usual battery of questions. Somewhere near the end of the interview, Shawna asked the examiner: "Do you love me?"

The little girl's confusion was perfectly understandable. Considering her life history up to then, she probably had no idea who loved her and who didn't.

The little girl, born out of wedlock on December 6, 1967, was ten months old when her birth mother, then named Rena Scott, gave up custody of the toddler to one of her older brothers and his wife. Then Shawna was handed off to a friend of that family, who in turn handed her to another of Rena's brothers. Her mother then took her back briefly but handed her off to the same older brother again. Rena eventually got her back again, only to give her up to another couple, family friends who adopted her for good, as it were. All that by the time she was five years old.

The little girl soon picked up shoplifting. Her adoptive parents were frequently called to come pick up Shawna by store owners who caught her in

the act. Her mother had to watch her closely if they ever went shopping together. She also had sticky fingers with friends and family: when she was
seven, she sneaked off during a dinner at the home of family friends and
stole a diamond necklace worth several thousand dollars. When she was
caught with the necklace at home, she had a phony excuse. She always did.

The rap sheet followed in logical consequential order: Shawna committed
her first felony at age eleven, breaking into her elementary school, trashing
classrooms and burglarizing lockers and stealing classmates' expensive belongings. Two years later, she was charged with theft in another case, but
the charges were dismissed.

Nonetheless, that was the final straw for her adoptive parents, who took
Shawna to the Crisis Intervention Office in Everett and left her there, stat-
ing that they wished to relinquish all their parental rights to the troubled
girl. She kept their last name as her own. The change did not alter her behavior significantly: five months later, she was convicted of a theft charge
for shoplifting. A year after that, she was convicted of a duplicate charge,
followed by a burglary charge for breaking into a home and stealing a bong
and pot. Three months later, she was convicted of taking a vehicle without
the owner's permission, and five months after that, she was convicted on
two separate crimes: theft for a dine and dash at an Everett restaurant and
prostitution when she was busted streetwalking in Everett.

At the time, she was all of fifteen years old. Before she had even turned sixteen, she was busted for hooking in Seattle, too. That was followed by a steady
string of busts, beginning the spring of '84, for a series of petty crimes: She got
caught stealing a dress and two pairs of earrings at the Bon Marché. Stealing
a Pontiac from an Avis shop in Seattle, then getting caught on the other side
of the Cascade Mountains, in Chelan County. Stealing a credit card, though
that charge got dropped. Charged for prostitution again in Seattle, with accompanying obstructing-an-officer and knife-possession charges.

That one got dropped when the arresting officer, a man named Rodriguez,
failed to appear in court. Shawna and her attorney claimed the detective had
broken the law by squeezing her breast, after she had placed his hand on it.
Without their chief witness, the judge had no choice but to dismiss.

Shawna was working the strolls of Seattle at the same time they were being
stalked by the Green River Killer, Gary Ridgeway, who eventually confessed to
murdering seventy-one women. She in fact was a good friend of Tammie Liles,
another Everett woman who disappeared in 1983 and whose remains were
later found, along with other Ridgeway victims, down in Tigard, Oregon.

Indeed, Shawna liked to tell friends she was the only victim of the Green

River Killer to have survived, regaling them with a tale of awakening nude, beaten, and half-strangled next to the Green River itself and flagging down a car for help. Like most of Shawna's stories, it had about a 99 percent chance of being 100 percent bullshit.

||

That's really the problem with trying to tell the story of Shawna's career before she became a Minuteman leader: beyond the public record—the thirteen arrests, the shunting from home to home, the five different names she used before becoming Shawna Forde—trying to discern the truth is like entering a hall of mirrors, a maze of deceit and half-truths and self-serving distortion, disorienting enough to make *Rashomon* seem like a simple puzzle. That's especially true of any part of the story told by Shawna herself, who is capable of telling the truth—when it serves her purposes—but who otherwise is such a prodigious and pathological liar that sorting the nuggets of truth out of the mountains of mendacity would test the skills of a forensic scientist.

The version of events told by her family members and friends is only somewhat less problematic: while Shawna's family deserves great credit for trying to be forthcoming and truthful about their daughter and sister, inevitably self-interest taints their story as well, particularly given that what they have to tell is a painful admission of mistakes and unthinkable behavior, not to mention their own victimization.

Certainly, the adults in Shawna's upbringing played an outsize role in making her the monster she became: she was abandoned, abused in every way—physically, emotionally, sexually—and practically feral by the time she was adopted. Indeed, a survey of the shambles that was Shawna's childhood years is really a classic, clinical litany of the predictable way that adults damage children, who grow up to be damaged adults who in turn cause tremendous harm and, in the case of antisocial personalities like Shawna, poison the lives of every person they touch.

Yet if the utterly toxic kind of nurture that Shawna received as a child made that outcome predictable, it was perhaps her nature that determined it with finality. Because from the time she was a toddler, people sensed there was something Not Quite Right about the little girl. Shawna unnerved adults with her clinical, calculating demeanor.

"She could look right through you even when she was tiny," says her mother, Rena. "There was something about her that was just . . . out of place. This was before I adopted her over to my sister-in-law. My sister-in-law noticed it, and we would sit and talk about it.

"And neither one of us could figure out just what it was, but there was just something about Shawna that was different. There was something, and we didn't know what it was. And it would give people the creeps.

"It was weird. It was just like she could just look right through you and just know everything about you. You know? It can be unnerving, especially out of a kid that was that little."

Rena herself was deeply troubled. She says she had been raped repeatedly by her stepfather as a teenager while her own mother, aware that her daughter was being violated, looked the other way. As a young woman, another family member had sexually assaulted her as well, she says. She married shortly after completing tenth grade and, over the next six years, produced four children, including her son Merrill. She finally left her philandering husband in 1965 and filed for divorce, which turned into an ugly battle for the control of the children.

In the meantime, she had met Shawna's father, a man named Shane, and moved in with him without marrying. They were together for three years, producing a son named Scotty in 1966 and Shawna in 1967. Her first husband used the illegitimate pregnancies to persuade the judge in their case that Rena was an unfit mother, and he won custody of their four children. He took off with the children and kept their location hidden, eventually relocating to Phoenix with the kids in 1969 without letting Rena or anyone else know where he was going, she says.

Distraught, Rena tried to kill herself. "I was in a bad state," she recalls. "My husband had run off with my kids, and I tried to commit suicide over that. And it didn't work. I was a basket case. I was in bad shape."

Her family members, especially one of her older brothers, decided it was time to take charge of her two children. "He was threatening to make my life a living hell, that he was going to go to the police and have me put in jail," she says. For what, she says, she didn't know: "I was young and stupid and afraid." She acquiesced, a mistake she came to regret the rest of her life.

Her brother handed the children off to a married couple of friends, people who were also members of the Jehovah's Witnesses congregation to which they all belonged. Eventually this arrangement fell apart when the couple divorced. Scotty was returned to Rena, who then turned around and adopted him out to another family, while her brothers resumed Shawna's guardianship.

Rena had by then married a man named Ken Caudle, who is still her husband to this day, and given birth to two children. She was finally able to get Shawna back from her older brothers in July 1971, but it did not last. The child she got back was still disquietingly calculating, but there were other disturbing behaviors. "She would take and smear the walls with her feces," says Rena. "Stuff like that. I didn't punish her for it. My husband gave her a couple of spankings for doing it, but neither one of us understood why she was doing it. We didn't even know it was a sign of abuse. We just didn't have that knowledge."

Rena now believes Shawna had been sexually molested by a family member sometime in those years out of her custody, in part because Shawna years later told her it had happened. She wasn't sure if she should believe it but says it was later corroborated by another family member, who had been an older child at the time and had witnessed it.

Even more disturbing than the acting out was the way the three-and-a-half-year old Shawna was interacting with her younger siblings, especially the infant girl they had named Rena. The Caudles had bought a little train that ran on a track in their living room that was big enough for children to ride. Shawna liked to ride on the engine. One day she ran it off its track and drove it to where little Rena lay on the floor and tried to run her over. Shawna also was caught biting the infant.

"And then one day I came out and she was sitting on the couch kind of straddled over Rena, and she was holding a pillow to her face," Rena says. It was the final straw. "That just scared me. I talked to my doctor, I went to everybody, and I went to the brothers in the Kingdom Hall and talked to them. And they say, 'Well, you know, you haven't had her very long. She really doesn't know you real well yet. Have you thought about maybe finding a home for her where there's just no other children—to make it safe?'

"And they didn't know any better than I did what to do. So that's when I started looking."

Rena was told about a family in their congregation, Harold and Patricia Breitgham, who were looking to adopt. "So I got acquainted with them. We went to a lawyer and did all the paperwork. It was legal. I took her out to their house, and I got her settled."

Rena remembers the parting starkly: "The day I left her with the Breitghams, I stayed for several hours and put her clothes away, that sort of thing," she says. "And she helped me. I told her that she would be staying there with these people, and that they were going to be her new family.

"She didn't show anything outward. Nothing was showing outward then. She was a little quiet, of course, which is natural. I had a hard time keeping the tears in. I know that she could tell I was upset.

"But I hugged her and kissed her and slowly edged my way out, talking to her the whole time. And then the Breitghams picked her up, and they sat her down, talked to her and got her distracted, and then I left the house. And that was the last time I seen her until she was eighteen."

Shawna would later claim that about six months after moving in with the Breitghams, when she was four, Harold, an engineer at Boeing, began molesting her almost daily, requiring her to perform oral sex on him in the afternoons. At other times, she claimed, they would take long drives to Yakima where he forced her to ride naked with him and perform sexual acts.

However, at other times, Shawna recanted these claims, and the Breitghams and their family members vigorously denied them all along, asserting that Forde was a pathological liar who wanted to hurt people who had later abandoned her. Certainly there is no police record indicating that Harold Breitgham was ever caught molesting Shawna—though in March 1979, when Shawna was eleven, the Breitghams were referred by Child Protective Services to the Luther Child Center for an examination after being accused of neglecting Shawna. A counselor who examined her reported that he believed Shawna was a victim of sexual molestation and abuse, though there was no indication that she had been victimized by the Breitghams.

What is unquestionably a fact is that Shawna's career as a petty criminal began while in the care of the Breitghams and blossomed into full-on criminality in spring of 1979, when she broke into her school, thoroughly trashed the place, and broke into lockers. As she explained in her own handwriting while entering a guilty plea in September: "On May 26, I broke two windows and went inside Lowell School. I was still inside when the police came." The little girl with a felony conviction was dropped off at the door of the Deaconess Home for Children in Everett a few days later by her adoptive parents, abandoned yet again.

Shawna was returned to the Breitghams in June of the next year because the children's home, where her own mother had once been placed as a teenager, closed its doors for good. She remained in their home under promises to behave, but when she was charged with shoplifting the following spring, they drove her down to the offices of Child Intervention Services and abandoned her there, this time for good.

Now a ward of the state, Shawna Breitgham went on to collect a long rap sheet of petty crimes by the time she was eighteen. In August 1986, she married a man named Jack Darling and moved to the remote Alaskan fishing village of Emmonak. The crimes became more infrequent thereafter—usually depending on her economic condition—but they never went away, either.

||

Shawna was pregnant when she married Jack Darling, and in January 1987 she gave birth to a baby girl they named Angelique who lived only a few weeks.

It was declared a case of sudden infant death syndrome. In a rural town of seven hundred people, cases such as that are rarely questioned. But within Shawna's family, stories persisted. Rena says that Jack Darling later told her a story about coming home and finding Shawna asleep on the bed and the infant dead in its bassinet, a pacifier in its mouth, held in place by a string around its neck; he said he removed the pacifier and cleaned the child up before calling EMTs. Shawna also confided to another of her eventual ex-husbands that she had been going through postpartum depression, desperately did not want the child, and strangled it with a pacifier.

The marriage in Alaska was almost immediately on the rocks; both Shawna and Jack drank a lot, and they fought a lot. In 1988, she moved back to Everett with Jack in tow; they rented an apartment, and he got a job at Boeing. She looked up Rena for the first time since she was three and a half. By then, Rena's life had stabilized, and she was delighted to have a second chance with her daughter, an opportunity to repair her biggest mistake.

"They came down, and they stayed at our house for about three weeks, until they found a place of their own," Rena recalls. "And then they moved into it, and in the process of it she told me she wasn't looking for a mother—she was looking for her father. So I gave her all the information on her dad, told her where she could find him. She went, and the first time she met her dad, I took her to meet him, because she was nervous about him."

Not long after arriving, Shawna moved out and got her own apartment, and Rena helped her move. By then, she had found a new boyfriend, an unemployed barfly named Tony Eddy, who was also still married to another person. She became pregnant that spring by Tony, and doctors told her it was a boy.

Perhaps remembering how Angelique had worked out, the pregnancy sent her over the edge. One day in early June 1989 she showed up at the workplace of Eddy's then-wife and began stabbing herself in the abdomen with a small knife, shouting out the woman's name. "She just went totally psycho out there," the woman later recalled. Police and EMTs arrived and carted her away, though her wounds were only superficial. Tony Eddy sought a restraining order against Shawna.

As a result of that incident, Shawna wound up being charged with forgery. That's because when Shawna received some court paperwork related to the restraining order, she altered it to make it appear that Tony Eddy now owed her money. In August 1989 Snohomish County slapped her with a felony charge and issued an arrest warrant.

In December of that year, awaiting trial, Shawna gave birth to her son with Tony Eddy, Devon. Four months later, she finally filed for divorce from Jack Darling, and in June 1990, it was granted. Shawna then turned around and convinced Tony Eddy to marry her in August of that year. With their chief witness now married to the accused forger, Snohomish County was forced to drop the charges against Shawna before the year was out.

Once again, it was a messy marriage. They had a daughter they named Jaszmin, born in October 1991. And while Shawna loved to play the doting mother, she also liked to spend Tony Eddy's money as if it were water. Tony liked to drink too, and Shawna claims he was abusive. In November 1993, he lost his job at Boeing, and a month later, Shawna left him, taking the two children with her. The following February, Shawna claims she went to work as a counselor at a Boys and Girls Club in Alderwood, a suburb south of Everett, though no one has ever been able to confirm that. Her divorce from Tony Eddy was finalized in July, and she was granted custody of the children.

Some years later, Shawna would tell people that she was a "grunge rock promoter," a claim that eventually grew into a story, repeated endlessly by both Shawna and gullible reporters, that she had helped Nirvana and knew Kurt Cobain personally. But in point of fact, during the years 1990–1994, when grunge rock and the Seattle music scene were at their zenith—Cobain committed suicide in April 1994—Shawna, the mother with two toddlers, was nowhere near at hand, let alone even involved in the music business. It's doubtful she ever heard Nirvana perform live.

Shawna met another Boeing worker around this time, James Duffey, who subsequently married her in Wichita, Kansas, in August 1994 while he was on a short-term transfer to the Boeing plant there. Duffey doted on her two children, and they took his surname as their own. Shawna went to work at Boeing too, and things were going well in her life for a change. Or so it seemed.

From the time she had moved back to Everett from Alaska, Shawna worked at reviving her relationship with her mother and the rest of her family, including her half brother Merrill. She and Merrill met for the first time in 1988, when her marriage to Jack Darling was falling apart, and she had taken a bus down to Idaho and lived for awhile with Merrill and another brother on the Wyoming border. Merrill had gotten a taste of the manipulative side of Shawna back then, and when they reconnected in the early '90s, she was much the same, only with a greater level of sophistication.

"She was doing the manipulation thing back then without anybody even knowing that was what she was doing," Metzger says now. "She literally controlled our whole family. I mean, if she wanted to have a problem with someone and not speak to them, she could set it up. She could destroy relationships, and she could put them together, just as easy. She liked playing God that way."

What she was gifted at, he said, was making it look like the source of a destructive in-family story was anyone but her, when in fact she concocted them at will. "That was Shawna," he says. "Of course, it took us awhile before we could figure her out. Eventually everybody did. I was a little more forgiving than most of my other siblings were, so Shawna and I maintained a relationship. And eventually it became a pretty good relationship, I thought."

Rena had moved to California in the early '90s, and Merrill had a home not far from hers in the Redding area. Shawna began showing up on a regular basis, often with the kids in tow. And often, she would leave the kids with him or with Rena. Uncle Merrill became a second father to the children.

Shawna was not a good mother, though she took great umbrage if you hinted otherwise and often loudly pronounced her love for her kids. "She would take her kids when they were little and she would lock them up in their bedroom, she would tie the doorknob to a hook so they couldn't open the door," says Rena Caudle, who says she was only told of this a few years later. "Devon had to take care of Jaszmin when he was five years old, and she'd go out and party at night."

Gradually, the marriage to Jim Duffey crumbled. Some years later, Shawna told a court-appointed mitigation specialist that she just fell out of love with him, even though he was a good provider and she always had extra money to do things with.

Her mother watched it happen from a distance, and with a sense of déjà vu. "Shawna's very narcissistic," she says. "Extremely narcissistic. And she also has a sense of entitlement that's very strong. Because each time she has married, she has left the men in deep, deep debt. Thousands of dollars in debt.

"I think when she left Jim, he was around sixty, seventy thousand dollars in debt, that was caused from her and her spending. And you don't want to turn Shawna loose with a credit card. Because I've seen how she is with a credit card. And there was a time when Shawna wouldn't even wash her clothes. She'd just go out and buy new when they got dirty."

Above all else, Shawna was a relentless manipulator, her mother says: "Another way that Shawna would get people hooked, too, is she would befriend them. And do all kinds of things for them. And then when she learned something bad about them, she would use it against them, more or less threaten them: 'Well, if you don't do what I want, this is what's gonna happen.' She was good at that."

At times Shawna seemed to evince empathy for her friends and family, but eventually, many of them concluded that this was simply part of her manipulation. "Shawna was good at making people think she was on their side as a way of getting them to reveal their weaknesses," her brother Merrill says. "Then once you let your guard down, she had you."

Moreover, she tended to avoid actual expressions of affection. "If you tried to show Shawna love, she would run from it," one of her friends told Scott North.

Serendipitously, the marriage to Jim Duffey crumbled just about the time she met John Forde.

|| 

By 1999, Shawna was indeed in the music-promotion biz. She had a little bar-band booking business called Northwest Rhythm that she ran on her own, and it sometimes booked gigs for a band that was a grunge-mainstream rock blend, though really she booked anyone who would sign up for her services. One of her clients was a '70s disco covers band. It was a small-beer operation that handled bar gigs, never bigger venues. And that was pretty much the extent of her real-life career as a "grunge music promoter."

But it was also how she met John Forde. Like many of the men in Shawna's life, Forde worked at Boeing. He moonlighted for fun as the drummer in a mainstream rock band called Wood. One night after a show at the Diamond Knot Brewery on Camano Island, a few miles north of Everett, Shawna pulled aside the lead guitarist in the band to see if she could recruit the band to her list of clients. John thought she was attractive and wound up chatting with her. The next week she went to a Wood performance at a Mukilteo drinking hole called the Monkey Trap. Shawna brought a rose. After that, she and John started chatting by email, they met up for drinks, and their relationship was off and running.

Shawna was still married to Jim Duffey, but the marriage was already thoroughly on the rocks; they still shared a multistory house, but Duffey slept in the upstairs bedroom while Shawna occupied a downstairs room. For the first few months of their relationship, that was where she and John Forde slept together.

Her friends could always tell that Shawna was about to get married again, because that was when she always got around to finally filing for divorce from her current husband, no matter how long it had been crumbling. Shawna almost never finalized the end of a marriage until she had another one lined up. And so it was with Jim Duffey: after roping in John Forde, she filed to divorce Duffey in late December 1999, and it was granted in late March 2000. She and John Forde were married in July.

No doubt what most attracted Shawna to John Forde was his utter nor-malcy: there was no drama in his life. Other than a minor marijuana bust in his teens, John—who spent a number of years in the army and then eventu-ally landed a job at the public utility company Seattle City Light—was the picture of stability and decency. This was something new to Shawna, and she wanted it badly. The problem was that Shawna and normal just didn't fit.

Even before they were married, there were signs of trouble. For one thing, Shawna was content to coast on John's income. He'd call from work at ten in the morning, and she would just be making coffee; when he got home, she would be gone and wouldn't tell him later where she had been. She told him he was being "controlling" just for asking.

Northwest Rhythms was not working out so well. John collected money and toted up the receipts. He tried to help her run it as a business, but she had no idea how. For Shawna, it was just another in a series of failed careers. At times, he would come home and find his basement full of strange men, and Shawna would act as though it were just a normal part of doing business. But for all that, John says he never saw the business actually make any money.

Instead, she ran through his money like it was going out of style but then would brag about her success as a rock promoter, even though John never saw it. She would bring home bags of groceries and claim she had been given them as tips.

There were other sour notes. She and John would take trips in the car with her two children, and she was prone to ruining the trips by shouting at the kids or slapping them.

They were married at the Everett Elks, where John had a membership. Shawna started hanging out there, meeting some of the older, very conservative clientele. It was there, John says, that Shawna began picking up her ideas about immigration; prior to that, he said, she had mostly been a liberal Democrat.

One day, shortly after they were married, Shawna sold her former house with Duffey and announced she was going to go to beauty school in Cali-fornia. She went down south for a few weeks with Jaszmin in tow, long enough to drop her off at her mother's. Then she came back to Everett and enrolled instead at the Everett Beauty Academy.

In June 2001, Shawna decided to organize a protest of the school for its training methods. As the story in the *Herald* explained:

> A group of about 35 beauticians-to-be walked out of the Everett Beauty Academy Thursday in protest, claiming they are not getting the necessary training promised when they paid $7,500 for the 1,800-hour program.

"Now they are making us do the waxing without any training, and two girls already messed up somebody's face," said student Shawna Forde, who is heading up the protest. "You just can't give a leg wax or bikini wax without the proper training. You could hurt a client."

The students, Shawna said, wanted more instruction on haircuts and other beauty techniques; they wanted the school shut down on Saturdays so they could get hands-on training with a model; they didn't want to have to pay for products used on clients; and they felt they shouldn't lose hours for failing to clock out for lunch. Forde also objected to how the academy brought in salon owners to talk to the students, and all they did was tell them how to get jobs out there. "They're wasting our hour when they're supposed to be talking about the theory of hair," Forde said. "And trust me, there's a lot to it."

She didn't last much longer at the school. One day she brought in alcoholic Jell-O shots to share with her fellow students, and she was summarily dismissed. Barely skipping a beat, she turned around and enrolled this time at the Everett Community College's beauty school, which was similarly intolerant of her behavior. But this time she stuck it out and got her beauty license, though it was not without at least some personal drama at home.

License in hand, Shawna proceeded to run through employers at a wide variety of salons in the Everett area. She got fired from all of them—for a variety of reasons. Once she got the boot at a Supercuts, where several hundred dollars had mysteriously vanished from the safe, and Shawna complained bitterly that she was being unfairly blamed for it. Those kinds of dramas happened around her all the time. One year, she worked at six different salons. She kept John in the dark; she would leave for work, and he would try to reach her on the job and learn that she wasn't working there and hadn't been for weeks.

Each time she was fired, John said, she would disappear down to California for a week or so, and he wouldn't hear from her for days. Most of the time, he wasn't even aware she'd been fired. She'd leave the kids with him and leave no word where she was going.

The marriage was heading for the rocks. Then, when she returned from one of her California jaunts in early 2006, she announced that she had figured out what she wanted to do with her life.

She had been listening to conservative talk radio on the trip and had been listening to talk about the Minutemen and their exploits.

"She said, 'I know what my calling is,'" John Forde recalls. "'And it is going to be to save this country from illegal immigrants.'"

# 9

# O Canada

The Canadian border near Blaine, 2006. DAVID NEIWERT PHOTO

The Canadian border, at certain stretches in northern Whatcom County, is a six-foot-wide ditch running between a pair of parallel two-lane country roads. You could walk across it with a long hop, and hardly a soul would notice.

Except on this day in early May 2006, because the Minutemen are out here, observing.

A silver-haired, hawk-eyed retiree named Larry Pullar, wearing a ball cap emblazoned with the logo of Operation Secure Our Borders, has set up his observation post right at a corner of one of these roads on the American side. The view is not quite the polar opposite of the kind the Minutemen had in Arizona, but close: the sky is gray and damp today, while the road is lined with green grass and tall trees. On the other side of the border is a dairy farm. You can tell that it's Canada because the traffic sign opposite Pullar's car warns of a bump two hundred meters ahead.

Mostly, Pullar sits in his silver PT Cruiser and waits for reporters to come around and ask questions. He's posted a small American flag next to his rear bumper and has a Minuteman sign in his rear window, so reporters driving the back roads looking for border watchers can spot him. He tells everyone that he watches for what he calls "suspicious behavior."

Pullar recalls a December patrol, when he called Border Patrol about a car that was behaving oddly; agents subsequently made an arrest. "We never heard back about it," he adds. "But I do know there have been five incidents we reported, and that was one of them."

Still, Pullar admits that he's not really on the border to report on bad guys in the act. "Our government is not controlling the borders," Pullar says. "Essentially, nobody's doing it, and it's been that way for years. It's just time for people to come out and make a statement that it's time to do something."

That's what he and his fellow Minutemen all say they're doing: making a statement about border security. Or illegal immigration. Or both. It's not really clear.

After all, there are no hordes of Canadians coming over the US border illegally, brown-skinned or otherwise. The biggest border problem with Canada involves drug trafficking—and drugs usually come through ports of entry or remote wilderness areas.

Nonetheless, the Minutemen are here. Pullar is part of a crew of about twenty people, average citizens from a broad array of backgrounds, who have gathered on this typically overcast spring day at a property just outside of the town of Ferndale.

They call the headquarters of the Minutemen's operations in Whatcom County—a piece of farmland on a road about four miles off the freeway and about ten miles south of the border, complete with an equipment shed that doubles as a gathering place and a camper trailer that serves as their communications center—Camp Standing Bear. There are a number of vehicles scattered around the lot, and not all of them appear to be Minutemen's.

The land is owned by Claude "Bear" LeBas, the ex-Customs agent who joined Tom Williams in Arizona for the original Minuteman Project in April. They've decorated it with a couple of flags: one, a yellow "Don't Tread On Me" flag popular for years with the militia movement, well before its later adoption by the Tea Party; the second, a white banner commemorating "Operation Iraqi Freedom 2003." The flags greet visitors as they pull up onto the farm and find a place to park.

The operations are on LeBas's property, but Tom Williams is overseeing the Minuteman operations here, as he has done since September. He spends much of his morning greeting participants and briefing them in the equipment shed, helping them to pick watch stations along the Canadian border from a big board they've erected on the wall. There are about eight of them to choose from, and so watchers will try to coordinate times and stations from the board.

Gary Cole, national operations director for the Minuteman Project and Chris Simcox's chief paid babysitter—for the time being, at least—has come to Whatcom County to observe the goings-on. He says the Minutemen here in Washington State are making an important point: "What we are doing is we are showing that we want the national attention on the fact that the borders are wide open. . . . You look out here and you drive the border, anybody with three IQ points to rub together could figure out, 'Hey, somebody who means us damage could come across this border.' And there's nothing being done by the United States government to stop that."

Cole sounds as though he's been absorbing Glenn Spencer. "It is an invasion," he insists. "Of course it is. What else would you call it? It's an invasion—when people from another nation cross your borders."

It's pointed out that this isn't an armed force sent by a government, which is usually what we call an "invasion."

"I've seen Mexican military setting up camps less than a half a mile from the American border that are in support of people getting ready to come across that night. Now that's military support of a group of people that are going to come across that border," he replies. "If we put 3,000 people a night into Mexico, what would they call it?"

Cole insists the Minutemen are not about xenophobia but national security: "There is no way that I kind of think of that we can carry on a national discussion of national security, homeland security, without first of all settling border security. The only way that you'll have border security is if you have good neighbors that respect your borders.

"I'm a good neighbor to that guy. He knows he doesn't have to put up a wall or a big fence or guard dogs or anything else to keep me from walking over there and stealing his pickup truck or taking his flowers or doing anything else. I'm a good neighbor, and he doesn't need to worry about that.

"Our problem is that we don't have a good neighbor, particularly to the south. To the north, I think they're really trying. I've been on a lot of radio talk shows in Canada where the Canadian people are very worried about the thing I just talked about earlier—the opportunity for terrorism to come across this border is greater even than coming across the southern border."

Well, yes. Not only is the opportunity greater, the Canadian border right here in Washington State is, as a matter of fact, the only place where an Al Qaeda terrorist has been known to attempt a border crossing with explosive materiel. That was in 1999, when the would-be LAX Millennial Bomber, Ahmed Ressam, attempted to cross from Victoria to Port Angeles and was caught by an alert Customs officer.

The Ressam case is particularly instructive, because it revealed that—in contrast to Mexico, where no Al Qaeda cells have been known to exist— there exists an established network of Islamist operatives in Canada. If you're going to make the argument that the borders need securing in order to protect us from terrorists, the logical focus would be on securing the Canadian border.

Indeed, if you go out driving along the Canadian border near Blaine, Washington, in the area where the Minutemen held their border watches, the border really does consist of a six-foot-wide ditch. It's in a remote part of the county, and though Border Patrol vehicles can be seen driving past from time to time, it's the kind of place where someone with a well-laid plan could easily slip over late at night.

There are a lot of places like this along the US-Canada border, which at about 4,000 miles is more than twice as long as the 1,500 miles or so we share with Mexico. What's even more common, in sparsely populated regions of the Northwest especially, are large, mountainous tracts of wilderness and desolate open range where security is nearly nonexistent at worst and widely sporadic at best.

In other words, there are many more opportunities for Islamist terrorists to enter the United States from Canada than there are from Mexico. Crossing the Canadian border in untracked areas, unlike the Mexican border, is neither terribly hazardous nor even particularly daunting.

However, most terrorism experts will tell you that terrorists prefer to travel incognito with fake papers and are most likely to try crossing through a regular port of entry with those papers. Remote border crossings are a real risk for such operatives because they become more exposed out in the open, rather than simply mingling in with the thousands who cross borders legally every day.

And the logistics involved in patrolling four thousand miles of border, of course, requires a strategy of outsmarting potential threats such as terrorists. Setting citizens out on the border is probably not the way to do it. And even Gary Cole admits that.

"What we are doing is we are showing that we want the national attention on the fact that the borders are wide open," he says. "To say that we are going to stand out here on one of these roads and be able to spot a whole bunch of people is, at very best, an overstatement. It's not going to happen."

For the people out there with binoculars, however, there's always hope.

||

The Washington Minuteman Detachment, as they officially call themselves, began organizing the summer of 2005, after Williams and LeBas returned from Arizona. They remained in touch with Simcox and company and began taking the necessary steps to set up Minuteman watches on the Canadian border, at Simcox's behest. He wanted a presence on the Canadian border as a way to refute his critics' contention that his focus on the Mexican border was evidence of the Minutemen's innate racism.

Their first official border watch at a Lummi Indian Reservation site in September 2005 drew only a handful of volunteers and fairly light media coverage. A month later, the Minutemen convened on LeBas's place outside of Ferndale and drew a number of TV and newspaper reporters and even more volunteers. They were off and running.

Whatcom County was an interesting choice for the Minutemen's first Canadian border watch. The shadow of the militia movement of the 1990s looms large here, because this was the home of the Washington State Militia, another self-described "neighborhood watch" that turned out to have been building pipe bombs and planning their detonation. Some eight members, including the militiamen's leader, a navy veteran named John Pitner, were arrested by federal agents on a variety of explosives, weapons, and conspiracy charges in 1996 and eventually convicted of most of them.

So there is a sense of déjà vu hanging over this latest gathering of "Patriots," though neither Williams nor LeBas ever refer to their group as a "border militia," as Chris Simcox did with his old Civilian Homeland Defense outfit. On the other hand, Claude LeBas's place has the familiar appearance of the Northwest compounds used by some of the 1990s militia groups, including the Freeman compounds in Montana and Bo Gritz's separatist community in northern Idaho: the rough edges; the clusters of cars, RVs, and trailers; the flags and signs.

Inside the communications center—a twenty-foot camper trailer owned by Claude LeBas—the flavor is different. The paranoia and unfriendly vibe that is often part of militia compounds is replaced here by a jovial and friendly atmosphere.

Part of the group's "make a statement" mission is media outreach, and it's clearly scoring in this regard. The first weekend of its April 2006 watch draws several Seattle TV news stations and a variety of newspaper reporters. The Minutemen track the number of reporters they speak with, and tailor their talk for cameras and tape recorders.

Headquarters is the communications center, crowded with radio and computer equipment. Minutemen here keep in touch by radio with the twenty or so members on border patrol; computers track the border watches at eight sites along the Canadian border and tie into the national network. People wander in and out, joke a bit, or hang outside the trailer and chat.

The Minutemen gather for "musters"—opening and closing organizing sessions—inside a large farm-equipment shed next to the trailer. A section has been portioned off with temporary walls that display maps showing the border-watch sites, along with posters like one with a picture of the Beverly Hillbillies, identified as the Department of Homeland Security. On rainy days, there's a blast heater running, and a table with a coffee pot and doughnuts.

After seeing everyone off to their morning assignments, Tom Williams pours himself a cup of coffee, sits down at the table, and leans back, smiling. A veteran of the Vietnam War, he is wearing a military vest adorned with patches covering a bright red Marines T-shirt and matching ball cap. He has a neatly trimmed grey beard and straightforward, engaging eyes. He's affable and pleasant, rather more like Jim Gilchrist than Chris Simcox.

Williams says he first moved to the Bellingham area in about 1995, after visiting on business and liking what he saw. Eventually, he found a place in Deming, just east of Bellingham, where he still lives. He's surprised to be told that John Pitner, the ex-militiaman, is his neighbor there. He says he's retired now, disabled by a combination of old war injuries and post-traumatic stress disorder—a syndrome on which he also happens to be an expert, having written a text on the subject.

He heard about the Minutemen in 2005, when he watched a television interview with Gilchrist, and was impressed. Since he was planning a trip to Arizona that spring anyway, he began making inquiries. A friend, retired FBI agent Jim Horn, with whom he had served as a Marine officer, knew Gilchrist and told him the group was credible. Williams wound up making the trip to Arizona with Claude LeBas in tow and likewise eventually played a role in the Great MS-13 Panic.

At the end of April 2005, they packed up and went home. En route, they encountered some Border Patrol officers at a checkpoint. According to Williams, the officer checking their rig saw they were Minutemen and called to his fellow officers. "And they all come out and clap and wave and yell at us. That was a good, good feeling, when that happened."

After returning home, Williams and LeBas were contacted by Gary Cole to organize a Washington Minuteman Detachment. They advertised for recruits and were up and running by September. Williams says he maintains the same kind of vigilance over his outfit as he did in Arizona, weeding out the gun nuts and extremists. His average recruit, he says, is "a sixty-two-year-old, former military and law enforcement, disabled or retired guy."

Border protection is what draws most of them. "Some people are getting pretty hot about the illegal immigration, and getting some resolution to the illegal aliens. But you know, universally, what keeps us together is border protection, and to support the Border Patrol. We wouldn't be here if the individual agents didn't think we were doing some good."

Williams, for his part, is stumped about how to respond to the growing concerns within the larger Bellingham community, particularly its growing Latino-immigrant bloc, that the Minutemen are part of a movement that scapegoats ethnic minorities.

He pauses. "I don't know. Like I say, I don't want somebody coming across this border and blowing something up again. I was there at Oklahoma City, and it may not have been somebody who snuck across the borders, but that sort of thing obviously happened at 9/11. If it hadn't been for 9/11, we wouldn't sitting here.

"We all know that this is awfully symbolic. Minutemen aren't going to catch them anyway—they're just going to observe and report."

||

His sentiments are echoed by other Minutemen. "We're just making a statement that the border should be secure," says Gerrit Terpsma, a retiree in his mid-seventies. Today, he and fellow border watcher, Dieter Pressler—both naturalized citizens (Terpsma still carries a stout German accent)—are well bundled against the rain that is keeping them inside Terpsma's red '85 Ford pickup. The spot they're watching is similar to the others, situated along another pair of parallel roads.

Terpsma is defensive about what he and his fellow Minutemen are up to: "The other people say we are intimidating them," he says. "We're not intimidating anybody!"

Border concerns have also drawn Benjamin Vaughan and his wife, who are parked at the end of a dead-end road with a smattering of homes, watching a wooded copse. They spend rainy days inside the van, listening to books on tape and watching for any border activity. "I've seen people cross," says Vaughan, another military retiree who lives in Bellingham. "Only problem was, they were going the wrong direction [into Canada]. It was like one of those things down south where you got a whole family group, about four adults and maybe three or four kids. That was what I saw, and it was going north." They notified the Border Patrol and left it to them to call Canadian officials.

Vaughan sports a body brace to help with a lingering back injury; getting around isn't easy for him. Still, after 9/11, he says, he grew seriously concerned about border control. "The only thing I do is support the [US] Border Patrol," he says. He refers to his old military service for his motivation: "I've got six grandkids, and I've still got the heart that says I signed up, and I've never quit."

While this talk of border concerns and 9/11 pervades discussions with Minutemen, if you speak with them long enough, the subject of immigration inevitably emerges.

"I see the nation descending into poverty, philosophically, and part of it is illegal immigration, a big part of it," says Eric, a clean-cut, tall, twenty-something Bellingham man who declines to give his last name as we chat outside the Minutemen's trailer. "It's also outsourcing, increasing corporate power, excessive corporate power, that kind of stuff. What I can do here, since I'm so close to the border, is help out with the immigration issue." His fiancée, he says, can't understand why he does it.

"Illegal immigration is my concern," he says. "Now, how to control it, of course, is to have better border security. That's what the purpose of border security is—preventing drugs and illegal immigration to enter. If we could help, then supposedly activity decreases on the border when we're out here. It's very boring. It's hard to stay awake."

At the border-watch site at Peace Arch State Park, the main border crossing in Blaine, Terry Schrader—a sharp-eyed, middle-aged man from the Olympia area with a graying blond beard—keeps watch on another border ditch that runs the length of the park—though the site is deserted on this rainy day.

"I was just a normal person a few years ago, have Mexican friends, my best friend is a Colombian guy," Schrader says. "Moved here many years ago. We worked together for years.

"But I've just seen the hordes of Mexicans in particular showing up in my little town . . . just the hordes of Mexicans coming in and taking over several occupations. In particular, construction, which I used to do—used to build houses.

"I'm building a new house right now. Trying to get a few subcontractors here and there, so I call them, and I say, 'Do you hire Mexicans?' Most of 'em say they do. Building trades like insulation, drywall, roofing have pretty much been gutted by the illegal trade. And they're not—the guys running the businesses aren't Mexican—they're American, speak English, hire illegals. So it looks sorta legal on the surface."

Some Washington Minutemen, indeed, were pursuing punitive measures against undocumented immigrants. Bob Baker, a Mercer Island resident and member of the Washington Minuteman Detachment, had that spring filed Initiative 946 on behalf of another organization, Protect Washington Now. Modeled on Arizona's successful anti-immigrant initiative, it required that the state deny "non–federally mandated" public benefits to undocumented immigrants and that state and local government employees ascertain applicants' immigration status before they apply for welfare and other benefits.

Minuteman Spencer Cohen of Seattle, a political consultant who was a frequent attendee at Minuteman musters through the month of April, returned home to begin organizing his own kind of watch in Seattle: he hung out near day-laborer pickup sites, photographed the people who picked up workers, and then posted them on a website.

This kind of activism, particularly the way it scapegoated a vulnerable minority, sent up red flags for many people in Bellingham, the home of Western Washington University and in many regards a deeply liberal town. The underlying emphasis on illegal immigration, in the minds of many Latinos, conveyed the message that they are the problem and not border security.

"I can understand, obviously, why they're scared to death. They're here illegally. Of course, they're scared to death," Tom Williams says. "What I'm getting from the phone calls, what I'm getting is an increased level of support from people that identify themselves as silent majority, saying, 'I don't want to see these Mexican flags.'

"I don't like people to be afraid of me. But I want the border secure. I want those Border Patrol agents to get what they need to do the job. They're fine, hard-working men and women, you know, they're just like our troops in Iraq, and half of them were troops in Iraq. They need what they need to do their job."

Williams acknowledges that some of the fears in Bellingham, given the history of militias in Whatcom County, aren't completely groundless. He says he'd like to find common ground with the Latino activists but blames them for creating the gap in the first place.

"Here's what happens from a psychological standpoint," he says, calling on his background. "It's called cognitive dissonance. What happens is, the more you have to solidify your position, the more polarized it gets, the more I get called a violent racist vigilante. . . . The fact is that he polarized me. He's painted me into a corner, poking a stick in my eye. And the more he pokes a stick in my eye, the more I am going to get against illegal immigration."

||

The first note of opposition was sounded by the Bellingham City Council in October 2005, with a nudge from the Whatcom County Human Rights Task Force.

Barbara Ryan, the council president, sponsored a task-force resolution regarding the presence of the Minutemen, decrying "the activities of self-appointed militia or vigilante groups or individuals with limited training and no legal authority" and pointing out that "the existence and activities of vigilante groups or individuals in other regions have created fear, an atmosphere of racism and violence, and increased suspicion, intolerance and even hate in those regions."

The opposition quickly went statewide. The Washington State Democratic Central Committee passed a nearly identical resolution, and two local groups formed specifically to oppose the Minutemen: the Coalition for Professional Border and Law Enforcement and Not in My County. A host of local and regional human rights groups joined in as well. The American Civil Liberties Union organized teams of legal observers to watch the watchers and make sure that no one harassed Latinos.

Bellingham resident Aline Soundy told the *Bellingham Herald* she was openly skeptical of the Minutemen's claims that they were only concerned with border security: "I understand the security issues with terrorism, but this isn't about terrorism. They're not here to protect us from terrorists but from illegal aliens."

The opposition did not go unnoticed. In Seattle, conservative radio hosts pounced on Ryan's resolution, particularly the language suggesting that the Minutemen were racist. In short order, she was appearing on national right-wing talk shows, where she found she was being used as a whipping post for defenders of the Minutemen. She also found that her home address and phone numbers were posted on at least one white-supremacist website, and she was inundated with hate mail and phone calls, some of them threatening.

It all came to a head in late April 2006, at a town-hall gathering in a Bellingham church, which hosted an official meeting of the state Human Rights Commission. About two hundred people showed up for what became largely a series of harangues against the border watchers.

The testimony, for the most part, was reasonable and well-intended. Researcher Paul de Armond explained that the Minutemen represented the latest cycle in a recurring wave of far-right activism that had been part of western Washington society for decades, including the Bellingham-based Washington State Militia. The specter of this not-so-distant earlier ugliness weighed on many of the concerns voiced that night by members of the Latino community, and it raised the temperature accordingly.

"Latinos have been many times persecuted," said Larry Estrada, a Western Washington University professor. "We have been under the gun by vigilantes, and that's not going to happen any more. . . . We say to the Minutemen, 'Not in our city, not in our county, not in our neighborhood.'"

Others pointed out that while the Minutemen might eschew racism publicly, their entire existence was part of a larger movement opposing Hispanic immigration, often by scapegoating Latinos. "The Washington Minuteman Detachment is nothing more than a clever PR campaign attached to anti-immigration legislation," said David Cahn of the local Community to Community Development organization.

Others were more conciliatory, noting that the local detachment was not necessarily a pack of racists. Rosalinda Guillen, a Latina community leader and founder of the Coalition for Professional Border and Law Enforcement, welcomed the twenty or so Minutemen who clustered in a section of the pews.

"It's preferable that you meet us and get to know who we are," she said.

As the charges of racism mounted, though, the hyperbole grew. "I ask the law enforcement: What is your plan when the lynching happens and what is your plan when the intimidation happens?" Another critic suggested that the Minutemen admired the Nazis his father fought against in World War II.

But others defended the Minutemen, particularly the most prominent member in the room: Chris Simcox himself. And it was a revelation.

Everyone knew Simcox from his TV appearances: a little scruffy, T-shirt, jeans, and ball cap, maybe with a gun down the front of his pants.

The Chris Simcox who showed up in Bellingham was a transformed man: clean-cut, healthy-looking, with a straightforward demeanor. The team from Diener Consulting—the DC-based public-relations firm that Simcox hired the previous year—had clearly done a first-rate makeover job.

Simcox claimed the mantle of the civil rights movement and emphasized how many lives the Minutemen ostensibly had saved. He also told the commission that the remark about shooting border crossers on sight actually was a case of "clever editing": "I said drug dealers should be shot on sight."

Simcox had been in town to meet with the Whatcom outfit and attended the meeting out of curiosity. He was one of the last speakers at the gathering, and he was adamant that the charges of racism were groundless.

"I don't think I've been in a room full of such fear and hate such as I have tonight in my whole life," he said, to a round of applause. He went on:

We are nothing more than a neighborhood watch group. If we were not, we would be in jail, what with the scrutiny of the FBI, the Department of Homeland Security, all law enforcement whom we've interfaced with, we wouldn't be in business if we had ever done anything wrong. That's a fact. In fact, since October of 2002, we have assisted Border Patrol with apprehending—not us, we've assisted Border Patrol in locating, and they apprehended 10,007 people since yesterday. That represents people from twenty-four different countries, including Switzerland, Germany, Poland, and Russia. We don't discriminate on the color of anyone's skin. We watch the border. We answered our civic duty and our call of our nation and our president to be vigilant, to be observant, and to report suspicious illegal activity to the proper authorities, which is what we've done. I don't care what color your skin is, where you come from, or what language you speak or what your purposes are. If you're breaking into our country in a post–September 11 world, you are a potential problem and should be reported to proper authorities. . . .

Too bad racism has entered this debate, because it has nothing to do with race. It has to do with forcing our federal government to do its job. Washington, DC, has failed us miserably—I agree with many of the discussions tonight about NAFTA and the injustices that have been perpetrated by our government. We need a good housecleaning in Washington, DC. We need to stand together as American people. We do need to resolve this mess that has been created by elected officials. We choose to do it by protecting our neighbors on the borders of the south, and certainly, for those of you who think we are looking for illegal aliens on this northern border, it is a symbolic stance, a First Amendment stance, about our federal government failing us miserably. Let's hope we can work together, let's hope we can solve this problem.

Some of the Minutemen's defenders tried to shame the crowd for what they saw as a kind of reverse prejudice: "Ask yourselves: 'What would Martin Luther King say?'" retorted one.

At the evening's end, the commissioners offered their thoughts. Ellis Casson, a Seattle pastor who actually knew King, offered a response to this earlier challenge.

"I knew Dr. King," he said. "I think I know what he would say." He shook his head slowly.

"'Here we go again.'"

||

Outside the meeting room as the gathering broke up, another reporter and I managed to snag Simcox on his way out the door to ask him a few questions. He was, as almost always, happy to oblige.

I asked him about the concerns that the Minutemen are attracting extremists: white supremacists and other neo-Nazis. In this corner of the world, that's a well-grounded concern.

"They're totally unfounded," he said. "Again, wild allegations to create fear in the community that have no basis in fact. All of our volunteers are thoroughly screened—they go through criminal background checks, psychological vetting; we have an Internet-based search system where we look for their email addresses, their names, or anything on any site that could be racist. We go to great lengths to make sure we screen our people. I have never talked to anyone in our organization who has ever been connected to any group like that, and I wouldn't tolerate it if it were."

Well, what about Laine Lawless?

"She was with us for two months," he claimed. "And we quickly vetted her out. That was because of her rhetoric. And we did more research into her background. She was quickly dismissed."

And with that, he ducked out the door, before I could point out that Lawless had been with his old Civilian Homeland Defense outfit for much longer than two months.

A woman who had been part of Simcox's entourage—a short, stout woman with a smiling demeanor—sidled up to me afterward and asked for my business card. I handed her one and asked her name.

"Shawna Forde," she said. She shook my hand and followed Simcox out the door.

A month later, I spotted her among a small cluster of counterprotesters in downtown Seattle at an immigration-rights rally. At the time, just another face in the crowd.

# 10

# The Fence to Nowhere

The official border fence at Sasabe, Arizona.
DAVID NEIWERT PHOTO

Jim Campbell was a contractor before he became an Arizona retiree, and so he happens to know a little about getting construction projects completed. He also happens to be an avid supporter of efforts to stem what he and thousands of others see as an unholy tide of illegal immigrants streaming over the borders.

So when Chris Simcox's Minutemen announced plans to build a section of fencing along the Arizona-Mexico border designed to prevent illegal crossings, it seemed like a good time to step up and make a difference.

A couple of years later and $100,000 lighter, Campbell's not so sure. In fact, he bluntly calls the people running the Minuteman border-fence project "a bunch of felons."

When he first contacted Minuteman officials in early May 2006, he was enthusiastic about his vision: "Miles and miles of steel!" he emailed the project's overseers. "I feel so fervently about this critical point of the project: the ground breaking, that (assuming the 'payback' arrangement is firmly structured), I'd even come up with a lot more money after I can see the steel orders."

Campbell offered to donate $100,000 immediately so they could act quickly to obtain supplies of steel posts in enough time to get them in the ground as the first step in building an "Israeli style" security fence. To do so, he took out a loan on his home in Fountain Hills, Arizona, and wired the money to the Minuteman Civil Defense Corps's parent organization, the Beltway-based Declaration Alliance.

But it quickly became apparent to Campbell, when he attended the Minutemen's big, public groundbreaking ceremony on May 27 (dutifully reported by numerous news organizations), that the five-strand barbed-wire fence being erected by volunteers was a far cry from what he had thought he was funding. After a flurry of negotiations with MCDC president Chris Simcox, he agreed to go out and purchase some $63,000 worth of steel posts with his own money before supplies evaporated—believing he'd be reimbursed out of the money he'd already laid out.

A year later, having gotten nowhere with both MCDC and Declaration Alliance officials in getting his money back—and having seen the Minutemen's fence-building plans go nowhere—he filed a lawsuit for $1.2 million seeking reimbursement and damages. In a letter to his lawyer outlining the sequence of events, he observed that the ongoing recalcitrance of Simcox and company made it "more and more likely that my donation (in what I anticipated would be a monument to the financial and personal sacrifice of thousands of like-minded patriots), will have been squandered in a seemingly well-intentioned but short-lived 'monument to deceit' on the border. It is clear to me now that this fence project was conceived as a grand facade—a scheme—to attract endless streams of donations from the public who placed blind faith (as I did) in both the sincerity and trustworthiness of its promoters."

||

This was the inner world of the Minutemen, where all-American values provided a nice storefront for a financial black hole into which hundreds of thousands of donors' dollars were vacuumed and from which nothing seemed to emerge.

In that regard, they actually fit into a long tradition of right-wing political organizing that runs from the resurrected Klan of the 1920s to the tax-protester scams of the 1980s and the militias of the 1990s. That is to say, in the end these groups are mostly scams, brewed up by a handful of bunkum artists—using a heady concoction of jingoistic fervor, bigoted xenophobia, and paranoid conspiracism—and served up as a means to salve all that ails the patriotic soul, but having mostly the mysterious effect of separating their fellow right-wingers from their money.

But then, the Minutemen themselves were a product of that tradition: Simcox had founded his original operations, after all, as a "border militia," and both he and Jim Gilchrist made frequent references to their members as part of the Patriot movement. Likewise, when Gilchrist ran for Congress in 2005, it was under the banner of the militia-friendly Constitution Party.

Word of their final divorce in December 2005 filtered around quickly. Observers initially assumed it was a result of a clash of egos—and there was plenty of evidence to support that—but in reality the split was over money, and specifically how the Minutemen should go about handling the hundreds of thousands of dollars in donations that were flowing in.

As part of Gilchrist's unsuccessful run for Congress that fall, he had hired as his consulting team the same conservative Beltway organization, Diener Consultants, that had assisted the Minuteman Project. At about the same time, Gilchrist and Simcox began talking with the Diener team and an associated outfit run by Alan Keyes called the Declaration Alliance about handing over the Minutemen's financial and public relations operations to them. But Gilchrist came away from his congressional campaign with a bad taste in his mouth—he later told his board members that the Diener/Keyes outfits "stole my money"—and wanted nothing further to do with them. Simcox, on the other hand, wanted to continue.

So each man went his separate way. The Minutemen had already split into two organizations—Gilchrist's Minuteman Project and Simcox's Minuteman Civil Defense Corps—each organized around different strategies: the MMP was to focus on challenging and exposing employers who hired undocumented workers and to encourage public activism, while the MCDC envisioned itself as a national enterprise that would recruit Minutemen to hold border watches in every border state. And after the Diener fallout, they officially had nothing to do with each other. Yet in the end, the paths each followed into dysfunction and paralysis were remarkably similar.

||

Following their supposedly distinct missions, Simcox's MCDC organized a follow-up border watch in Arizona in April 2006 and border watches in places like Washington State and Vermont. Gilchrist, in contrast, was primarily occupied that spring and summer with making speaking appearances around the country and promoting the book *Minutemen: The Battle to Secure America's Borders*, which he cowrote with Jerome Corsi (who'd achieved notoriety two years before as the coauthor of the "Swift Boat veterans" book attacking Democratic presidential candidate John Kerry's military-hero credentials). At one of these he got into an ugly confrontation with students at Columbia University, who invaded the stage where Gilchrist was speaking and forced him to flee. And that fall, with a congressional race already under his belt, he raised the possibility of a presidential bid under the banner of the far-right Constitution Party by flying out to Florida to meet with party officials (though nothing came of the talk).

Meanwhile, besides organizing border watches, MCDC was even more active in raising funds by recruiting new Minutemen around the country in places as disparate as Illinois, Washington, and New Hampshire. The donation money began pouring in—but that was only the beginning of the MCDC moneymaking operation.

Now that it was thoroughly enmeshed in the Keyes organization, all the donations to MCDC were flowing into a web of nearly a dozen organizations revolving around Declaration Alliance, including Diener Consultants; a Texas outfit called American Caging that acted as the escrow agent and comptroller for the operation; Renew America, a Keyes-run "grassroots organization" whose website featured a Minuteman message board; and a direct-mailing company called Response Unlimited.

The latter is especially illustrative of how the machine worked. Headed up by Diener's Phil Sheldon and a man named Philip Zodhiates, Response Unlimited makes its money by brokering mailing lists—hundreds of them, gleaned from right-wing organizations and political campaigns, and made available to fundraisers and organizers who can select a list of thousands of names based on their specific interests. Besides the MCDC and readers of the conservative *Weekly Standard*, among the lists offered by RU is one culled from readers of the notoriously anti-Semitic weekly the *Spotlight*. Also among their clientele: Bob and Mary Schindler, the parents of Terri Schiavo, who sold RU the list of names they had collected during their campaign—which briefly became a national right-wing cause célèbre—to prevent authorities from letting their daughter die as a means to end her vegetative state.

So when unsuspecting supporters of the Minutemen sent in their checks to Simcox's outfit, that was just the beginning of how MCDC made money from them. Their names became part of the MCDC mailing list that Response Unlimited then sold to various fund-raising organizations. So when those same donors suddenly found their mailboxes being filled with pitches from a variety of other right-wing causes, few of them might have guessed it was because they'd sent in a donation to the Minutemen.

There was also a distinct change in tone and style for the rough-and-ready culture the Minutemen had cultivated. The shift was embodied in the complete makeover of Simcox under the guidance of the Diener team. On the Arizona border, he'd been a rough-shaven, foulmouthed bomb-thrower who posed for pictures in T-shirt and ball cap with a pistol jammed down the front of his jeans. After joining up with Diener, he became scarcely recognizable as the carefully dressed, carefully groomed, and carefully spoken leader of the Minutemen, smooth and reassuring in his public appearances and on TV.

The association with Keyes's organizations raised hackles within the ranks of the Minutemen. Some of the volunteer border watchers began exchanging emails containing information about Diener Consultants, Declaration Alliance, Renew America, and Response Unlimited denouncing the associations, since these groups were perceived within the ultraright ranks as being "neoconservative" (a euphemism for "Jewish") organizations whose interests were inimical to theirs. Jim Gilchrist, who had washed his hands of the Keyes groups, sent out a bulletin making clear that his Minuteman Project no longer had any associations with Simcox and his organization.

Jerry Seper of the *Washington Times* reported on the dissent and quoted Keyes dismissing the MCDC's critics as anti-immigrant racists "and other unsavory fringe elements attempting to hijack the border security debate to further their individual agendas."

In April 2006, Simcox hit on the idea of building a "state-of-the-art" security fence along a section of the Arizona-Mexico border and told Seper he had more than $200,000 in donations for the cause. He described the project as one that would "feature separate, 14-foot-high fences on both sides of the border, separated by a roadway to allow the passage of U.S. Border Patrol vehicles, with surveillance cameras and motion sensors."

It was this description that enticed Jim Campbell into joining the cause, ponying up his $163,000. But there was one problem: the ranch owner on whose property Simcox had worked out a deal to build the fence had no interest in an "Israeli style" security barrier: he only wanted a standard five-strand barbed-wire fence to keep out Mexican cattle—certainly nothing that would deter illegal border crossers. And so that was in fact what was eventually built—though the steel Campbell bought was used to begin work on a short section of "demonstration" fence at another ranch. (The only work done on it to date involves putting some of those posts in the ground.)

It was at about this same time—in mid-May 2006—that the shit began hitting the rank-and-file fan.

It shortly emerged that Gary Cole had been removed as MCDC's national operations director the previous summer for "asking too many questions about the money"—namely, the "tens of thousands of dollars" in donations he had personally collected during the original Minuteman Project. However, Simcox had persuaded him to stay on as an overseer of his other border projects in places like Washington State and New Mexico: "I didn't want the thing to fail because it is much too important, so I came back to help out," Cole told Jerry Seper of the *Washington Times*. "But that doesn't mean my concern went away."

Since then, Cole said, nothing had changed. "This movement is much too important to be lost over a question of finances," Cole said. "We can't demand that the government be held accountable for failing to control the border if we can't hold ourselves accountable for the people's money. It's as simple as that."

The exodus continued. Vern Kilburn, one of the leaders of Simcox's Texas operations, resigned that spring, citing "professional differences with the management and business practices" of MCDC's national headquarters. He said Simcox and company had "no acceptable answers" to his concerns about accountability, ownership, management, and the distribution of money for the Texas Minutemen. Kilburn said that his outfit had only received a couple of $1,000 checks for operations from MCDC headquarters while piling up thousands more in expenses, adding that he wasn't alone: local Minuteman leaders all around the country "are having similar problems concerning money or the lack of."

Kilburn said he tried to stay on with the Minutemen in some other capacity, but Simcox fired him. Kilburn concluded by saying he "pretty much had my fill of the Minutemen as far as Chris Simcox goes."

Mike Gaddy had been coordinator of field operations for the Minuteman Project in Arizona and had similar concerns. At one point, he even offered to personally pay for an audit to blunt the growing discontent among the Minuteman rank and file. Simcox rejected that too.

"He told me what he did was his business," Gaddy told Jerry Seper. "Something is seriously wrong. I saw firsthand the dedication of the men and women who volunteered to stand these border watches, sometimes under very difficult circumstances, and proudly came to the conclusion that this is what America was all about. But a number of people I thought I could trust have since disappointed me."

Simcox, when confronted by Seper, was full of promises but simultaneously evasive. "I agree that the Minuteman volunteers and those who donated money to us have a right to know how much has been collected and on what it has been spent, and I know there is a lot of concern in the ranks regarding finances. That's why I sought capable accountants to get those answers, and I intend to make them public as soon as they are available.

"I can't wait for the final audit to answer and embarrass our critics, those who have tried to destroy this organization," he said. That audit, of course, was never conducted, or at least its results were never publicized.

Alan Keyes himself came to Simcox's defense by suggesting his critics were racists and white supremacists who wanted to take over the border-watch movement: the internal critics, he said, were "decidedly racist and anti-Semitic," people who had been removed for violating the Minutemen's standards.

"I personally applaud Chris Simcox for his diligent adherence to a rigorous standard that weeds out bigots from the upstanding, patriotic mainstream Americans who participate in the Minuteman citizens' border watch effort that I am proud to support," he told Seper.

Things turned south for good when a group of state-level MCDC organizers held a meeting to air their grievances over the way Simcox was running the operation: promised funds never delivered, his heavy-handed leadership style, and the general lack of accountability and transparency, especially as far as finances were concerned. They particularly wanted to know what had become of the $1.6 million that Simcox had told the press the organization had brought in, since they were seeing precious little of it spent at the operational and state levels.

Simcox abruptly fired them all the next week. So the dissenters, led by Simcox's former Arizona chapter head, Stacey O'Connell, regrouped and within a couple of months had formed a rival organization calling itself the Patriots Border Alliance. O'Connell continued to openly criticize Simcox and the MCDC over its murky finances, appearing on radio talk shows and circulating what information he could glean about the MCDC's money.

O'Connell, who describes himself and Simcox as formerly close friends ("Our wives were close—they went shopping together, they'd come over to our house, we'd go to theirs"), says the rift was "painful," but "it opened my eyes to many things that were going on within. I have enjoyed my time in the past year picking him apart on certain things, because I cannot stand somebody that continuously lies. I joined an organization that I thought stood for the rule of law and was transparent and was part of the American spirit. And to watch what has happened over the past couple of years has really faltered the ideas of the movement. And that has to do with one man, and that man is Chris Simcox."

In the end, any examination of the MCDC's finances was limited by the financial information it provided to the public, and that was precious little. Its 2006 financial-disclosure form claimed it had brought in about $600,000 in donations and spent about $650,000, but a closer look at the form revealed a number of open-ended expenses (such as $103,000 in "field operational expenses") vague enough to drive a Hummer through.

Tracking the money was made even more obscure by the Byzantine maze around the organization, but the general picture that emerged was that after the money passed through the maze, more than 60 percent of it was skimmed off for a variety of expenses, some of it legitimate (such as printing and mailing costs), some of it so vague and open-ended (such as consulting fees and caging costs) that it would take a forensic accountant with access to bank files to sort through it. That meant only a percentage of the donation monies went to the MCDC and its supposed fence project. The MCDC claimed that the administrative cut was as low as 32 percent, but closer examination of the actual returns indicated that it was more likely in the 60 to 80 percent range, and possibly higher. Which in turn may explain why the rank-and-file members at the field level were seeing so little of the money that Simcox claimed was rolling in.

Certainly there was a significant gap between his public claims of having raised $1.6 million for the border fence and what his financial-disclosure forms showed. The picture was further confused by a 2006 Declaration Alliance disclosure form claiming it paid out over $3 million to the MCDC as a "program service expense" that year.

A look at Declaration Alliance's 2006 public filings indicates that, of all the money raised for the border fence, only a small amount (if any at all) went toward its construction. The forms for the Declaration Alliance—through which all the border-fence donations were directed—show that it brought in nearly $5 million that year for all its programs. What percentage of that $5 million consisted of border-fence donations is unclear, but considering that the fence appeals began in May 2006 and remained the MCDC's (and Declaration Alliance's) chief fund-raising focus in the ensuing months and even years, it is nearly certain that those donations provided at least a majority of that money, if not nearly all of it. (The year before this, Declaration Alliance's total budget was only about $20,000.)

It also shows that $3.19 million went to the MCDC. But for what? The Declaration Alliance largely spent the money on printing, consulting, and similar activities. The only indication on the form that any actual money went back to the MCDC in the field is $143,000 listed as "operational expenses," though this money reportedly was for MCDC border watches, not the fence project. If any of those millions of dollars actually went toward building a border fence, it's difficult to ascertain where they are and how much was disbursed—though a look at the disclosure form for the Minuteman Foundation, the MCDC entity set up specifically to handle the fence project, shows a mere $87,500 in total revenues from donations for 2006. If that's the actual revenue coming from that $3.19 million the Declaration Alliance says it spent on the MCDC, then we're talking about less than 3 percent coming back to build the fence.

In other words, the best rough estimate is that about 97 cents of every dollar Jim Campbell spent on the fence went toward printing, mailing, consulting, and whatever black hole MCDC and Diener had created for those funds. So only 3 cents went toward building a fence.

Without offering specifics, Simcox denies what the financial-disclosure forms seemed to show. "I know there's a lot of controversy over the funding," he tells me. "But it's just absurd. Every penny that we raised went into the surveying, the engineering, and the construction of what we could build with what we brought in. It's difficult to complete a project when you don't have the funding."

||

While Simcox faltered under the weight of members demanding transparency in the MCDC's finances, his former cohort, Jim Gilchrist, found his organization embroiled in a strikingly similar controversy, one that would leave his group, the Minuteman Project, likewise paralyzed.

The problem began in November 2006, when Gilchrist began bouncing checks. The MMP's board of directors—particularly Marvin Stewart, a black anti-immigration activist who had accompanied Gilchrist on a number of his public and TV appearances—grew concerned and began asking to see bank statements, as well as a copy of the organization's bylaws. Gilchrist promised and hemmed and hawed but never delivered any of the requested documents, though he did eventually reveal to the board that he had opened a separate bank account into which he was depositing donations while writing checks on the original account, which had been allowed to run dry.

The more the board looked into the way Gilchrist was handling the MMP's finances, the more alarmed they became. They discovered that one of Gilchrist's lieutenants, Steven Eichler, had opened a merchant banking account into which donations were being directly deposited, and that deposits had been made into the personal account of one of Eichler's associates. There were separate accounts for Gilchrist's book-promotion work and for an MMP foundation whose existence the board hadn't known about.

The issue came to a head in a series of board meetings in December, the first of which Gilchrist did not attend and at which Stewart raised the possibility that funds had been embezzled. Gilchrist did show up at the follow-up meeting on December 29, however, and accused the board of acting like a "lynch mob," warning, according to the meeting's minutes, that "if you do not give me everything I want I will not do anything for the Minuteman Project again and I will burn it to the ground!"

The wrangling continued over the next few weeks. Finally, when the board gathered to meet on January 26, it found Gilchrist had locked up the Minuteman Project offices, so the remaining members—Stewart, Barbara Coe, and Deborah Courtney—retired to a nearby sushi restaurant and conducted the meeting. At its conclusion, they voted to terminate Gilchrist as the MMP president and to dismiss two of his lieutenants for fiduciary misdeeds.

Three days later, Gilchrist showed up at the board's meeting at the MMP offices and announced, "You are all fired! You are all fired!" The board members responded that he lacked the power to do so. The board met again on February 2, a meeting at which Gilchrist came accompanied by two "bodyguards" who prevented anyone "unwanted" from attending and who periodically interrupted the proceedings; eventually, sheriff's deputies were called, and the board finished up its business and left.

From there, the matter descended into a blizzard of lawsuits, with Gilchrist first claiming he had become the sole member of the board of directors and accusing the board of attempting to hijack his organization. He eventually dropped that suit, but the board meanwhile countered with one of its own accusing Gilchrist and his cohorts of fraud. That lawsuit trundled through Orange County's court system for nearly a year before the judge in the case dismissed it, at least partially at the plaintiffs' behest, in

May 2008. Shortly after the dismissal, the board (this time with a new lawyer) filed a fresh version of the case; that one eventually went Gilchrist's way, and he regained full control of the MMP.

Meanwhile, the recriminations flew, particularly online, where Gilchrist and his remaining followers posted extended attacks on the characters of the board members. Gilchrist continued filing his own lawsuits. Barbara Coe, who stepped down from the MMP board to protect her own organization (the California Coalition for Immigration Reform), even went so far as to post an appeal for donations to a defense fund to deal with Gilchrist's lawsuit against her.

When he talked about the case, Gilchrist waxed paranoid. "There's an agenda," he told me. "I talked with the folks at the law firm we use and they are suspicious about—there's gotta be some reason why three or four people who are unemployed, who have nothing to gain by trying to take my project—which they're not gonna take, legally, they're not gonna get it—they have nothing to gain, they have everything for our adversaries to gain. And that is to jam the Minuteman movement—not just my project, but the entire movement across the country. And they've been very effective at that.

"It appears that somebody is pulling strings, but nobody knows who they are."

For their part, the MMP board members insisted that their actions were about financial accountability. "If we were mean and vicious and dumb, we would want Gilchrist in jail," said Paul Sielski, board member Deborah Courtney's husband and one of the plaintiffs. "But at the end of the day, we don't want him to go to jail, because how's he going to pay us back?" Sielski said all he and Courtney wanted was to recover their funds and expose Jim Gilchrist's mismanagement of the Minuteman Project.

Finally, in December 2009, the Orange County judge hearing the matter issued a ruling granting Gilchrist control of the MMP. The next month, he issued a permanent injunction barring the board members from bringing any further action in the matter.

The broken promises and vicious infighting meant, unsurprisingly, that the Minutemen's original mission—watching the border—receded utterly to the background for both organizations. In 2007, the MCDC claimed some two thousand volunteers at various border watches, though the on-scene reports indicated far fewer participants. In 2008, the activity dropped further, so that the annual April border watch attracted only a few dozen participants and no media coverage. Likewise, Jim Gilchrist's plan to target employers of undocumented immigrants, Operation Spotlight, vanished into nothing.

Gilchrist took to lamenting the Minuteman movement's direction. In early 2008, one of his lieutenants penned a column wondering aloud on the MMP's website whether the movement was "doomed," given the willingness of Simcox and other critics to turn on Gilchrist after he endorsed GOP presidential candidate Mike Huckabee. Gilchrist and Huckabee, he said, "are threats to the continued financial security and commercial enterprises of these professional extremists and charlatans who make an earnest market in soliciting public donations to stop the illegal alien invasion crisis."

For his part, Gilchrist has even publicly regretted what he called a "Saddam Hussein mentality" within the ranks of the Minutemen, particularly some of the smaller, independent offshoots that have adopted the Minuteman name but none of Gilchrist's comparative restraint: "In retrospect, had I seen this, had I had a crystal ball to see what is going to happen . . . Am I happy? No," Gilchrist told *Orange County Register* reporter Amy Taxin in June. "Am I happy at the outcome of this whole movement? I am very, very sad, very disappointed."

||

His concern may have been disingenuous, but it was far from groundless.

All along, there was a problem with neo-Nazis and other extremists silently and surreptitiously joining the Minutemen's ranks, aided and abetted by the group's much-touted but essentially nonexistent "screening" efforts. Simcox's proclaimed efforts to "weed out" any racists or white supremacists were, at best, a sham, and potentially a scam as well, since Simcox charged new members fifty dollars each, a portion of which was supposed to pay for a "background check" that may have been nothing more than a Google search, if even that. Nor was Gilchrist's organization immune to infiltration by white supremacists.

But this only hinted at the broader problem: By promoting an explicitly armed vigilante response to illegal immigration, in addition to the ordinary citizens they drew to their cause, they were riddled throughout by people with violent dispositions, people who advocated violent solutions to the immigration issue. A lot of people thought it was time to start shooting border crossers on sight. And even more loved nothing more than to dehumanize Hispanics.

This was the chief danger the breakdown of the larger national Minuteman organization represented: as more and more splinter groups broke away, and as they distinguished themselves among their peers by indulging in increasingly outrageous rhetoric and behavior, the likelihood of violence rose exponentially. Just as Gary Cole had feared, the splinter groups began spinning out of control.

One of these was an outfit calling itself the San Diego Minutemen, run by a man named Jeff Schwilk, who started up his organization in 2005. It was inspired by the Gilchrist-Simcox project in Arizona but never affiliated with either's group. Like the California Minutemen, San Diego Minutemen operated without official blessing. This was fine with Schwilk, who found the original Minutemen far too namby-pamby for his decidedly confrontational tastes.

One of Schwilk's favorite tactics was to try to scare immigrants by traveling to places where day laborers hung out seeking work and threatening and intimidating them, shouting epithets, calling them "wetbacks" and the like. Then the Minutemen would chase down would-be day-labor employers: they drove SUVs equipped with flashing amber lights and frightened the potential employers away.

Casey Sanchez of the Southern Poverty Law Center observed Schwilk and his cohorts in action:

> At another day labor site that day, a Minuteman is yelling at immigrants. "Hey, putas," the man shouts, calling them whores, before he remembers that Spanish has gendered word endings and starts calling the men "putos" instead. The word translates best into the English-language epithet, "faggot." A motorist who's stopped by the Arco station to top off his tank leans out his window to tell off SDMM leader Schwilk. "Hey, Billy boy," he begins.
>
> Furious, Schwilk demands that the man get out of his car. Then the SDMM boss pulls out a can of Mace. "Bring it on, bitch," Schwilk says. "Bring it on." The man drives off instead.

On another occasion, Schwilk was videotaped pulling down the tents and makeshift shelters of a migrant workers' camp in McGonigle Canyon near San Diego. He came under police investigation on suspicion of having taken part in vandalizing the same camp a couple of months later.

Schwilk was prolific in sending out emails promoting his outfit's cause. His philosophy: "We are lock and load centrists! . . . We are for Compassion, Law Enforcement, Reason—and, as a last resort, bullets." His mails regularly described Latino immigrants (or *degrados*) as being like "human cockroaches" and other kinds of vermin. "We're dealing with animals here, and animals in-stinctively pick off the stragglers," he advised someone about dealing with mixed-race crowd situations. "Especially Third World animals."

Then there were the spin-offs of the spin-offs.

The *New York Times* profiled a California border watcher named Britt Craig, who appeared to be running a completely solo border watch outside of Campo. This probably would not be exceptional, except that Craig re-fused to recognize the leadership of the Campo unit of Jim Gilchrist's Min-uteman Project—namely, a fellow army veteran named Robert Crooks, who went by the nom de guerre Little Dog. He so openly and aggressively in-sulted Craig on emails to his charges—calling him, among other things, "a swine who lives in a cat box"—that it eventually came to fisticuffs on the main street in Campo. Craig broke Crooks's glasses after the man refused to apologize for the insults.

Crooks, a fifty-seven-year-old with a white walrus mustache, had a falling out with Gilchrist a year later and formed his own outfit, calling it the Mountain Minutemen. Crooks sent Gilchrist a taunting email, telling him he was a weakling who could "Talk the Talk" but not "Walk the Walk."

Attached was a video, shot through a night-vision scope, watching two or three men in the distance atop a hill, on the other side of a barbed-wire fence, surveying the ground. "All right, come on across, motherfuckers," a man says quietly off camera. "Yeah, go that way. I dare you to go that way. That's my fucking trail, bitch!" He keeps muttering for several minutes, call-ing his targets "cockroaches." Then he shouts out: "Hey *putos* ["faggots"], one, two, three!"—followed by the chambering sound of a shotgun shell, then a blast and a flash.

"This video shows how to keep a Home Depot parking lot empty," Crooks told Gilchrist. Gilchrist, whose Minuteman Project had earlier pro-vided Crooks's group with supplies, responded by banning Crooks from contact with his own group. When reporters asked Crooks about the video, he denied being the shooter.

A week later, a second video featuring the same night scope and the same shooter surfaced, and it was far more disturbing, because it purported to show the actual shooting of a border crosser with a backpack. This time, the night scope zooms in on a single figure trudging along on a trail with a load on his back. The same voice as before starts talking off camera: "I got him. He's low crawling. Guy with a backpack. I betcha it's probably full of dope."

Once again, the man shouts, just as the figure tops a hill: "Hey, *puto!*" The dark figure dives behind an outcropping of rocks, then pops up his head, and peers in the direction of the shooter. "I got him," the shooter says. "He's prairie doggin' now. He heard me."

This time, he is in a conversation with another Minuteman on a walkie-talkie. "All right, where you at? What's your twenty?" his cohort can be heard asking.

"He's up there on the, uh, smuggler's trail."

After a few seconds of static: "I don't have a visual."

The dark figure begins to creep from behind the rock. "You know what? I'm going to take a fucking shot," the first voice says. This is followed by the flash and bang of two quick rifle rounds. The man with the backpack appears to fly backward suddenly, out of view.

"Oh fuck, I got him dude!' the first voice says. "I fuckin' got him!" He pauses, breathing heavily. "Dude, what are we gonna do?"

On the other end, the voice replies: "Get the shovel, get some lime, and hey, grab me a twelve-pack, too, while you're up there."

The video then suddenly segues to a daytime shot, with the same cameramen walking up to what appears to be a gravesite marked with a crude cross. Our narrator offers his final respects: "*Adios*, asshole!"

There was a brief uproar about this video, until Crooks admitted shortly thereafter that they had made it all up. "Who in their right mind is going to shoot a smuggler, videotape it, then post it to YouTube?" Crooks said.

What was clearly not faked was the narrator's chilling lacking of humanity—the viciousness with which he waited for the right moment to get off a round. What was clearly real was his wish that he could shoot one of these border crossers, and his belief moreover that we ought to be doing that. In the first video, he mutters, after firing off a round and yelling obscenities at the border crossers: "And that's how you get rid of Mexicans!"

||

Jim Campbell was finally reimbursed in September 2007 for his $63,000 outlay for the pipe, but he wanted his $100,000 back, too. His lawsuit was dismissed, so he tried to get criminal action brought against Simcox and the MCDC operation. His pleas, however, went unanswered.

Meanwhile, nothing like Simcox's promised "high-tech, double-layered gauntlet of deterrent" ever came close to being built. "We're still hoping to finish that, basically, standing as a monument," Simcox said, but added that it wasn't necessary anymore, and that fundraising for the project had come to a halt. (At the time he told me this, the MCDC's website still asked visitors to "Donate to Build the Minuteman Border Fence.")

Simcox said the Minutemen declared victory when Bush signed the Secure Fence Act in the fall of 2006, which authorized the construction of over seven hundred miles of double-reinforced fence along the US-Mexico border. "That was really the purpose—to challenge them to do that," he told me. "I just don't think we're going to get any more funding, to tell you the truth, because people see that the government's doing it. Mission accomplished."

# 11

# The Distaff Minuteman

**Shawna on the border.** MAURICE SHERIF PHOTO

Aside from her brief stint as a beauty-salon protester, Shawna had never been even remotely involved in politics before she decided to join the Minutemen. She had been a vaguely supportive Clinton Democrat when John Forde first met her. But hanging out at the Elks Club and listening to talk radio had introduced a new worldview that she now embraced with a true believer's fervor.

At first, it seemed that Shawna hung out with the older men at the Elks as simply a new twist to her longtime habit of worming money out of men. "She was thinking, thinking way out there how to take advantage of this," John says. At the same time, it became clear that she was adopting their ideas as her own. Her ardent embrace of the Minuteman movement was of a piece with her usual pattern: it was a wide-open opportunity for a manipulator like Shawna, while its politics and rhetoric came readily to her—indeed they were practically tailored to her personality.

One of the chief attractions the movement had for Shawna was that, as with her little taste of protest in 2001, it gave her a chance to lead by being a loudmouth—something she was skilled at. The Minutemen, John Forde says, gave Shawna permission to go activist. "That gave her the avenue to be militant," he says.

A significant aspect of the scapegoating rhetoric common to right-wing nativist movements—rhetoric that is almost wholly structured around building outrage and anger in their audience and overwhelming rationality—is a kind of competitive escalation: the more outrageous and inflammatory the rhetoric, the greater influence you wield, and the greater following you attract. In a can-you-top-this political environment, a lifelong topper like Shawna will always flourish. And she did.

Shawna began showing up at Washington Minutemen events sometime in the spring of 2006, appearing first at the border watches at Claude LeBas's place near Ferndale, where she was noted more for networking than for actually participating in the border watches. Her friends Bob and Kathy Dameron first met her in Ferndale. She also appeared at Minuteman protests at day-labor pickup sites in Seattle. And she threw herself into supporting Minuteman Bob Baker's efforts to gather enough signatures for his Initiative 946. In order to qualify for the ballot, the measure needed some 224,000 valid signatures by state voters.

Hal Washburn, Washington Minuteman Detachment's vetting director, first met Shawna at an anti-immigration rally in Olympia that June, but he had heard about her beforehand from Bob Baker, for whom she had been helping organize signature-gathering efforts. "He had told me about her," Washburn said. "He kind of recommended her to me."

The Olympia event, featuring nativist pundit Frosty Wooldridge and his Paul Revere Ride—a cross-country tour featuring motorcycles and bicycles, with pit stops in cities stretching all across the country—was rife with the kind of extreme rhetoric that was a common flavor at Minuteman rallies. Wooldridge, author of a 2004 book titled *Immigration's Unarmed Invasion: Deadly Consequences*, built his tirades around lurid tales of the evils brought to America by Latino immigrants, including diseases, crime, Santeria rituals, animal sacrifice, you name it.

Wooldridge indulges in classic eliminationist rhetoric, words designed not merely to demonize and dehumanize their targets but to conceptualize them as objects fit only for extermination and removal. He has a particular fetish about diseases, warning that "you're breathing air that may be carrying hepatitis" simply by shopping at a Wal-Mart or going to a movie, and claiming that tuberculosis, head lice, and hepatitis are showing up in classrooms, and that a deadly parasite that will destroy your heart is showing up in the nation's blood supply. Wooldridge calls all this the immigrants' "disease jihad."

"I don't want to see my country taken over . . . and have them make the Southwest a slime pit Third World country like Mexico," Wooldridge once proclaimed. He described California as a place "with its nightmare gridlock, schools trashed, hospitals collapsing, drug gangs and overall chaos generated by a Third World mob of illegal aliens."

Just as he launched his tour that May, Wooldridge penned a classic eliminationist essay titled "A Day Without Illegal Aliens," which concluded that ridding the nation of all twelve million of its undocumented workers would end a plague of crime and disease, but most of all, "America would not suffer balkanization, language apartheid, cultural apartheid, angry non-citizens, chaotic schools and bankrupted hospitals. Benefits gained include more jobs for Americans, peaceful communities, less drunks on highways, less burglaries, less rapes, greater honesty in business, fair wages paid to Americans and SO much more."

In fact, virtually none of these claims are accurate. Numerous studies have concluded definitively that immigrants commit crime at much lower rates than native-born Americans, that they do not bring in diseases at an appreciable rate, that the taxes collected (as required by law) from their paychecks more than outweigh whatever social-benefit costs they incur, and that they remain eager adoptees of the English language. However, nativists like Wooldridge operate in a fact-free milieu in which emotions—particularly anger and resentment and fear—remain far more powerful and persuasive. Indeed, while Wooldridge is an oft-published author of many articles and books, and claims to have bicycled a hundred thousand miles over six continents, he in fact has no known expertise in immigration other than his opinion. Which, for the Minutemen, was all that was really needed.

Shawna Forde also had no fear of expressing her opinions, and they were invariably as inflammatory, xenophobic, and racially tinged as Frosty Wooldridge's—whose views, after all, were in fact fairly typical of the kind of rhetoric that was heard among the Minutemen, both at the leadership level and among the rank and file as well.

She also figured out that a little drama could get people's attention. In August, she sent out an email, distributed widely among Washington Minutemen, narrating a tale of her close confrontation with scary Mexican men at an Everett Starbucks. It was penned in Shawna's inimitable writing style, which was a blizzard of run-on sentences, misspellings, malapropisms, and nonsensical grammar:

Not paying attention ofcourse, I go to my vehicle and go to put some bags away but first I have to take out all the signs that Bear loaned me (secure our boarders) So I'm standing their holding these signs my girl-freind is on the other side of the car when all of a sudden (on her side) comes about 5 or 6 mexicans. They start yelling at her saying she is a white bitch and what is the problem with her, next thing I see is her falling against my car *sucker punched* I'm still standing their holding these signs thinking well I have protection in my car. I open my door *or at-tempt too* and BLAM it's kicked shut I turn around and I'm face to face with a pair of dark brown eyes that are filled with pure hate.

So I'm racing in my mind to get a grip fast I lock eyes with this mexi-can male and thought well shit if I throw down with him atleast I go out fighting. So I stood toe to toe with him it was truly one of the most in-tense encounters, it's like he wanted to rape me or kill me probably bolth. I swear the world totally dissapeared for that momement from his hate filled energy with sexual tension *it was bizarre*, my fear, that turned to anger (within seconds) mind you I'm still holding the signs *thanks bear* All of a sudden out of nowhere is a flash of green and the next thing I know there's 8 to 10 Army guy's kicking the shit out of these mexicans in the starbucks parking lot yellin !how dare you touch this or any american woman! it was a rumble. Cars are honking people are gathering, (I'm still holding the sign *secure our borders* My girlfriend is bleeding she splits totally freaked out. I tell the army guys (their dressed in full fatigues and were in two convoy trucks they were at the other end of the lot *checking us out* when they saw my friend get hit and the confrontation and all jumped from their trucks to come to our aid) that they better split I knew the cops would be there soon.
God bless our military.

The email caused a brief sensation among the Minutemen—who touted the supposed incident as evidence of the threats they had to endure as a re-sult of their activism—and helped bolster Shawna's cred among their ranks. A little while later, hearing Tom Williams complain about having to field so many media calls, she volunteered to be the Minutemen's state media li-aison. After a little consideration, they agreed.

At first, Shawna impressed everyone with her zeal and energy. "She was adamant about the country, patriotism. She was constantly going all over the state getting things done," Bob Dameron says.

Yet almost immediately, there were questions and objections. Shawna's tough-chick demeanor had also grown into a reputation among the Minutemen as a bit randy. "There were a lot of questions, whether her morality could be trusted," Dameron says later. "They got to the point where they didn't trust her."

Shawna's old habits promptly manifested themselves among the Minutemen. One day during a border watch at Claude LeBas's place in Ferndale, LeBas's sister caught Shawna up at their house, rummaging through bedroom dresser drawers. She didn't show up at any border watches after that. (LeBas thinks she was already making plans to form her own Minuteman organization even back then; he believes Shawna was looking for his membership roster for the Washington Minuteman Detachment.)

She also loved to manipulate the Minutemen the way she had done with her family and friends for years: spread malicious gossip or concoct stories of backstabbing in the ranks, and spread the tales without making herself appear to be the source. "She was always in the middle of things, stirring up trouble," Hal Washburn says. "Turning people against each other. Things like that."

Friction had been growing among the state's various Minutemen. Dameron, who had founded a Yakima chapter to help organize activities on that side of the Cascade, firmly believed that they should be focusing their efforts on educating local governments and stopping employers from hiring "illegals." The Minutemen who had been running border watches, though, were equally insistent that they maintain their traditional missions. The debate was a perfect opportunity for Shawna to manipulate the tensions to her own end.

Washburn says it grew to the point that the state Minuteman leadership—mostly Tom Williams, Claude LeBas, and himself—decided to demote Shawna as media director and create the position of "events coordinator" as one where they could manage her better. She was required to call Washburn weekly and report in. "Over the phone it was all wine and roses, but I had gotten onto her by that point, and you couldn't believe a word she said," he says now.

Bob Dameron steadfastly defended her. After all, as he pointed out, she was one of the state's only Minutemen to travel around and make appearances at city councils and town halls, to organize events elsewhere, and to generally promote "boots on the ground" political activism. "She was doing all of that, and I didn't see anybody else doing those things in the state," Dameron says.

It nearly came to a head at the very moment of Shawna's greatest triumph, accidental as it was: On November 14, 2006, KCTS-TV—the state's largest

PBS affiliate, based in Seattle—broadcast a town-hall discussion of immigration in Yakima at the studios of KYVE-TV, hosted by reporter Enrique Cerna and featuring a panel of representatives from a variety of perspectives. Shawna, dressed neatly and wearing fashionable glasses, appeared as the spokesperson for both the Minutemen and the Federation for American Immigration Reform.

Neither organization, in fact, was aware that she was to be its representative for this program. Originally, Bob Baker—who belonged to both groups and in fact was the state FAIR representative—was scheduled to make the show. However, Baker's professional life as an airline pilot intervened at the last moment; he was called in to work, and suddenly KCTS needed a replacement. It's not entirely clear how Shawna was chosen. "I certainly didn't recommend her," Baker told me several years later. "I don't know how she got put on the panel."

Cerna himself explained: "What happened was that he wasn't able to make it . . . and then they had to scramble on that day to find somebody, and then, I don't know how they picked her but they ended up picking her. And so, the day that we did it, it was kind of a last-minute thing. There were a lot of phone calls. So they put her in there, and we didn't really know a lot about her. And it was very quickly apparent that she was very, um, right-wing."

Indeed.

For the most part, the panel was a reasoned discussion of immigration that tried to deal with the concerns of all sides—at least, until Shawna entered into the discussion. Then, the bomb-throwing style she had picked up from nativists like Frosty Wooldridge was on prime display:

> CERNA: Shawna, let me ask you about the issue of economics. You've heard constraints from growers, you know, that the apple harvest is very important in this state, particularly in this region. What do you say to the growers?
> FORDE: We've got a prison system. Let's utilize it.

It's hard to say whether Shawna was advocating imprisoning farmers who used undocumented labor, or if she simply thought the immigrants themselves should be imprisoned. But it sounded good, and it blew up the debate afterwards—which took an accusatory and angry turn at that point—quite nicely.

Shawna later wrapped up by claiming empathy for the people affected negatively by illegal immigration as a justification for targeting Latinos:

FORDE: I'd like to see two things on there. Not just about the people who came here legally, and are here legally, but how about the Americans who have been affected and died because of the illegal invasion in our country? How about our sovereignty?

And securing our borders and protecting our nation is extremely important. And I know the Minutemen and many organizations will not stop—we will start at the local level and work our way up—we will not stop until we get the results that we need to have.

While the show was being broadcast, Bob Dameron—who was going to drive Shawna home from the TV studio—received a call from Hal Washburn: claiming to be a Minuteman spokesman without anyone's authorization was the final straw. Dameron was ordered to fire her. "I was looking for a way to get rid of her at that point, and that was Bob's assignment," says Washburn.

Dameron balked: "She had done such a good job that we could not do that." After the show, on the drive back to his home, he told Shawna he had been ordered to fire her, but he wouldn't do it. Shawna thanked him and headed home.

On the drive out of Yakima that evening, Shawna totaled her Honda Civic by running it into a guardrail. She was taken to a local hospital with minor injuries. She claimed that Mexican truck drivers had forced her off the road, but troopers investigating the accident determined that Shawna had simply lost control when she came upon trucks driving fifty-five miles per hour. The drivers' ethnic backgrounds were not included in their report, however.

The accident forestalled the Minuteman leaders' efforts to oust her. In the meantime, she went to work. In early December, she sent out a fundraising email to all Washington State Minutemen asking them to donate to a fellow Minuteman who was about to lose his home—but who insisted on remaining anonymous.

"She said he was too proud to have his name mentioned," Hal Washburn recalls. "And she did this without our knowledge. She just sent an email out to all the Minutemen here in Washington.

"It was supposedly a Minuteman over in the Yakima area who was unemployed and was ill. She had run into him and his wife, and they were going to lose their house and this and that, and they needed money. So all of a sudden, I got the email too, asking money be sent to her for the benefit of this fellow. So I actually sent her some money, but at the same time, we talked to her about it—'Don't ever do this again without our knowledge. And we want to know who this person is.' And she wouldn't tell us."

At the same time, Shawna opened up a secret channel of communications with Chris Simcox's MCDC office in Tombstone. She had been emailing MCDC's office manager, a woman named Phyllis Gross—who told Shawna she considered her "an outstanding asset in my humble opinion and professional judgment"—and with her encouragement, dropped a message to Simcox, portraying herself as "media director" for the Washington State MCDC chapter and urging him to look hard at the lack of leadership in the state. She added: "If Hal Washburn or Bear find out I have contacted you or had any correspondence with Phyllis I will be in jeopardy of being kicked out of the MMCDC due to the fact this goes against very direct orders that I am never allowed communications with HQ."

Simcox wrote back: "Thanks for the heads up on your concerns Shawna. Thank you for everything you are doing. . . . You call us any time you need something. I'm investigating beginning tomorrow. Send me what you have and we'll make a trip up there to hold some meetings to get things back on track."

Forde wrote back in early January 2007, outlining in a lengthy email her "plan" for the state, urging Simcox to consider creating two outfits in the state: one dedicated to running border watches, headed by the current leadership, and a second one devoted to "internal" watches, harassing day laborers and people who employ undocumented immigrants—to be headed up by herself, naturally. She complained that the current leaders were threatening to throw her out of the organization: "They do not like the fact that I'm trying to organize and get thing's done they see it as a pain in their necks and would like it to be quiet and everyone just go to the border once a month and keep it simple. They always talk about doing things but it never transpires."

Simcox wrote back enthusiastically: "Shawna, Thanks for the info, we'll get this done asap. I'll call you tomorrow evening to discuss. Please contact Carmen Mercer about finances and raising money-since we are a non-profit corporation it's not all that simple, we'll help you out with internal chapters. Look forward to working with you. I think it best we send a national person up there to help show you how to develop chapters as we have done all over the country."

Within a few days, he sent out a missive to the Washington Minutemen announcing exactly that change. Naturally, this caused a major eruption within the organization: nearly the entire leadership of the state chapter—

including Washburn, LeBas, and Williams—threatened to resign, along with a large number of members, if Simcox carried out the reorganization and promoted Forde to head up the new "internal" chapter. After much internal wrangling, Forde backed out and announced she was "stepping down" as "internal chapter director."

"I feel that somewhere this has just gone wrong," Forde wrote Washburn and others. "You . . . think I just want to be in charge. In fact I don't want to be in charge! I'm terrified for our future and the country that my children will be forced to live in. All I ever wanted to do is get out there and 'DO.'"

A few weeks later, the disgruntled state leadership officially fired her from their organization. "It was February 3 when we canned her," Washburn recalls. "Carmen Mercer [MCDC operations director in Tombstone] came up. We went out to dinner over in Tukwila. Carmen was staying at a hotel over near the airport. Anyway, Bob Dameron was there, myself, Bear. Tom was not there. And Shawna, of course. Carmen wouldn't let us fire her without her coming up and making the final decision. So that's what that was all about.

"Things got a little heated at the dinner, and she accused Bear of using Minuteman money for his own personal expenses up there in Ferndale. And I jumped all over her when that happened. We had had some problems with her concerning money.

"Shawna ended up storming out. And then she called Carmen from her cell phone an hour or so later, and Carmen got rid of her the next morning."

It didn't matter. Forde had decided at that point to form her own Minuteman organization; she had come to recognize that the movement's larger leadership vacuum was a perfect opportunity for someone with her own organizing skills and energy. A lot of rank-and-file Minutemen were unhappy with the way things ran in the state. Knowing this, Shawna saw a prime opportunity to make her own destiny.

||

Shawna had first met Mike Carlucci in 2006, when she hired him, in her capacity as a Washington Minuteman Detachment official, to review their security procedures and to identify areas where the organization might have liability exposure.

Carlucci, a respected private investigator and a conservative with shared views about immigration, reviewed a plan Shawna had prepared to limit the MCDC chapter's exposure. What he wound up telling her was that she needed to strictly vet anybody who wanted to be involved with her organization—that unless everyone on the border had a complete background check, they would be vulnerable to bad actors who attached themselves to the group and then committed crimes.

He outlined a worst-case scenario for them: "I used the hyperbolic statement: 'What if somebody goes and breaks in and tries to rip off something and kills people?'" Carlucci recalls.

Prophets, however, are most often ignored, especially by the people their prophecies are about. Shawna thanked him for his input and promised to put it into action. Instead, the security plan was shelved. It had probably crossed Shawna's mind that such procedures might not work to her advantage: the MCDC's vetting procedures to date had not yet uncovered her long criminal background, since whoever was doing the background checks had not looked into any other names but Shawna Forde. Prior to that identity, Shawna had used five other surnames, and most of her criminal past was hidden under them.

Carlucci had observed the growing rift between Shawna and the state MCDC leadership up close, and it was clear to him that what rubbed the leaders wrong the most was that she was an assertive, brassy woman who was pointing out to them, bluntly, their own organizational failures.

At first, he says, "they were letting her do anything she wanted to do because she was the only one that was a worker. Everybody else wanted to be out there on the border with their AK-47s."

Shawna was pushing for a more active approach to fighting illegal immigration, which didn't go down well with the faction that was content setting up border watches. "They were pissed off at her because she was trying to bring balance to the Washington branch of the MCDC," Carlucci says. "That's what she was doing."

Worker bees like Shawna are highly valued in volunteer-oriented organizations. Which was why, when it all blew up, Chris Simcox in fact tried desperately to keep Shawna on board with his organization. Mike Carlucci sat in on the conference calls and heard it.

"I was there when they were begging Shawna to stay on board, and to weather out the storm, and to work with them," Carlucci says. "I mean, begging her to do that. Begging Shawna not to be pissed off, not to leave, not to start MAD, but to hang in there with them and they would get this ironed out. Chris Simcox, for crying out loud, was apologizing to Shawna and asking if there was anything that he could do to keep her on board."

The split between Simcox and Gilchrist had been growing into a rivalry, and he feared losing Shawna to the other side, so even after she had been fired by the state MCDC, he was scheming up ways to keep her in his organization.

"Simcox was trying to move fast," Carlucci says. "In these conversations with Shawna up here, he wanted to make her a hybrid. He wanted to kind of put her in charge and make her not tell anybody that she was in charge. Kind of a power behind the throne. He belabored that in conversations with Shawna."

It didn't work. Shawna had grander plans. She politely declined and then went out and started building her own border militia.

||

At about the same time she was being tossed from the MCDC, more drama erupted in Shawna's personal life. First, in late January, she was arrested for shoplifting a carton of chocolate milk worth $3.18 from an Everett grocery store. She claimed it was all a misunderstanding, that she had simply walked into the Starbucks next door and had forgotten to pay.

Then, on March 20, 2007, her then-seventeen-year-old son, Devon Duffey, walked with two other men into the Everett beauty salon that Shawna co-owned with a gay man named Lonnie Hernandez. (This had been an unlikely partnership, built more out of necessity than harmony: Shawna had bought into the shop with Hernandez largely as a way to have a chair in his business.) Devon pulled out a baseball bat, walked up to Hernandez, and proceeded to beat him badly: the man required twenty-seven stitches in his scalp and was hospitalized. Shawna was not at work that day.

When police caught up with Devon, he admitted to the beating and led police to the weapon he had used. At first he told police that he beat Hernandez because he was gay, but when it became clear that such an admission had transformed the act into a hate crime, he changed his story. Suddenly, it was because Hernandez had supposedly stolen money from his mother.

Shawna denied that she had ever told her son any such thing, telling the court Devon had not lived with her for more than a year, and she "refused to allow him to live at home due to his dishonesty, lack of respect, theft of property from the home, and concerns about substance abuse."

Devon was given jail time for the beating, which was stiffened further when he was busted for shoplifting while awaiting trial. In December 2007, Devon would be arrested for burglarizing a Marysville home and sent away to prison for an even longer stint.

||

Shawna named her new group with the intention of giving it a nice, angry-sounding acronym, conveying the anger of "ordinary citizens": Minuteman American Defense, or MAD.

"We started Minuteman American Defense because we wanted to take it to a more aggressive and more active level than what was currently happening with MCDC," she later told a radio interviewer.

"She had maybe fifteen or twenty members, but it gave her a lot of credibility," Hal Washburn says.

Bob Dameron cobbled together a website for MAD and signed up as a cofounding member. Forde told him she wanted to use the site to promote herself, but he balked at some of her more outrageous demands. Her vision for the site was to feature videos and photos of Shawna tracking immigrants in the desert, peppered with her first-person accounts of the undercover investigations she began claiming she was conducting.

By forming MAD, Forde in essence took a side in the burgeoning feud between Chris Simcox and Jim Gilchrist, throwing in her lot with Gilchrist. And indeed, in the months after she and MCDC parted ways, she cultivated a friendship with the Minuteman Project leader. Working with an Edmonds conservative named Doug Parris, Forde organized in late June 2007 an Illegal Immigration Summit in Everett featuring herself and Gilchrist.

Parris operated a website called The Reagan Wing, and he liked to organize conservative events in Snohomish County. He wanted to put together an event focused on immigration-related issues. He later told Scott North that Shawna approached him that spring, presenting herself as uniquely qualified to help and noting that she had support from some Republican leaders in Snohomish County, was the leader of Minuteman American Defense, and owned a company specializing in "Take Back America" T-shirts. Forde touted her contacts with Gilchrist in pitching the idea to hold her summit at the Everett Elks Lodge, where she also had contacts.

"Shawna came in and was dynamic, engaging, flashy; made all sorts of claims about what she could produce in terms of the Minutemen side," Parris said.

Parris also succumbed to Shawna's paranoid style of activism. In May, his website featured an urgent report on a potential security threat that was being confronted by Forde at the Everett city library. The dispatch read:

> The Reagan Wing has learned that Minutemen American Defense is, at this minute, positioning personnel at the Everett Public Library in direct response to confidential pleas from Library staff to counterract aparent Terrorist Surveilance from that location, of the Port of Everett. Men described as 'Middle Eastern' have, over a period of days or weeks, repeatedly attended the Library without either reading or checking out books, ac-

cording to the sources. They have, instead, busied themselves with noting the position of seagoing vessels, port infrastructure and photographing the whole Port of Everett, clearly visable from the Library windows. "You can see everything from Bainbridge Island to Mukilteo and every Navy ship," said a Minuteman, from a cell phone on site. "This is the perfect place to plan a terrorist attack."

Once Parris gave her the green light on their Immigration Summit, it was full speed ahead. Shawna made decisions about the invited speakers and ticket sales without even consulting Parris. Naturally, he raised questions. Naturally, Shawna threw a fit and walked out, saying she was done.

And naturally, on the day of the forum—June 30, 2007—she was there, ready to take the stage, large and in charge. Parris was a little nonplussed but proceeded anyway.

Forde told Parris she wanted to rearrange the speakers' lineup. Parris said no. So she stalked up from behind Parris and snatched the event clipboard out of his hands and then started off in the other direction, telling everyone she was changing things. She didn't get far: Parris promptly snatched the clipboard back and assured everyone the schedule would proceed according to the original plan.

"It was at that moment that our relationship was over," he says.

It didn't matter, however, because the show went on, and Shawna got to share the stage with Gilchrist. She gave a brief talk explaining how she came to take up arms on the border: "I was in the mall one day and, hey—nobody's speaking English. I realized we had a serious problem. I just got tired of pushing one for English. I decided to do something about it." She also led the audience in a rousing cheer: "Take Back America!" they shouted. And you could buy a T-shirt afterward.

Gilchrist was similarly xenophobic, warning of a "tsunami of immigration" that threatened to swamp the nation's very existence. Predicting that Spanish would become the official language of the United States by 2030 if things didn't change, he warned: "This is how a nation is conquered without firing a shot."

Part of the event's promotional material said Shawna was a onetime "grunge rock promoter," a description she had given Doug Parris, which was then uncritically picked up by various media outlets reporting on the event, as well as a number of reports about Shawna afterward. Thus was born the legend of Shawna Forde's grunge-rock career, one that she herself began to eagerly feed and build on.

Unsurprisingly, it emerged shortly afterward that Shawna appropriated a significant chunk of money from sales of the thirty-dollar forum tickets. Doug Parris thought about filing a complaint with the obviously uninterested Everett police, but didn't. He was just glad to be shut of Shawna Forde.

||

While Jim Gilchrist was in town that last weekend of June 2007, Shawna drove him up to Claude LeBas's place near Ferndale, where the Washington Minuteman Detachment was holding one of its semiregular border watches.

LeBas says it was a quiet weekend, but he and Tom Williams and Hal Washburn were all there when a rental car pulled up and Jim Gilchrist emerged, unannounced. He walked into the operations center and began chatting everyone up, apparently intent on trying to draw them into his fold. But LeBas spotted Shawna out in the car.

"She was hiding in the car when they pulled up," he says. "And Gilchrist came in, and we talked and what not. And I saw her peeking out the window of the car. So I got up, and I walked out there. and I said, 'What the hell are you doing here? You're not welcome here.'

"And then Gilchrist said, 'Well, she's with me.' And I said, 'Well, if she's with you, then you're not welcome here either.' And then I said, 'But I'll tell you this: You better watch your back.'"

Gilchrist got back in the car and drove off with Shawna.

||

Shawna had developed another project that summer: running for Everett City Council on an anti–illegal immigration platform. If only she hadn't been caught shoplifting.

She filed for the nonpartisan seat in June, her ambitions fired by having arranged the Gilchrist appearance at the Everett Elks. After the big show, she began campaigning in earnest, emphasizing immigration at every speaking stop. She also promised to allow Everett cops to arrest suspected illegal immigrants.

However, her chocolate-milk shoplifting charge came up in court on August 1, just as the campaign season was beginning, and it was in the local news. Her opponent, incumbent Drew Nielsen, pointed it out to reporters.

Shawna decided around then that it was time to go to Arizona for border duty with MAD.

She had already lined up her next sucker: a Yakima-area conservative named Scott Shogren. She had used some of Shogren's money to cofound

MAD, and then convinced Shogren to finance her next big project: a documentary about the Minutemen, filmed by Minutemen and with their cooperation, down on the Arizona border. Shogren willingly handed over large sums of money in the summer of 2007 to Shawna for this project. He won't say now how much it was, but the outlay probably ran into five figures.

Shawna took that money and ran down to the border with it, Bob Dameron in tow. The plan was for Bob to be Shawna's cameraman for the documentary. In August 2007, they headed to Glenn Spencer's hundred-acre ranch in Hereford, where a number of fellow Minutemen had decamped as well. Dameron only brought along a pup tent, while Shawna quickly arranged to find other accommodations. She convinced Spencer to let her occupy a motor home he had on the property for guests: "What she told me is that she had all these contacts with the media," Spencer says, "and that we weren't getting any coverage at all, and she was going to bring the media down here to explain what the American Border Patrol was doing.

"That's what she promised me, and I thought, 'Well that's a pretty good trade-off: I'll let her stay here; she's going to help us get some exposure.'"

Shawna took Bob Dameron to his tent site, dumped him there with his belongings, and drove off. He spent five weeks living there, joining his fellow Minutemen on desert patrols and videotaping them for the documentary that never came to be. He had to rely on strangers for rides into town to buy food. He saw Shawna only occasionally in all that time; she seemed to be accommodating other Minutemen in her borrowed RV.

"That was the most humbling experience of my life," Dameron later told Scott North. "I learned to trust God."

Shawna was very much enjoying herself, because she was getting to network with all the Minuteman movement bigwigs, including Spencer. Jim Gilchrist showed up. Shawna was photographed that summer with Gilchrist: together they admired Spencer's remote-controlled airplane and then scanned the horizon in search of border crossers.

That November, not having campaigned much at all, Shawna nonetheless attracted 5,892 votes to Drew Nielsen's 10,943 in the Everett City Council election.

||

Forde kept in touch with Gilchrist and subsequently arranged for him to make an appearance in February 2008 at Central Washington University in Ellensburg, about a hundred-mile drive from Seattle. Gilchrist at the time was embroiled in heated lawsuits and disputes with his former board of directors over ownership of the Minuteman Project, and he no longer had any functioning presence on the borders; Forde offered to step up and take on the job. Gilchrist became so enamored of Forde that, on February 9, he directed his staff to "put Shawna in the website as our border patrol coordinator."

A mutual-admiration society had developed. When word of Shawna's appointment to the border-patrol position circulated among other nativist groups, Gilchrist and the Minuteman Project were roundly criticized. Shawna warmly defended Gilchrist in an email to him:

> I just have to sit back and laugh about all this they are idiots and I love throwing your name around and watch the tempers fly hahahaha, You are a powerful man when in name only you can stir a state, I just am amazed sometimes I've never been attacked so much for a associate, But you are my Friend and I'm proud to be associated with you so Fuck em!!

Gilchrist flew in to Sea-Tac Airport on February 26 and was met by Forde and her driver—who happened to be Mike Carlucci. She had asked him to provide security for Gilchrist for the visit, and he agreed. He came to deeply regret it.

Shawna and Gilchrist engaged in animated conversation all the way out to Ellensburg. The focus of the conversation was on finding ways to finance the movement. "It was all about money—money, money, money," says Carlucci.

The previous October, Gilchrist had snared headlines and cable-TV coverage when students had stormed the stage in angry protest during a speaking appearance at Columbia University. Gilchrist had been escorted away before anyone could harm him. It had apparently given him ideas. On the drive over to Ellensburg, he told Shawna he hoped to create a similar disturbance in Ellensburg.

"He wanted to be able to sue the university for not providing adequate protection," Carlucci says. "And they talked about that on the way over."

Sure enough, after Gilchrist had given his talk, he began bantering with some of the students there to protest him. "Jim Gilchrist actually provoked students, looking to incite someone to assault him," Carlucci says. "We were in this student union building with all these kids, and he was willfully, knowingly, and wantonly trying to provoke these guys, to the point that they cut the event off sooner than planned."

The whole experience convinced Carlucci he wanted nothing further to do with these people. For one thing, he was wholly unimpressed with Jim

Gilchrist. "He was a terrible public speaker," Carlucci says. "How he obtained a position of movement prominence is beyond me.

"But what concerned me was that he was calling people idiots, stupid, assholes—he wanted the guy to physically assault him. I went and apologized to the campus police for bringing Jim Gilchrist to their campus—that's how bad it was."

Carlucci thought the experience couldn't get any worse. It did.

On the drive back to Seattle, Shawna and Gilchrist had another animated conversation. In this one, she was outlining more ways they could make money. Including robbing drug dealers.

"They were discussing in what I thought was a hyperbolic way, doing what she wound up doing—by taking on people who were selling drugs and taking the money from their organizations," Carlucci says. "She was thinking about that shit in a role-playing way back then, and doing a gallows laugh.

"They were talking incredibly inappropriate shit all the way back. And I'm sitting there hearing it all.

"They discussed taking out drug dealers on this trip, in a hyperbolic fashion. But it was almost like she was bouncing it off Gilchrist and seeing how he responded."

Jim Gilchrist heatedly disputes that this conversation occurred. He flatly denied ever talking to Forde about her plans to rob drug dealers when asked about it by a reporter for the SPLC, saying, "This is bullshit," and claiming that Forde was simply a member of the audience.

Gilchrist also claimed, in published comments about the matter, that he had spoken with Mike Carlucci, and that they "both agree" that the reportage on these conversations was "made up": "[Neither] I, nor Mr. Carlucci ever had any discussion with Shawna Forde about her agenda to rob drug dealers," he wrote.

However, when asked about this by the SPLC reporter, Carlucci stood by the original reportage, saying it "was consistent with my comments in the interview."

# 12

## Adrenaline Rush

A border fence decorated by the Minutemen.
MAURICE SHERIF PHOTO

Shawna and the Belgian documentary maker have been talking music. Grunge rock, specifically. Nirvana, even more specifically. Shawna has been telling him how she knew Kurt Cobain personally. As he films her, "Smells Like Teen Spirit" comes up on the CD player in Shawna's Honda Element. They are sitting out in the Arizona desert. He asks her to name her favorite Nirvana song.

"I like a lot of them, but I love 'Teen Spirit,'" she says. "I really do. I love 'Teen Spirit.' That was like his first hit. His big one, you know?"

She pauses briefly, thinking. "I like all of 'em. Because if you listen to the words behind it—and he always talks about killing himself or shooting himself—because he was always really infatuated with death. But he never thought he would kill himself. I don't think he ever thought he was going to kill himself. But I think everyone knew he would eventually."

Sebastien Wielemans had written to Shawna several weeks before organizing the trip from Brussels to Arizona. He was employed by a Canadian broadcaster making short documentaries and was intrigued by the idea of a border project. He arrived at Shawna's camp south of Three Points in mid-October 2008.

As with the Nirvana talk, much of what Shawna says on the resulting video is pure bullshit, intended to impress her international audience. Shawna emphasizes her concern for rape victims and the women crossing the border, and she talks about how all the Minutemen want to do is "save the country."

There is a rare glimpse of honesty from Shawna, however, when she talks about why she goes out on border watches: "It's an adrenaline rush. You get addicted to it. It's an addiction. I'm an addict. I'm an adrenaline junkie." She giggles at that, then turns serious.

"So, you know, what do you say? I mean seriously. I think once you've lived certain ways, it's really hard to go and be humdrum. OK, I'm just going to sit at home, or I'm just going to work my nine to five Monday through Friday and have my weekends off, and in the evening I'll watch my favorite TV show and I'll go to bed by ten p.m. I mean, who—I'll never live that way. I'd rather die. I'd rather die. Put a bullet in my head. Because—forget it. Because to me, that would be death to me too."

As it happened, her husband, John Forde, agreed. He had just filed for divorce from her that week.

||

After Shawna's jaunts down to the desert in August 2007, John Forde had pretty much had his fill of his absentee marriage. He gave Shawna an ultimatum: either she started acting like a wife and contributing to their household instead of running off to the desert, or he would divorce her. Forde says he wanted to stay married, but it was up to Shawna to change things. And for awhile, she did; for much of the late part of 2007, she backed out of Minuteman activities.

In the meantime, she continued her pattern of getting into trouble and then claiming victimhood. "Every single time it was always somebody else's fault," John recalls. "It was never Shawna's fault."

Shawna worked for awhile at the Sears hair salon at the mall in Lynnwood. During that time, she kept coming home with Sears goods, including a large painting and various tools and gewgaws. John asked where she was getting it all, and she claimed it was all on the square.

Then one day she came home and grabbed everything she had brought home from Sears and put it in the car and had John drive her to the mall. She now explained that it really was all stuff that she'd purchased using her friend's employee discount, and that she wasn't going to let her friend get into trouble. She said that she'd worked it all out with the security people and everything was taken care of.

John, naturally, knew better than to believe her: "I kept saying, Shawna, everything is drama here."

Even more dismaying to John was the transformation in his wife since she had joined the Minutemen. He attended a couple of their gatherings, including an MCDC event in Yakima and the Immigration Summit at the Elks Lodge. He walked out of that one after about an hour: "It just wasn't my scene."

The vitriol the movement promoted bothered him the most. "It just is disgusting, the anger," he says. "I wanted to help her, but it is not my cup of tea to run around and do battle and be angry."

It obviously was Shawna's. Gradually there was an increase in Shawna's venom: "She began to get filled with hate and using the n-word," he says. It got to the point that he told her, "You aren't the person I knew."

She was giving voice to these sentiments on her blog—titled "Shawna's Corner" and written in her inimitably semi-illiterate style—at the MAD website. "See, there is a new white girl in town . . . this one is not afraid and will not tolerate this, not while I'm on post," she wrote. "We can all live in fear or we stand strong and tall and look the criminals in the eye and say 'No more.' I did not get involved in this movement to be a wallflower and as most of you know me you know I'm a hands on kind of gal. We have to do this so if you have area's that are known to be [drug] traffic area's and full of illegal's make a stand start with local law enforcement, take pictures and build a case file."

A vein of ethnic hatred and paranoia emerged as well. She began making offhanded remarks about "subhuman Mexicans." "After they cross the border," she wrote of immigrants, "they are taking over area's of our cities, neighborhoods, schools with their way of life witch is: 1 Corruption 2 Lie's 3 Drug dealer 4 welfare fraud 5 stealing 6 Filthiness 7 Gang code of ethics 8 violence 9 no respect for existing Americans 10 Hate. I could continue this list I have seen first hand and have been getting to know people in the Hispanic community so that when they say we should respect the plight of these pour people do not be fooled for one moment they think we are weak and stupid plus we don't speak their language so they operate their own life styles under the radar. I would say 90% of all patrons here are illegal some just got her yesterday. These are not proud people they are nothing more than thugs."

The hiatus from the Minutemen ended soon after Jim Gilchrist named Shawna Forde his "director of border operations" in February 2008 and she hosted his visit to Ellensburg. He assigned Shawna to lead a Minuteman Project unit down at an April border watch in Campo, California, led by Britt Craig, the Minuteman who, only a few years before, had defiantly declined to recognize Gilchrist as an organizational leader and had gotten into a tussle on the street with the local MMP leader.

It's unclear whether Shawna actually went down to Campo in April. She did, however, show up there in August. Craig's wife, Deborah, later explained in a statement: "In August of 2008, Shawna Forde came [to] the border at Campo, CA and contacted Campo Minuteman Britt Craig. She did not make any comments to indicate she was unstable or violent. She had a Minutemen Civil Defense Corps badge so she presumably had been vetted by the group. Minutemen Civil Defense Corps charges a fee and does a background check."

The statement added that Forde and Britt Craig went to their operations center, dubbed Camp Vigilance, in separate vehicles, "where she was given full access by the caretaker. She purchased a bulletproof vest from the caretaker and indicated she planned to spend the night. She indicated that she primarily did her border watching in AZ, that she had her own group, Minutemen American Defense, and we did not hear [from] her directly again."

Chris Simcox's MCDC organization in Tombstone also organized a border watch in Arizona that April, held at a private ranch about forty miles south of Three Points called King's Anvil Ranch, right in the middle of the Altar Valley. Lasting only a week, it was part of MCDC's announced strategy of holding more frequent border watches of shorter duration.

They held another "muster" at King's Anvil in mid-June. Reportedly, Shawna Forde showed up there, too, presenting herself as Gilchrist's MMP representative in the field. She and her cohorts were asked to leave, MCDC officials later claimed.

"They had a military, bad-ass posture about them," Chris Simcox later told a reporter. "She had made a comment at that time that they were going to be stopping any drug dealers that they came into contact with. They were going to be carrying long arms and not be letting people pass."

Simcox claimed that MCDC officials kicked Forde out of the camp and contacted the Border Patrol, whose agents "went out and talked to them. And they B.S.'d them [the agents] as well," Simcox said.

But Shawna was evidently inspired by the Altar Valley ranch watch, because she then set about organizing her own watch in the Altar Valley that fall. This was to be a monthlong affair, headquartered at a desert-ranch RV park about eleven miles south of Three Points called Caballo Loco, which MCDC had also used as a camping facility for its musters.

In the meantime, with her daughter, Jaszmin, in tow, she returned to Glenn Spencer's ranch outside of Hereford in August and once again took up occupancy in the guest RV. By this time, however, he had gotten wind of Shawna's multiple sexual dalliances during her previous stay, and he asked her to leave after a little while. She asked if she could leave Jaszmin behind at the RV for a few weeks while she did more scouting work for her fall event. He refused and says he instructed his staff not to let her return.

Shawna instead returned to Everett and dumped Jaszmin with some friends. She showed up at the Caballo Loco the first week of October in her shiny new copper-colored Honda Element. She had paid $30,000 for it.

She arrived knowing her marriage with John Forde was finished, obliterated by this latest spate of border-watching travel and absence from their home. Before she left, he told her he was filing for divorce.

"Are you sure this is what you want?" she had asked.

"Yes," he answered. "I want you out of my life. I want this madness to stop."

||

It was at the Caballo Loco that Shawna Forde won most of her media attention before the murders in Arivaca. Sebastien Wielemans was only one of several European documentarians to shoot footage of Minuteman American Defense's Delta One Operations (as Shawna had taken to calling them) in Arizona. Another crew from Norway also arrived and obtained similar shots of Shawna and her ragtag crew cruising the desert.

Shawna explained her philosophy to the filmmakers: "We're not a Third World country. We're not getting people—scientists and doctors—here, OK? We're getting the poorest of the poor. We're getting Third World values into a first-rate country, which is dropping all of our rates way down.

"This is my country first. If you want to become an American, there's a process you need to go through, because a lot of people do go through that process. So it's important for us also to secure these borders. I think after

9/11, I think it made us realize what a target we are, and how many people out there want to see us dead. And I'm not sure what part of 'I want to kill you' we don't understand, but I understand it. And because I do understand that, I want to do my part in helping to get these borders secured and educate Americans on the issues of the southern border. And there's a lot of issues down here."

This was also where Chuck Stonex first met Shawna Forde and became part of her organization. You can see Stonex in some of the documentary footage, defending their presence in the desert and decrying illegal immigration.

Shawna posted a number of videos from her Altar Valley operations. The handheld clips often focus on the garbage left in the desert by border crossers. One notable video shows Forde claiming to have found a "rape tree," a spot where the illicit coyotes would assault their female clients. The weirdest video, by far, features Shawna claiming that Border Patrol had found bodies of drug mules duped by terrorists into carrying radioactive materials hidden inside their marijuana loads. Forde explained that the smugglers' bodies couldn't be touched because "the radiation is so heavy [it] will kill you on contact."

A Boston-based photographer named Andrew Ong came out to try to document the Minutemen's activities. His shots—which later ran as a gallery at the online magazine *Daily Beast*—show Shawna stalking through the sand in high heels and tank tops.

Ong told Scott North that Forde spent the bulk of her time on the border laboring over emails or posts for the MAD website. Ong photographed Shawna's grand new tattoo: shoulder-to-shoulder ink across her back, the Minuteman American Defense logo—an eagle crest with the legend on its chest "Rule Of Law"—demonstrating her final allegiance.

In an eerily prescient scene, he also captured Shawna wading into a vacant desert home, gun in hand, wearing a dress and high heels, as she and her fellow Minutemen search for illegal immigrants. She was locked and loaded.

Ong tagged along on one of Shawna's night patrols, for which Shawna furnished some night-vision equipment. As the patrol stopped to check a brushy area for smugglers, Ong watched Shawna pick up a couple of rocks and heave them over the heads of her Minutemen.

One of the rocks hit a hard object, producing a sound like a ricocheting bullet. Sure enough, the Minutemen were convinced they were being shot at and scrambled for cover. Forde was back behind them, quietly laughing. She saw the look on Ong's face.

"Have some fun, Andrew," she said, grinning. "Have some fun."

The next day, Forde ordered the Minutemen to report the incident to the Border Patrol, saying they had been shot at. She also posted a video of the incident on YouTube as evidence of the hazards Minutemen faced while patrolling the nation's borders.

Indeed, Shawna and the Minutemen eagerly regaled the Norwegian film crew with the tale of their harrowing close call a few days later. Stonex, who was one of the Minutemen in the group, described the event from his clearly gullible perspective: "We got ready to come out, and we spotted some fresh tracks, the driver seen some fresh tracks, and we got out and was investigating the fresh tracks, and probably got twenty-five, thirty yards down this little wash, and all of a sudden there was a gunshot and a ricochet that kind of fell between me and the cameraman. And we never did figure out who it was, but it was close. Some say it was a warning shot. I say it was a bad shot."

It was also an opportunity to tout their own bravery. "I was out there with a flashlight," Stonex added. "I mean, I was the prime target, I was the one that was fully armed. But that's the risks we take here on this border watch. Right now it's mostly drug cartels out here instead of people looking for a better way of life. It's just these guys trying to destroy somebody's better way of life."

Stonex said it had been awhile since he had been shot at. "It was my first experience since I left Vietnam," he told the filmmakers. "So you know, hey look—it's what price are you willing to pay to protect your country? Here you got a problem going on here. You got drugs coming over from Mexico and South America by the truckload. I'm willing to pay whatever price I have to protect my family and my country, you know."

Shawna made sure the journalists knew what stakes were at play: "Shootings and deaths occur on a daily basis out here," she told them.

The whole scene left Andrew Ong shaking his head. "It was very, very bizarre," he said. "It was not at all what I expected."

||

Much of the reason Shawna got such an adrenaline rush from her life as a Minuteman was that it so closely approximated the kind of tough-guy action movies she loved to watch. She was out on the front lines, stalking the desert with a gun, making headlines, getting media attention. But up until the fall of 2008, all of her talk about investigating drug-cartel activity in the area had been mostly just that—talk.

Then she finally had a breakthrough that October in Arivaca. She made a connection with a drug-cartel figure. They had a little macho showdown at the bar. They shared some cocaine. Then he showed her his stash house. She took pictures. It was all incredibly exhilarating.

At least, that was the picture she painted in a breathless email she sent to a handful of Minutemen, including Jim Gilchrist, on November 3. She described how she had descended into the murky underworld of drug smuggling in Arivaca, leaving her deeply fearful: "Everyday I almost expect it to be my last. I have moved Jaszmin 'daughter' to a safe and undisclosed location," she explained.

I met my contact in a Catina in Arivaca he had received a call I was in the area with a couple of others so he came to check me out, When this happened I order my guys around in front of him so he recognized that I was a leader " it's a respect thing" anyway I knew in my gut he was important but when we made eye contact it was confirmed he had eyes of a killer. I ordered my guys to leave me there so I could work it out. I wanted a knife so went to car with them and had them give me a knife which was a sorry excuse for one but I took it and put it into my bra, armed with a cell phone a lipstick and now a knife I went back in.

Wow as soon as they left it was on I was surrounded by the most dangerous looking group of drug cartel that you see in movies and it was not a flirt session it was "Who are you, why are you in Arivaca? and they were hitting me hard and fast so I could see the leader sitting and watching me from the side to see how I would respond, I turned to one on my left told him to back off my grill and to go sit the fuck down because he was annoying me.

I seen the leader nod and then he started to laugh and came and sat by me next thing I know I'm in a conversation with him and we had the whole side of the bar to ourselves they all went elsewhere just from a nod. He was testing me so he asked if I wanted to get high I said sure, This is not a place or time to be holier then thou. So we got up went outside in the courtyard and I followed him to the bathroom on our way down my knife fell out of my bra he saw it fall I quickly recovered it and said ohh "my lipstick" I did not think he was paying that close attention.

we get in the bathroom and he takes out his 45 slides it back to cock it and looks me dead in the eye. If I could share with you the feeling in that 8x10 room "chilling" then I looked him straight in the eye and say nice gun. He puts it down on the sink we laugh "nervous laugh"

At that point, as Shawna described it, they went back to the bar, and then after a nighttime walk about the town, he took her to his "stash house." At one point, she claimed, he asked to see her knife and laughed at what she produced, then gave her a better-quality switch blade of his own. "So we connected and were relaxed," she reported. "I am planning on going back today sometime and hang I need to get his address and more pics."

Shawna attached the photos from the stash house with the email, which was titled: "Stash house Do not share these!!!!!!!!! it would be my life." Naturally, this meant that it was immediately distributed widely among the Minutemen, both in Washington State and elsewhere. As with many of Shawna's emails, it caused a brief sensation in those circles.

It later emerged, of course, that the "cartel guy" with whom she had shared cocaine was none other than Albert Gaxiola. For some reason, she thought he was honcho of some sort, while in reality he was about a third-tier gofer, in charge of other gofers. But she didn't need to know that. He was going to be her connection in Arivaca. If he played his cards right, she was going to be very useful.

||

Shawna was not able to hang out in Arizona for very long after her big break-through, however. There was a little problem with money: she didn't have any. There was also the problem of the impending divorce from John Forde. The two were closely related.

John knew the divorce was the right thing when all of his family members—including his children, who despised Shawna—started reconnecting with him, now that Shawna was out of the picture. "The people in my family were like, 'Oh, thank God. Thank God,'" he says.

In order to make the divorce possible, John had to take out a second mortgage on their properties. He learned in the course of doing so that Shawna, who always had cash on hand, was living on credit. She'd bought the Element entirely on a line of credit and had not made any payments on it.

He also discovered that Shawna had just been stuffing all of her bills into a shoe box. So he took them all, created a spreadsheet, got a high-interest loan, and paid them all off, including her jewelry bills; he even got her current on her car payments. So when Shawna returned to Everett in early December, she had her economic house largely in order, thanks to John.

Even so, she kept after him. "She kept wanting more money," John recalls. "I said, 'Listen, I'm not going to give you more money.'"

In the meantime, Shawna had found a new boyfriend. His name was Thomas Wayne Gibler, a slender, six-foot man with tattoos and a rap sheet longer than Shawna's. Gibler in fact had fourteen felony convictions to his name, including a panoply of assault and drug charges as well as a high-speed police chase. The state had designated him a high-risk violent offender and placed him under active supervision. Apparently, he was just what Shawna was looking for; she introduced him to several people in Snohomish County as her boyfriend.

John, however, had not met him. At least not yet.

The divorce was being handled by a legal outfit called Peaceful Separations in Everett. One day, Shawna came in to sign some papers in the divorce and wound up chatting up the paralegal handling the papers. "She asked the woman, 'What would happen if John died, or something happened?'"

In fact, Washington is what is known as a "community property" state— that is, a spouse is entitled to all of a decedent's property if that person dies intestate, without a will. As it happened, John was worth close to a half-million dollars at the time. If that fell to Shawna, it would be her biggest haul ever: "She would have got the most money had I died compared to anything she has done—big time," John says.

The paralegal thought that Shawna's query was odd and brought in the lawyer because of it. The attorneys in turn gave John a heads up that Shawna was floating those kinds of questions and advised him to keep trickling money to her so that he could get out of the situation as quickly and cleanly as possible. So he did—not large sums, but enough, he thought, to keep her at bay.

John felt liberated too. It was December, Christmas was approaching, and he was enjoying life for the first time in awhile, going skiing and hanging out with his old friends. Some of them started telling him stories about Shawna, stories they had kept quiet about out of respect for John's marriage. Now that it was over, they were telling him the truth. The more he heard, the more relieved he was to be done with her.

It had mostly been amicable. The only bump in the proceedings came when John rekeyed the locks to their duplex. Shawna complained bitterly to him, calling from what she said was an attorney's office and insisting that she had a right to be in the home until the divorce was final. She threatened to bring cops if he didn't give her a key. He caved and gave her a key to the back door.

Other than that, the proceedings were going smoothly—almost too smoothly for anything involving Shawna. "My buddies even said, 'John, something is going on. It is too easy,'" John recalls.

On the afternoon of December 22, he got what he thought was a strange call from Shawna. "She asked if I was going to be home," he recalls. "She was going to pick up some of her stuff." She asked him when he was going to be home, something she'd never done before.

The whole situation felt ominous to John. He had felt twinges of fear and found himself looking out his window irregularly. What he suspected was that if Shawna wanted to hurt him, she would trash one of his Porsche Boxsters, in which he took a great deal of pride.

John knocked off work at five p.m. as usual and went home to their duplex. He was still in his work clothes, sitting on the couch, watching the evening news with Charlie, his Jack Russell terrier, snuggled next to him, when the stranger walked in.

The living room and kitchen were on the second floor of the duplex, so the man—a thin Caucasian of average height, mustachioed, his hands in his pockets—had entered from below, through the back door. At first, having heard nothing until the man suddenly appeared from the stairwell, John thought it was simply someone who had come in the wrong door and into the wrong home.

Then the shooting began. "He came around the corner, and within seconds he pulled out his right hand and started shooting," John recalls. "It was one second, maybe two. I was ready to say something, and he started to shoot."

Being shot, John says, is not the way it is in the movies. When you're hit by a bullet, he says, you're done; your body gives out, and you can't move. "You are down for the fucking count, let me tell you," he says. And you observe the strangest things.

John was looking at the man's clothing. It was cheap clothing but brand new: a tan windbreaker, tan pants, tan ball cap. "It looked as if he'd picked it all up at JCPenney or Sears in the work-clothes section," John recalls. "The first thing I thought was Shawna got him an outfit to kill me at Sears. She had a card."

The man did not handle the gun professionally, either: he fired from a crooked arm at his waist, like they do in old noir films. That may be why John survived.

The first shot hit his left arm, then the next shot hit his right arm. One of those rounds passed through the arm and pierced his lungs. The man fired three more rounds into John's torso, with one hitting his lower right abdomen, another hitting his liver and diaphragm, and one more round lodged in his back. Thinking he was done, the man turned and fled back down the stairs.

John lay there, stunned, helpless, smelling his own flesh smoldering where the bullets had entered, knowing he was now bleeding, profusely, to death. At first all he could do was wonder: "All I could think of was 'What did I do? What did I do?'" But as he realized who the only person who might want him dead might be, he turned angry, and that probably saved him.

John had a lifelong dread of being shot. "I know what bullets do to you. You don't die right away. That's the horror in my mind of being shot. You know you are going to die." Lying on the couch, he realized: "My worst nightmare has come true."

At first he tried making noise to attract his neighbors' attention, but when there was no response, he realized he could reach the phone, since he had not been shot in either leg. He half-walked, half-crawled to where the phone was and, using the remnants of his bloodied hands, dialed 911.

He was intent on letting them know right away that he knew Shawna was behind it all. "I just started screaming my name, my address, her name, her address. I'm shot. I'm hit I'm dying. Get somebody here."

"I said her name a hundred times: 'I'm getting a divorce. She's trying to kill me. Nobody would do this to me. Shawna Forde is trying to kill me.'"

He doesn't remember how long it took for the ambulance to arrive, but it seemed to take forever, especially because they tried entering through his front door and had to jigger the gurney around on his stairs; he recalls that on the way out, they nearly dropped him over the side of the exterior stairs. He finally lost consciousness en route to the hospital and thought he was dying as he did so. He was in excruciating pain and barely able to breathe, and as blackness closed in, he thought he saw the white light so many people with near-death experiences describe.

Doctors went to work immediately, even though they did not give him much of a chance: he had lost too much blood, had suffered too many egregious injuries. Still, John was alive the next morning, and the next, and the next. He remembers none of it, though.

Shawna in fact was taken into custody that evening and questioned about the shooting. She denied having anything to do with it and suggested that it was likely the work of drug cartels in Arizona that she had angered. She was released that night and told to stay in town.

She wasted no time. The next day, she and Tommy Gibler moved into the duplex, ignoring the crime-scene tape. She had John's wallet and credit cards and promptly began using them. She never went up to John's hospital room to visit him or check on him.

It wasn't until four days after the shooting, the day after Christmas, that John's family learned he had been shot and was in critical condition in the hospital. Shawna hadn't bothered to contact them. They only found out because one of John's commuting buddies had pieced everything together and tracked him down to the hospital. The buddy had then contacted Shawna to get John's computer and cell phone back, but Shawna wouldn't let him have the latter. Still, he was able to get the phone numbers for John's family, and he called them to let them know. They all came to the hospital within the hour, found that John had been registered under a wrong name, and bulled their way up to see him.

John was in a medically induced coma at the time. All he remembers is being on a long spiritual journey and seeing the world from a removed state, and then realizing he was still alive and wanted to live. A short time later he woke up.

The doctors who had worked on him were amazed, and they came by frequently to tell him how lucky he was. "You are a miracle," they told him. "It is just a miracle you are alive."

Indeed: John was out of the hospital in twelve days. He retreated to a safe place out of town and began piecing things back together, while Shawna and Tommy Gibler helped themselves to his old residence. While he was recovering, he discovered that Shawna had forged his name on a check for $3,000 from his credit union and had freely used his debit and credit cards and rung up several thousand dollars' worth there. He also figured out that, prior to her most recent Arizona sojourn, she had obtained a $9,000 loan on their joint account without his knowledge, also using a forged version of his signature.

John had long since stopped being amazed at Shawna's audacity. Indeed, she had already moved on to what she liked to call "the next level."

||

After her initial interview with Everett detectives about the murder attempt on John Forde, Shawna began assiduously avoiding any kind of follow-up interview, finding one excuse after another to put police off. "We've made several attempts to schedule a meeting with Ms. Forde. We've not been successful," an Everett police spokesman told Scott North two months later.

Exactly a week after John was shot, Shawna called Everett police from the duplex and claimed she had been beaten and raped. Officers arrived to find her on the kitchen floor, her knees to her chest, sobbing and moaning and saying she had been raped. There was a little blood on the shower curtain, but police could find few signs of injuries.

Shawna was so groggy-seeming that they wondered if she was on drugs; her eyelids were fluttering, and she appeared to be slipping in and out of consciousness. They loaded her onto a gurney. But just as she was being wheeled out the door, she ordered the crews to stop for a minute. She needed her purse.

One of the investigating officers noticed that cuts on Forde's forearms and thighs—which she later told investigators were wounds from the knife her attackers used—were in fact oddly superficial and shallow, consistent with the injuries seen when people deliberately hurt themselves. Police call these "hesitation wounds." They had in fact already scabbed over and appeared to be at least a day old.

The next day, even though she had not yet given a statement to police about her rape, Shawna got on the phone and called Scott North at the *Herald*, asking if he was going to report on her rape in the Everett paper. "I was assaulted. I was raped. I was beaten. I was cut with a knife," she told him. She knew the rape kit would come back negative, as it eventually did, but that it would be several weeks before anyone would find that out.

North made a few phone calls and figured out that there was a deeper problem with Shawna. He is a veteran newsman and had spent at least a portion of his time as a reporter in the 1990s dealing with the outbreak of right-wing extremists—militiamen, tax protesters, and "constitutionalists"—who had beset portions of Snohomish County and western Washington generally, so he was aware of their proclivities. Moreover, his news sense, honed by thirty years of experience, told him that there might be a real story there—just not necessarily the one Shawna Forde wanted to tell everyone.

Shawna's version, of course, had in short order been blasted out on the MAD website. She posted it the day after she called North, giving her own harrowing account of her vile mistreatment at the hands of likely Latino gang members. It included photos she had taken supposedly showing her bruises, though even an untrained eye could see that these looked suspiciously like makeup jobs.

The *Herald* ran a story the next day. Jim Gilchrist's Minuteman Project website picked up and promoted Shawna's version of the story, as did the right-wing blogosphere, which began recounting her tale unquestioningly. (At Sound Politics, the leading right-wing political blog for Washington

State politicos, the contributor "pudge"—who had posted Shawna's account uncritically—scathingly attacked anyone who questioned her story, or worse yet, suggested she might have had a hand in John's shooting.) A conservative webcast called No Compromise Radio conducted an interview with Shawna in which she described three or four assailants shooting her husband and then a like number coming back to beat and rape her.

Shawna had by then gained a large number of enemies among the ranks of Minutemen and other nativists—most notably, Jeff Schwilk of the San Diego Minutemen as well as William Gheen of American Legal Immigration PAC—who castigated Gilchrist for his gullibility. "Jim!" shouted one Schwilk missive. "Don't be a moron!"

Shawna was dismayed that anyone could suggest she had anything to do with John's shooting or that she had faked her rape, calling such notions "ridiculous." She had her defenders, too, including Chuck Stonex, who told the *Herald*: "It happened. Absolutely. I have no doubt in my mind that it happened."

Jim Gilchrist defended her just as vociferously. He told her critics (and his) that what mattered more was her ability to overcome a troubled past. "She is no whiner," he wrote. "She is a stoic struggler who has chosen to put country, community and a yearning for a civilized society ahead of avarice and self-glorifying ego."

When detectives finally spoke to her on January 13, Shawna told them she had been feeding snacks to Charlie, John's dog, when a Hispanic man appeared out of nowhere and punched her on the left side of her face, near her eye. "I just went down immediately," she told them. "Bam! I just remember hitting the, I mean, and then everything was like really dizzy, just starry, you know, like I was seeing stars you know, like they say you see stars? Well, you do."

There were two, maybe three attackers, she said. One of them had on a black ski mask, but she could tell he was Hispanic. The second was a young white male with a scraggly beard and mustache, who used a knife to threaten and subdue her. They were speaking both English and Spanish, saying things like "*chinga la puta*" and "let's drown the bitch." They then proceeded to rape her anally and vaginally, she said, using a miniature souvenir baseball bat. The attack lasted about fifteen or twenty minutes.

Investigators asked if she knew her attackers. "No," she replied. "But I do remember hearing like some 'weezie' or 'weasel' or something. . . . So, I don't know what this is about."

Someone had written the number thirteen on her kitchen floor in black magic marker. The police asked her why they might have done that.

"I think that somebody did that just to be a jerk," she told them. "And just maybe to scare me or to make me think it was something else. . . . I didn't really make a lot of it to be honest . . ."

"So even now you're not making a big deal out of that?"

"No, because after, If you really think about it, and after I've thought about it and talked to people—if it was, I mean there are MS-13 in north Everett, I mean they're out, they are there . . ."

"But had you had anything to do with them?"

"Well, other than going after their cartel operations, no. But you know, I'm not one of their friendliest people. They don't like me, I mean; you know I'm not probably on their top list of favorites."

"Aren't you more concerned with illegals crossing the border; just to come over here to work?"

"No. I'm more concerned about the drug cartels."

Two days later, on January 15, Shawna's mother, Rena Caudle, got a strange call at her California home from her daughter. "She called me that evening, and she says, 'There's somebody following me in a white car,'" Rena recalls. "And she says, 'I'm going to duck into this alley here and see if I lost them. And I'll call you back later.'" Then she hung up.

A little while later, Kathy Dameron got a similar call in Yakima from Shawna in Everett. She said she was walking back from the Eagles lodge, and they started shooting the breeze. The only thing that was odd was that Shawna kept telling her where she was at the moment.

Suddenly, it got tense. "Oh my God, there is a car following me," Shawna told Kathy. Then she said there were two cars—one light, one dark. Shawna said she was ducking into an alleyway and then said she thought she had lost them. Then Shawna cried out: "Oh my God! Oh my God! Oh my God! Oh shit!"

Kathy Dameron hung up and called the Everett police directly and told them what she had heard and Shawna's location. She called Shawna back immediately.

Shawna answered and told Kathy she had been shot in the arm. "The cops are on the way," she told Kathy.

Kathy recalls, "She said one shot had gone past her head; that she was turned sideways, and two went into her arm."

Police arrived and took Shawna to the hospital and gathered witness statements. Nobody had seen the shooting, but some of the neighbors had heard gunfire and had come out to investigate.

Jim Gilchrist expressed his surprise at the spate of violence directed at

Shawna. "I don't think this is a hoax. I don't know what to think," he said. "I'm certainly in shock. We have to let law enforcement play it out and see what is going on."

||

The shooting was the final straw for her brother, Merrill Metzger, who knew that Jaszmin was living with Shawna at the time. He drove up with his son from California the next day to retrieve his niece and bring her down to the family in California, so she could be safer.

Shawna had told him that Scott North had written a story about the attempt on John's life that included a police sketch of the gunman, taken from John's description. When he arrived in Everett and they had settled in on the couch at Shawna's place, where she was hanging out with Tommy Gibler, he got curious.

"So I asked her for that article, and we were both, my son and I, sitting there looking at the drawing," Merrill recalls. "And I looked up, and all of a sudden Shawna looks at me and she said, 'That drawing kind of looks like you.'

"And I said, 'No, not really.' We were laughing.

"And I said, 'Actually, it looks like him'"—he pointed to Gibler—"the guy that was there with her. Immediately the laughing was over."

They drove home the next day. "When I got out of Everett, and I was back home with my niece, I called the Everett Police Department, and I told them, 'Hey, that guy that's with Shawna right now fits that description of the shooter to a T.'"

Everett police, however, have never made an arrest in the attempted murder of John Forde. Even though John eventually made a positive identification to police, and neighbors who saw the gunman climb over John's back fence that night have done so as well, a police department spokesman insists that—short of finding the gun used and the clothes worn—there is not enough physical evidence to bring a case to court.

||

On February 5, Shawna Forde came in to the offices of the *Herald* for a two-hour interview. Scott North had conducted a thorough investigation of her the previous two months and had uncovered all the secrets of her past: her felony conviction at age eleven, her career as a prostitute and petty criminal, her many lies and deceptions.

The interview was conducted in a special room and was video recorded.

What's most remarkable, watching those videos now, is how utterly unflappable Shawna was as North laid out before her the devastating results of his investigation. And at the end, she just smiled confidently and said, "It's not about the past. It's about what we do today, and trying to secure the borders tomorrow."

The story ran on February 22 on the front page of the Sunday paper. Shortly thereafter, Shawna—who never did give police that follow-up interview for detectives about John's shooting—took off for Arizona again, and this time she did not come back.

# 13

# The Bad Boy

Jason Eugene Bush's booking photo.
COURTESY PIMA COUNTY SHERIFF'S OFFICE

No one, except Shawna Forde and Jason Bush themselves, really knows how the two of them met. Shawna has largely remained mum on the matter, though she wrote to a friend in Everett that "he was sent to me by a national leader so I assumed he was okay." Jason Bush later claimed, in an interview with Kim Smith of the *Arizona Daily Star*, that they had never met in person until that day in late May 2009 when she picked him up at his girlfriend's house in Meadville, Arizona, and drove off with him into the night. He also claimed that they had initially made contact while he was conducting "research" using information from the Southern Poverty Law Center's profile of Shawna, which had appeared in the *Intelligence Report* in Spring 2008. He also claimed to have had contact with Chris Simcox and his Tombstone-based Minuteman Civil Defense Corps, and to have come into contact with Shawna through Simcox.

The problem with believing anything that comes out of Jason Bush's mouth, however, is that there's an overwhelming probability that it is false or at best a grotesque distortion. In that regard, he and Shawna were a perfectly toxic match. Indeed, their ability to lie successfully to each other—each had completely conned the other, just as both of them were conned by another prodigious liar named Albert Gaxiola—played a critical role in the tragedy that followed.

What we do know is that Shawna became enamored of her new recruit, Gunny, sometime in May and decided to name him her "Operations Director." In an announcement on Jim Gilchrist's Minuteman Project website, she touted his vast military record, including his six overseas tours and various medals: "He received a Purple Heart, Silver and Bronze star, Combat Infantry Badge and a Presidential citation for his actions in the Special Forces. He will be in charge of all operations on the Southern Border, assisting in command decisions Recon and Tactical training."

Of course, for reasons of "operational security," she couldn't reveal his real name: Jason Eugene Bush.

Gunny had a packet of military identification papers to back up all of his claims, too. They were very convincing-looking, certainly good enough for Shawna to be convinced. Chuck Stonex, an actual veteran, was taken in by them too.

Like so much that surrounded Shawna Forde, it was all a lie—but on a scale that made Shawna look like a mild-mannered scofflaw. She had met her match and then some.

Jason Bush had in fact never served a day in the military, let alone in a combat unit. He instead had a long record as a career criminal. He had spent much of the 1990s as a violent white supremacist living in the Pacific Northwest. And he was a serial killer.

All of which, in the end, made him just perfect for Shawna's needs.

||

Jason Bush even tried telling a few people that he had served in Vietnam, which was not remotely possible, since he was born August 11, 1974, well after military involvement in that conflict had ended. But, like the name Gunny, it probably just sounded good.

Though he was born in LaGrande, Oregon, Bush says he spent most of his childhood years in Sandpoint, Idaho, and then switched back and forth between there and Benton County, Washington, after his parents divorced and he was placed in foster care. It was in Benton County, as a thirteen-year-old, that he first began running afoul of the law: stealing a microrecorder, charged with a weapons offense for bringing a bayonet along on a school field trip, charged with another weapons offense for bringing a knife and razors to school—all before he had turned fourteen. Then he moved back to Sandpoint, and in a few years he was committing petty crimes there—mostly a string of five burglaries, as well as writing bad checks.

In 1994, when Bush was nineteen, he was arrested in Kansas for burglary. While he was doing time there, he grabbed a female corrections officer and threatened to kill her with a toothbrush. He was charged with battery against a police officer in the process and wound up doing real prison time. He later claimed that it was while in prison in Kansas that he became an Aryan Brother—a member of the white-supremacist prison gang. When he got out and returned to Idaho in 1996, he was promptly busted on the old bad-check charges and wound up being placed on probation in Idaho. In May 1997, he got a job as a welder at Far West Iron Works in Wenatchee, Washington, and moved there.

In addition to whatever ideology he picked up in Kansas, it was clear that sometime during his residency in northern Idaho he had been exposed to the white-supremacist ideology of the Aryan Nations, the Hayden Lake–based Christian Identity organization that had been producing criminal misery of various kinds in the Panhandle since the late 1970s. Everyone who knew him in Wenatchee during that time remembers him as a big, violent, scary neo-Nazi of the classic skinhead mold, wearing leathers and combat boots intending for stomping foes in a fight.

That played out the night of July 24, 1997, when Bush and one of his skinhead pals were stalking the streets of Wenatchee and came upon a homeless Latino man named Hector Lopez Partida sleeping on the street, huddled under a few blankets. Jason Bush picked up a slab of concrete and threw it atop the blankets, and then, after his buddy kicked the man a few times, he piled on top of him with a knife and began stabbing.

Lopez Partida stood up and screamed and staggered away, bleeding. He collapsed a little way away and was barely alive when paramedics arrived a little later. When asked who had stabbed him, he only was able to gasp, "*Gavachos*" (white guys). He died a few minutes later. Jason Bush and his buddy had run away by that time, though Jason tore off his bloody shirt and left it at the scene.

Jason decided he was hungry after that, so they went to a diner and ordered a big meal, even though Bush had the man's blood on his jeans. "Jason ate food like nothing had happened," his buddy told the FBI later.

It's possible the killing was just for fashion's sake. The next day, Bush and his buddy traveled to Hayden Lake to participate in the annual Aryan

Congress, the big Northwest gathering of white supremacists that always featured cross burnings and long sermons from Aryan Nations chief Richard Butler. Both men were wearing yellow laces in their Doc Martens boots—the skinhead way of making the statement that the wearer had killed a minority.

Bush bragged openly to his neo-Nazi friends, including an acquaintance named Jonathan Bumstead, about having killed a Mexican man. A couple of months later, on the night of September 21, Bush and three of his gang headed out into the countryside for "target practice." The foursome had scarcely emerged from the car when there was a gunshot. The other two men came running and found Jon Bumstead lying on the ground, wounded in the back and bleeding and moaning for help. As they watched, Bush walked up to him and shot him point-blank in the head.

Bush coolly collected his shell casings and the shotgun Bumstead had been carrying, then turned his gun on the other two and threatened to kill them if they ever told anyone. He told them Bumstead was a "race traitor" who had a contract on his life put out by the Aryan Nations.

The other two men never believed him. Their impression was that Jason Bush just killed Jon Bumstead for fun.

"This isn't the first time I've killed somebody, and it won't be the last time," he told them—perhaps as a way of threatening them into silence. It worked: neither man came forward until after the murders in Arivaca, when Jason Bush was safely behind bars.

||

Jason Bush claimed he had mental problems. At least, he told the court that was why, on November 28, 1997, he got in a truck full of welding equipment owned by his employer and drove off with it. When he was arrested a week later, he had dyed his hair red.

Bush filed a request for a psychiatric examination, claiming he had long ago been diagnosed with schizophrenia and bipolar disorder. "For most of my life since the age of eleven or twelve, I have had an experience of being outside myself, of watching another person take over my body," Bush said in a 1998 court declaration. "I start going haywire and I don't know what I'm doing or why. It's like being in a daze. I don't know why it happens and it scares me. It's like someone else crawls under my skin. It is very frustrating."

His family members told authorities that Bush had long been prescribed medication to treat his mental illness, but when he went off the regimen, he "lives in a fantasy world."

However, there is no discussion of any mental illness in any of Bush's previous corrections records, including those from his juvenile years. The psychiatrists who did examine him in January 1998 concluded that he was in fact perfectly competent to stand trial and understood fully the difference between right and wrong. The implication of those findings was that Bush wasn't so much mentally ill as he was a manipulative and violent psychopath.

Bush promptly substantiated such a diagnosis: in March 1998, while still being held in the Chelan County jail, he viciously assaulted another inmate. Bush simply walked into the man's cell and began hitting him until the other inmate lost consciousness. He told fellow inmates he did it because he thought the man was gay.

By the time all the cases for which he had been arrested—which did not, however, include the two murders—had been processed through the court system, Jason Bush faced six years in prison. He served most of that term, and with time off for good behavior, he was back on the street by September 2003, living in Sandpoint again. Along the way, he had picked up a number of tattoos including one reading "white power," another declaring that he was an "Aryan Brother," one reading "Special Forces," a "Recon Viper" tattoo, and a spider web on his hand. This last one was common among white supremacists who had done prison time, but it also is known to signify that the wearer has killed a brown, black, Jewish, or gay person.

After that, Bush mostly stayed out of trouble. He stayed in northern Idaho until 2005, then drifted for several years, and eventually got a job doing maintenance work at the Skywalk on the Grand Canyon in Arizona sometime in 2008. He was working there when he met his girlfriend, Melinda, who worked in sales at the tourist attraction. In October, she "fell head over heels in love" with the big man, who talked often about his past military service and showed her the dossier of papers he had to prove it. She left her then-husband and got her own place in Meadview, a tourist town close to the Grand Canyon, in December. Jason Bush moved into her home in January.

While on a trip to Texas in August 2008, however, he assaulted a man near Waco and was charged with a felony, but the next month in court, it was pleaded down to a misdemeanor and a fine. Still, the charge was a violation of Bush's probation, and his employer was informed. They looked into his background further and found a number of inconsistencies that he refused to explain. The Skywalk management fired him in March 2009.

Bush told Melinda he was going to reenlist. He told a number of other people that, including the owner of a local convenience store—whom he then ripped off by cashing bogus money orders for a total of $2,000.

"He was a huge con artist," Tracy Van Wormer, owner of Meadview Market, later told a *Green Valley News* reporter. "I'm sitting on about $2,000 worth of counterfeit money orders from him." The bank returned them, telling her they were old money orders that had been washed and rewritten.

Bush used his convincing-looking military papers to become a member of the local VFW post, largely so he could enjoy their cheaper drinks. The post's senior vice commander, Lavern Allsman, told the reporter he had been taken.

"He said he was in Vietnam," said Allsman of the thirty-four-year-old Bush. "It looked good on paper."

Finally, on May 26, 2009, Bush followed through and headed out to reenlist—or so he told Melinda: "I came home from work one night and he said he was leaving today," she later testified. "He said somebody was going to pick him up."

At around eleven p.m., a copper-colored Honda Element pulled up in her driveway. A short, stout woman with blonde hair emerged. Jason introduced them: "This is Shawna," he said. They shook hands, and then Bush piled his gear in his car, and they drove off together, leaving Melinda behind, waving good-bye through her tears.

||

Shawna Forde had been in Arizona and elsewhere around the West, including California, Las Vegas, and Denver—anywhere but Everett, where detectives still wanted to talk to her about her now-ex-husband's shooting—for several months by then. She quietly left Everett sometime in late February or early March and went to see her old friend and fellow Minuteman, Kathy Dameron, in Yakima. They had become so close that Shawna called Kathy her "second mom."

It only lasted a couple of days. Kathy already suspected Shawna of having pilfered some of her pain medications the previous November, after she had helped Kathy clean the Dameron home. This time she caught her red-handed.

Kathy did an inventory and discovered that almost half of her oxycodone prescription was missing, as well as some muscle relaxers. Her suspicions aroused, she went to Shawna's purse and did a quick search. It didn't take her long to find all the missing meds. She took them back and put them in her medicine chest.

Shawna was out at the time, and when she returned, she went into the bedroom where she was staying and closed the door. Kathy could hear her frantically searching through her purse. Then she came out and looked Kathy squarely in the face.

"I've been busted, haven't I?" Shawna said.

Kathy was resolute: "Yes, you have."

"I'm sorry, Mom," Shawna said.

Kathy just shook her head. "Not good enough," she said. The next day Shawna drove off in her Honda Element. It was the last time Kathy saw her.

||

Shawna had much weightier matters on her plate than the detritus of destroyed relationships back in Washington, anyway. Inspired by her secret meetings with the shadowy drug lord in Arivaca named Albert, she started making plans to move ahead with the scheme she had outlined for Jim Gilchrist: funding their movement by ripping off border drug smugglers.

She showed up at Rena Caudle's home in Redding in early April and stayed there for nearly a week, visiting with her half brother Merrill Metzger as well. She started boasting to them of her upcoming plans.

First on her list, she told Merrill, was a robbery: "She was telling me that she was going to rob some store down in Arizona that kept $40,000 in cash under the counter for all the illegal Mexicans to cash their checks.

"I told her, 'That's dangerous, Shawna. You could go to jail for that. That's robbery, whether it's illegal immigrant money or not, it's still robbery. You could get your ass shot and killed.'"

She was just getting warmed up. Her big plan, she told him, was to finance her own paramilitary activities by hitting the Mexican drug cartels. "She sat right here on my couch and told me about how she's got these guys, and they're going to rob drug cartel dealers of their cash and their drugs and sell the drugs and use the money to fund their group," Metzger recalls. "She wanted to buy some big, huge, thousand-acre ranch down there in Arizona, and she was going to start a compound. And they were going to start some kind of a militia, kind of like Blackwater. She wanted to start an outfit like that, that went in and rescued people who were kidnapped and stuff by people from the Mideast.

"And I thought, 'This is absolutely absurd.' But I didn't put it past her, because I knew Shawna was capable of doing anything that she put her mind to, because she had in the past. And so I told her, 'You're talking dangerous stuff.'

"She talked about not only robbing drug dealers but starting a revolution against the government."

Rena Caudle says that Shawna told her exactly the same thing on that visit. "I honestly didn't know what to think," she says. "With Shawna, you just never knew."

Shawna was not just telling her family about her militia plans. She was also talking to a Colorado Minuteman named Ron Wedow—codenamed Raven.

Wedow had been involved in Minuteman activities since 2005, when he participated in a border watch in Texas. He had first met Shawna Forde while on a Minuteman operation near Sasabe in 2007 and had remained in email contact with her off and on over the ensuing months.

In late April 2009, Shawna Forde contacted him by phone. "She called and told me about a deal she had going involving machine guns, rocket-powered grenades, drugs and money," he later testified. "They were in a house in Arivaca."

Forde wanted to put together a commando squad to hit this house. She also bragged about her drug-cartel connection, embroidering her original tale. "She told me she had met a cartel guy at a bar," he said. "She took a cigarette out of his mouth and stomped it on the floor. After that he was impressed with her."

Shawna told Wedow that she and the "cartel guy" had reached an agreement: he would give her a heads-up about illegal border crossers if she would look the other way when it came to his drug-smuggling operation. "I thought I was being set up," Wedow said.

Forde was seeking to build a specialized team equipped for such an operation. "She wanted to know if I had a team that could go down there and take this house down," he said. "The family was a front."

He told her he thought it was possible, but he wanted to bring in a Colorado friend named Bob Copley who went by the code name Anglo. "I was going to put her in touch with him," Wedow testified.

Copley, in fact, was a former law enforcement officer who had previously worked with the FBI as an informant. Wedow called him immediately.

The three of them agreed on a May meeting at a truck stop in Aurora, Colorado. Wedow said he didn't really want to attend—"I had better things to do," he said—but he wound up going anyway. Shawna was going to lay it all out in detail.

||

If the Minutemen were a movement almost perfectly tailored to the personality and peculiar talents of Shawna Forde, then there was nothing that quite embodied her hopes for mainstream acceptance like the Tea Party.

As with most conservatives, Forde was dismayed at the election of a black Democrat, Barack Obama, to the presidency in 2008, and so she eagerly joined up the following winter as right-wing ideology got a fresh rebranding under the banner of the populist Tea Party. Her family members said she was very keen on the protests being planned—and assiduously promoted on right-wing outlets like Fox News—for that April. She wrote about the potential of the movement to advance the Minuteman cause on "Shawna's Corner."

And then she turned up at the Tax Day Tea Party in Phoenix on April 15. She was one of a long list of second- and third-tier speakers who lined up to have their three minutes at the microphone during the daylong event.

In the context of some of the day's more incendiary speakers, Shawna's remarks don't really stand out—other than that she called for a citizen revolt, perhaps of the kind she was in the process of enacting. She posted the text on the MAD site the next day:

> I wish I had words of wisdom or even some false hope to produce, but I don't. The only conclusion I have drawn is that you and I are not alone in our fear for a future but look left and right every American around you is sharing in this fear.
>
> It is time for Americans to revolt.
>
> It is more than words. It is about action. Share your opinions with your neighbor. Go to the offices of those elected officials. Be active, and stand even on a corner with a sign if that's as far as you can take it. But do not go into your house and draw your blinds and wish it away. This is the time for all Americans to join organizations and REVOLT!!!
>
> Refuse to be part of a system only designed to enslave you and you children!
>
> Times will get worse before they get worse.
>
> Say no to illegal immigration!

On her website, she signed the message: "Lock and Load, Shawna Forde."

Shawna also turned up in a YouTube video taken that day in Phoenix. A counterprotester, wearing an orange ball cap, can be seen holding a sign reading, "Republicans Borrowed Hundreds of Millions of Dollars Today!" As the Tea Partiers who surround the man harass him, he defends President Obama from onlookers who call him a "piece of shit."

Shawna can be seen chiming in: "You want to say that about amnesty? You want to let fifty million illegals take our jobs? So I bet you're going to be behind him then, right?"

A few days after that event, Shawna traveled to Denver and met with other Minuteman movement followers. In an April 24 message on the MAD website, she wrote, "It has been a wonderful experience here in Denver," remarking on the significant presence of Latinos in the city. She also noted: "We have a strong border crew here that will be working on future operations to help assist along the southern border to assist Border Patrol."

Forde announced she would next travel to Las Vegas "to talk with many Americans there who are suffering from the loss of jobs that have been taken by illegal Aliens."

In the meantime, she had fallen into a couple of strange online feuds. First she got into a conflict with Bob Dameron over control of the MAD website, which she felt should feature more stuff about her. Dameron, on the other hand, felt it should be more issue-oriented and emphasize the volunteers who made it work. They got into an argument over the phone in April, and Bob hung up on her.

So then Bob got an email from Shawna, forwarding another email with a header from Scott Shogren, the original financier of MAD and the never-finished Minuteman documentary. In prose remarkably similar to Shawna's unique style, it complained along the same lines as Shawna's issues with Dameron's handling of the website. So then Dameron and other MAD members began exchanging emails with Shogren, or so they thought.

Shogren, again in eerily Shawna-like prose, sturdily defended the MAD "national director," as she had taken to identifying herself: "One thing I admire about Shawna she walks the talk and does not quit execpt now she may be out for good. She is tirered of being the only one willing," Shogren told Chuck Stonex. He also castigated Bob Dameron: "I'm not interested in huis bad mouthing a woman that has put her life and sweat into this she may not be perfect but she atleast gets it done and between Jim and I she has followed every order without bitching or complaining ever. So the last thing we want to deal with is whinning from others Shawna has nothing to say sorry for or needs to say nothing to us."

In early May, Scott North also received a peculiar email supposedly from Scott Shogren, urging him to investigate Shawna, knowing that North had done previous work on right-wing extremists for the *Herald*:

*I wanted to contact you on this matter you seem to have done a in depth background on her 25 years ago I really think you should look at doing a very serious piece on her border activity. I believe she is also linked to the Aryan Nation that has gone underground since Hayden Lake she is personal Friends with Augusta Crist the National leader.*

*My interest in her is that I have been investigating militia developments in America as a project for a documentary and I don't know about you but the more I research Shawna the more layers I find and I think she is one scary individual. very interesting, very interesting, "but scary." I'm not experienced enough yet as you are but when I graduate I plan on going into the Field of investigative reporting.*

North later contacted the real Scott Shogren, who assured him that he had written none of these emails. Shawna had, in fact, hijacked his online identity and posed as him in the exchanges. North still is perplexed about why Shawna would try to attract his attention this way. Most likely she believed even negative coverage could work to her benefit—especially if it helped her grow her niche reputation as a racist badass.

||

Shawna also got into an online squabble with her onetime friend Joe Adams—largely because Adams in fact maintained ties with federal law enforcement officers. And some of his contacts in those circles were warning him away from Shawna.

Adams is something of a shadowy figure himself, with a background as a CIA operative and drug smuggler. He was indicted in 1988 for violations of the Neutrality Act as a result of his work helping to fund (often through drug smuggling) and organize the right-wing Contra death squads in Nicaragua in the 1980s, and he later became a private investigator with ties to the Jimmy Hoffa family. He was naturally attracted to the Minutemen and first joined Chris Simcox's Minuteman Civil Defense Corps in 2006, but he then left (saying MCDC was "a bunch of people who want to do a good job but don't know what they're doing") to eventually form his own offshoot, which he called Project Bluelight (a name suggesting that it operates with the tacit cooperation of law enforcement, "blue light" being law enforcement lingo for proceeding with the blessing of police).

Adams first met Shawna at a Minutemen gathering at the Caballo Loco RV Park in March 2008, when she showed up to promote MAD at a Bluelight border-watch operation. A journalist from Illinois interviewed the two of them together on patrol.

Shawna had come running to Adams shortly after her legendary meeting with the "drug cartel" guy in Arivaca. "She came into my campsite and said, 'Do you want this information?'" Adams later told Tim Steller of the *Arizona Daily Star*. "She tells me how she's infiltrated these drug dealers in Arivaca. And I'm like, 'Are you crazy? You're going to get killed.'"

Shortly afterward, Forde sent him her long email with the photos from inside the stash house attached. Adams turned around and reported Forde to federal Department of Homeland Security agents with whom he was in contact. Now these same sources were advising Adams to distance himself from Shawna.

That spring, Adams heard that Shawna and some of her Minutemen were dropping his name to other federal law enforcement officers, so he fired off an email on May 11 warning her to stay away:

> *Here is what I am suggesting; 1. Stop dropping mine and Project Bluelight's name to give you and your amateur operation credibility. 2. Stay in Washington and off the border for the good of the movement. Shauna, you are a dangerous sociopath and anyone who would listen to your bullshit is an idiot. You do not know what you are doing, and you put people and the border movement in harms way. You have no knowledge of any Bluelight Operation. My Scouts and I have worked very hard to develop a solid professional relationship with DHS and cannot afford to associate with anyone who would jepardize that work. I will give you the health tip of the week, do not contact me or any of my Scouts again. It would further be advised to never speak of Bluelight again. Go away. Good luck in prison.*

Shawna was unimpressed and defiant in her response. "Shaking in my boots asshole," she replied. "If I'm a sociopath then your a lunatic. Your rant and raves I find ridicules and threatening me Joe? uhmm and I'm the dangerous one? Yeah okay."

Adams answered that he merely "meant it as a warning that certain government officials have you in their sights. I have been sticking up for you for months and people couldn't understand why. I would like to think you mean well, but I can no longer risk the association. I always liked you as a person, but you are your own worst enemy."

Now Adams started receiving emails from "Scott Shogren," who stuck up for Shawna as "one Marine to another." "Shogren" wrote Adams: "Shawna has been under the microscope many times and is used to it she runs with some high profile hitters and was raised in the Gambini family 'Brooklyn' I will say this she has helped us out with operations and intel on more then one time and has never given us up."

At first, Adams appeared to have succumbed. "Don't get me wrong, I still like Shawna as a person," he replied to "Shogren." "But professionally I have to distance myself from her. From one Marine to another, I tried to defuse the problem that a particular government agency has with Shawna as much as I could. If I do not distance myself from Shauna, my relationship with that agency will cease to exist."

"Shogren" answered: "she follows orders from some big brass I cant tell you but she operates under orders as well she is the shit magnet and we need her for that. I give her projects to work and they get done. she uses her good looks to all of our advantage she can get Intel like I have never seen haha."

At that point, Adams probably realized he was in fact corresponding with Shawna herself, and the exchange ended. Then he received an email from Shawna in late May:

*After consideration with our crews we have decided to take you up on your offer.*

*we have 40 acre ranch and 5/ 8 men crews in the valley and I do not want any relationship with you or your crew you stay in your area and we will stay on the border.*

*We will never mention you and expect my name never to cross your lips if asked you know nothing.*

Adams replied: "That makes perfect sense to me. Good luck to you all." That email was dated May 30.

||

On May 15, Shawna traveled to Aurora, Colorado, to meet up with Raven and Anglo—Ron Wedow and Bob Copley—in person so that she could map out her Arivaca plan for them. They met at a truck stop just off of Interstate 70.

There were five people at the meeting: Shawna, Wedow, Copley, and two men who went by the undercover names Bandana Dave and Sio.

Forde, according to Wedow's later testimony, eagerly tried to sell her plan by playing up how much money there was to be had by hitting the target home in Arivaca. "She talked about millions of dollars being kept there," he said. "She said that at any given time there were two to three million dollars in the house. After the house was secured, her team would take the drugs, money and guns and they would meet at a later time."

Wedow tried to question Forde closely regarding her information; Shawna assured him the information was solid. "She told me she had it under surveillance," he said. "She started talking about drug money and home invasions. I let it roll from there."

Shawna also drew a sketch of Arivaca for the men, including the location of the target house, just northeast of the main town site, which she said was "under surveillance." They kept it and later gave it to the FBI, which for reasons yet unexplained misplaced it.

The men were intrigued, but the whole thing smelled fishy to them. Talking among themselves, they were especially concerned about Shawna's plan calling for their team to enter and secure the house first, after which her team would follow. It smelled like a setup to Bob Copley: "Our feeling was not knowing her team that they might come in and take us down leaving the impression that we were the only ones participating in the operation," he would later testify.

Shawna had originally contacted the men about a September operation, but she wanted to do this one now, while the money was still at the house. Shawna assured them that she planned later operations that fall, and they could take part in those if they liked. After some discussion, three of the men—Wedow, Copley, and Bandana Dave—said they'd like to wait a bit. Sio, apparently, agreed to join Shawna's team for the Arivaca "mission," and so she bought him a bus ticket for Tucson to come join them in a couple of weeks. He never used it.

Shawna parted amicably with the men and headed back to Arizona in her Honda. They all promised to stay in touch, and they did. Shawna did not suspect that when they did next, the FBI would be listening.

||

It's difficult to tell whether Shawna really believed that there was $3 million to be had inside Junior Flores's home or whether she was just inflating everything in the retelling, as was her habit. Obviously, she believed there were large sums stashed there for the taking, regardless of whether they were in the millions or the mere thousands.

The person telling her that, all along, was Albert Gaxiola, who had given her Junior's name and address in the first place. Shawna had been hanging out off and on in Arivaca throughout the month of May, staying with Gaxiola. They were sleeping together, and he was telling her all about the drug scene in Arivaca. In return, she made him an honorary Minuteman, giving him patches and bumper stickers that he tucked away in his desk drawers. She also got him a real-looking Border Patrol shirt complete with patches.

Oin Oakstar and Albert had been talking all that spring about how to consolidate power in Arivaca. Oakstar says he drew up a hit list of smugglers they wanted to take out—with Junior and Victor Flores atop it—and Albert adopted it as his own. Weighing on their minds in particular was the fact that they had ripped off one of Junior's dealers for $500 worth of pot: "Once we had gone that far either he was going to kill us or we were going to kill him," Oakstar testified. "Albert thought we should kill him. We discussed having it done by somebody else. We also discussed doing it ourselves."

Shawna and her Minutemen had dropped into their lap, telling them of grand schemes to take out drug houses: a gift bedecked in camo gear, the answer to their dilemma, a way to outsource the violence, a patsy for their own schemes. Albert was probably being helped by his drug-smuggling employer, Rita, who introduced Shawna around town as a Minuteman. It was Ralph and Rita, after all, who most wanted Junior Flores out of the picture but were prevented by their own superiors from indulging in any violence.

Shawna probably believed, too, that Gaxiola would honor their arrangement to help capture illegal border crossers, just as she had agreed to look the other way when his smuggling activities crossed her path.

But in the end, it was the money that mattered. The money that was never there.

# 14

# The Next Level

A child's lamp in the yard of the Flores home. DAVID NEIWERT PHOTO

Shawna liked to share her operating philosophy for Minuteman American Defense with her recruits: "Life out there is a jungle, and we've got targets," she told them. "We're going to finance and rock the world."

She also had a simple explanation for why she inspired so much fear and loathing, even among the ranks of Minutemen: "I'm the one person they know is willing to take it to the next level, and that scares a lot of people," she told Ron Wedow.

No one was really sure what she meant by "the next level." Over a matter of minutes during the early morning hours of Saturday, May 30, 2009, she showed them.

||

Shawna Forde and Jason Bush appear to have arrived in Tucson sometime on Wednesday or Thursday. They picked up Albert Gaxiola's teal-colored Chevy

Astro van at the home of his girlfriend, Gina Moraga, leaving Shawna's distinctive copper-colored Honda parked somewhere nearby.

The van had tinted windows. Albert had obtained it sometime earlier, using it to haul loads of marijuana to and from his safe house. It looked like a nice, unobtrusive family vehicle, and the darkened glass helped obscure anything in the back end. It was nearly a perfect car for his purposes.

Shawna and Jason arrived in Arivaca that Friday morning at around ten a.m. and promptly went to Albert Gaxiola's house on Second Street. Albert was out in the backyard when they arrived. Oin Oakstar was there, too.

Albert stayed behind while Oin Oakstar gave them a tour of the target. Jason Bush drove, Shawna rode shotgun, and Oakstar guided them from the backseat. They drove around behind the Flores-Gonzalez property on the paved Arivaca Ranch Road, then turned up the aptly named Hardscrabble Road, a bouncy dirt track riven at the far end by the same wash that ran behind the house. At the end of Hardscrabble they took the hard right onto Mesquite Road, slowly came up over a short, bumpy rise, and then were at the home of Junior Flores and Gina Gonzalez.

Gina was out in the yard, on the other side of the wire fence, with Brisenia. They were looking for her car keys, which had strangely vanished the day before. The occupants of the van didn't see Gina until they were over the rise and suddenly upon the place. Oin Oakstar ducked down behind the seat so she couldn't see him, because he knew she would recognize him.

It was only a little odd: tourists and various other lookie-loos were known to wander past the place from time to time, lost and wandering, though hardly anyone ever turned up Hardscrabble the way this van had to have come. Gina didn't recognize the van, or the big man driving it or the blonde woman in the passenger seat either. She waved the same greeting wave that everyone in Arivaca uses: brief, simple, friendly.

Shawna tersely smiled and waved back. The van drove on slowly. Gina watched after them and the little cloud of dust they left behind and wondered what that was about. She shrugged and returned to her search.

Inside the van, everyone breathed a sigh of relief at the close call. They drove Oin Oakstar home to his girlfriend's place; then Jason and Shawna went back to Albert's place in town and mostly hung out there for the remainder of the day, resting and getting their guns and ammo ready. Oin Oakstar began drinking.

||

It had been a hot, sunny day in the implacable Arizona desert, and so night-fall's gracious descent came like a blanket of cool relief. It was home for the night creatures of the desert—the bats, the owls, the pumas. And it was cover for night creatures of the human kind.

Four people—Shawna Forde, Jason Bush, Albert Gaxiola, and a fourth, Spanish-speaking man who has never been identified—emerged from Gax-iola's house after nightfall. Albert was wearing his faux Border Patrol uniform; Jason and Shawna were decked out in camo gear. Albert had an AK-47; Jason Bush was armed with a shotgun whose action was held together with duct tape, and a .45 caliber handgun with a ten-round clip. Shawna had her own special: a silver .357 revolver with pearl grips. It's unknown what the fourth man was bearing. They piled the guns in the back end of the van and drove to Oin Oakstar's place to pick him up.

There was a problem, though: Oakstar had been smoking weed, drinking, and thinking. The planned "mission" made him nervous: Oakstar, like Raven and Anglo, smelled a setup. He suspected that Gaxiola and his new friends were going to make him a patsy for whatever went down in the Flores-Gonzalez home that night.

Most of all, he later testified, he thought doing a home invasion with family members present was a violation of the Arivaca Rules, which above all kept people's families out of what was otherwise simply business. "Women and children are not part of it," Oakstar testified. "There's no reason to bring them into it."

He had no great love for Junior Flores, but he says he knew this was trouble. So he drank and smoked: "It just felt wrong. What he [Albert Gaxiola] had suggested or wanted to do felt wrong to me," he testified. "I used alcohol and drugs as an excuse not to go."

When the teal van arrived to pick him up, they found Oakstar in his girlfriend's living room saying he was too wasted to go. After some discussion, they agreed that he would be a liability and left without him.

The four Minutemen arrived at the Flores-Gonzalez property sometime around midnight and appear to have first parked just down the ridge on Hardscrabble Road, at the point where the wash crosses the road. They had a good view of the rear of Junior's home from that vantage and could watch as lights went on and off.

Shawna painted Jason Bush's face black, her beautician's makeup skills coming in handy. When she was done, she was impressed with her own handiwork: "Jesus, you are one scary dude," she told Bush. Shawna liked to reassure "her guys" that way. She was also right.

They agreed on the most important part of the plan, there in the darkness of the teal van: there would be no survivors.

||

Junior Flores finally turned off most of the lights in the house sometime around twelve thirty. Brisenia was sleeping on the love seat with her puppy, and Gina had fallen asleep. He settled in to watch a movie on the TV in their bedroom, something he did to help him go to sleep.

Then it came: the loud banging on the front door, the shouting voices, someone shining a bright light. Junior got up, dressed only in his boxer shorts, and looked out the bedroom window; then he shook Gina gently awake. "I think the police are here," he told her.

Junior padded down the hall and into the living room, where Brisenia was still slumbering. His little girl was a deep sleeper.

Before he answered the door, he walked into the kitchen and turned on a light. Then, in the washroom adjacent, he reached into a cupboard and pulled out his own .40 caliber handgun. Not sure what was happening, he placed it on the kitchen counter and then went to answer the door before the banging woke Brisenia.

They were still shouting and pounding: "Open up! This is the Border Patrol! We are seeking a fugitive on these premises! We have you surrounded! Open up!"

Night visits from the Border Patrol were not unheard of for the Flores-Gonzalez home. The wash behind their home was frequently used by border crossers trekking up toward Tucson, and so there had been the occasional knock on the door from Border Patrol officers asking permission to cross their property in pursuit of someone they were tracking. But Border Patrol officers were always very polite.

Not these night visitors. When Junior Flores opened his front door—leaving a screened steel security door still closed between himself and whoever was outside—someone outside shone a bright light into his face. He held his hand up to shield his eyes.

"What do you want?" he asked.

"This is the Border Patrol!" shouted a woman's voice. "We have tracked a fugitive onto these premises! We need to conduct an immediate search!"

"OK, wait just a sec, let me get some pants on."

"Do not move, sir, or we will shoot you where you stand!"

Junior froze. "Open up immediately!" the woman demanded.

"Don't you have a warrant or anything like that?" he asked.

"We don't have time for that! We are in hot pursuit of a federal fugitive!"

Junior hesitated and then opened the screen door and let them in. Gina, who had thrown on a T-shirt and jeans, now arrived in the living room just as Shawna Forde and Jason Bush swept into her home, brandishing their guns and shouting.

Shawna wore a brunette wig and had to sweep it out of her face constantly. She was shouting: "Everybody down! Down on the couch!" Jason Bush, looming over everyone with his blackened face and glaring eyes, and brandishing the shotgun, frightened everyone into obedience. Junior Flores sat down on the big couch, his back to the kitchen wall. Gina sat down on the love seat next to Brisenia and covered her protectively. Her puppy had scurried out the door. Brisenia still slept, her nine-year-old's dreams not yet interrupted by the real-life nightmare in her living room.

Shawna was demanding to know where their second daughter was: "Where is she? The second one?" she demanded. "She's not here," both Junior and Gina insisted.

Jason Bush set the shotgun down on a shelf near the door and withdrew his .45 from its holster, flicking the safety off. Junior Flores at first was too overwhelmed by the shouting and the guns, but now he could see that something was not right here.

"Wait a minute," he said to Shawna. "You haven't shown me any identification papers or badges or anything. How do we know you're Border Patrol?"

"We don't have time for that!" Shawna spat back.

"Well, you know," Junior continued, "that gun"—and he pointed to the shotgun with duct tape on the action, lying where the big man in blackface had set it down—"that's not like any gun any Border Patrol would ever use."

Jason Bush swerved menacingly and raised his handgun, pointing it at Junior as he sat on the couch. "Don't take this personally," he told Junior Flores, "but this bullet has your name on it." And he fired.

The bullet hit Junior in the lower left chest and passed through his torso, exiting through his back and into the couch. It also threw him back and stunned him.

Gina shrieked and jumped up from the couch, rushing toward her fallen husband and Jason Bush. Bush pivoted and fired three shots at her: the first hit her in the shoulder and exited near her breast, the force spinning her backward; the second hit her in the thigh and dropped her in a heap onto the floor, at the head of the love seat where her daughter was now stirring from her slumber. The third shot missed her, narrowly, altogether. She curled into a fetal position and pretended to be dead, but she was conscious and aware of everything now.

Junior managed to stand up, and began grappling with Jason Bush, who stood a good eight inches taller and outweighed Flores by a hundred pounds or more. It halted the volley of shots for a moment, but Flores knew it was a futile struggle and begged Bush: "Please don't hurt my wife." That they could harm his daughter was yet inconceivable.

Bush won the brief tussle by shooting Junior in the right hand as he tried to wrest the gun away. His hand flew back, and Bush shot him in the right forearm, through the center of the tattoo he had dedicated to Gina. Junior fell back onto the couch again, helpless now. "No, no," he begged. Bush shot him twice in the lower throat, through the middle of his clavicle, and then finished him off with a shot through his right temple.

Gina, lying on the floor, could hear Junior's dying breaths, and finally, a gentle death rattle.

Brisenia was wide awake now, shaken finally from her dreams by the sound of Jason Bush unloading his magazine into her father. She began screaming and crying.

More people were coming into the house now: Gina could hear the voices and footsteps, the fat loud woman shouting commands. She could hear two men speaking Spanish in her kitchen; Gina does not speak Spanish herself, but she understands it, and she could hear the men dividing up the task of searching the house. One of the voices sounded unsettlingly familiar, like her onetime friend Albert Gaxiola.

She lay there, praying that they would just find whatever they had come for and leave. That was her only hope: she knew if they discovered her alive, it would be all over for her and possibly Brisenia too.

Voices in the back of the house were shouting out to Jason Bush in the front room as he stood there, guarding Brisenia. She was crying still, and he was telling her everything would be all right, that no one would hurt her, in a reassuring voice. The voices in the back of the house were searching for Alexandra. "She's got a sister!" someone said. "Find her!"

Jason Bush started querying Brisenia. "Where's your sister?"

"She's at my nana's. She's not here."

As they were speaking, Gina could hear Bush take out his empty magazine from the pistol he had used to kill her husband.

He pointed at Gina, curled up on the floor. "Who's that? Is that your sister?"

"No, that's my mom. Why did you shoot my mom?" she cried.

Bush said nothing. "Why did you shoot my poppa?" she asked.

Still he said nothing. "Are you going to shoot me?" she asked. She was sobbing.

"No, honey, don't worry. We won't shoot you."

Then Gina could hear the unmistakable sound of a fresh magazine sliding and clicking into place.

"Please don't kill me," Brisenia pleaded.

"Don't worry. We won't kill you."

Barely moments after this last reassurance, there was a gunshot: Gina, through clenched eyes, could see her daughter's body fly backward onto the love seat. Then there was a second shot.

Bush's first shot was fired from about three feet away and entered through the center of Brisenia's nose and exited out the back of her skull, killing her instantaneously. He made certain of his deed by pressing the nose of the .45 to her left cheek where she now lay on the love seat and firing a second shot into her head: the escaping gases from the gun blew apart the left side of her face and sprayed blood everywhere.

Now there was silence in the house except for Shawna's shouted commands and the men shouting their replies. Gina could hear them ransacking the house: furniture was being overturned; drawers and cupboards were being searched.

Finally, after what felt like an eternity but was probably only a few more minutes, Shawna announced that it was time to leave. For a minute Gina could hear them talking outside, and then it seemed as if the people who had murdered her family were gone.

||

Gina Gonzalez pulled herself up on the love seat and riveted her attention on Brisenia. She was bleeding profusely from her face.

"I sat up and grabbed Brisenia. I was telling her not to die on me," she testified later. "She was shaking really hard."

On a windowsill next to the love seat was a wireless phone handset. In a panic, she dialed 911.

"911, where is your emergency?"

"Ma'am, somebody just come in and shot my daughter and my husband."

Now it came out in a rush, her panic and fear. She asked for medical advice for her daughter: the woman on the other end told her to leave Brisenia where she was. She began trying to explain what had happened, and it felt as though in her confusion and pain she couldn't get it all out right. The police were on their way, and a little of her fear subsided.

And then Shawna Forde walked back in. Albert Gaxiola had none-too-brightly left his AK-47 sitting atop the kitchen stove, and she had come back to retrieve it. She was no longer wearing the brunette wig, and her short blonde hair was showing. She also was no longer carrying her silver revolver; if history is any guide, she had probably shoved it down the back of her pants.

What she did have when she entered the house was a big, self-satisfied smile. And when she saw Gina Gonzalez, sitting on the little sofa next to her dead daughter, talking to police on the phone, it went away instantly. Her face fell, and she exclaimed: "Oh, shit!"

Gina shouted into the phone: "They're coming back in! They're coming back in!"

Shawna ran back out through the front door, still shouting: "She's still alive! You guys need to get back in there and finish the job!"

Gina did not need to hear this to know she had to act quickly. On her one good leg and still clutching the phone, she hopped the six feet or so to the kitchen entrance and another few feet into the kitchen. She saw the AK-47 sitting on the stove, but more importantly, she saw the .40 caliber semiautomatic handgun Junior had gotten out and placed on the counter next to the sink. She grabbed it in her hand just as her legs gave out beneath her and she crumpled into a heap on the kitchen floor.

She could hear somebody coming in the front door, and so she crawled another six feet or so over to the space at the end of the sink, in front of her back door, and curled up in the corner there. She set the phone down and clutched the gun in both hands. From that position, she could see, to her right, all the way through to the front door and, to her left, the kitchen entrance from the living room.

As she huddled there, a figure—Jason Bush's—peeked around the corner from the living-room entrance. Then his hand, clutching a gun, reached around the corner, and he began firing blindly, wildly missing. Gina began firing back, just as blindly. Bush's left foot was sticking out a little around the corner. They exchanged several rounds, and then she heard a yowl and a shouted curse. With a roar of pain, Jason Bush went fleeing out the front door, limping. Gina could see him as he fled.

Then, at the same door, just as Jason Bush exited, she saw another face poke around the corner—a familiar face, like Albert Gaxiola's. He was wearing a Border Patrol uniform. Now Gina just began firing in their direction blindly, shouting: "Get the fuck out of here! You've done enough!" Amid the gunfire, Albert aimed the shotgun blindly back in her direction and fired. The round went into the kitchen wall and lodged in the refrigerator on the other side.

Then they were gone. For good. Gina could hear the 911 call taker trying to talk to her. She picked the handset back up and began their long conversation and her interminable wait for help to arrive. And the horror of it all began to sink in.

For Gina Gonzalez, the night would offer only two consoling graces, one large, one small: Her oldest daughter was still alive; in the coming weeks and months, this would help keep Gina Gonzalez alive and strong, strong enough to see justice for her dead daughter. And by fighting back, she had unknowingly chased the Minuteman movement out into its long overdue night.

||

When Jason Bush went fleeing in a hail of curses and gunfire out the front door of the Flores-Gonzalez home, streaming blood from the wound in his calf that Gina Gonzalez had inflicted, he left a trail of blood all the way out to the fence around the house and then into the road in front, where the teal van was waiting to pick him up. He dove into the back seat. In a few hours, detectives would be collecting the many viable samples of his DNA he had trailed behind him.

Shawna was not far behind. As she climbed over the fence, though, her silver pearl-handled revolver—with her fingerprints and DNA on it—fell out. Detectives would find it lying next to the fence.

Albert was the last in. He jumped in the driver's seat and drove off quickly up Mesquite Road, past the community center, and up toward the town.

They dropped off the fourth man somewhere and retreated to Albert Gaxiola's house in the teal van. Shawna and Gunny went inside, and she started to tend his wound. He had bled all over the back seat of the van, and left some bloody smears on the headrest in front of him and the door frame.

It's not clear why, but they had decided to hole up at Albert's house while he drove into town in the Hyundai Tiburon owned by his girlfriend, Gina Moraga, who later testified that she was present that night. But the carburetor was acting up, and the engine was flooded and would not start. Albert lifted the engine lid and began fiddling with the engine, removing the air filter to try to get the carburetor working. He banged the lid closed and then reopened it several times. Gina Moraga sat in the driver's seat and turned the key.

Albert's elderly neighbor, Inga Hartman, had trouble sleeping that night. She was awake at one fifteen a.m. when she started hearing the banging noise from next door. She opened up her front door to have a look. There she saw Albert and Moraga trying to get the vehicle going.

The engine was chugging and belching thick exhaust. Hartman was revolted by the stench and closed her door, going back to her living room and her book. After about twenty minutes, the noise stopped. A little later, she heard a car drive away.

Eventually, they got the car running, and Albert and Moraga drove into Tucson. The car broke down there at a gas station, and he and Gina spent much of the morning trying to get it running again. Shawna and Jason holed up at his place and awaited help in the morning from Oin Oakstar and Chuck Stonex.

When Albert arrived in Tucson, though, they discovered that he did not have the keys to Shawna's Honda. They huddled by cell phone: Albert did not want to drive back to Arivaca in his rig, and so they decided to wait for Chuck Stonex and Laine Lawless to arrive, so that Shawna could hand her keys off to them. One of those two could then take the keys to Albert, and he could drive down the next day.

In the distance, they could hear the sirens of arriving ambulances and police cars, the whupping of the helicopter as it flew Gina Gonzalez away to a Tucson hospital. They stayed huddled inside Albert's home, watching TV and sleeping and talking over their exploits, quite proud of themselves. Normal people might have been tormented by the cold-blooded reality that they had murdered little Brisenia Flores. But they never were normal, and that was why she was dead.

# 15

## Justicia

Shawna Forde during her trial, January 2011.
JONATHON LEFAVIRE PHOTO

Nineteen months elapsed after her arrest in June 2009 before Shawna Forde's case went to trial in January 2011. Prosecutors announced shortly after the arrest that they would be seeking the death penalty in the case—which, as always, introduced numerous complications and process delays.

One of the complications arose from Gina Gonzalez's early interviews with detectives as she recovered from surgery in her hospital room. The Monday after she was shot, while she was still dazed with physical and emotional pain and the painkillers, they had shown her a photo lineup of possible suspects. A photo of Shawna Forde was among them. Gina had narrowed it down to three women—including Shawna—but couldn't definitively say, since the hair color wasn't right for any of them.

Shawna's defense team, led by two respected Tucson attorneys, Eric Larsen and Jill Thorpe, made clear at the outset that they intended to make Gina's ambiguity a centerpiece of their legal strategy. If she could not definitively identify Shawna and place her at the scene of the crime, they might be able to convince a jury that she actually wasn't there.

Knowing that Gina Gonzalez likely would be present, Shawna's attorneys intentionally began limiting her court appearances. The official reason was that they didn't want potential jurors to see her wearing prison scrubs. Instead, she was arraigned by video camera and made a number of other court appearances by telephone.

But at the September 2010 hearing to have the trial delayed, Shawna appeared in person, her hair—which had been blonde for as long as anyone could remember—now transformed by prison life to its natural mousy brunette.

Gina Gonzalez was there that day, as she was for every single day of any court proceeding involving her family's murderers. She recognized Shawna this time. There was no doubt in her mind now that authorities had arrested the woman who invaded her home that night.

It wasn't so much the appearance that she recognized, she told a detective later: it was her "smile and demeanor," something "she can't get out of her mind. . . . It's a mean demeanor, and she has an evil eye."

That was enough to convince the defense attorneys to conduct all future court appearances telephonically when they could. They also tried to have Gina Gonzalez disqualified as a potential witness on the basis of her remarks to the detectives. That motion was denied.

||

It was an eventful nineteen months in Arizona, as it happened. The nativist politics that had brought forth Shawna Forde and the Minutemen was reaching its apotheosis, embodied in an anti-immigrant bill passed by the Arizona legislature in April 2010 titled SB 1070, whose entire purpose was to not merely encourage but require local and state law enforcement officers to enforce federal immigration laws—particularly to take into custody anyone who could not prove their American citizenship.

The bill had been largely written by an operative for the Federation for American Immigration Reform—the outfit Shawna had once claimed to represent on that Yakima town-hall broadcast—and its chief sponsor was one of the most notorious nativists in Arizona, state senate president Russell Pearce, who had a history of dalliances with Arizona neo-Nazi figures and outrageous anti-Latino pronouncements. Pearce is also a longtime ally of another noted Arizona nativist, Maricopa County Sheriff Joe Arpaio.

The fears about border-related crime from illegal crossers that were rhetorical grist both for the Minutemen and for the bill's proponents came starkly to life on March 27, when a third-generation Cochise County rancher named Robert Krentz, out on his ATV repairing fences on his ranch, encountered a stranger. He called in to his brother Phil on his walkie-talkie: "I see an immigrant out here, and he appears to need help. Call the Border Patrol." Several hours later, Krentz's body was found near the ATV. Whoever had shot him had killed his dog too. Footprints from the crime scene were tracked to a bridge crossing into Mexico.

The story was immediately seized on as a manifestation of the problems on the Arizona border, particularly the dangers posed by all those immigrants out wandering in the desert—not just by state media, but nationally. Fox News in particular ran numerous segments on the crime, but all the cable networks were not far behind. Right-wing anti-immigration pundits played up the story as proof that the Obama administration was failing to secure the border.

The problem was that the case was never solved. At first the assumption was that the killer had been either a random immigrant border crosser or, more likely, a drug mule. (The day before the murder, federal agents had busted eight smugglers on the Krentz ranch with 250 pounds of marijuana.) However, as the investigation proceeded, even those assumptions came into question: by mid-May, investigators were telling reporters that they were now looking at someone residing in the United States as their chief suspect.

By then, however, SB 1070 had passed the Arizona legislature and was signed into law by Governor Jan Brewer on April 23. Over a thousand people—almost evenly divided between those opposed to it and those who supported it—gathered that day at the state Capitol in Phoenix to register their feelings. But that was only the beginning.

There was an immediate national outcry. President Obama called SB 1070 "misguided" and said it would "undermine basic notions of fairness that we cherish as Americans, as well as the trust between police and our communities that is so crucial to keeping us safe." Boycotts of Arizona were organized by Latino organizations, and protests were held—not just in Phoenix, where thousands rallied in opposition, but also in cities around the country. In Los Angeles, they numbered over fifty thousand.

The Major League Baseball players' union—whose members include some of the most prominent and wealthy Latinos in America—registered their concern that hundreds of Latino players, many of whom are noncitizens, might be subject to the new law. Phoenix Suns players, who voiced their opposition to the law, wore their "Los Suns" jerseys to register their support of the Latino community. Many of their fans were angered by the gesture. A number of cities—including Los Angeles, San Francisco, Seattle, Oakland, Minneapolis, Saint Paul, and Denver—also announced they would boycott Arizona over SB 1070.

Tea Partiers got into the act as well. On Memorial Day, when thousands of opponents, mostly Latinos, marched five miles in the high heat in Phoenix, Tea Party groups from St. Louis and Dallas organized a sundown rally at Diablo Stadium in Tempe. Joe Arpaio was the keynote speaker.

The national uproar took several weeks to settle down. Eventually the furor subsided after a federal judge issued an injunction in late July prohibiting the most contentious aspects of the law——particularly the components that would have encouraged racial profiling—from being enforced.

Still, SB 1070 hovered over the state like a toxic cloud for months to come. In the November 2010 election, it became a contentious component for Arizona voters, particularly in Representative Gabrielle Giffords's Tucson-based district. Giffords, a moderate Democrat, had not supported the boycotts against the state (unlike her Arizona colleague Raul Grijalva). Giffords told reporters she understood her constituents were "sick and tired" of the federal government's failure to secure the border, adding that the situation was "completely unacceptable"; she said SB 1070 was a "clear calling that the federal government needs to do a better job." But Giffords declined to support the law, saying it "does nothing to secure our border" and that it "stands in direct contradiction to our past and, as a result, threatens our future." That position—her Tea Partying Republican opponent was an ardent backer of SB 1070—became a key issue in her reelection campaign that fall. Giffords was accustomed to winning handily, but that year she won by a little over 1 percent of the vote.

The murders in Arivaca became a small part of the debate. The opponents of SB 1070 pointed out that the anti-Hispanic mind-set—and the rhetoric accompanying it—was creating a climate in Arizona that seemed to be creating permission for violence against Latinos, even American citizens like the Flores-Gonzalez family. Signs began appearing at the anti–SB 1070 protests calling for people to "Stand Up Against Anti-Latino Violence."

"Justice for Brisenia," the signs demanded, above a stylized portrait of the nine-year-old. "We Will Not Forget You."

||

Shawna's trial was scheduled to get underway on Tuesday, January 11, 2011, at the modern, sparkling-clean Pima County Courthouse in the heart of Tucson's downtown. Three days before that, though, Jared Lee Loughner exploded.

Gabrielle Giffords was holding a meet-and-greet event for constituents outside a mall Safeway in the northern part of town, when Loughner—a mentally ill twenty-two-year-old with a hate-filled fixation on Giffords— walked up to her, pulled out a 9mm Glock, and shot the congresswoman point-blank through the skull. Then, enabled by a thirty-three-round magazine in his Glock, the shaven-headed college dropout waltzed through the crowd and gunned down eighteen more people. When he ran out of bullets, he dropped the fresh magazine he had carried with him, and a bystander grabbed him. Even more bystanders took him down: one whacked him in the back of the head with a chair, and a seventy-four-year-old retired colonel, despite having been shot himself, tackled him to the ground.

Five people died, including a federal judge named John Roll and one of Giffords's staffers. Giffords herself, miraculously, survived after undergoing emergency surgery, though it took months of therapy before she could speak and walk again, and she would eventually be forced to retire from Congress. The most famous of the victims—because her story was so heartbreaking— was a little eight-year-old girl named Christina Taylor-Green, who had come to the rally with her elderly neighbor because she was interested in politics and wanted to meet the congresswoman. Loughner had shot her once in the chest.

The day after the shootings, Pima County Sheriff Clarence Dupnik held a press conference at which he discussed the climate of violent hate talk that seemed to be pervading Arizona at the time and how it had contributed to the tragedy: "When you look at unbalanced people, how they respond to the vitriol that comes out of certain mouths about tearing down the government— the anger, the hatred, the bigotry that goes on in this country is getting to be outrageous." He added that Arizona had unfortunately become "the capital" of this toxicity: "We have become the mecca for prejudice and bigotry."

On Monday, the community still in turmoil, Shawna Forde's defense team attempted to have the trial postponed because of the tragedy. Jill Thorpe argued that jurors might draw an emotional parallel between her client and Jared Lee Loughner. "Sheriff Dupnik blamed the nation's vitriolic political rhetoric, saying Arizona has 'become the mecca for prejudice and bigotry,'" Thorpe said. "Obviously, there are people who would characterize the border-watch movement as motivated by prejudice and bigotry and that their activities usually involve members carrying guns."

She also noted that the intense media attention brought on by the tragedy was not likely to wane in the coming days: "The defense urges that this community—a community who will be deciding Ms. Forde's guilt or innocence, and if convicted whether she should receive the death penalty—needs some time to heal and for any 'dots' that might be connected between the January 8 events and Ms. Forde to subside," Thorpe wrote.

At first, Judge John Leonardo ruled against Thorpe's motion, and the trial was then scheduled to begin on Wednesday. But the next day, it emerged that a family member of one of the attorneys had developed an emergency medical problem. In light of that, and the discussions of the day before, Leonardo decided "the atmosphere is not conducive to going forward," and he reset the trial's start for Monday, January 17.

The community was still reeling from the Giffords tragedy that Monday. Christina Taylor-Green's funeral had been held that weekend, and it drew thousands, as well as national media coverage. The national media were still in town when the Shawna Forde trial started, and a few reporters wandered by to take it in.

More than a few people noticed the difference in how the media had covered the respective deaths of Christina Taylor-Green and Brisenia Flores: even in spite of the dramatic recording of Gina Gonzalez's 911 call, media coverage of the Shawna Forde case had been muted at best and utterly nonexistent at outlets like Fox News. At the trial, family members wondered aloud if it was because Christina was white and Brisenia brown.

Terry Greene Sterling, a longtime Arizona journalist, now a professor at Arizona State and a contributor to the *Daily Beast*, covered Shawna's trial for the duration. She talked to a producer from a major news network who told her that her superiors had briefly considered paying more attention to the Forde case, even making it an "emphasis" story. But they had backed away because they had decided the Flores-Gonzalez family wasn't sympathetic enough: the reporter said they were considered to be "trailer trash."

||

Opening arguments were as expected. Prosecutors Rick Unklesbay and Kellie Johnson recounted in detail the horrific early morning home invasion in Arivaca and described some of the witnesses and what the jury would hear from them—most notably Gina Gonzalez herself. Eric Larsen, of course, proclaimed his client's innocence: "Shawna Forde was not involved in this crime," he said. "The state's case looks good as an umbrella, but it has a lot of holes."

Larsen made much of the fact that Gonzalez had not been able to definitively identify the "short, stocky white woman" who entered her home that fateful night. "Gina Gonzalez eliminates Shawna Forde as being the person in that home," he claimed.

But when Gina Gonzalez herself took the stand that afternoon for the first time, her testimony was not so cut and dried. A petite, strikingly pretty woman, she spoke quietly and firmly throughout her testimony, describing the murders of her husband and daughter in even but emotion-laden tones. Her piercing gaze sent the unmistakable message that she was intent on justice. But her bearing, and her answers, had a steely integrity that spoke even greater volumes.

The jury of twelve women and two men first heard Gina's desperate 911 call, which set the stage for everything to follow. Gina's panicked voice was still ringing in everyone's ears when she took the stand and told her story, including her conditional identification of Shawna Forde as the woman who staged the home invasion.

Gonzalez said that it appeared to her that the woman was wearing a wig when she entered the first time: she was always brushing her hair out of her face, and it was "brownish." She said that when the woman came back into the house the second time, there was no wig and her hair was blonde.

Prosecutors asked Gina if the woman who had been in her house was in the courtroom. "She's sitting over there," she said, pointing to Shawna. "The one with the glasses on." Then she seemingly contradicted herself: "I don't know her and I can't say she's the person that came into my house."

Gina kept explaining, on cross-examination, that the woman at the defense table simply "looked like" the woman who was in her home, "but she's different now." It seemed like a simple and honest enough answer.

Prosecutors, however, did not need Gina Gonzalez's word to convince jurors that Shawna was the leader of the home invaders. There was the physical evidence, such as the jewelry and clothing belonging to Gina found in Shawna's possession. Prosecutors also introduced a letter from Shawna to her son, Devon Duffey, in prison, asking him to lie about where she got that jewelry and claim he had given it to her. (Shawna's DNA and fingerprints were in the teal van, too, along with Jason Bush's blood—the same blood found at the crime scene, though for reasons that were never explained, this was not introduced as evidence in Shawna's trial; likewise, the silver revolver with Shawna's DNA on it, found out at the fence around the Flores-Gonzalez property, went unmentioned until Albert Gaxiola's trial in June.)

Oin Oakstar testified too. Long-haired, bearded, and gap-toothed, he was no one's ideal of a credible witness. But his description of the plot to "take out" Junior Flores had a ring of truth to it, self-interested as it was: certainly the details meshed with everything the jury had learned so far. Most of all, it was Oakstar's depiction of life in Arivaca that stayed in everyone's mind. "Rural is putting it mildly," he said. "It's mostly ranchers, miners and drug smugglers. Almost the entire economy is based on illegal activities."

And then there was his remark about hearing of the deaths of Junior and Brisenia Flores that morning, before Shawna called him: "Automatically, I assumed it was Shawna and Jason."

The jury also heard from Ron Wedow and Bob Copley—Raven and Anglo—who described Shawna's plans for a home invasion in Arivaca. They also heard Shawna's taped conversations with Wedow, her boasts that she was "taking it to the next level."

She could also be heard boasting: "We did a couple of operations without you." Shawna, as always, was her own worst enemy.

||

Laine Lawless had been making a nuisance of herself since nearly the moment Shawna was arrested. She created a website, "Justice for Shawna Forde," devoted to her theory that Shawna had been set up by a federal conspiracy to discredit the Minuteman movement. She visited Shawna more than two dozen times after her arrest.

In December 2010, she had filed a complaint against Eric Larsen and Jill Thorpe, claiming that they were doing inadequate work, mostly by failing to follow through on the important leads her "investigative" work had produced. Judge Leonardo had to call a session with all the attorneys and Shawna present in court, where she assured everyone that she was pleased with her representation: "Absolutely 100 percent, and I always have been." Lawless's complaint was dismissed.

Because she had played an important role in bandaging Jason Bush's wound and transferring Shawna's keys to Albert Gaxiola, Laine Lawless was designated a potential witness in the trial and placed on a list of people who, accordingly, were not permitted in Judge Leonardo's courtroom. On Tuesday, January 25, Lawless ignored this order and showed up in the courtroom seats anyway.

Judge Leonardo promptly ordered her from the courtroom. Lawless objected. "I was told I was not going to be a witness," she claimed. Leonardo replied: "If you expect to be a witness you should not be discussing your testimony with anyone."

Lawless muttered, "I have not discussed any potential testimony," and walked out.

Two mornings later, she returned, carrying a couple of bags of clothing, which she handed to Jill Thorpe, and seemingly left. But then, as prosecutors were getting to the day's second witness, the white-haired Lawless came back in, wearing a black wig, dark glasses, and a dark overcoat, and took a seat.

Reporters in the gallery seats immediately recognized her and were trying to get the attention of court officials when a detective turned around, realized who it was, and got Unklesbay's attention. He promptly asked the court to stop proceedings, and the jury was led from the courtroom. "Ms. Lawless is standing here in some sort of disguise," Unklesbay explained to Judge Leonardo.

Leonardo explained to Lawless that she was in apparent violation of his earlier order regarding witnesses and demanded to know why. Lawless was defiant. "I am a citizen reporter and have First Amendment rights to be here as any other reporter here," she insisted.

The judge then tried to determine if, in fact, Lawless remained under subpoena and was informed that she was by both defense and prosecution teams. "Despite what she may believe, we have not made any decisions as to whether she would be called as a witness," Kellie Johnson told Leonardo.

It emerged that, according to Unklesbay, the previous witness had told him that as she had waited for her turn to testify, Lawless had been discussing the case in the hallway outside the courtroom with someone else. He asked Leonardo to order Lawless to stay away from the courthouse altogether, unless she was summoned to testify. Larsen chimed in, asking that she be ordered to desist from blogging about the case or doing radio interviews. She was interfering with his work. "She has had conversations with my client at the jail about daily court events," he said.

Leonardo agreed to all these requests by the lawyers. Then he reiterated his earlier order not to discuss her testimony. Lawless asked if he was issuing a gag order. "You may call it what you want, but that is my order," Leonardo said.

She was then escorted from the courtroom and the courthouse itself by the very detectives who had investigated the murders.

||

Shawna's demeanor changed very little over the course of the trial. She always tried to exude calm confidence, seeming to be at ease with her attorneys, appropriately serious when the testimony called for it, smiling and chatting in between. When the autopsy photos of Brisenia's ruined face were projected onto a large screen for all to see, she looked down and looked grave.

Still, when the defense's turn came, her attorneys announced at the outset that Shawna would not be testifying. Instead, Larsen and Thorpe attempted to exploit Gina Gonzalez's somewhat ambiguous identification of Shawna Forde, even proposing an elaborate theory that the woman who had been in the Flores living room that night was not Shawna, but rather Albert Gaxiola's girlfriend, Gina Moraga.

It was clear that this theory did not fly with jurors, however. The defense rested the morning of Thursday, February 10, and closing arguments were heard that afternoon. The jury began deliberating Friday morning. They returned Tuesday morning, February 14, and, having spent seven hours reviewing the evidence, delivered a guilty verdict on all eleven counts. They also declared Shawna eligible for the death penalty. It was Valentine's Day.

It did not seem to register with Shawna. As she was led out of the courtroom, she looked up and maintained a not-quite-smile of self-assurance, shuffling down the corridor with shackles on her ankles.

The next two weeks were devoted to the jury's most momentous decision: whether Shawna Forde should live or die for her crime. The so-called penalty phase of the trial featured a parade of experts of various stripes, including a forensic psychologist who laid out for the jury Shawna's sad and tawdry, profoundly abusive childhood, as well as her criminal history afterward and the trail of broken relationships she left in her wake.

One psychologist testified that, during her clinical examination, Shawna had expressed empathy for Gina Gonzalez: "She said she had lost a child and knew what it was like to lose a child," she said. The psychologist did not mention that this was the same child that Shawna had told close confidants she had strangled with a pacifier, though probably this was because she did not know it.

Another psychologist testified that he had tested Shawna and determined that she had an IQ of about 86, in the lowest eighteenth percentile. Rick Unklesbay informed him that, after this test, Shawna had bragged on a phone call to a friend from her cell she had "duped the shrink" by deliberately seeking a low score, because she didn't want them to know how smart she really was. She really had a 132 IQ, she said.

The psychologist smiled wryly. "I wouldn't buy that," he said. "Her ego is much more important to her than anything else."

Jill Thorpe, in her closing argument, broke down and essentially admitted that her client had been at the scene of the crime. "When she was in the

Flores home when Junior was shot, when she was in the back room as Brisenia was shot by Jason Bush—does she have the ability to develop a different strategy?" she asked, urging the jurors to consider her 86 IQ as the real problem.

It went over about as well as the "Gina Moraga did it" gambit. The decision was handed to the jurors on Friday, February 19; they returned on Tuesday and in short order announced that they had consigned Shawna Forde to Arizona's death row.

||

Jason Bush's trial got under way on Friday, March 18. Exactly one week later, on March 25, the jury found him guilty of two counts of first-degree murder. It took only three days of evidence presented by the prosecution, and a little under four hours of jury deliberation spread over two days, to get there.

Having seen the outcome of Shawna Forde's trial, Bush's defense attorneys—Richard Parrish and Chris Kimminau—decided on a different strategy. Instead of trying to prove their client's innocence, they would simply try to keep him off death row. Given the amount of physical evidence that Jason Bush left at the scene of the crime in the form of his blood trail, combined with Gina Gonzalez's identification of Bush as, once again, someone who "looked like" the person who shot her and her family, any effort to clear him of guilt had a negligible chance of success at best.

So when the prosecution was finished presenting its evidence, after three days of testimony—including, once again, Gina Gonzalez, who had resumed her daily position in the front row of seats at the trial—Bush's attorneys had engaged in only a minimum amount of cross-examination, mostly evidence pointing toward mitigating circumstances in the case. At the same time, the evidence—Gina's 911 call, her description once again of the nightmare home invasion and the injuries she sustained, the blood trail, the autopsy photos of Junior and especially of Brisenia—packed an unbearable emotional wallop. It was no surprise, then, that the jury—four men, eight women—spent so little time finding him guilty a week later, or that it only took them fifteen minutes of deliberation to subsequently rule that he was eligible for the death penalty.

The defense team's work was cut out for it in the penalty phase, when Parrish and Kimminau struggled furiously to paint Jason Bush as a mentally ill, damaged man deserving of some measure of sympathy and compassion. "Mr. Kimminau was very, very careful to avoid during the entire presentation of the state's case any inference that what was done by Jason Bush was proper and excusable or justified," Parrish reminded the jury in his opening remarks.

He suggested that the jury had been led into a bias against Bush: "You were shown photographs of every wound, every bullet that goes into one of the victim's bodies. You were shown the face of a little girl that is destroyed by bullets," he said, his voice raised. "Why? Is it not enough to say that two people, without justification, were murdered? No. You have to be taught to really hate Jason Bush."

Parrish outlined a history of abandonment and abuse not terribly dissimilar from Shawna Forde's, claiming that when Jason Bush reached age eleven, his parents legally disowned him. "His father put him into a mental institution where he was sexually assaulted and abused by the older boys," he said. "While it is true that the acts he committed are incredibly terrible it is also true that from early on in his life everyone literally abandoned him."

Bush had spent a good deal of time in prison, Parrish said, but he had not received any help. "They marched him from psychologist to psychiatrist who didn't help him because they don't do that in these institutions," he said. "Psychologists and psychiatrists in these institutions where kids go and then adults go are there to protect the institution. They don't have the training to cure. They march him from place to place, from prison to prison, from jail to jail and they bring him here and they say, 'Here, you kill him.'"

They paraded a series of psychologists before the jury, including one who suggested that Bush might be a paranoid schizophrenic. Dr. B. Robert Crago, clinical director of Neurobehavioral Health Services in Tucson, had performed a quantitative EEG—a test for evaluating brain function, based on brain electrical activity mapping—on Bush prior to the start of the trial.

Crago displayed a graphic showing nineteen channels of electrical activity from Bush's brain. "In Mr. Bush's case I was asked to decide if there was any evidence of abnormalities and if so what would they be consistent with," he testified. "The impression was, that first of all, this is a very deviant EEG. The test cannot say that he is paranoid schizophrenic. The test can only say deviant."

It was interesting testimony but not enough to shake from the jurors' minds the image of little Brisenia with holes in her face. On April 6, after another three and half hours of deliberation, they reached the verdict of death for Jason Bush, and Judge Leonardo sentenced him to death row.

||

Albert Gaxiola's lawyers stayed with a more traditional defense strategy: to establish question marks throughout the evidence, enough to sustain the jurors' reasonable doubts about their client's guilt. This time, there was a modest measure of success.

Gaxiola's trial began on June 7, a Tuesday, and prosecutors Unklesbay and Johnson largely proceeded over the next two weeks to lay out the evidence in the same fashion as they had in the previous trials: the jurors once again heard Gina Gonzalez's 911 call; once again heard Gina describe, in heart-rending fashion, the murders of her husband and daughter and her own shooting; once again saw the autopsy photos of Brisenia and Junior; once again heard Oin Oakstar describe the plan to "take out" Junior Flores.

However, the testimony proceeded at a snail's pace—Gina's testimony took more than three hours and was spread over two days—as Gaxiola's defense team, Jack Lansdale and Steven West, pored over every piece of evidence and tried to find holes, or at least question marks, at every step. They questioned cell-phone records, DNA evidence, and the veracity of Oin Oakstar. (The only exception to this came during the autopsy testimony, which the defense team hurried to get through; Albert Gaxiola was clearly shaken by the evidence.) When the prosecution rested on June 16, they continued largely in the same vein: providing evidence and countertestimony that might raise reasonable doubts about the prosecution's evidence. Gina Moraga, for instance, testified that she was with Albert Gaxiola throughout the day and night of May 29 in Arivaca, that they had nothing to do with the murders, and that Shawna Forde had not been there at his home that night.

There were also numerous defense motions for mistrial, all of which were denied. For the next two weeks, Lansdale and West worked to undermine the prosecution's evidence. But after closing arguments were heard on June 30, the jurors proceeded to hold five hours of deliberation and, on July 1, pronounced him guilty of all eight charges, including two counts of first-degree murder, promptly decreeing that he was eligible for the death penalty.

The penalty phase proceeded largely as it had in the previous trials, with jurors hearing from psychologists and family members (including Gaxiola's estranged father, who testified that his son had been recruited into the drug trade by his mother) about his abusive and twisted upbringing. The only difference this time was that Albert Gaxiola actually spoke in court: taking advantage of his right to "allocate"—in which a convicted defendant is given the opportunity to make a personal statement on his own behalf to mitigate his impending punishment—Gaxiola made a brief set of remarks that were addressed not to the jury but to the Flores family, indicating his deep remorse: "There's nothing that I can do or say that can relieve the pain and suffering from the loss of a loving husband or the loss of a precious daughter. All I can say is that I am truly sorry."

In closing arguments, Lansdale contended that his client had simply been along for the ride with Shawna and Jason and had no intention of ever letting things go as far as they did and was shocked and appalled at the murders. He asked the jury to do the right thing: "We feel at the end of the day that when you evaluate all of the facts and circumstances you have the right to use that term mercy," he said. "This is not an eye for an eye, tooth for a tooth situation. This is not a cold-blooded killer. This is not a worst of the worst situation."

It seemed to have an effect. On July 15, the jury gave Albert Gaxiola a sentence of life in prison without parole for the murder of Junior Flores and could not reach a verdict on Brisenia's murder, largely because two sides could not agree on whether or not it warranted the death penalty. This meant that if prosecutors wanted to obtain the death penalty for Gaxiola in Brisenia's death, yet another trial would be required. Prosecutors consulted with Gina Gonzalez and then told Judge Leonardo they were content to withdraw the death notice in Brisenia's case.

Leonardo then sentenced Gaxiola on August 14 to "natural life in prison"—meaning he could never be released under any circumstances—for Brisenia's murder. He was the only one of the home invaders—besides the yet-unidentified fourth man—to escape death row.

||

That final hearing on August 14 marked the end of a long and difficult journey for Gina Gonzalez, who did not miss a single day of court proceedings in the three cases—including jury selection—over the two years and ten weeks since the murders of her daughter and husband.

She was usually accompanied by a family member, most often her mother, though her younger sister and other relatives frequently joined her on the front row of wooden seats, nearest the jury, in the tiny gallery of Judge Leonardo's courtroom. From time to time her surviving daughter, Alexandra, made an appearance too.

Her testimony in the three trials often repeated itself, but she never lost either her passion for telling the story or her steely self-assurance, molded by the intense physical and psychic pain of her ordeal. There were tears at times—especially when she was trying to describe her futile attempts to revive her daughter—but they were brief, brushed aside with a determined look. Her victim's statements, given during the penalty phase in each trial, were also somewhat similar, though shaped to each case's circumstances. The most striking was the statement she gave at the end of Albert Gaxiola's trial:

As you can probably imagine, the murder of my husband and daughter on May 30, 2009, has changed my life forever.

I went to bed with my family as I normally would on any given night, not imagining I would never wake up from this never-ending nightmare.

The defendant and my family hung around together, we laughed, he played video games with my daughters, told them how beautiful they were, how well-behaved they were, how their hair always looked nice. The memory that sticks out most in my mind is when the defendant would throw Brisenia up in the air, catch her and make her laugh.

We were all friends. How could someone who loved my family plot their final destiny? How could someone who loved my family stand by and allow a child he made laugh be murdered?

Brisenia was a beautiful little girl. I can't possibly understand what she could have done to deserve this. What could I have done to deserve this? What could my husband have done to deserve this? What did Alexandra, my oldest daughter, do to deserve the loss of her little sister, who was her best friend and her father, who she misses very much?

I am still in denial about the whole thing. I can't believe someone I loved and trusted could have done something like this. For the longest time, I never thought the defendant would have been capable of doing something like this . . . almost wiping out my entire family.

It saddened me to know that Brisenia's face had to be reconstructed for her funeral. It was very hard to see my child in the casket. It was also hard to see my husband in the casket. But it was more difficult to comprehend that I may know the person who did this to them. I continue to have a hard time re-directing my grieving for both my husband and daughter. It's all so overwhelming!

Who put Junior's name on the bullet and didn't care what happened to my daughter and me?

The defendant knew my history with Junior. He knew we had been together since he was 15 years old. When my husband was murdered, we were two-and-a-half months short of being married 13 years. We had built our lives together and we were looking forward to growing old together. He had a great sense of humor, was a great cook and he loved his little girls very much.

It's hard for me to understand how this all happened. I have so many questions that will remain unanswered. I just need to know "Why?" Even though knowing why still wouldn't be good enough. It still won't bring them back.

My life is ruined. I now know that evil lives among us and it comes in many forms. It can even befriend you, gain your trust and kill your family.

For Shawna Forde, she had a simple question: "What could a nine-year-old possibly have done to deserve getting shot like that?" she asked. "I don't understand how someone could have that much hate in her heart."

||

Shawna Forde gave only one interview to a reporter from the mainstream media after her trial: a courthouse interview with Terry Greene Sterling on the afternoon of the day she was found guilty. Clad in black-and-white-striped jailhouse pajamas, Forde told Sterling she was "extremely saddened" by the verdict, which she found "surreal," even though she said she took it like a "pro."

Shawna brought up her long-dead baby daughter, the one she'd told close confidants she had smothered in a fit of postpartum depression, in a bizarre attempt to express her empathy for Gina Gonzalez. She told Sterling she had "lost a daughter" and thus knew from experience that Gonzalez will feel pain "the rest of her life."

"I know in her mind," Forde said of Gonzalez, "I am guilty and she hates me. I know her tragedy is extremely sad."

But the empathy only went so far. Forde said that on the other hand, "people shouldn't deal drugs if they have kids."

"I wish I could say I was sorry it happened," Forde said. "I am not sorry on my behalf because I didn't do it."

She was strangely resigned to her future on death row. For Greene Sterling, she put on a brave face about the prospect of being executed by lethal injection. If that happens, she said, "I'll move on to my next journey. We're all going to die. And it only happens once."

# 16

## The Nativist Legacy

The front door of the Flores home. DAVID NEIWERT PHOTO

They don't call themselves Minutemen anymore, because of Shawna
Forde—or more precisely, thanks to Gina Gonzalez and her will to
fight. There are still border watchers out there, and the shells of the national
Minuteman organization linger on in a zombielike half-life. But the Minutemen and their nativist supporters have gone on to greener, Tea Partying
pastures now.

When Shawna and her cohorts were first arrested in June 2009, the national Minuteman organization leaders engaged in a mad scramble to distance themselves from her. Chris Simcox claimed that his Minuteman Civil
Defense Corps had expelled her in less than six months, amid what reporters
described as "allegations of lying and pretending to be a senior leader."

"We knew that Shawna Forde was not just an unsavory character but
pretty unbalanced, as well," Simcox said. Not only that, he claimed that this

proved his organization had done a good job of weeding out extremists from within its ranks.

Evidently it had slipped Simcox's mind that not only had he been the person who promoted Shawna Forde to the new position of state "internal operations leader" for MCDC in Washington—thereby inspiring a revolt by his established state leadership—but also he had fought to retain Shawna, pleading with her to remain a "power behind the throne" at MCDC.

Similarly, Jim Gilchrist took down material from his Minuteman website supporting Forde's MAD and announced his "condolences to the victims," declaring that Forde and her associates were "rogues" and insisting that his relationship with her was never "extensive." "They happened to use the Minuteman movement as a guise, as a mask," he said.

Conveniently forgotten was the fact that he had functionally outsourced all of his border-watching activities to Shawna Forde and MAD and made her his national border-operations chief, that he had regularly promoted her and her border watches on his own Minuteman Project website, that he had passed along money to Shawna Forde to help finance her activities in Arizona, and that he had been in regular, ongoing contact with Shawna Forde, up until and including the very morning she was arrested.

Simcox's MCDC spokesperson, Carmen Mercer, decried the media coverage of the Forde case in a press statement. "The media continues to flame the fires of ethnic friction and faux racism through their ridiculous reporting that this is a Minuteman crime—the media is irrational and reckless in perpetrating this despicable propaganda," she declared. "The Arivaca home invasion had nothing to do with the Minutemen, nothing to do with race or illegal immigration, it had to do with psychopathic criminals preying on other criminals."

It seemed not to occur to Mercer—who, like Simcox, had fought to retain Shawna Forde in a leadership position in Washington and had even flown to Seattle to try to mend fences in the state MCDC—that the politics and rhetoric of the Minutemen had everything to do with why they not only attracted but were vulnerable to the predations of psychopaths like Forde and Bush. It was indeed a psychopathic crime—and it was also a Minuteman crime. These were not mutually exclusive aspects of the murders in Arivaca but indeed quite complementary—perhaps even inevitable.

||

Despite the strenuous efforts to distance their brand name from Shawna Forde, the damage was done. A number of Minutemen created new border-watch organizations that simply avoided the name. One of these was Al

Garza, Simcox's former right-hand man at MCDC, who started up an out-fit called the Patriots Coalition.

"A lot of people felt, well, you're a Minuteman, you're a killer," Al Garza told Gaiutra Bahadur of the *Nation*, and then blamed not Shawna Forde nor her enablers but the movement's critics: "The name Minuteman has been tainted by organizations that didn't want us at the border, that say we're killers, that we've done harm."

Explained Garza, when he announced his new organization: "Unfortu-nately, the public perception of the Minutemen has been tainted by our de-tractors and the media, which has successfully been enflamed by the internal and unnecessary strife. I do not see an end in sight for the problems plagu-ing what was once the greatest citizen movement in America."

A study conducted by the Institute for Research and Education on Human Rights (IREHR) examined the larger decline of the American nativist move-ment after 2010 and used the Minutemen as an exemplary case study:

> Several factors, including negative in-fighting and lawsuits, have con-tributed to the Minuteman Project's decline. One incident seemed to have had an outsized impact. In June 2009, Shawna Forde, who had been one of [Jim] Gilchrist's local chapter leaders, and two of her cohorts, broke into the home and brutally murdered Arizonan Raul Flores and his nine-year-old daughter Brisenia. The murders created a lot of negative public-ity for the gun-toting border vigilantes of the Minuteman groups, not unlike the way the bombing of the Oklahoma City federal office building in 1995 damaged the public reputation of the militias.

The Minuteman Project fell the hardest. Gilchrist wrote a year-end fund-raising letter in 2009, after the Arivaca murders, fretting about the loss of volunteers. He confided: "It has been a hard year for me here at Jim Gilchrist's Minuteman Project."

The Minuteman Project continues to operate but at a reduced level. With no Shawna Forde, it has no active border-watching operations. As the IREHR study noted, of the seventy-seven local chapters active in 2010, only thirty-four remained active in 2011.

The same was true of Chris Simcox's Minuteman Civil Defense Corps. The IREHR study reported that "of the 115 groups connected to MCDC and the Minuteman Project in 2010, only 53 showed any signs of activity in 2011, a 54% overall decrease in local groups in one year."

The decline followed sharply in the wake of Forde's arrest. First came the finger pointing and internecine warfare that erupted over Forde, particularly between American Legal Immigration PAC's William Gheen and Jim Gilchrist, who continues to claim that his associations with Forde were "not extensive." Gheen urged Gilchrist to step aside: "Do the movement a favor and announce your resignation," he wrote. Another California nativist, Chelene Nightingale of Save Our State, also attacked Gilchrist in an email posted briefly at the Minuteman Project website: "As a mother I am sick to death that a little child was murdered! Murdered at the hands of people that were endorsed on the Jim Gilchrist MMP site. Wasn't it bad enough that your forum is a sewer full of lies and bashing of patriots? Or are each of you being paid by say the SPLC, La Raza to destroy the movement with your filth and personal connections?" Gilchrist dismissed their attacks as the product of jealousy.

In the spring of 2010, Chris Simcox's Minuteman Civil Defense Corps announced that it was closing up shop. The precipitating event was an email that Carmen Mercer sent out to members in mid-March, announcing: "This March we return to the border locked, loaded and ready to stop each and every individual we encounter along the frontier that is now more dangerous than the frontier of Afghanistan." Mercer said she received a "dramatic" response to the email from members—many of whom, evidently, responded that they intended to show up at the border fully armed—which in turn inspired the MCDC board to dissolve itself because of fears that they would not be able to control participants, and they might be held responsible for people who failed to follow proper "rules of engagement."

"I'm afraid that for many citizens, the passing of health care against the will of the people and now indications that Obama will try to pass amnesty may be the straw that will break the spirit, or may be the straw that ignites frustration that we, as an organization, may not be able to manage or contain," Mercer wrote in announcing the dissolution of the MCDC. "This organization has grown too big for its own good; or rather, the problem has grown too big and serious for us to manage. I predict soon the violence will spill over the border (it already is) and I predict Americans, on their own, will lock, load and do what the feckless cowards in Washington refuse to do."

She told KOLD-TV in Tucson that it was just a tactical maneuver to avoid legal liability for any future Shawna Fordes: "The movement itself, the organization itself, is not going to go away, [it's] just the dissolving of the corporation." She warned future would-be Minuteman offshoots: "It only takes one bad person to destroy everything we've built in the last eight years."

Chris Simcox, who briefly flirted with a primary challenge to Senator John McCain in 2010, has largely vanished from public view since April

2010, when his estranged wife, Alena, obtained a protection order against him; her complaint claimed Simcox "brandished a gun and threatened to shoot her, their children and any police officers who tried to protect them."

Jim Gilchrist remains adamant that the Forde affair had little or no effect on his organization. "The Minuteman Movement was not seriously interfered with by whatever Shawna Forde and her two accomplices did," he wrote in response to reportage on relationship with the MAD founder. "The Minuteman Movement was put into a temporary tailspin by some selfish opportunists posing as immigration law enforcement advocates whose true interest was in hijacking the movement for their own financial and egotistical interests, in my opinion."

He claimed simultaneously that Forde was acting all on her own and that she was in touch with many others in the movement as well: "Shawna Forde and her two thugs were lone wolves who operated their own organization distinct and separate from other immigration activist groups. She also regularly communicated with many of the hundred or so similar groups established around the country," conveniently forgetting that none of those other organizations named Forde their national border-operations director, either. "Simply, the murderous trio used a feigned participation in the immigration law enforcement movement as a convenient veil to cloak some sinister plans to rob drug dealers and coyotes."

Local Minuteman organizations suspended operations in the wake of Forde's arrest, and most of them have not returned. Scott Anderson, leader of the MCDC's Green Valley chapter—which had never had any connection to Forde—announced he was suspending its border-watch activities immediately after the arrests. "I figured something like this was going to happen," he told a local reporter. "We're all going to be painted with the same broad brush." The group has never returned to action.

There are still some border-watch outfits trying to organize recruits, but none call themselves Minutemen anymore, and they operate on the fringes even more than MAD did. At least one of the new border-watch outfits, led by Arizona white supremacist J. T. Ready, openly courted the most radical segment of the American right, including neo-Nazis from the National Socialist Movement and biker gangs. Ready named his organization the U.S. Border Guard, but his operation came to an abrupt end on May 2, 2012, when he went on a shooting rampage against his girlfriend and her family in the home they shared, killing four people (including a fifteen-month-old toddler) before turning the gun on himself.

Another splinter border-watch group, calling itself the Cochise County

Militia, proposed an outfit remarkably similar to Shawna Forde's vision for MAD: reforming itself into a local Blackwater-style organization. According to the Southern Poverty Law Center, CCM's founder, Bill Davis, told his supporters in an April 2010 email—just as the fight over SB 1070 was heating up—that his Tombstone-based militia would be forming a private military company, which Davis insisted is "completely legal!!!"

In the email, Davis said he preferred combat veterans for his venture but would consider others. The work was unpaid. "We can be considered paramilitary, but not vigilantes, mercenaries, etc.," Davis wrote.

On the other hand, his website's discussion of weapons insisted that "we don't want to appear as a para-military group in any way."

At the same time, the site's sentiments about border crossers were unmistakable: "Thirsty Illegals Are Just Dying To Be Caught," it announced, over photos of men armed with combat rifles. Davis also outlined some of his rules of engagement in a newsletter: "Be polite . . . be professional . . . be ready to kill all you Meet!"

||

Shawna Forde had early on recognized the potential of the Tea Party—a much broader expression of right-wing populism, but borne of the same political currents that produced nativist movements like the Minutemen. And in the months and years since her criminal spree permanently tainted the Minutemen, many of the former Minuteman movement leaders have been steadily remaking themselves as Tea Party activists.

"The Forde killings really made the whole movement sordid and these guys [Minuteman leaders] needed to find somewhere else for their ambitions," Heidi Beirich, codirector of the Southern Poverty Law Center's Intelligence Project, told the IREHR researchers. "Rebranding themselves as Tea Party figures is their effort to stay relevant. They saw the rising populism as a good thing to latch onto, so they just toned down their anti-immigrant messaging a bit and synced themselves with the larger Tea Party agenda."

Glenn Spencer explained it more benignly: "Many of the so-called Minuteman groups died off, mainly due to lack of focus of the organizations. Sitting on the border in a lawn chair does not fire the hearts of men. Those who were drawn into the political arena by the border issue naturally gravitated towards better organized groups of people concerned with the overall failure of our government to work in the interests of the people, of which the failure to secure the border is just one example."

Indeed: in the summer of 2010, Spencer hosted Tea Party tours at his

Arizona ranch, which you could sign up for through the Maricopa County Republicans website. Perhaps more notably, in August of that year, he hosted a "United We Stand" Tea Party rally at his ranch. The line-up for the rally was a virtual who's who of Arizona's nativist politicians and activists: Sheriff Joe Arpaio, SB 1070 author Russell Pearce, US Senate wannabe J. D. Hayworth— who was challenging incumbent Senator John McCain that year in the GOP primary, accusing him of being "soft" on immigration—and Republican congressional hopeful Pamela Gorman, who had gotten some attention for her campaign video showing her emptying a number of rounds from her machine gun into the Arizona desert.

It was a mutual affair: the Tea Party movement's national leadership largely embraced the Minutemen's nativism. One of the movement's chief publicity draws is its national Tea Party Express bus tours, and in October 2010, the tour featured Joe Arpaio. At a stop in Las Vegas, Arpaio came on-stage before a crowd of some two thousand as a Tea Party band sang: "We stand with you Arizona / The rule of law in this land / What part of 'illegal' don't they understand?"

One of the movement's leading national bodies, the Tea Party Patriots, held their national convention in Phoenix in February 2011, drawing about two thousand people. The conference site was chosen specifically to support SB 1070, and the nativists were front and center: both Joe Arpaio and Russell Pearce were featured luminaries for the gathering.

Arizona Governor Jan Brewer welcomed the convention to Phoenix by thanking the Tea Party: "You didn't have to choose our home. . . . I know you are here because we share a common cause in taking back our country. We want our borders secured. We want the federal government out of our daily lives."

As the IREHR study observed, "both the Patriot Action Network and Tea Party Nation continued to promote an explicitly racist brand of nativism. Tea Party Nation Founder Judson Phillips, for instance, called for a return to the racist 1924 National Origins Act, and warned that immigrants are causing 'White Anglo-Saxon protestant extinction.' He called for gutting the 14th Amendment's birthright citizenship rights."

Meanwhile, despite his years of Latino bashing and hatemongering, Glenn Spencer has so successfully mainstreamed himself that in March 2011, he was called as an "expert witness" to testify before the Arizona Senate's Border Security Committee, chaired by Sylvia Allen, a nativist Republican from Snowflake. After a couple of Democrats walked out in protest, the committee heard Spencer promote his so-called sonic barrier technology— which purportedly would detect unlawful border crossers—with the help of an associate, who gave a live demonstration to the remaining senators. Spencer ultimately admitted there were a couple of flaws: for one thing, it would cost approximately $100,000 a mile. It is also unable to distinguish between cows and human beings.

When it comes to Shawna Forde, Spencer prefers not to discuss the matter. What he has told reporters is that his American Border Patrol operation continues to grow, despite the setbacks. "Our supporters come from all over the United States, and the Shawna Forde thing was just a local thing. It did make some national news but not much. . . . It had no impact on us whatsoever."

||

While Glenn Spencer clearly had a skewed view of what constituted a "local thing"—considering the Shawna Forde saga stretched all the way to the Canadian border, with numerous points in between—he was correct in the sense that the story never made it much out of the local-media orbit in terms of coverage. National media covered the case briefly—often with their facts wrong—at key junctures, but the amount and intensity of that coverage were insignificant compared to similar reportage on the Robert Krentz murder or other notorious cases outside of Arizona.

Millions more people, for instance, were intimately familiar with the relatively mundane contents of accused (and eventually acquitted) child killer Casey Anthony's jail-cell phone calls than had ever heard Gina Gonzalez's desperate and dramatic 911 call. And this did not go unnoticed with at least one significant segment of the populace: Hispanic Americans.

Many Latinos were left wondering why the media could obsess over the Krentz and Anthony cases but could not drum up any outrage over the deaths of Brisenia Flores and her father. "A prevalent impression by those in the Hispanic community concerned with the Shawna Forde case is that, despite the fact that an innocent child was murdered, public condemnation of this senseless act has not been forthcoming," wrote Salvador Ongaro of Los Abogados, Arizona's Hispanic bar association, in an email to Terry Greene Sterling.

The claim that Forde wasn't really a Minuteman—despite overwhelming evidence that she was a longtime player in the movement, elevated to positions of power by various national leaders—meanwhile enjoyed a long half-life in the national media. When Bill O'Reilly hosted a segment discussing the story on his Fox News show in February 2011, for instance, both of the "legal analysts" featured in the segment, Kimberly Guilfoyle and Lis Wiehl, insisted that Forde was not really part of the movement. "She was not part of the Minutemen," Wiehl told O'Reilly. (O'Reilly himself described the

Flores-Gonzalez home as "an illegal alien house," even though both Junior Flores and Gina Gonzalez qualified by any criterion as multigenerational American citizens.)

When Shawna was convicted in February 2011, the Latino-rights organization Presente—which had created the striking "Justice for Brisenia" signs seen at a number of anti–SB 1070 rallies—issued an incisive commentary on the view from within its community:

> Though we received a verdict that condemned these atrocious murders, we also recognize that the Brisenia Flores' case is not the isolated incident that some media reports make it out to be. Rather, it has galvanized the attention of the entire Latino community across the country as it reflects the anti-immigrant, anti-Latino hatred organized by extremist groups. Latinos—the fastest-growing and largest ethnic minority group in the U.S.—understand and experience the phenomenon of hatred that has rapidly expanded in the nation. In fact, Latinos are closely watching media outlets that provide a platform for hatred promoted by extremist groups like MAD and the Federation for American Immigration Reform—a group Forde represented on a PBS show, for instance. Latinos are closely watching those media outlets that irresponsibly allow hateful groups to attack Latinos and immigrants, fanning the flames of fear and violence in our communities.

Much of the media calculus in its handling of the Flores murders appears to have been founded on two key narratives favored by media outlets: it ran directly counter to the long-running narrative depicting the Minuteman movement as a collection of friendly neighbors out watching the border in their lawn chairs, and most significantly, it was concluded by the people calling the news shots that because Junior Flores was in fact a marijuana smuggler, he had essentially asked for the fate that descended on his family. After all, weren't drug-related murders a common occurrence on the border?

In the context of Arivaca—where marijuana smuggling has been part of the cultural and economic landscape for more than four decades and where someone like Junior Flores was simply an everyday businessman—this judgment was absurd and amoral. It was also not grounded in the realities of their everyday lives. As Dan Shearer at the *Green Valley News* discovered when he began examining the facts on the ground, these kinds of crimes are decidedly not very common, even on the border, despite the media hype and the hysteria stirred up by Minutemen like Shawna Forde. She may have fully believed, as she told the Norwegian documentarians, that life is cheap on the border: "Shootings and deaths occur on a daily basis out here." They do occur—but neither that frequently, nor are they greeted with a shrug.

In much of the rest of the country, where that context does not exist, this assessment might be considered reasonable. But even then, it begs the question of whether involvement in the drug trade is an excuse for wanton murder, especially when the victim has done nothing more than smuggle marijuana—which, while still illegal, is regularly consumed by over seventeen million Americans, has been tried by 42 percent of Americans, and is now legal for medicinal purposes in sixteen states. More American teenagers smoke marijuana than smoke tobacco. It would be one thing if Junior Flores had been a murderer or violent thug himself, but he was not. Making Flores accountable for his own murder and that of his daughter is only a vaguely mitigated—not to mention grossly disingenuous—instance of blaming the victim.

Moreover, it occludes the reality that the perpetrators were not drug smugglers but leading exponents of a movement predicated on demanding a strict adherence to American laws, even when it was self-evident that those laws are both antiquated and destructively dysfunctional. The Minuteman American Defense logo featured the motto "Rule of Law" at the center of its crest, and it was clear that Shawna Forde's incendiary rhetoric, like that of her fellow Minutemen generally, reflected her belief that the righteousness of her mission had come to supersede all other legal and moral considerations. Indeed, she not only lowered her organization to the level of drug cartels but then behaved in a manner that even violated those cartels' dubious codes of behavior.

The Minutemen, in reality, were keen on the "rule of law" only insofar as it applied to keeping out what Shawna called "subhuman Mexicans." In the end, Forde's fetish for lawfulness was only a pretext for carrying out an agenda based on bigotry—and she was hardly alone in that regard.

Carlos Galindo, a Phoenix radio host, told Terry Greene Sterling before the Forde trial that he had reminded his listeners of Brisenia Flores "on a regular basis at least two or three times a week" since the murders occurred and had criticized Latino leaders for failing to voice sufficient outrage.

"This was a horrible, tragic, and absolutely race-based coldblooded murder," he said, "and we allowed the far right to muddy it up and say her dad was a drug dealer and Brisenia was collateral damage. When we don't counter that, we allow continued violence against all Arizonans."

Kat Rodriguez, program director for the immigrant advocacy group Coalición de Derechos Humanos, found the nativists' scramble to disown Shawna Forde somewhat amusing. "The fact is that they've all gone into CYA—cover your own ass—mode," Rodriguez said.

She observed that all of these nativists—the Minuteman leaders, Glenn Spencer and his fellow nativists, as well as the Tea Partiers—share the real guilt of stoking Shawna Forde's demons and giving her a platform of power. "The anti-immigrant rhetoric, the fervor, the lies that continue to be told . . . she would not have been able to do those kinds of things, say those kinds of things, get the traction she had, had she not enjoyed this status that was implied by being part of the Minutemen Project."

As Presente observed in its commentary on Shawna Forde's convictions: "The details revealed in the murder trial . . . reflect the deepening and mainstreaming of the most noxious and dangerous strands of hatred in the United States." Because the American media responded as if it were just another drug-related home invasion, they only contributed to that deepening.

||

The Minuteman movement began crumbling apart even at the moment of its greatest triumph—the media circus in Naco in April 2005—in large part because of the kind of personalities that it attracted: contentious, prone to anger, hypercritical, paranoid, grandiose, egocentric people who found it almost impossible to coexist after only a few weeks of fitful cooperation. The strife and dissension, over issues ranging from strategy to finances, not only continued but intensified over the ensuing years, assuring that the movement would continually splinter, inevitably creating radicalized organizations like MAD, increasingly unleashed from the restraints that national organizations labored under in order to mainstream their movement.

It attracted these kinds of personalities in large part because they reflected both the politics and the rhetoric the movement employed in its appeals: resentment and anger were common features of their rhetoric—indeed, the more inflammatory the speech, the greater its audience seemed to be. The core of the Minutemen's politics was scapegoating: blaming Latino immigrants for being forced into circumstances that they did not create and that were for that matter created by Americans as much as Mexicans. By insisting on "securing the borders" before fixing the problems that had made the borders so insecure, most of them a product of antiquated immigration laws, they actually ensured that the borderlands would remain a volatile place.

The sum of the Minuteman movement's achievements was thus nearly nil: in the seven years between its inception and its final demise, nothing changed in American immigration policy, other than that the Obama administration, in an effort to prove its good-faith effort at securing the borders, doubled the number of Border Patrol agents and deported more immigrants—some

396,000 by October 2011—than any administration in American history. Yet that wasn't even nearly enough to satisfy Obama's critics. Tea Partiers and assorted nativists continue to claim that Obama is "soft on immigration" and viciously disparage his immigration policies. In the meantime, any effort to reform the nation's immigration laws has been stonewalled, especially after Tea Party–led Republicans took control of the House in 2010.

The only thing that did change was that the American economy took a nosedive in 2008, and the resulting recession wiped out many of the five hundred thousand or more unskilled-labor jobs that the economy had at one time produced annually. The demand for immigrant labor thus declined sharply, while simultaneously the Mexican economy began to recover from its long, NAFTA-induced downturn. The end result was that many fewer people were attempting to cross the American border, either through the desert or other means, in search of work. The Minutemen had nothing whatsoever to do with this change.

The Minutemen's failure was not merely a product of internal dissension or obstructive politics, however. The movement crumbled under the weight of the extremists it attracted, despite numerous warnings—not merely from its critics—that because of its agenda and its politics, it ran a nearly in-eluctable risk of becoming a haven for violent racists. Though the Minutemen often proclaimed their efforts to "weed out" racists from their ranks (begging the question: Why did they need to do so in the first place?), movement leaders never took seriously the need to thoroughly vet the backgrounds of their recruits, not to mention their leaders. If they had, people like Shawna Forde would never have been accepted in the first place. Whatever procedures they had were grossly inadequate—though perhaps that is because many of their leaders would not have survived a thorough check, either.

It was far easier—and in the end, more effective—to simply complain that their critics were intent on depicting them as "racist vigilantes," even as many of them turned a blind eye to overt racism within their ranks, not to mention outright vigilante immigrant hunters like Shawna Forde. The com-plaint became an oft-repeated bitter joke for Minuteman spokesmen, to the point that many reporters simply began to take it for granted that the move-ment was devoid of racists and *cazamigrantes*.

Moreover, as the case of Shawna Forde—as well as the larger movement's internal dynamics—amply demonstrated, the movement was vulnerable to the depredations of people with personality disorders. Just as it attracted contentious and angry people because so much of its appeal was contentious and angry, it also attracted toxic personalities—borderline personalities, narcissists, and psychopaths—because so much of its rhetoric reproduced their interior lives.

Psychologists recognize a variety of personality disorders, divided into roughly three categories described in the *Diagnostic and Statistical Manual of Mental Disorders*:

The borderline personality: "The major symptoms of this disorder revolve around unstable relationships, poor or negative sense of self, inconsistent moods, and significant impulsivity. There is an intense fear of abandonment with this disorder that interferes with many aspects of the individual's life. This fear often acts as a self-fulfilling prophecy as they cling to others, are very needy, feel helpless, and become overly involved and immediately attached. When the fear of abandonment becomes overwhelming, they will often push others out of their life as if trying to avoid getting rejected. The cycle most often continues as the individual will then try everything to get people back in his or her life and once again becomes clingy, needy, and helpless."

Narcissistic personality disorders, which "revolve around a pattern of grandiosity, need for admiration, and sense of entitlement. Often individuals feel overly important and will exaggerate achievements and will accept, and often demand, praise and admiration despite worthy achievements. They may be overwhelmed with fantasies involving unlimited success, power, love, or beauty and feel that they can only be understood by others who are, like them, superior in some aspect of life. There is a sense of entitlement, of being more deserving than others based solely on their superiority. These symptoms, however, are a result of an underlying sense of inferiority and are often seen as overcompensation. Because of this, they are often envious and even angry of others who have more, receive more respect or attention, or otherwise steal away the spotlight."

Antisocial personality disorder, which is the category that earns one the label of "psychopath" or "sociopath" (the distinction between these two lying in whether the symptoms originate from the subject's innate nature or with his environment, or some combination of both). Its symptoms include "a longstanding pattern . . . of disregard for the rights of others. There is a failure to conform to society's norms and expectations that often results in numerous arrests or legal involvement as well as a history of deceitfulness where the individual attempts to con people or use trickery for personal profit. Impulsiveness if often present, including angry outbursts, failure to consider consequences of behaviors, irritability, and/or physical assaults."

It is this last category that is most germane when dealing with the case of Shawna Forde, because her known history—embodied both in her public criminal history and in her private life as described by family, friends, and acquaintances—most closely fits that particular constellation of symptoms.

Dr. Robert Hare, a University of British Columbia psychologist, compiled a checklist of the major traits of psychopathy in the 1990s (since revised modestly) that has become a major tool for clinicians and law enforcement officers in dealing with the depredations of psychopaths in the past decade and longer. Hare's checklist has played an important role in investigations into such noteworthy crimes as the Columbine High School massacre and the Green River Killer case.

Reviewing Hare's checklist is nearly a summation of Shawna Forde's biography. He cites two key factors: a personality built on "aggressive narcissism" and a "socially deviant lifestyle." The traits of the first factor include a glibness and superficial charm; a grandiose sense of self-worth; pathological lying; cunning and manipulative behavior; a lack of remorse or guilt; shallow affect in interpersonal relations, in which genuine emotion is short-lived and egocentric; a callousness and lack of empathy; and a failure to accept responsibility for one's own actions.

A psychopath's case history manifests a "socially deviant lifestyle" if it demonstrates a need for stimulation and a proneness to boredom; a parasitic lifestyle, sponging off the work of others; poor behavioral control; a lack of realistic long-term goals; impulsivity; irresponsibility; juvenile delinquency; and early behavior problems. Other traits, uncorrelated to either of the two chief factors, include promiscuous sexuality, many short-term marital relationships, and criminal versatility.

Shawna's personal history is replete with multiple examples of each of these traits. Family and friends, enemies and allies alike have described Shawna's ability to charm people, often with the intent to manipulate, often by lying. Her own pronouncements bespoke a wildly overinflated sense of self-worth and grandiosity—especially when it came to the Minuteman movement—and she never, ever took responsibility for her own miscreant behavior. Nearly everyone who knew her described how she would simulate empathy as a way to draw out people's vulnerabilities, exposing them to her manipulations. And while at times she could be genuinely empathetic and remorseful, her history is littered with criminal callousness, culminating in three acts utterly devoid of remorse or compassion: the probable attempt to have her estranged husband, John Forde, killed for the sake of his money; her robbery of her friends Pete and Lyn Myers; and ordering Jason Bush to shoot Brisenia Flores as she pleaded for her life.

Similarly, Shawna frequently spoke of her constant need for an "adrenaline rush" such as the one her Minuteman work provided her; she constantly sponged off men, particularly her husbands, while flitting from job to job, and when she couldn't soak her four husbands, she wrangled money out of various other men, notably including her colleagues in the Minuteman movement. She seemed unable to control her impulses, particularly when it came to shoplifting—even while she was bidding for respectability in the form of a city council seat—and was a profoundly irresponsible parent and spouse, dumping her children with other people willy-nilly and indulging frequently in extramarital affairs and one-night stands. She was always concocting one grandiose scheme after another and substituting that for anything resembling realistic life goals, and then was incapable of even taking the initial steps toward achieving those grand plans. She was, of course, a troubled child and not merely a juvenile delinquent but a teenage prostitute. And finally, she was nothing if not a versatile criminal, indulging in theft, prostitution, fraud, embezzlement, assault, robbery, and eventually murder.

The likely presence of a central psychopathic player—and the likelihood of the symbiotic impetus given to her crimes by the introduction of another psychopath, or at least a willing and eager enabler, in the form of Jason Bush—brings to mind another great national tragedy, the 1999 killing rampage by two teenage boys, Eric Harris and Dylan Klebold, at Columbine High School in Colorado, in which thirteen people died and another twenty-one were injured. As Dave Cullen explored at length in his remarkable study of the incident, *Columbine*, the conclusion of investigators was that Eric Harris was a cold-blooded psychopath, while Dylan Klebold likely suffered from a personality disorder and played a key role in enabling Harris's massacre plans.

In that regard, it might be plausible to consider the Minuteman movement itself a victim of a psychopath in the form of Shawna Forde, destroyed by her insensate criminality. The problem with making such a claim is that, unlike the administrators at Columbine High School—who, if guilty of anything, had failed to adequately recognize the threat posed by a psychopath like Eric Harris—the Minutemen and their leadership in particular not only made rhetorical appeals nearly certain to attract psychopaths but embraced, encouraged, and inflamed Shawna's own fast-rising arc of radicalization. They empowered her psychopathic behavior even as it became manifest in the movement's own broiling inner turmoil. The Minutemen were not Shawna Forde's victims but her enablers.

The rhetoric of the Minutemen and their related nativist organizations— including, nowadays, the Tea Party—appealed to psychopaths like Shawna Forde and Jason Bush because it reflected so much of their interior psyches and moreover provided an irresistible opportunity for grandiose self-inflation and validation.

Minuteman rhetoric often reflected the very traits of personality disorders, particularly in its political mind-set, which sought to blame weak and helpless (contemptibly so, from the nativist view) others for their own, often self-inflicted, national problems. It was frequently grandiose, particularly in its claims to be preventing terrorist attacks and its larger claims to be in the act of "saving America"; it indulged a marked propensity to lie and dispense false information, ranging from Glenn Spencer's Ebola rumor and Reconquista claims to Chris Simcox's bogus border-fence scam to Jim Gilchrist's bathetic, and ultimately futile, attempts to distance himself from Shawna Forde. The Minutemen also frequently distorted facts, if they did not outright falsify them, in order to manipulate public sentiment, and they did so remorselessly. Most of all, despite occasional lip service to the plight of immigrants, the Minutemen's rhetoric was profoundly lacking in empathy for the targets of their ire; indeed, the more callous and cold-hearted the remark, the more widely it was circulated. If ever there was a movement tailored to recruit and promote psychopaths, it was the Minutemen.

||

Shawna Forde's symbiotic embrace of the Minutemen was not accidental nor even the random result of circumstances, as is often the case with psychopaths and the means they employ to their often criminal and sometimes violent ends. It was a virtual inevitability, given the nature of their politics, agenda, and rhetorical fuel.

What movements like the Minutemen most offer psychopaths like Shawna Forde is the opportunity to remake themselves into their own hyperinflated view of themselves as Heroes with a capital H, all without the hard work, sacrifice, and dedication that usually comprise the foundations of real heroism. This is something the Minutemen shared in common with nearly all brands of right-wing extremism: a core ethos dedicated to constructing and establishing their own heroic identities, a grandiose kind of self-validation.

The Minutemen in particular were noteworthy in promising a path to heroic status. The Arizona desert is an exotic and adventurous place, still largely wild and always potentially dangerous all on its own. Add to that the thrill of hunting down and catching lawbreakers in the act, and you have something straight out of a testosterone-fueled action film. All in the name of saving America from "illegals."

As James Aho described it in his study of the behavior of right-wing extremists, *This Thing of Darkness*, an essential component of constructing a heroic identity entails identifying and naming the enemy:

> The warrior needs an enemy. Without one there is nothing against which to fight, nothing from which to save the world, nothing to give his life meaning. What this means, of course, is that if an enemy is not ontologically present in the nature of things, one must be manufactured. The Nazi needs an international Jewish banker and conspiratorial Mason to serve his purposes of self-aggrandizement, and thus sets about creating one, at least unconsciously. By the same token, the radical Zionist locks himself in perverse symbiosis with his Palestinian "persecutors," the Communist with his "imperialistic capitalist running dogs," the capitalist with his Communist "subversives." . . .
>
> . . . Whether embodied in thing or in person, the enemy in essence represents putrefaction and death: either its instrumentality, its location (dirt, filth, garbage, excrement), its carriers (vermin, pests, bacilli), or all of these together. . . .
>
> The enemy typically is experienced as issuing from the "dregs" of society, from its lower parts, the "bowels of the underworld." It is sewage from the gutter, "trash" excreted as poison from society's affairs—church, school, workplace, and family.
>
> The enemy's visitation on our borders is tantamount to impending pestilence. . . . The enemy's presence in our midst is a pathology of the social organism serious enough to require the most far-reaching remedies: quarantine, political excision, or, to use a particularly revealing expression, liquidation and expulsion.

American nativist movements—and the Minutemen are no exception—have traditionally identified immigrants of various stripes as the enemy: in the 1840s, it was the Irish; in the 1880s, it was the Chinese; in the 1890s, it was the Germans; in the 1920s, it was the Japanese. And since the 1970s, but most acutely in the past decade, it has been Hispanics.

One of the most invidious and pervasive means of demonizing Latinos has been to emphasize their legal status in the labels used to describe undocumented immigrants. It's hard to conceive of a more innately dehumanizing term than "illegal aliens"—not only are they assumed to be criminals, but it is suggested that they are something other than fully human (indeed, the phrase has its origins in the eugenics era, used primarily to describe Asian immigrants, whose full humanity was very much in doubt among the racial thinkers of the West at the time). Yet it is bandied about with abandon by politicians, media pundits, and editorial writers.

The same is true of the offhanded label "illegals," which reduces a human being entirely to his or her legal status as a citizen. Moreover, it is applied almost entirely to Latinos, even though they are not the only people breaking the law under our current immigration scenarios. No one calls the CEOs of the agribusiness corporations that hire large numbers of undocumented immigrants "illegals," even though they have just as surely broken the law. Only slightly less noxious is the phrase favored by news reporters, "illegal immigrants," which at least accurately describes the person but presumes to judge his or her legal status without ever being subjected to a court hearing—something a news reporter would never do in any other context.

The pervasiveness of this kind of language in the mainstream media not only legitimizes the nativist worldview but fuels the self-proclaimed heroism of right-wing populists who dehumanize them by rote. After all, who does not believe in the rule of law? The unquestionable virtue of their mission and their superior status as citizens readily flow into the hands of people who then set themselves up as above, and beyond, the law—arbiters not just of right and wrong but of life and death.

This has profound consequences for Americans, both on a mass political level and on the local, personal level. Naming the enemy is the first and most important step down a path that has historically led to tragedy, even genocide. Right-wing populist movements have a history, both in America and elsewhere, of producing human destruction: in the United States, the Ku Klux Klan of the 1920s, which played a central role in the lynching era and the enforcement of Jim Crow laws, is the chief exemplar, while in Europe, the Nazi Party's bloody reign of terror produced one of the great tragedies in human history.

Naming an enemy inevitably creates a demand to exterminate it—and just as inevitably, this is justified as serving a greater "good." Ervin Staub observed this in his study of genocide, *The Roots of Evil*:

The essence of evil is the destruction of human beings. This includes not only killing but creating the conditions that materially or psychologically destroy or diminish people's dignity, happiness, and capacity to fulfill basic material needs.

By *evil* I mean actions that have such consequences. We cannot judge evil by conscious intentions, because psychological distortions tend to hide even from the perpetrators themselves their true intentions. They are unaware, for example, of their own unconscious hostility or that they are scapegoating others. Frequently, their intention is to create a "better world," but in the course of doing so they disregard the welfare and destroy the lives of human beings. Perpetrators of evil often intend to make people suffer but see their actions as necessary or serving a higher good. In addition, people tend to hide their negative intentions from others and justify negative actions by higher ideals or the victims' evil nature.

If nativist sentiments in America ever were to build beyond short-lived, self-destructive movements like the Minutemen, the potential for large-scale evil, as Staub defines it, would grow exponentially. When such movements remain small and naturally attract psychopathic elements by practicing a politics that sneers at empathy as weakness, the tragedies they produce will generally be on a small scale like the murder of Junior and Brisenia Flores or numerous other acts of violence against Latinos inspired by inflammatory nativist rhetoric. Translated to a larger scale as a mass movement, where those same antisocial personalities obtain real power, these propensities will produce tragedy on a much larger scale.

The antidote to the poisonous mass politics of ethnic resentment, however, lies not with an opposing mass politics but in the personal choices Americans make as individuals. We can each choose not to scapegoat immigrants for our economic problems, and we can reject the arguments of those who do. We can choose not to indulge in the language of dehumanization that reduces human beings to the level of vermin and diseases, and we can reject and disempower those who insist on promoting eliminationism. We can choose to find real, common-sense solutions to the challenges of immigration that respect the dignity of immigrants, rather than the punitive, destructive, and ultimately futile twin courses of mass deportation and militarization of the American border. We can choose to retain our humanity. As long as we do that, nativists and their politics of inhumanity will not win.

What ultimately will empower those choices is the knowledge of what happens when we go down the road taken by the nativists, when we lose our collective and individual humanity, when we become the demonic. The grave of a little nine-year-old girl and her father in Sahuarita, as we have learned, becomes a marker along that path.

||

Shawna Forde remains on death row in Arizona, only the third woman to achieve that distinction in recent times. She has some female company there in the form of another child killer, Debra Ann Milke, who was convicted in 1991 of ordering the execution-style murder of her four-year-old son, Christopher. Milke too continues to proclaim her innocence. The third woman on death row is Wendi Andriano, who back in 2000 tried poisoning her cancer-stricken husband and, when that didn't work, stabbed him in the neck and struck his head twenty-three times.

Shawna insists on screening her media interviews through Laine Lawless, who still operates her Justice for Shawna Forde website, exploring the ostensible conspiracy to frame the Minuteman movement and Shawna, and who so far has refused all requests. Jason Bush and Albert Gaxiola, likewise, have declined all interview requests. In the meantime, the automatic appeals hearings in the death sentences for Forde and Bush were scheduled for the fall of 2012.

Then there is the human wreckage Shawna left in her wake, whose stories really are more meaningful:

John Forde: Having recovered miraculously from his five gunshot wounds—though his body has enough scar tissue to frighten a biker—John is back at work and once again enjoying his life in Everett. He has a new home, and goes skiing and bicycling with friends, often the same folks who helped him get through his recovery and ensuing year of physical therapy. He tears up when talking about these friends: "They saved my life, and anything I can do for them will never be enough." Charlie, the Jack Russell terrier who sat beside him as he was shot, is still his happy-go-lucky companion.

Pete and Lyn Myers: Because they no longer had their $12,000 tucked away, the Myerses lost their home in Shasta Lake to foreclosure in 2010. They are now living in a trailer home near Redding. Their developmentally disabled son was forced to move in with his grandparents.

Gina Gonzalez and Alexandra Flores: The widow of Junior Flores and their daughter have retired quietly to a community south of Tucson, where Gina makes her living doing cleaning work. Alexandra is attending the local high school. Both, unsurprisingly, have also declined all media interviews.

Shawna Forde left behind a number of other victims, of course—some of whose names and stories we will probably never learn. It can also be said that she made an entire town her victim: Arivaca.

||

Two and a half year after the murders, the cloud over Arivaca is beginning to lift. But it is only beginning.

As much as the murders themselves, it was the things that were written and said about Arivaca in their aftermath that created this cloud. Perhaps the nadir was Oin Oakstar's testimony in Shawna Forde's trial depicting the town as nothing more than a nest of drug smugglers. As one Arivacan told me: "That may have been true for Oin Oakstar. That was his world. For the rest of us, it's a very different story."

In early November 2011, community leaders—most notably Clara Godfrey, the aunt of Albert Gaxiola—organized their sixteenth annual Folklorico Festival, a celebration held downtown in observance of Día de los Muertos, celebrating, as the poster said, "the Sweet Things in Life." People in the town saw it as a chance to come together, play guitars under the trees, and eat good food. A sign of healing.

It was a sunny but chilly Saturday, which meant that the local farmers' market—set up in an open space to the east of La Gitana Cantina, roughly in the same area as the Buffalo Soldiers' parade grounds—was open for business. There was a variety of fresh produce for sale, including some wonderfully rich local honey. Along the main street, local food vendors were setting up their trailers, offering everything from tamales to Sonoran tostadas to barbecued meat on a stick.

Most of the action for the celebration took place off the main drag, however. The events kicked off a little after noon as Clara Godfrey—dressed in a black-and-white pants suit and a red flat-rimmed hat, her face painted with a skeletal white mask, a second skull mask attached to the back of her head, so that she was the visage of two-faced death—led a procession of similarly costumed revelers in the annual parade through the ancient Arivaca Cemetery.

There were about thirty of them, mostly children, many of whom were thrilled at the opportunity to wear their Halloween costumes a second time.

One boy came as Spider-Man; others just wore their ordinary Saturday clothes. Another boy came dressed all in black, a cowled death mask hiding his face, a fiery skull emblazoned in gold on his chest.

As the procession reached the end of the cemetery, there were prayers and brief honoraria to the recently interred. Then the celebrants shared a repast of pumpkin-and-cream cake and punch.

Clara Godfrey spent much of her time doting on the children. She persuaded the boy in the death mask to try the cake, though he was reluctant at first to remove the mask. She also posed for pictures with two of the local high school students who had been named royalty for the celebration.

As the procession returned to the town site, most of the celebrants gathered in a little square just off the main street, behind the artists' co-op. There was music and a sizzling grill cooking up steaks and pork for tacos. Clara led the children in several rounds of Musical Chairs, and she gave out a number of festival awards. Later in the afternoon, there was live music, featuring local musicians, and people danced and laughed and sang along.

And yet despite the smiles and music and good food, a certain tension lingered. An elderly lady, who had grown up in Arivaca and planned to die there, talked to me about the town in the aftermath of the Flores murders. Things are better, she said, but not finished, either. "I think the people who brought that down on us are still here," she said, looking up and down the street.

Indeed, while the good feelings were a sign of healing, of the community coming back together, yet there was also a tinge of fear, inspired perhaps by the knowledge that somewhere out there, there was a fourth man who took part in the murders, never identified, much less caught. And maybe more.

There was also an undercurrent of sadness and regret. Perhaps that was because it was Dìa de Los Muertos, the Day of the Dead, when you honor the dead. In Arivaca, in addition to the dead whose well-decorated graves Clara Godfrey led those marchers past, there were the unspoken dead—the man and his daughter buried in another town miles away—who also lingered in the memory.

You got the sense that not all the pages in this chapter have been turned here in Arivaca. But then, stories like this are never really over.

# ACKNOWLEDGMENTS

This book would not have been possible without the groundwork laid by two people, both daily news reporters working ingloriously in the journalistic trenches:

Scott North, a veteran reporter and editor at the *Herald* in Everett, Washington, who happens to be a longtime friend and colleague. It was North who first exposed Shawna Forde as a pathological fraud, even before she became a child killer, and it was North who uncovered the entire story of her career in crime in the aftermath of the Flores murders. Scott was also the first to interview the first known victim in her spree of murderous violence, John Forde, and to track down the turmoil of her upbringing. North shared his notes and information with me freely, and this book would not have existed without his hard work and upstanding diligence. It also helps that Scott North is as decent a man as they come; not only did it open many doors for him, it also drove him to pursue this story deeply.

Dave Ricker, a part-time reporter for the *Green Valley News and Sun*, the biweekly paper published out of Sahuarita and the hometown paper for Arivaca. Ricker was the only reporter who covered nearly every day of all three of the Tucson trials in the Flores murders, and his dogged pursuit of the story revealed a hundred nuances and previously unknown details, especially as the facts of the case played out in the courtroom. I met Ricker while covering the trials myself and was impressed by his attentiveness to detail and his keen insights, and I was deeply appreciative that he was willing to share notes, details, and a broad range of background information with me as I put this book together.

Two of my other colleagues at the Tucson trials—Terry Greene Sterling of the *Daily Beast* and Kim Smith of the *Arizona Daily Star*—deserve special thanks; covering trials is always a cooperative venture, and we all wound up getting help from each other and helping in turn.

I also owe a thanks to Ricker's editor at the *Green Valley News*, Dan Shearer, who was himself the first reporter on the scene the morning of the murders; Dan was kind enough to share his insights about those events with me, as well as his perspective on daily life in that part of Arizona.

There are a number of other reporters who delved this story in some depth, and I hope their fine work is reflected in this text too—notably Tim Steller of the *Arizona Daily Star*, Rick Anderson of *Seattle Weekly*, and Stephen Lemons of *Phoenix New Times*.

Several independent sources were invaluable in obtaining a fuller picture of Shawna Forde and her operations, especially private investigator Michael Carlucci, who spent many hours with me poring over the facts and details of the case. I also deeply appreciated the time and insights provided by her mother, Rena Caudle, and her half-brother, Merrill Metzger, and by her ex-husband, John Forde, whose courage and strength are truly an inspiration.

Many people in Arivaca were kind enough to lend me their time and their perspectives, and many made me feel as welcome as possible, given the unhappy and delicate nature of the interviews I was conducting. A number of those people asked to remain anonymous, and so they shall. Those who did not include Mary Noon Kasulaitis, the town's librarian and bona fide historical expert, who assisted me greatly in understanding the town's long history. Photographer Karl Hoffmann was especially helpful in introducing me to folks around Arivaca and getting a sense for the lay of the land, and he has my deepest thanks for that. Among the people who knew Junior and Brisenia Flores, I owe special thanks to Andrew Alday and Alan Wellen, who were willing to speak their minds publicly. Finally, I owe special thanks to Ellen Dursema of the Arivaca Community Center, who helped me get oriented when I first arrived in town and who gave me important insights into the personality of her young friend Brisenia Flores.

There are many people who have written about the Minuteman movement over the years, and their work was also essential in putting this text together. Most important of these is the staff at the Southern Poverty Law Center, which remains the most assiduous, detailed, and dependably factual of all the organizations that gather and publish information on the radical right in America. In addition to my friend Mark Potok, who heads the SPLC's intelligence project, I owe special thanks to the many SPLC reporters who over the years have tracked the activities of the Minutemen, especially Heidi Beirich, Susy Buchanan, Dave Holthouse, and Casey Sanchez.

I have a debt of gratitude to the many people who have worked with me on the story of the Minutemen and, later, of Shawna Forde over the years.

Leading the list is Esther Kaplan at the Investigative Fund of the Nation Institute, who funded and edited my investigative work into the Minutemen's finances, as well as my coverage of the Forde trials; and Joe Conason, who has consistently championed my work at the Fund. I'm also grateful to the editors at *American Prospect*, who published the financial investigation in 2009, and Joshua Holland, my editor at AlterNet, who published my initial report on the Forde case in 2012. Finally, I owe thanks to the editors at *Seattle* magazine who published my initial foray into reportage on the Minutemen in 2006.

My agent, Jill Marsal, played a key role in shaping this manuscript, and her insights, as always, have proved invaluable along the way. Carl Bromley, my editor at Nation Books, has been a fantastic cohort and a wise counselor.

I'd also like to thank my copy editor, Beth Wright, for her sharp-eyed, sensitive, and creative input, and my friend Beth Nauman-Montana for her superb indexing. And I'd like to thank the people who read the manuscript in process and offered me their edits and their insights, notably my wife, Lisa Dowling, and her mother, Diana Dowling. Lastly, I need to thank my daughter, Fiona, for giving me all the inspiration a father could wish.

October 2012
Seattle

# NOTES

## Chapter 1

2 **Tanya Remsburg had:** This account is drawn from the transcript and audio recording of Gina Gonzalez's phone call to 911 on the morning of May 30, 2009, and from the testimony of Tanya Remsburg in the trials of Shawna Forde, Jason Bush, and Albert Gaxiola, in Jan., March, and June 2011. Remsburg declined numerous requests for interviews and left the Pima County Sheriff's Department in spring of 2012. The audio recording of the call can be heard at crooksandliars .com/david-neiwert/why-did-they-kill-my-family-victim-m.

7 **Brisenia Flores loved animals:** Drawn from Gina Gonzalez's testimony in the trial of Albert Gaxiola, June 8, 2010.

11 **That may have been why:** Drawn from the testimony of Border Patrol officer Don Williams on June 9, 2011.

13 **At first only Detective Garcia:** Compiled from the transcript of Detective Charles Garcia's interviews with Gina Gonzalez on May 31 and June 1, 2011, and from Gina Gonzalez's testimony of June 8, 2011.

16 **She saw a speck of something:** Drawn from the testimony of Pima County Detective Jill Murphy on June 9, 2011, and the notes of Pima County Detective J. Sabori on June 2, 2009.

18 **Detectives asked Albert Gaxiola:** From the Detail Incident Report provided by Pima County Detective Robert Svec, June 8, 2009.

## Chapter 2

19 **Robert DePugh:** There have been several good accounts describing DePugh's career, most notably J. Harry Jones, *The Minutemen* (Garden City, NY: Doubleday, 1969), as well as James Ridgeway, *Blood in the Face: The Ku Klux Klan, Aryan Nations, Nazi Skinheads, and the Rise of a New White Culture*, 2nd ed. (New York: Thunder's Mouth Press, 1995), 129–133; Rick Perlstein, *Before the Storm: Barry Goldwater and the Unmaking of the American Consensus* (New York: Hill and Wang, 2001), 149; and Kevin Flynn and Gary Gerhardt, *The Silent Brotherhood: Inside America's Racist Underground* (New York: Free Press, 1989), 22–23. See also David A. Neiwert, *In God's Country: The Patriot Movement and the Pacific Northwest* (Pullman: Washington State University Press, 1999), 52–55.

20   **One Minuteman:** Keith Gilbert remained active on the racist-right scene in the Pacific Northwest for many years and is currently in prison on a weapons violation. See Maureen O'Hagan and Michael Ko, "Two Play Key Role in White Supremacist's Rise," *Seattle Times*, Feb. 17, 2005; as well as the papers in that case, which detail Gilbert's background extensively and are available online at www.splc.org/pdf /roosevelt_motionforsj1.pdf. Gilbert is identified as an active member of DePugh's Minutemen organization in Flynn and Gerhardt, *The Silent Brotherhood*, 23–24.

21   **At the time, Duke:** Michael Zatarian, *David Duke: Evolution of a Klansman* (Gretna, LA: Pelican, 1990), 198.

21   **The idea of an anti-immigration:** Leonard Zeskind, *Blood and Politics: The History of the White Nationalist Movement from the Margins to the Mainstream* (New York: Farrar Straus Giroux, 2009), 34–35.

22   **On October 25:** Tyler Bridges, *The Rise of David Duke* (Jackson: University Press of Mississippi, 1994), 67.

22   **Duke later mused:** See "Klan Border Watch Edition," *Crusader* 27 (October 1977): 3. Cited in Zeskind, *Blood and Politics*, 35.

22   **David Duke's star:** Martin A. Lee, "Insatiable," *Intelligence Report* 109 (Spring 2003). See also "David Duke Pleads to Mail Fraud, Tax Charges," Associated Press, Dec. 18, 2002, www.usatoday.com/news/nation/2002-12-18-david-duke_x.htm.

23   **This reached its apotheosis:** The best account of the career of Robert Mathews and the Order can be found in Flynn and Gerhardt, *The Silent Brotherhood*.

23   **Thus was born:** See esp. Daniel Levitas, *The Terrorist Next Door: The Militia Movement and the Radical Right* (New York: Thomas Dunne Books/St. Martin's, 2002), 292–295.

24   **The most prominent of these:** See the Southern Poverty Law Center profile of Spencer at www.splcenter.org/get-informed/intelligence-files/profiles/glenn-spencer, as well as its Winter 2005 *Intelligence Report* piece describing the nation's leading anti-immigration hatemongers, titled "The Nativists," leading off with Spencer (www .splcenter.org/get-informed/intelligence-report/browse-all-issues/2005/winter/the -nativists-0?page=0,13).

25   **Eventually Spencer's theory:** See my rebuttals of the Malkin and Reynolds posts at dneiwert.blogspot.com/2006/04/reconquista.html, dneiwert.blogspot.com /2006/05/reconquista-redux.html, and dneiwert.blogspot.com/2003/09/this -smear-must-stop.html.

26   **He was profiled in 2000:** See Tim McGirk and Ronald Buchanan, "Border Clash: Private Citizens Are Deputizing Themselves as Border Patrollers to Capture Illegal Aliens Pouring Across from Mexico in Record Numbers," *Time*, June 26, 2000. For more on Roger Barnett, see Max Blumenthal, "Vigilante Injustice," *Salon*, May 22, 2003, www.salon.com/2003/05/22/vigilante_3, and Bob Moser, "Arizona Extremists Start Anti-Immigrant Citizen Militias," *Intelligence Report* 109 (Spring 2003), www.splcenter.org/get-informed/intelligence-report/browse -all-issues/2003/spring/open-season?page=0,3.

27   **In May 2000:** See Armando Navarro, *The Immigration Crisis: Nativism, Armed Vigilantism, and the Rise of a Countervailing Movement* (Lanham, MD: AltaMira, 2009), 167.

27   **Foote explained in a 2003:** Kevin Strom, "War on the Border: An Interview with Jack Foote," National Alliance/American Dissident Voices, radio broadcast of Dec. 20, 2003, transcript at www.natvan.com/adv/2003/12-20-03.html.

28   **When accused of harboring:** See Moser, "Arizona Extremists Start Anti-Immigrant Citizen Militias."

28   **Nethercott already had quite:** See Anti-Defamation League, "Extremists Declare 'Open Season' on Immigrants: Hispanics Target of Incitement and Violence," May 23, 2006, www.adl.org/main_extremism/immigration_extremists.htm, and "Neo-Nazi Leads Recruitment Drive for New Border Militia," Sept. 10, 2004, www.adl .org/PresRele/Militi_71/4563_71.htm.

29   **Glenn Spencer was already:** Navarro, *The Immigration Crisis*, 168–170.

29   **Things turned rocky:** "Cops, Neighbors Fire Back at Arizona's Border Vigilantes," *Intelligence Report* 116 (Winter 2004).

29   **Spencer's plan was:** Navarro, *The Immigration Crisis*, 169.

29   **Casey Nethercott, however:** "E-mails Reveal Discussions on Group; Sheriff Says Concerns About Ranch Rescue Unwarranted," *Sierra Vista Herald*, Dec. 20, 2003.

29   **It was kind of a bad month:** Luke Turf, "Ranch Rescue Member held in Texas Case," *Tucson Citizen*, Nov. 26, 2003, www.azcentral.com/news/border/articles /1126ranch_arrest.html.

30   **In February 2004:** Luke Turf, "Vigilantes Threaten Mexican Military," *Tucson Citizen*, Feb. 14, 2004.

30   **His new recruitment chief:** See Anti-Defamation League, "Neo-Nazi Leads Recruitment Drive for New Border Militia."

30   **Nethercott denied that anyone:** Jim Becker, "Militia Group Near Douglas Denies White Supremacist Ties," KOLD-TV News 13, Sept. 16, 2004, www.kold.com /story/2316649/militia-group-near-douglas-denies-white-supremacist-ties.

30   **A couple of weeks later:** See "Jury Acquits Border-Watch Group Member," Associated Press, Feb. 23, 2005.

31   **(Eventually Nethercott would:** See Bill Hess, "Militia Leader Booked into Texas Prison," *Sierra Vista Herald*, April 22, 2005, and Mark Lacey, "Arizona Man Looks to Law in Bid to Retrieve Ranch," *New York Times*, May 27, 2011, www.nytimes .com/2011/05/28/us/28arizona.html.

31   **Within the year:** See the SPLC's filings on the case at *Leiva v. Ranch Rescue*, www.splcenter.org/get-informed/case-docket/leiva-v-ranch-rescue.

31   **In August 2005:** Andrew Pollack, "2 Illegal Immigrants Win Arizona Ranch in Court," *New York Times*, Aug. 19, 2005, www.nytimes.com/2005/08/19/national /19ranch.html.

31   **Chris Simcox liked to pose:** Probably the best-distributed example of Simcox posing with a pistol stored in the front waistband of his jeans can be found at cdna .splcenter.org/sites/default/files/imagecache/gallery_detail/images/media/chris -simcox.jpg.

32   **When Chris Simcox first arrived:** This account is largely drawn from Susy Buchanan and David Holthouse, "Minuteman Civil Defense Corps Leader Chris Simcox Has Troubled Past," *Intelligence Report* 120 (Winter 2005), www.splcenter .org/get-informed/intelligence-report/browse-all-issues/2005/winter/the-little -prince, and Blumenthal, "Vigilante Injustice," as well as Simcox's own speeches and video appearances. See also Dennis Wagner, "Minuteman Leader Found New Calling After 9/11 Attacks," *Arizona Republic*, June 1, 2006.

32   **It's certain that he:** See Tom Beal and Ignacio Ibarra, "Border Trek Delivered Simcox to His Cause," *Arizona Daily Star*, Dec. 6, 2002.

36   **Borane also made:** See Tim Vanderpool, "Just a Minute, Men: Weekend Border
     Warriors Create a Rift Between Cochise County Politicos," *Tucson Weekly*, March
     31, 2005.

36   **Joanne Young:** See Dan Baum, "Patriots on the Borderline: Toting Guns, Cameras
     and Mighty Convictions, Small Bands of Americans Are Patrolling the Southwest
     in Search of Illegal Immigrants," *Los Angeles Times Magazine*, March 16, 2005,
     www.latinamericanstudies.org/immigration/borderline.htm.

36   **It probably didn't help:** See Buchanan and Holthouse, "Minuteman Civil De-
     fense Corps Leader."

38   **The underlying problems:** The history of the Immigration Act of 1924 has been
     ably discussed in a number of works, particularly Roger Daniels, *The Politics of
     Prejudice: The Anti-Japanese Movement in California and the Struggle for Japanese
     Exclusion* (Berkeley: University of California Press, 1962), esp. 98–103, and Page
     Smith, *Democracy on Trial: The Japanese American Evacuation and Relocation in
     World War II* (New York: Simon and Schuster, 1995). See also David Neiwert,
     *Strawberry Days: How Internment Destroyed a Japanese American Community* (New
     York: Palgrave Macmillan, 2005), 57–66.

38   **The deadly crisis:** See Navarro, *The Immigration Crisis*, 125–130. See also Terry
     Greene Sterling, *Illegal: Life and Death in Arizona's Immigration War Zone* (Guil-
     ford, CT: Lyons, 2010), x–xiii.

39   **At first, the Border Patrol:** See William Clayton Jr., "'Our Border Can Be Con-
     trolled,' Says Analysis of Two Crackdowns: Study Looks at El Paso and San
     Diego," *Houston Chronicle*, June 1, 1995, A15.

39   **Hardly anyone observed:** See Navarro, *The Immigration Crisis,* 128–130.

39   **The numbers kept growing:** Ibid., 126–127.

40   **One coyote told:** See the 2005 documentary film by Joseph Matthew and Dan
     DeVivo, *Crossing Arizona.*

41   **So when the wave:** See *GAO-06-770 Illegal Immigration: Border-Crossing Deaths
     Have Doubled Since 1995*, US Government Accountability Office, Aug. 2006,
     www.gao.gov/new.items/d06770.pdf. See also Karl Eschbach, Jacqueline Hagan,
     and Nestor Rodriguez, "Causes and Trends in Migrant Deaths along the U.S.-Mexico
     Border, 1985–1998," Center for Immigration Research, University of Houston,
     web.archive.org/web/20070926034617/www.uh.edu/cir/Causes_and_Trends.pdf.

42   **These frightened ranchers:** See Beal and Ibarra, "Border Trek Delivered Simcox
     to His Cause."

42   **Dobbs, whose *Moneyline*:** The statistics on Simcox's appearances were compiled
     through online searches of the CNN transcript files and Lexis/Nexis searches of
     CNN programming.

42   **The latter segment:** See *CNN Newsnight*, Jan. 23, 2003, transcript at transcripts
     .cnn.com/TRANSCRIPTS/0301/23/asb.00.html.

43   **Soon he was expanding:** Buchanan and Holthouse, "Minuteman Civil Defense
     Corps Leader."

43   **He told Nikolaj Vijborg:** See Nikolaj Vijborg, *USA Under Attack*, 2008.

44   **Dubbed Proposition 200:** See Navarro, *The Immigration Crisis*, 284–287.

44   **In reality, a number:** *The Economic Impact of Arizona-Mexico Relationship*, Thun-
     derbird School of International Management, 2003.

45   **Officials at PAN:** See Byron Wells, "Migrant Foe Tied to Racism," *East Valley
     Tribune*, Aug. 16, 2004.

45 **The campaign attracted:** See *Crossing Arizona* for the footage of Anderson's rant.

46 **Putnam's recurring theme:** Jim Gilchrist acknowledged Putnam, who died in 2008, as a seminal figure in promoting Simcox's border watches and inspiring the Minuteman idea in his book, cowritten with Jerome R. Corsi, *Minutemen: The Battle to Secure America's Borders* (Los Angeles: World Ahead, 2006), 5–6. Putnam's archives at NewsMax—the right-wing magazine where he spent his declining years—also provide a sense of his agenda. The piece defending Simcox can be found at archive.newsmax.com/archives/articles/2003/4/18/24422.shtml.

46 **Gilchrist had grown up:** Gilchrist provides most of these biographical details in the book he cowrote with Corsi, *Minutemen*.

## Chapter 3

49 **Chuck Stonex was just:** The conversation with Shawna Forde was reconstructed from Stonex's description of it during his testimony in the trial of Albert Gaxiola on June 9, 2011.

50 **That October day:** See the footage of Stonex being interviewed in the documentary by Belgian filmmaker Sebastien Wielemans, *A Cycle of Fences*, which can be viewed online at vimeo.com/20137911.

51 **In the interim:** Taken from Shawna Forde's announcement on May 15, 2009, on the Minuteman American Defense website.

54 **Oin Oakstar had gotten:** Reconstructed from Oakstar's testimony in the trials of Shawna Forde and Albert Gaxiola, Jan. 31, 2011, and June 14, 2011.

56 **The first reporter:** Taken from the author's interview with Dan Shearer, Nov. 3, 2011, as well as Shearer's reportage.

58 **"It was a real shock"** : Author's interview with Andrew Alday, Nov. 4, 2011.

58 **Shawna also called:** Author's interview with Rena Caudle, Feb. 11, 2012.

60 **There were also a few things:** See Susy Buchanan and David Holthouse, "Border Guardians Founder Laine Lawless Calls for Violence," *Intelligence Report* 122 (Summer 2006), www.splcenter.org/get-informed/intelligence-report/browse-all-issues/2006/summer/going-lawless.

64 **Down the road in Amado:** See Jaime Richardson, "Mother Shot Intruder; Funeral Set for Girl, Dad," *Green Valley News*, June 12, 2009.

65 **Police descended:** Gates described these events in an email he sent to various Minutemen, including Shawna Forde, on June 4, 2009, after word had spread among Tucson-area Minutemen that police were seeking Shawna.

65 **Sometime that afternoon:** John Forde produced this letter, with its Palm Springs postmark, during interviews with Scott North and the author (March 7, 2012).

65 **She also fired off:** A confidential source provided the author with a complete set of Shawna Forde's pre-arrest emails.

67 **On Saturday, Shawna Forde:** Author's interview with Caudle.

68 **Pete Myers was:** Author's interview with Peter Myers, Feb. 11, 2012.

70 **At the Alamo Motel:** See Christine Clarridge, "Ex-Everett Woman Charged in Arizona Slayings Now Suspected of Two Crimes in California," *Seattle Times*, June 17, 2009.

71 **Shawna had also been:** See the testimony of Ron Wedow during the trial of Shawna Forde, Feb. 1, 2011. See also David S. Ricker, "FBI Informant Links

Shawna Forde to Arivaca Activities," *Ricker's Radar Screen*, dsricker.wordpress
.com/2011/02/01/fbi-informant-links-shawna-forde-to-arivaca-activities.

73  **Detectives, however, were monitoring:** See Suzanne Adams, "Murder Suspect
Nabbed in Meadview," *Daily Miner* (Kingman, AZ), June 16, 2009, www.king
mandailyminer.com/main.asp?SectionID=1&subsectionID=1&articleID=31978.

73  **That is where Pima County detectives:** Testimony of Detective Christopher
Hogan, Feb. 2, 2011, in the trial of Shawna Forde. See also David S. Ricker, "The
Prosecution Case Is Almost Complete," *Ricker's Radar Screen*, Feb. 2, 2011,
strega5742.blogspot.com/2011/02/prosecution-case-is-almost-complete.html.

73  **Spencer said he was:** See Glenn Spencer, "Full Disclosure About Shawna Forde,"
*American Border Patrol*, June 22, 2009, www.americanpatrol.com/ABP/NEWS
/2008-UP/090622-FORDE/FordeShawna090622.html.

73  **Among the people Forde:** From Shawna Forde's email to Jim Gilchrist and
Stephen Eichler, dated June 12, 2009, with the subject line "Re: I need the contact info and intro."

74  **They also caught up with:** See the testimony of Detectives Paul Montano and
Christopher Hogan on Feb. 2, 2011, in the trial of Shawna Forde.

74  **At the press conference:** See coverage of the arrests, including Jamar Younger, "3
Arrested in Killings of Dad, Girl in Arivaca," *Arizona Daily Star*, June 13, 2009.

*Chapter 4*

76  **As word spread:** See Tim Vanderpool, "Just a Minute, Men: Weekend Border
Warriors Create a Rift Between Cochise County Politicos," *Tucson Weekly*, March
31, 2005.

76  **Las Vegas radio:** Mark Edwards is credited by Gilchrist with having given the
Minutemen a critical and timely boost in his book, cowritten with Jerome R.
Corsi, *Minutemen: The Battle to Secure America's Borders* (Los Angeles: World
Ahead, 2006), 5–6. See also Edwards's online radio archives at thewakeupamerica
.com/MARK_EDWARDS_SHOW_ARCHIVES.htm.

76  **Among the first in line:** From *Lou Dobbs Tonight*, CNN, Jan. 25, 2005, transcript at transcripts.cnn.com/TRANSCRIPTS/0501/25/ldt.01.html.

78  **Lou Dobbs continued:** The April 14, 2005, leprosy report by Dobbs became a
crucial factor in his eventual removal from the CNN roster, in no small part because CBS's Lesley Stahl later grilled Dobbs about the matter in a famous *60 Minutes* interview that ran May 6, 2007 (video and extensive quotes from the interview
in Daniel Schorn, "Lou Dobbs, 'Advocacy' Journalist?" CBS News, Feb. 11, 2009,
www.cbsnews.com/stories/2007/05/03/60minutes/main2758082.shtml), followed
by a *New York Times* piece that further ran down Dobbs's mendacious reporting
(and his response to attempts at holding him accountable); see David Leonhardt,
"Truth, Fiction, and Lou Dobbs," *New York Times*, May 30, 2007. The Southern
Poverty Law Center also played a significant role in bringing pressure to bear on
Dobbs; see its report, "Bait and Switch," June 7, 2007, www.splcenter.org/get
-informed/news/bait-and-switch.

78  **Fears about:** See the "Rumor Mill" at Spencer's American Border Patrol site:
americanpatrol.com/COMMENTARY/RUMOR-MILL/00RumorMill-Current
.html. See also Ellen Miller, "Web Site Rumor of Virus Stirs Fears," *Rocky Mountain News*, Feb. 18, 2005.

79  **Three weeks before:** From *Lou Dobbs Tonight,* CNN, March 21, 2005, transcript at transcripts.cnn.com/TRANSCRIPTS/0503/21/ldt.01.html.

80  **Two days later:** See "Bush Decries Border Project," *Washington Times,* March 24, 2005, www.washingtontimes.com/news/2005/mar/24/20050324-122200-6209r /?page=all. See also Chris Strom, "Activists to Flock to Border, Set Up Citizen Patrol," *Government Executive,* March 28, 2005, www.govexec.com/federal-news /2005/03/activists-to-flock-to-border-set-up-citizen-patrols/18864.

80  **The day of the kickoff:** See *Lou Dobbs Tonight,* CNN, April 1, 2005, transcript at transcripts.cnn.com/TRANSCRIPTS/0504/01/ldt.01.html.

81  **The project had in fact:** See Amanda Susskind and Joanna Mendelson, "Extremists on the Border," *Los Angeles Daily News,* May 15, 2005, www.adl.org/ADL _Opinions/Extremism/20050515-LA+Daily+News.htm.

82  **Chris Simcox was:** The original KVOA story can be found online at www.alipac .us/f12/minutemen-say-no-thanks-white-separatists-744.

82  **"I wonder what:** See Claudine LoMonaco, "Minutemen Gather in Tombstone for Border Watch," *Tucson Citizen,* April 2, 2005.

82  **Jim Gilchrist had an idea:** See "Gang Will Target Minuteman Vigil on Mexico Border," *Washington Times,* March 28, 2005, www.washingtontimes.com/news /2005/mar/28/20050328-125306-7868r.

82  **The first day of registration:** See Spiff, "Firsthand Report of Today's Minuteman Project Activities," *Free Republic,* April 1, 2005, www.freerepublic.com/focus /f-news/1375805/posts.

82  **Up till then:** Author's interview with David Holthouse, Dec. 28, 2011. See also Holthouse's own reportage for the Southern Poverty Law Center, particularly "Minutemen, Other Anti-Immigrant Militia Groups Stake Out Arizona Border," *Intelligence Report* 118 (Summer 2005), www.splcenter.org/get-informed/intelligence -report/browse-all-issues/2005/summer/arizona-showdown?page=0,1.

84  **Buchanan joined:** See Marc Cooper, "Lawn Chair Militias: Surviving a Weekend with the Arizona Minutemen," *L.A. Weekly,* April 7, 2005, www.laweekly.com /2005-04-07/news/lawn-chair-militias.

85  **The day after registration:** Signage culled from news photographs of the April 2 event.

85  **The men said they were calling:** For more on the significance of David Lane's "Fourteen Words," see "Hate on Display: 14 Words," Anti-Defamation League, www.adl.org/hate_symbols/numbers_14words.asp. See also the Wikipedia entry on "Fourteen Words," en.wikipedia.org/wiki/Fourteen_Words.

87  **Gilchrist began holding:** See Holthouse, "Minutemen, Other Anti-Immigrant Militia Groups."

88  **The college had been:** See "History of Miracle Valley," Miracle Valley Bible College, miraclevalley.us/gpage11.html, as well as "1982 Gun Fight," Miracle Valley Bible College, www.miraclevalley.net/subpage39.html. See also William R. Daniel, *Shootout at Miracle Valley* (Tucson: Wheatmark, 2009), and "Scandals: Miracle Valley Shootout," *Arizona Republic,* Jan. 6, 2012, www.azcentral.com/centennial /news/articles/2012/01/06/20120106scandals-arizona-miracle-valley-shootout .html. A video with archival footage of national news coverage of the shootout can be seen at youtu.be/K8dIbIzeVoI.

88  **So the opportunity:** The press release can be found online at www.miracle valley.net/gpage27.html.

89   **It finally exploded:** Author's interview with Holthouse.

89   **Among the Minutemen:** Author's interviews with Tom Williams (May 7, 2006) and Claude LeBas (June 4, 2012).

91   **The participants almost:** The original KPHO reportage has largely disappeared from the Web; some portions of the transcripts are preserved at dneiwert.blogspot .com/2006/05/real-minutemen.html. The station was barraged with angry protests from Minuteman supporters in the weeks following the stories' broadcast on April 7–8, 2005; an example can be found at www.ar15.com/archive/topic .html?b=1&f=5&t=341018. Jim Gilchrist and Jerome Corsi bitterly describe the reportage in their book *Minutemen*, 339–340.

91   **Over at Team 14's station:** See Holthouse, "Minutemen, Other Anti-Immigrant Militia Groups."

92   **On Fox's *Hannity and Colmes*:** See the transcript from April 8, 2005 show, www.foxnews.com/story/0,2933,153908,00.html.

92   **Nicely himself:** See Arthur H. Rothstein, "Success of Border Patrol Volunteers Is Disputed," Associated Press, April 22, 2005, www.boston.com/news/nation /articles/2005/04/22/success_of_border_patrol_volunteers_is_disputed.

92   **The Minutemen may have been:** Holthouse described this incident in the author's interview, but it is also described by several Minuteman sympathizers in their online accounts. See, for instance, Spiff, "Report of Some Activities of Day 10 of the Minuteman Project," *Free Republic*, April 11, 2005, www.freerepublic .com/focus/f-news/1381453/posts.

93   **"The Border Patrol didn't want:** See Holthouse, "Minutemen, Other Anti-Immigrant Militia Groups."

93   **The participants did not:** See Andy Isaacson, "Minutemen Do the Dirty Work That 'Government Won't Do,'" *San Francisco Chronicle*, May 8, 2005, www.sfgate .com/opinion/article/Minutemen-do-the-dirty-work-that-government-2672387 .php.

93   **As Marc Cooper:** See Marc Cooper, "The 15-Second Men," *Los Angeles Times*, May 1, 2005, www.latimes.com/news/opinion/la-op-minutemen1may01,0,26802 84.story.

94   **Lou Dobbs had been:** See *Lou Dobbs Tonight*, April 18, 2005, transcript at transcripts .cnn.com/TRANSCRIPTS/0504/18/ldt.01.html.

95   **That happened to be April 18:** See transcript at www.foxnews.com/story/0,2933 ,153908,00.html.

97   **Afterward, several higher-ups:** See Hernan Rozemberg, "Minutemen Bordering on Chaos," *San Antonio Express-News*, May 6, 2005, www.opensourcesinfo.org /journal/2005/5/8/us-immigration-news-5605.html?cmd=Open#16.

97   **Freshly out of prison:** See Anti-Defamation League, "Armed Vigilante Activities in Arizona," April 21, 2005, www.adl.org/learn/extremism_in_the_news/White _Supremacy/arizona_border_update52105.htm

97   **A few weeks later:** See Bill Hess, "Nethercott Opposes Minuteman Project," *Sierra Vista Herald*, March 20, 2005, www.alipac.us/f12/nethercott-opposes-minuteman -project-524.

98   **Then, as he watched:** See Jan Sturmann, "Minutemen, Migrants, and Seven Strands of Wire," *Spotlight*, April 2005, www.albinocrow.com/articles/0504A_illegal _migrants/0504A_illegal_migrants.htm.

98   **Nethercott jury-rigged:** See "Arizona Guard Militia Plans More Aggressive Border Action," KVOA, April 9, 2005, www.freerepublic.com/focus/f-news/1380371/posts.

## Chapter 5

101   **Shortly after the murders:** See Dan Shearer, "From the Editor: The Awful Truth About Arivaca, and Us," *Green Valley News*, June 16, 2009, www.gvnews.com/opinion/from-the-editor-the-awful-truth-about-arivaca-and-us/article_e0fe041f-868b-5a03-8380-d3a30a9af916.html.

103   **Eventually there was indeed:** See Mary Noon Kasulaitis, "Arivaca Yester Years, the Military in Arivaca: The Tenth Cavalry," Arizona Buffalo Soldiers Association, www.buffalosoldiersw.com/id20.html, and the Wikipedia entry for the Battle of Bear Valley, en.wikipedia.org/wiki/Battle_of_Bear_Valley.

105   **If you keep driving south:** For more about the Ruby-area hippie commune, see Bob Ring, "The Private Life of Ruby, Mining Ghost Town," Arizona History Convention, April 24, 2004, 10–11.

105   **"The hippies came here:** See Fred Brock, "Arizona Backroads at the Border," *New York Times*, April 4, 2008, travel.nytimes.com/2008/04/04/travel/escapes/04border.html.

105   **Clara Godfrey:** Joel Smith, James Johenning, and Bryce Goodman, *A Line in the Sand*, 2009, bcove.me/jrhefl3d.

106   **Allan Wellen:** Author's interview with Allan Wellen, Nov. 8, 2011.

107   **Tracy Cooper:** See Karl W. Hoffmann's documentary film, *Living on the Border*, 2009, www.livingontheborder.com/Living_on_the_Border/home.html.

## Chapter 6

114   **Before April was even out:** See "Comments from Congressional Immigration Reform Caucus on Minutemen," April 27, 2005, www.freerepublic.com/focus/f-news/1393637/posts.

114   **House Majority Leader:** See "Transcript of Interview with Tom DeLay," *Washington Times*, April 13, 2005, www.washingtontimes.com/news/2005/apr/13/20050413-111439-5048r/?page=all.

114   **Then there were the public endorsements:** See Peter Nicholas and Robert Salladay, "Gov. Praises 'Minuteman' Campaign," *Los Angeles Times*, April 29, 2005, articles.latimes.com/2005/apr/29/local/me-governor29.

115   **A few months later:** See Carla Marinucci, "Governor Defends Border Watchers," *San Francisco Chronicle*, Sept. 22, 2005, www.alipac.us/f12/governor-schwarzenegger-defends-border-watchers-again-8708/.

115   **Republican senator Wayne Allard:** See "Senator Suggests Deputizing Citizens for Border Security," KVOA, April 21, 2005, www.thehighroad.org/archive/index.php/t-135680.html.

115   **John Culberson:** See Alex Chadwick, "Texas Congressman Proposes Armed Border Militia," National Public Radio, Aug. 16, 2005, www.npr.org/templates/story/story.php?storyId=4801944.

115   **These ideas nearly:** See Chris Strom, "Border Patrol Seeks More Personnel, Might Enlist Citizen Patrols," *Government Executive*, May 13, 2005, www.govexec.com

/defense/2005/05/border-patrol-seeks-more-personnel-might-enlist-citizen
-patrols/19219.

115 **A couple of months later:** See "Border Patrol Looking to Involve Citizen Volunteers," NewsMax, July 21, 2005, archive.newsmax.com/archives/articles/2005/7
/21/110118.shtml.

115 **A day later:** See Anna Gorman, "No Plans for Citizen Border Patrols Seen," *Los
Angeles Times*, April 22, 2005, articles.latimes.com/2005/jul/22/local/me-border22.

115 **Meanwhile, Republican legislators:** See Fernando Quintero, "Lawmakers Tour Mexican Border," *Rocky Mountain News*, Oct. 5, 2005, www.alipac.us/f12/lawmakers
-tour-mexican-border-9226.

116 **Simcox and Gilchrist both hired:** See the various reportage on MCDC's history
with Diener Consulting, including the author's investigative piece, "Fence to
Nowhere," *American Spectator*, Sept. 19, 2008, prospect.org/article/fence
-nowhere-0. See also David Holthouse, "Angry Former Supporters of Minuteman
Civil Defense Corps Question Founder Chris Simcox's Accounting," *Intelligence
Report* 123 (Fall 2006), and Susan Carroll and Dennis Wagner, "Minutemen Are
Focus of Call for Cash Audit," *Arizona Republic*, Aug. 11, 2006, www.azcentral
.com/arizonarepublic/news/articles/0811minutemoney0810.html.

116 **Preparations continued apace:** See Brock N. Meeks, "'Minutemen' Gear Up for
Mainstream," MSNBC.com, June 10, 2005, www.msnbc.msn.com/id/8162019
/ns/us_news-security/t/minutemen-gear-mainstream/#.T_oD3fW-3Kc.

117 **McGauley said he agreed:** See "Texans Band Together in Minutemen Patrols,"
Associated Press, July 8, 2005, lubbockonline.com/stories/070805/sta_07080
5095.shtml.

117 **Meanwhile, Wanda Schultz:** See Scott Gold, "Border Watchers Gear Up for Expanded Patrol," *Los Angeles Times*, July 3, 2005, articles.latimes.com/2005/jul/03
/nation/na-minutemen3.

118 **One of the more active:** See Ben Ehrenreich, "Minuteman Divisions: Internal
Squabbles Tear at Anti-Immigrant Movement," *L.A. Weekly*, July 28, 2005,
www.laweekly.com/2005-07-28/news/minuteman-divisions.

118 **Chase had been a visible figure:** See the profile of Chase by Susy Buchanan and
Tom Kim, "The Nativists," *Intelligence Report* 125 (Winter 2005): 4, www.splcenter
.org/get-informed/intelligence-report/browse-all-issues/2005/winter/the-nativists
-0?page=0,4.

118 **It was also plain:** See Ehrenreich, "Minuteman Divisions."

119 **Still, he was dismissive:** See Leslie Berestein, "Border-Watch Squabble: Civilian
Patrols Mushrooming, Along with the Infighting," *San Diego Union Tribune*, July
6, 2005, www.freerepublic.com/focus/f-news/1437813/posts.

119 **Later that summer:** See Rene Romo, "Border Watchers Sought in Las Cruces;
Minuteman Leader Touts Oct. Project," *Albuquerque Journal*, July 11, 2005,
www.abqjournal.com/news/cruces/370822nm07-11-05.htm. See also Berestein,
"Border-Watch Squabble," and Anna Macias Aguayo, "Minuteman Patrols to Start
in New Mexico," Associated Press, June 11, 2005, www.abqjournal.com/news
/state/apborder06-11-05.htm.

120 **In California:** See Susy Buchanan and David Holthouse, "Groups in Texas, Calif.,
Imitate Nativist Extremist Minuteman Project," *Intelligence Report* 119 (Fall
2005), www.splcenter.org/get-informed/intelligence-report/browse-all-issues/2005
/fall/playing-rough?page=0,1.

120 **Ramirez, an American citizen:** See Meeks, "'Minutemen' Gear Up for Mainstream."

120 **Even though Simcox:** See Buchanan and Holthouse, "Groups in Texas."

121 **In the meantime:** A copy of Gilchrist's bulletin can be found online at dir .groups.yahoo.com/group/minutemencalifornia/message/465.

122 **And behind the scenes:** See Berestein, "Border-Watch Squabble."

122 **"There has always been:** Ibid.

124 **Afterward, Gilchrist declared:** Gilchrist's speech, titled "Jim Gilchrist's Victory Party Remarks," is available at www.jimgilchristforcongress.com/article.php?id =141.

125 **In California, the nativists:** See "Immigration Protesters Joined by Neo-Nazis in California," *Southern Poverty Law Center Bulletin*, Aug. 8, 2005, www.splcenter .org/get-informed/news/immigration-protesters-joined-by-neo-nazis-in-california. See also the author's blog posts at the time, notably "March of the Minutemen," dneiwert.blogspot.com/2006/01/march-of-minutemen_15.html, as well as the neo-Nazi Stormfront forum discussion of the incident at www.stormfront.org /forum/t221526-2.

125 **In Tennessee:** See Shasta Clark, "Minutemen Group Stirring Controversy in Hamblen Co.," WATE-TV, June 14, 2005, www.wate.com/Global/story.asp?S =3476855.

126 **One Minuteman who:** See KPHO report, "Beyond the Minutemen," April 27, 2006, transcript at www.tucsonnewsnow.com/story/4857876/beyond-the -minutemen.

127 **One of her fellow:** See Stephen Lemons, "Burn, Baby, Burn," *Phoenix New Times*, Feb. 15, 2007, www.phoenixnewtimes.com/2007-02-15/news/burn-baby-burn /full.

127 **Indeed, it turned out:** See Susy Buchanan and David Holthouse, "Border Guardians Founder Laine Lawless Calls for Violence," *Intelligence Report* 122 (Summer 2006), www.splcenter.org/get-informed/intelligence-report/browse-all -issues/2006/summer/going-lawless.

129 **That same April:** The "Border Patrol" game, created using the software Flash, can still be found online at www.resist.com/racistgames/playborderpatrol/borderpa- trol.htm. For more on WAR and Resist.net, see "Racist Skinheads: Understanding the Threat," Southern Poverty Law Center Special Report, www.splcenter.org/get -informed/publications/skinheads-in-america-racists-on-the-rampage.

## Chapter 7

131 **"Two days later":** Nearly the entirety of this chapter is based on interviews with local sources, several of them confidential, two of them from the law enforcement community. Those local sources who were willing to go on the record are properly identified.

136 **One of their chief interviewees:** The interview with Albert Gaxiola can be seen in the documentary *A Line in the Sand*, by Joel Smith, James Johenning, and Bryce Goodman, released in 2009. It is available online at bcove.me/jrhefl3d.

137 **Albert Gaxiola had been raised:** Information about Gaxiola's background and family is derived from the testimony of his sister, Sonia Muniz, during mitigation hearings in his murder trial, July 7, 2011, and by his father, Robert Gaxiola, in the

same trial, July 8, 2011. See David Ricker's coverage at his blog, strega5742
.blogspot.com/2011/07/gaxiolas-sister-testifies-about-their.html and rickersradar
screen.blogspot.com/2011/07/gaxiolas-father-attempted-to-kidnap-him.html.

## Chapter 8

147   **In January 1972:** Taken from testimony by mitigation specialist Margaret
      DiFrank, in the mitigation hearing for the death penalty for Shawna Forde, Feb.
      18, 2011.

147   **The little girl, born:** The first portion of this chapter is largely compiled from the
      author's interviews with Rena Caudle (Feb. 11, 2012) and Merrill Metzger (Feb.
      12, 2012), while the criminal background information on Shawna Forde was al-
      most entirely unearthed by Scott North, a veteran reporter for the Everett *Herald.*
      North generously shared his notes with the author, though North already covered
      much of this information in his superlative early exposé of Shawna Forde, "Trou-
      ble Finds Shawna Forde," *Herald* (Everett, WA), Feb. 22, 2009, www.heraldnet
      .com/article/20090222/NEWS01/702229930, published several months before
      the murders in Arivaca. See also Rick Anderson's excellent piece on Forde,
      "Lethally Blonde," *Seattle Weekly*, July 15, 2009, www.seattleweekly.com/2009
      -07-15/news/cover-story-lethally-blonde.

156   **Like many of the men:** This section about Shawna's part in John Forde's life is drawn
      largely from the author's interviews with John Forde, March 7, 2012, as well as from
      Scott North's interview with Mr. Forde, which North generously shared.

157   **In June 2001:** See Theresa Goffredo, "Students Take a Cut," *Herald* (Everett, WA),
      June 15, 2001, www.heraldnet.com/article/20010615/NEWS01/106150752.

## Chapter 9

Nearly the entirety of this chapter is drawn from the author's coverage of the Washington
Minuteman Detachment's activities in spring 2006 for "Borderline Personalities," published in Aug. 2006 in *Seattle* magazine. A large number of the quotes in this chapter were
not used in that piece, though some were.

162   **The Ressam Case:** See the special report by Hal Bernton, Mike Carter, David
      Heath, and James Neff, "The Terrorist Within," *Seattle Times*, June 23–July 7,
      2007, seattletimes.com/news/nation-world/terroristwithin.

## Chapter 10

173   **Jim Campbell was:** Author's interview with Jim Campbell, Aug. 2008. The
      MCDC's thank-you to Campbell for his donation is still online at www.minute
      manhq.com/hq/article.php?sid=93. See also Stephen Lemons, "Minuteman
      Leader Chris Simcox Sued by Pissed-Off Donor over Border Fence," *Phoenix New
      Times*, June 1, 2007, blogs.phoenixnewtimes.com/bastard/2007/06/minuteman
      _leader_chris_simcox.php, and Jonathan Clark, "Man Sues Minutemen over
      Fence," *Sierra Vista Herald*, May 30, 2007, www2.svherald.com/articles/2007
      /05/30/news/doc465d0fc256c9f078099071.txt. Most of this chapter is comprised
      of the author's original reporting, in a project funded by the Investigative Fund of

the Nation Institute: "The Fence to Nowhere," *American Prospect*, Sept. 19, 2008, prospect.org/article/fence-nowhere-0.

175 **As part of Gilchrist's unsuccessful:** For further reportage on the relationship of the two Minuteman organizations to Diener Consulting, see also David Holthouse, "Angry Former Supporters of Minuteman Civil Defense Corps Question Founder Chris Simcox's Accounting," *Intelligence Report* 123 (Fall 2006), and Susan Carroll and Dennis Wagner, "Minutemen Are Focus of Call for Cash Audit," *Arizona Republic*, Aug. 11, 2006, www.azcentral.com/arizonarepublic/news/articles/0811 minutemoney0810.html.

176 **At one of these he got into:** For a colorfully biased account of the Columbia affair, see Eliana Johnson, "At Columbia, Students Attack Minuteman Founder," *New York Sun*, www.nysun.com/new-york/at-columbia-students-attack-minuteman -founder/41020.

176 **The latter is especially illustrative:** See "Direct Mail Company Response Unlimited Sells Lists of Subscribers to Anti-Semitic Newspaper," *Intelligence Report* 121 (Spring 2006), www.splcenter.org/get-informed/intelligence-report/browse-all -issues/2006/spring/haters-for-sale.

177 **Jerry Seper:** See Jerry Seper, "Minutemen Not Watching over Funds," *Washington Times*, July 19, 2006, www.washingtontimes.com/news/2006/jul/19/20060719 -091346-2988r, and Jerry Seper, "Minutemen Skeptical of Ties with Keyes Project," *Washington Times*, July 19, 2006, www.washingtontimes.com/news/2006 /jul/19/20060719-114206-4187r.

179 **Simcox abruptly fired them:** See Stephen Lemons, "Monkey Knife Fight at the MCDC: Chris Simcox Puts the Smack Down . . . ," *Phoenix New Times*, May 24, 2007, blogs.phoenixnewtimes.com/bastard/2007/05/monkey_knife_fight_at_the _mcdc_1.php.

179 **O'Connell, who describes himself:** Author's interview with Stacey O'Connell, Aug. 2008.

181 **The problem began:** See David Holthouse, "Jim Gilchrist Fired by Minuteman Project," *Intelligence Report* 126 (Summer 2007), www.splcenter.org/get-informed /intelligence-report/browse-all-issues/2007/summer/minute-mess. See also Jennifer Dilson, "A Minuteman Meets His Hour of Crisis," *Los Angeles Times*, March 11, 2007, articles.latimes.com/2007/mar/11/local/me-gilchrist11.

184 **For his part, Gilchrist:** See Amy Taxin, "Minutemen Leader Laments Path of Anti-Illegal Immigration Groups," *Orange County Register*, June 25, 2008, www.ocregister.com/news/immigration-173479-gilchrist-border.html.

185 **One of Schwilk's favorite tactics:** See Casey Sanchez, "Police Investigate Activities of San Diego Minutemen," *Intelligence Report* 126 (Summer 2007).

186 **The *New York Times* profiled:** See Charles LeDuff, "Poised Against Incursions, a Man on the Border, Armed and Philosophical," *New York Times*, Aug. 14, 2006, www.nytimes.com/2006/08/14/us/14minute.html.

186 **Crooks, a fifty-seven-year-old:** See "Nativist Video Depicts Apparent Shooting," *Intelligence Report* 127 (Fall 2007), www.splcenter.org/get-informed/intelligence -report/browse-all-issues/2007/fall/nativist-violence.

187 **There was a brief uproar:** See Casey Sanchez, "Nativist Leader Now Says Video Is Fake," *Hatewatch*, Aug. 20, 2007, www.splcenter.org/blog/2007/08/20/nativist -leader-now-says-video-is-fake.

## Chapter 11

The majority of this chapter is compiled from information provided in the author's interviews with John Forde (March 7, 2012), as well as with a number of Shawna Forde's associates in the Washington Minuteman Detachment: Hal Washburn, Claude LeBas, and Michael Carlucci (June 4, 2012). The author also relied on Scott North's interviews with John Forde and with Bob and Kathy Dameron, whose interviews were published in North's comprehensive report on the Forde affair, "No Boundaries: Shawna Forde and the Minutemen Movement," *Herald* (Everett, WA), Oct. 25, 2009, www.heraldnet.com/article /20091025/NEWS01/710259945.

190   **Wooldridge indulges:** See particularly Frosty Wooldridge's book, *Immigration's Unarmed Invasion: Deadly Consequences* (Bloomington, IN: Author House, 2004), cited here. See also Susy Buchanan and Tom Kim, "The Nativists," *Intelligence Report* 120 (Summer 2005), www.splcenter.org/get-informed/intelligence-report /browse-all-issues/2005/winter/the-nativists-0?page=0,18.

191   **Just as he launched:** See Frosty Wooldridge, "A Day Without Illegal Aliens," News with Views, Sept. 25, 2006, www.newswithviews.com/Wooldridge/frosty 191.htm.

193   **It nearly came to a head:** Shawna's performance on the KYVE/KCTS town-hall program can be viewed at www.youtube.com/watch?v=ErqCmLiWQj8. The author's original reportage for Crooksandliars.com, where the quotes from Cerna and Baker originate, is at crooksandliars.com/david-neiwert/minuteman-tactical -leadermurder-susp.

199   **Then, on March 20, 2007:** See Scott North, "Trouble Finds Shawna Forde," *Herald* (Everett, WA), Feb. 22, 2009, www.heraldnet.com/article/20090222/NEWS01 /702229930.

200   **Parris also succumbed:** See Rick Anderson, "Lethally Blonde," *Seattle Weekly*, July 15, 2009, www.seattleweekly.com/2009-07-15/news/cover-story-lethally -blonde.

201   **It didn't matter:** See "Profiles of 20 Nativist Leaders," *Intelligence Report* 129 (Spring 2008), www.splcenter.org/get-informed/intelligence-report/browse-all -issues/2008/spring/the-nativists?page=0,6.

201   **Gilchrist was similarly:** See David Chircop, "Minuteman Rally Draws 100," *Herald* (Everett, WA), July 1, 2009, heraldnet.com/article/20070701/NEWS01 /707010347.

205   **Jim Gilchrist heatedly disputes:** See Leah Nelson, "Report: Minuteman Leader Knew Killer-to-Be Yearned for Violence," *Hatewatch*, July 25, 2012, www.splcenter .org/blog/2012/07/25/report-minuteman-leader-knew-killer-to-be-yearned-for -violence. See also Gilchrist's comment on the author's AlterNet report on the Minutemen, "How the Brutal Murders of a Little Girl and Her Father Doomed the Xenophobic Minuteman Movement," July 23, 2012, www.alternet.org/comments /story/156128/how_the_brutal_murders_of_a_little_girl_and_her_father_doomed _the_xenophobic_minuteman_movement#comment-599879535.

## Chapter 12

207   **Shawna and the Belgian:** Sebastien Wielemans's documentary featuring Shawna Forde, *A Cycle of Fences*, can be viewed online at vimeo.com/20137911.

208  **After Shawna's jaunts:** Drawn from the author's interviews with John Forde, March 7, 2012, as well as Scott North's interview with Forde, which North generously shared with me.

209  **She was giving voice:** Taken from Shawna's Web postings at the Minuteman American Defense site, archived by the author. All of these disappeared from the Web after Forde's arrest.

210  **The hiatus from the Minutemen:** See Scott North, "No Boundaries: Shawna Forde and the Minutemen Movement," *Herald* (Everett, WA), Oct. 25, 2009, www.heraldnet.com/article/20091025/NEWS01/710259945.

210  **It's unclear whether:** See Miriam Raftery, "Minutemen Leader Arrest in Murder of 9-Year-Old Visited East County Minutemen Training Camp," *East County Magazine* (San Diego), June 15, 2009, eastcountymagazine.org/node/1419.

210  **Chris Simcox's MCDC:** See the press release for these gatherings at the MCDC site, www.minutemanhq.com/state/read.php?chapter=AZ&sid=849, and www.minutemanhq.com/state/read.php?chapter=AZ&sid=928.

210  **Reportedly, Shawna Forde:** See Tim Steller, "Slaying Suspects' Pasts Troubled," *Arizona Daily Star*, July 13, 2009, azstarnet.com/news/local/crime/article_c293398d-edf5-5593-b8bd-e4b47bed3a27.html.

211  **In the meantime:** See Glenn Spencer, "Full Disclosure About Shawna Forde," June 22, 2009, *American Border Patrol*, www.americanpatrol.com/ABP/NEWS/2008-UP/090622-FORDE/FordeShawna090622.html.

211  **Another crew from Norway:** See the brief documentary, by Geir Terje Ruud and Bjørnar Tommelstad, online at www.vg.no/nyheter/utenriks/presidentvalg-2008/artikkel.php?artid=521638.

212  **A Boston-based photographer:** Andrew Ong's gallery of photos of Shawna Forde in action at the Caballo Loco can be found online at www.thedailybeast.com/galleries/2011/02/18/shawna-forde.html. See also Scott North's interview with Ong in "No Boundaries."

213  **Indeed, Shawna and the Minutemen:** See the interview with Stonex in the Ruud/Tommelstad documentary, www.vg.no/nyheter/utenriks/presidentvalg-2008/artikkel.php?artid=521638.

214  **a breathless email she sent:** Forde sent this email on Nov. 3, 2008, with the subject line "Stash house Do not share these!!!!!!!!!!!! it would be my life."

215  **Shawna was not able to hang out:** This section is entirely drawn from the author's interviews with John Forde and from Scott North's interviews with him as well, from which the majority of the quotes are taken.

224  **The story ran on February 22:** See Scott North, "Trouble Finds Shawna Forde," *Herald* (Everett, WA), Feb. 22, 2009, www.heraldnet.com/article/20090222/NEWS01/702229930.


*Chapter 13*

225  **Shawna has largely remained mum:** Letter from Shawna Forde to anonymous friend, postmarked July 27, 2009 (in author's files).

225  **Jason Bush later claimed:** See Kim Smith, "Arizona Daily Star Interview with Jason Bush," *Arizona Daily Star*, July 31, 2009, azstarnet.com/online/pdf/pdf_ea04988a-3095-11e0-aab7-001cc4c03286.html. See also Kim Smith, "Arivaca Suspect Denies Links to Killings, Aryans," *Arizona Daily Star*, Aug. 9, 2009,

azstarnet.com/news/local/crime/article_538ca40e-a451-588f-8e53-96c0b34c54c9
.html.

226  **Jason Bush even tried:** See Daniel Newhauser, "Arivaca Suspect Made Enemies in
Small Town," *Green Valley News*, July 11, 2009, www.gvnews.com/news/article
_e5e0e051-f7be-53e1-8afe-26de93857e25.html.

226  **Though he was born:** Most of Jason Bush's personal history was uncovered by
Scott North in his reportage for the *Herald*, notably "Records Show Suspect in
Arizona, Washington Murders Not Who He Claimed to Be," *Herald* (Everett, WA),
June 17, 2009, www.heraldnet.com/article/20090617/NEWS01/706179571, and
"Forde's Co-Defendant Has Long, Disturbing History," *Herald* (Everett, WA),
Feb. 1, 2011. See also Tim Steller's coverage for the *Arizona Daily Star*, notably
"Investigators Believe Serial Killer Sits in the Pima Jail," *Arizona Daily Star*, Dec.
13, 2009, azstarnet.com/news/local/investigators-believe-serial-killer-sits-in-the
-pima-jail/article_71c01fe7-deb3-5816-b478-e8cce66f8898.html, and "Slaying
Suspects' Pasts Troubled," *Arizona Daily Star*, July 13, 2009, azstarnet.com/news
/local/crime/article_c293398d-edf5-5593-b8bd-e4b47bed3a27.html.

227  **That played out:** See Dee Riggs, "Former Wenatchee Man Suspect in Fourth
Homicide," *Wenatchee World* (WA), July 28, 2009, www.wenatcheeworld.com
/news/2009/jul/28/former-wenatchee-man-suspect-in-fourth-homicide. See also
Steller, "Investigators Believe Serial Killer Sits in the Pima Jail."

228  **Bush bragged openly:** See Dee Riggs, "Prosecution Charges Bush with Murder,"
*Wenatchee World* (WA), July 31, 2009, www.wenatcheeworld.com/news/2009/jul
/31/prosecution-charges-bush-with-murder.

228  **Jason Bush claimed he had:** See Bush's court filing of Nov. 28, 1997, in the Superior Court of Washington for Chelan County, No. 97-1-00435-8.

228  **Bush filed a request:** See Bush's court filing of Jan. 7, 1998, in the Superior Court
of Washington for Chelan County, No. 97-1-00435-8, "Declaration of Jason Bush
in Support of Motion for Psychological Evaluation."

229  **Bush promptly:** See North, "Records Show Suspect."

229  **He was working there:** From the testimony of Melinda Williams, Jan. 27, 2011,
in the trial of Shawna Forde. See David Ricker's reportage, "Jason Bush: The Army
Veteran Who Really Isn't," *Ricker's Radar Screen*, Jan. 27, 2011, strega5742
.blogspot.com/2011/01/jason-bush-army-veteran-who-really-isnt.html.

229  **He told a number of other people:** See Newhauser, "Arivaca Suspect Made
Enemies."

230  **Shawna Forde had been:** See Scott North, "No Boundaries: Shawna Forde and the
Minutemen Movement," *Herald* (Everett, WA), Oct. 25, 2009, www.heraldnet
.com/article/20091025/NEWS01/710259945.

231  **Shawna had much weightier:** From the author's interviews with Rena Caudle
(Feb. 11, 2012) and Merrill Metzger (Feb. 12, 2012).

232  **Shawna was not just:** From the testimony of Ron Wedow during the trial of
Shawna Forde, Feb. 1, 2011. See also David S. Ricker, "FBI Informant Links Shawna
Forde to Arivaca Activities," *Ricker's Radar Screen*, dsricker.wordpress.com/2011
/02/01/fbi-informant-links-shawna-forde-to-arivaca-activities.

233  **She posted the text:** Forde posted the text of her speech on her email list to her
readers and wrote glowingly of the Phoenix Tea Party event in "Shawna's Corner"
at the Minuteman American Defense website. The video in which Shawna briefly
appears is at youtube.com/_fboeN50-34.

234   **In the meantime:** The email exchanges under the Shogren pseudonym and other exchanges with Bob Dameron, Chuck Stonex, and Joe Adams appear in Shawna Forde's complete email archives.

235   **Adams is something:** For more on Joe Adams's background, see Tim Steller, "To Ex-Mercenary, Shawna Forde 'Was Just a Pain,'" *Arizona Daily Star*, Oct. 11, 2009, azstarnet.com/news/local/border/article_2c4f9831-61b2-5dd5-84b4-232c 897c37f3.html.

237   **On May 15:** From the testimony of Ron Wedow, Feb. 1, 2011.

239   **Oin Oakstar and Albert:** See the testimony of Oin Oakstar in the trial of Shawna Forde, Jan. 28, 2011. See also David Ricker, "The 'Arivaca Rules' Were Broken on May 30, 2009," *Ricker's Radar Screen*, strega5742.blogspot.com/2011_01_01 _archive.html.

*Chapter 14*

This chapter was compiled from the testimony of Gina Gonzalez in the trials of Shawna Forde, Jason Bush, and Albert Gaxiola in 2011, with additional information from the testimony of Oin Oakstar on Jan. 28, 2011, and the confession of Jason Bush to Pima County detectives. See the testimony of Pima County detective Juan Carlos Navarro, March 23, 2011, in the trial of Jason Bush. See also Kim Smith, "At the Courthouse: Jason Bush Claims Gaxiola a Scary Guy," *Arizona Daily Star*, May 27, 2011, azstarnet.com /news/blogs/courthouse/at-the-courthouse-jason-bush-claims-gaxiola-a-scary-guy/article _c5459a06-88a3-11e0-b3fa-001cc4c03286.html. See also Patrick Oppmann, "Sheriff: Suspect in Arizona Border Slayings Confesses," CNN.com, July 17, 2009, articles.cnn.com /2009-07-17/justice/arizona.slaying.minutemen_1_shawna-forde-unmarked-police-car -deadly-home-invasion; and David Ricker, "Bush Confessed That He Shot Brisenia at Gunpoint," *Ricker's Radar Screen*, March 23, 2011, strega5742.blogspot.com/2011/03 /bush-confessed-that-he-shot-brisenia.html.

*Chapter 15*

252   **Knowing that Gina Gonzalez:** See Kim Smith, "Surprise Appearance," *Arizona Daily Star*, Sept. 27, 2010, azstarnet.com/news/blogs/courthouse/article_264d dfe8-ca95-11df-bc49-001cc4c002e0.html.

252   **Gina Gonzalez was there:** See Kim Smith, "Forde Backs Her Attorneys," *Arizona Daily Star*, Dec. 21, 2010, azstarnet.com/news/local/crime/article_de07d02d- 7c64-5aed-8e03-801288db0bd1.html.

252   **The bill had been largely written:** See George Talbot, "Kris Kobach, the Kansas Lawyer Behind Alabama's Immigration Law," *Alabama Press-Register*, Oct. 16, 2011, blog.al.com/live/2011/10/kris_kobach_the_kansas_lawyer_1.html. See also Kevin O'Leary, "Arizona's Tough New Law Against Illegal Immigrants," *Time*, April 16, 2010, www.time.com/time/nation/article/0,8599,1982268,00.html; and John Schwartz and Randal C. Archbold, "A Law Facing a Tough Road Through the Courts," *New York Times*, April 27, 2010, www.nytimes.com/2010/04 /28/us/28legal.html.

252   **and its chief sponsor:** For more on Pearce's history of ties to neo-Nazi figures, see Elise Foley, "Russell Pearce Distances Himself from J. T. Ready, Shootings in Gilbert, Arizona," *Huffington Post*, May 3, 2012, www.huffingtonpost.com/2012/05/03

/russell-pearce-jt-ready-gilbert-arizona-shootings-immigration_n_1474251.html,
and Stephen Lemons, "Russell Pearce Can't Shake His Ties to Neo-Nazi J. T.
Ready," *Phoenix New Times,* Aug. 23, 2012, www.phoenixnewtimes.com/2012
-08-23/news/russell-pearce-can-t-shake-ties-to-neo-nazi-j-t-ready.

253 **The fears about:** See Amanda Lee Meyers, "Killing Roils Immigration Debate:
Some Say Death Is Proof U.S. Must Do More to Secure Border," Associated Press,
April 9, 2010, www.msnbc.msn.com/id/36331490/ns/us_news-life/t/killing-roils
-immigration-debate.

253 **However, as the investigation proceeded:** See Brady McComb, "Focus in Krentz
Killing on Suspect in US," *Arizona Daily Star,* May 3, 2010, azstarnet.com
/news/local/border/article_35ef6e3a-5632-5e58-abe7-e7697ee2f0d5.html.

253 **Over a thousand people:** See Craig Harris, Alia Beard Rau, and Glen Creno, "Arizona Governor Signs Immigration Law; Foes Promise Fight," *Arizona Republic,*
April 24, 2010, www.azcentral.com/news/articles/2010/04/23/20100423arizona
-immigration-law-passed.html.

253 **There was an immediate:** See "Civil Rights Groups Fight Ariz. Immigration
Law," Associated Press, April 24, 2010, www.msnbc.msn.com/id/36735281/ns
/politics/#.UFYUQFEluSo; and Sophia Tareen, "Anger Over Arizona Immigration Law Drives U.S. Rallies," Associated Press, May 1, 2010, www.azcentral.com
/news/articles/2010/05/01/20100501national-immigration-protests.html.

253 **The Major League Baseball players' union:** See Kevin Baxter and Mike DiGio-
vanna, "Baseball Union Calls for Arizona Immigration Law to Be 'Repealed or
Modified,'" *Los Angeles Times,* May 1, 2010, articles.latimes.com/2010/may
/01/sports/la-sp-arizona-players-union-20100501.

254 **Phoenix Suns players:** See J. A. Adande, "Suns Using Jerseys to Send Message,"
ESPN.com, May 7, 2010, sports.espn.go.com/nba/playoffs/2010/columns/story
?columnist=adande_ja&page=Sarver-100504.

254 **A number of cities:** See Ethan Sacks, "Battle over Arizona's SB 1070: Oklahoma
Eyes Similar Immigration Law; City Councils Eye Boycotts," *New York Daily News,*
April 30, 2010, www.nydailynews.com/news/national/battle-arizona-sb-1070
-oklahoma-eyes-similar-immigration-law-city-councils-eye-boycotts-article-1.1699
48#ixzz26esNyEYc; also Alan Duke, "Los Angeles Approves Arizona Business Boycott," CNN.com, May 13, 2010, articles.cnn.com/2010-05-13/travel/los.angeles
.arizona.boycott_1_immigration-status-los-angeles-city-council-la-raza; and "Seattle
City Council Approves Arizona Boycott," Associated Press, May 17, 2010, seattle
times.com/html/nationworld/2011890438_apusarizonaboycottseattle.html.

254 **Tea Partiers got into the act:** See Randal C. Archibold, "Foes and Supporters of
New Immigration Law Gather in Arizona," *New York Times,* May 29, 2010,
www.nytimes.com/2010/05/30/us/30immig.html.

254 **Still, SB 1070 hovered:** See Erin Kelly, "Gabrielle Giffords, Jesse Kelly Race
All About Immigration," *Arizona Republic,* Oct. 8, 2010, www.azcentral.com
/arizonarepublic/news/articles/2010/10/08/20101008tucson-gabrielle-giffords
-jesse-kelly.html#ixzz26ew9boNk, and "Gabrielle Giffords Wins Re-Election
in Arizona," Associated Press, Nov. 5, 2010, www.azcentral.com/news/election
/azelections/articles/2010/11/05/20101105arizona-elections-gabrielle-giffords
-elected.html.

255 **Gabrielle Giffords was holding:** See "Arizona Congresswoman Giffords Shot;
Doctors 'Optimistic' About Recovery Chances," *Arizona Republic,* Jan. 8, 2011,

www.azcentral.com/news/articles/2011/01/08/20110108arizona-giffords-brk.html#ixzz26f0gXd3C, and Jessica Hopper, Kevin Dolak, and Lauren Sher, "Heroes of Tucson Shooting: 'Something Had to Be Done,'" ABC News, Jan. 10, 2011, abcnews.go.com/US/heroes-rep-gabrielle-giffords-shooting-tucson-arizona -subdued/story?id=12580345#.UFYg_1EluSo.

255    **The day after the shootings:** See Sandhya Somashekhar, "Sheriff Dupnik's Criticism of Political 'Vitriol' Resonates with Public," *Washington Post*, Jan. 9, 2011, voices.washingtonpost.com/44/2011/01/sheriff-dupniks-criticism-of-p.html.

255    **On Monday:** See Kim Smith, "Start of Arivaca-Killings Trial Delayed," *Arizona Daily Star*, Jan. 12, 2011, azstarnet.com/news/local/crime/article_b000e916-5368 -5fba-bd8b-1428057eb2db.html.

256    **More than a few people:** See Terry Greene Sterling, "Arizona's Other Shooting Horror," *Daily Beast*, Jan. 20, 2011, www.thedailybeast.com/articles/2011/01 /20/in-giffords-shadow-trial-of-arizona-minuteman-accused-of-killing-girl-begins .html.

256    **She talked to a CNN:** From the author's conversations with Greene Sterling.

256    **Opening arguments:** See Dave Ricker, "Forde's Trial for Murders of Arizona Father, Daughter Begins," *Herald* (Everett, WA), Jan. 26, 2011, www.heraldnet .com/article/20110126/NEWS01/701269808.

257    **But when Gina Gonzalez:** See Nicholas Riccardi, "Mother Describes Border Vigilante Killings in Arizona," *Los Angeles Times*, Jan. 25, 2011, articles.latimes.com /2011/jan/25/news/arizona-test, and Terry Greene Sterling, "The Minuteman Vigilante's Arizona Murder Trial," *Daily Beast*, Jan. 26, 2011, www.thedailybeast .com/articles/2011/01/26/minuteman-vigilantes-arizona-murder-trial-brisenia -flores-mother-testifies.html.

257    **Gonzalez said that it appeared:** See Dave Ricker, "Was Shawna Forde Wearing a Wig During the Arivaca Home Invasion?" *Ricker's Radar Screen*, Jan. 25, 2011, strega5742.blogspot.com/2011/01/was-shawna-forde-wearing-wig-during.html.

257    **Oin Oakstar testified:** See Dave Ricker, "The 'Arivaca Rules' Were Broken on May 30, 2009," *Ricker's Radar Screen*, Jan. 28, 2011, strega5742.blogspot.com /2011/01/arivaca-rules-were-broken-on-may-30.html, and Kim Smith, "Witness: Family Not On Hit List," *Arizona Daily Star*, Jan. 29, 2011, azstarnet.com/news /local/crime/article_de07d02d-7c64-5aed-8e03-801288db0bd1.html.

258    **The jury also heard:** See Dave Ricker, "FBI Informant Links Shawna Forde to Arivaca Activities," *Ricker's Radar Screen*, Feb. 1, 2011, strega5742.blogspot.com /2011/02/fbi-informant-links-shawna-forde-to.html.

258    **In December 2010:** See Smith, "Forde Backs Her Attorneys."

258    **On Tuesday, January 25:** See Dave Ricker, "Forde Supporter Enters Courtroom in Disguise," *Green Valley News and Sun*, Jan. 30, 2011, www.gvnews.com/news /forde-supporter-enters-courtroom-in-disguise/article_bdf9ef7c-2a7f-11e0-8abf -001cc4c03286.html, and Kim Smith, "Forde Murder Trial Comes to Halt as Witness Appears in Disguise," *Arizona Daily Star*, Jan. 27, 2011, azstarnet.com /news/local/crime/article_e9a7003a-2a4b-11e0-b26e-001cc4c002e0.html.

260    **It was clear that this theory:** See Kim Smith, "Forde Convicted in Killing of Arivaca Man, Daughter," *Arizona Daily Star*, Feb. 14, 2011, azstarnet.com/news /local/crime/article_6ae561fe-386c-11e0-9555-001cc4c002e0.html, and Dave Ricker, "A Pima County Superior Court Jury Has Returned Verdicts of Guilty on All Counts," *Ricker's Radar Screen*, Feb. 14, 2011, dsricker.wordpress.com

/2011/02/14/a-pima-county-superior-court-jury-has-returned-verdicts-of-guilty
-on-all-counts, and Dave Ricker, "Forde Is Now Eligible for the Death Penalty,"
*Ricker's Radar Screen*, Feb. 15, 2011, dsricker.wordpress.com/2011/02/15/forde
-is-now-eligible-for-the-death-penalty.

260 **One psychologist testified:** See Dave Ricker, "Forde Felt Remorse, According to
Testimony," *Green Valley News and Sun*, Feb. 17, 2011, www.gvnews.com/news
/forde-felt-remorse-according-to-testimony/article_7d94185e-3b0f-11e0-a3f1
-001cc4c03286.html.

260 **Another psychologist:** See Dave Ricker, "Forensic Neuropsychologist Testifies
That Forde Suffers from Brain Damage," *Ricker's Radar Screen*, Feb. 16, 2011,
strega5742.blogspot.com/2011/02/forensic-neuropsychologist-testifies.html.

260 **Jill Thorpe, in her closing:** See Dave Ricker, "No Decision Yet on Death Penalty
in Forde Case," *Herald* (Everett, WA), Feb. 19, 2011, www.heraldnet.com/article
/20110219/NEWS01/702199933.

261 **It went over:** See Dave Ricker, "Shawna Forde Has Been Sentenced to Death,"
*Ricker's Radar Screen*, Feb. 22, 2011, strega5742.blogspot.com/2011/02/shawna
-forde-has-been-sentenced-to.html.

261 **Having seen the outcome:** See Dave Ricker, "2nd Arivaca Trial Likely to Be
Quick," *Green Valley News and Sun*, March 21, 2011, www.gvnews.com/news/article
_352d8abe-53e2-11e0-8c58-001cc4c002e0.html, and Kim Smith, "Lawyer: No
Defense for Arivaca Suspect," *Arizona Daily Star*, March 16, 2011, azstarnet
.com/news/local/crime/article_532d6db0-7639-5166-b574-5b29545d73ef.html.

261 **it only took them fifteen minutes:** See Kim Smith, "Bush Guilty in Arivaca Double Slaying," *Arizona Daily Star*, March 26, 2011, azstarnet.com/news/local
/crime/article_65d8182a-8146-52c9-bc60-e36ce1a893f0.html.

261 **The defense team's work:** See Dave Ricker, "Bush Jury Has Been Taught to Hate
Him During the First Two Phases of the Trial," *Ricker's Radar Screen*, March 31,
2011, strega5742.blogspot.com/2011/03/bush-jury-has-been-taught-to-hate-him
.html.

262 **Dr. B. Robert Crago:** See Dave Ricker, "Jason Bush Is a Paranoid Schizophrenic,"
*Ricker's Radar Screen*, March 31, 2011, rickersradarscreen.blogspot.com2011/03/jason
-bush-is-paranoid-schizophrenic.html, and Kim Smith, "Bush's Brain Is 'Unusually
Deviant,' Psychologist Says," *Arizona Daily Star*, April 1, 2011, azstarnet.com/news
/local/crime/article_f583957d-e168-5432-a7fa-2d2e7f47ae0b.html.

262 **It was interesting testimony:** See Dave Ricker, "Bush Jury Sentences Him to
Death for the Murders of Raul and Brisenia Flores," *Ricker's Radar Screen*, April 6,
2011, rickersradarscreen.blogspot.com/2011/04/bush-jury-sentences-him-to-death
-for.html.

263 **Gina Moraga, for instance:** See Dave Ricker, "Gaxiola's Girlfriend Testifies About
the Night of the Murders," *Ricker's Radar Screen*, June 17, 2011, strega5742
.blogspot.com/2011/06/gaxiolas-girlfriend-testifies-about.html.

263 **But after closing arguments:** See Kim Smith, "Third Person Convicted in Killing
of Arivaca Man, Daughter," *Arizona Daily Star*, July 1, 2011, azstarnet.com/news
/local/crime/article_618c7a50-a439-11e0-bc8e-001cc4c002e0.html, and Dave
Ricker, "Guilty Verdicts on All Charges in Gaxiola Double Murder Trial," *Ricker's
Radar Screen*, July 1, 2011, strega5742.blogspot.com/2011/07/guilty-verdicts-on
-all-charges-in.html.

264   **In closing arguments, Lansdale:** See Dave Ricker, "Gaxiola's Fate Is Now in the Hands of the Jury," *Ricker's Radar Screen*, July 13, 2011, strega5742.blogspot .com/2011/07/gaxiolas-fate-is-now-in-hands-of-jury.html.

264   **It seemed to have an effect:** See Dave Ricker, "Gaxiola Escapes Death Penalty," *Green Valley News and Sun*, July 30, 2011, www.gvnews.com/news/gaxiola-escapes -death-penalty/article_ad2a1bdc-bafc-11e0-b9cb-001cc4c03286.html, and Dave Ricker, "Gaxiola Sentenced Natural Life in Prison," *Ricker's Radar Screen*, Aug. 15, 2011, strega5742.blogspot.com/2011/08/gaxiola-sentenced-natural-life-in.html.

264   **Shawna Forde gave only:** See Terry Greene Sterling, "Minuteman Murderer, Shawna Forde, Speaks," *Daily Beast*, Feb. 14, 2011, www.thedailybeast.com/articles /2011/02/15/shawna-forde-guilty-of-murder-exclusive-interview-with-arizona -minuteman.html.

*Chapter 16*

267   **When Shawna and her cohorts:** See Jonathan Cooper, "Arizona Killings Highlight Risk of Fringe Activists," Associated Press, June 20, 2009, www.statesman.com /news/content/news/stories/nation/2009/06/20/0620immigkillings.html.

268   **Similarly, Jim Gilchrist:** See Tim Steller, "Woman Held in Two Slayings an Outcast, Activists Say," *Arizona Daily Star*, June 28, 2009, azstarnet.com/news /local/article_b25e446d-02c9-5ee5-afa8-e89d558a2130.html.

268   **Simcox's MCDC spokesperson:** See Carmen Mercer, "Alleged Home Invasion Murder Suspects Criminals, Not 'Minutemen,'" *Borderfire Report*, June 19, 2009, www.freerepublic.com/focus/f-news/2276001/posts.

268   **One of these was Al Garza:** See Gaiutra Bahadur, "Nativist Militias Get a Tea-Party Makeover," *Nation*, Oct. 28, 2010, www.theinvestigativefund.org/inves tigations/immigrationandlabor/1420/nativist_militias_get_a_tea-party_make over.

269   **A study conducted:** See Devin Burghart and Leonard Zeskind, *Beyond FAIR: The Decline of the Established Anti-Immigrant Organizations and the Rise of the Nativist Tea Party*, Jan. 17, 2012, www.irehr.org/issue-areas/tea-party-nationalism/beyond -fair-report.

269   **First came the finger pointing:** See Sonia Schnerr, "Accused Nativist Murderer Finds Few Allies in Movement," *Hatewatch*, June 23, 2009, www.splcenter.org /blog/2009/06/23/accused-nativist-murderer-finds-few-allies-in-movement/.

270   **The precipitating event:** See Linda Bentley, "Minutemen Return to the Border—This Time Locked and Loaded," *Sonoran News*, March 17, 2010, www.sonoran news.com/archives/2010/100317/ftpgMinuteman.html.

270   **Mercer said she received:** See Linda Bentley, "Minuteman Civil Defense Corps Cancels Muster, Announces Dissolution," *Sonoran News*, March 31, 2010, www.sonorannews.com/archives/2010/100331/ftpgMinuteman.html.

270   **"I'm afraid that:** See "MCDC President Carmen Mercer's March 22 Email: 'We Are Dissolving the Corporation,'" *Arizona Daily Star*, March 23, 2010, azstarnet .com/article_27caa730-36d8-11df-b071-001cc4c03286.html.

270   **She told KOLD-TV:** See J. D. Wallace, "Border Watch Group Breaks Up," KOLD-TV, March 24, 2010, www.tucsonnewsnow.com/Global/story.asp?S=122 00645.

270  **Chris Simcox, who:** See "Minuteman Founder Fights Back Against Allegations," Associated Press, July 9, 2010, www.abc15.com/dpp/news/region_phoenix_metro /central_phoenix/minuteman-founder-fights-back-against-allegations.

271  **Jim Gilchrist remains adamant:** See Gilchrist's comment on the author's reportage at www.alternet.org/comments/story/156128/how_the_brutal_murders_of_a _little_girl_and_her_father_doomed_the_xenophobic_minuteman_movement #comment-599879535.

271  **Local Minuteman organizations:** See Daniel Newhauser and Dan Shearer, "Suspect in Murders Headed Minuteman Group," *Green Valley News and Sun*, June 12, 2009, www.gvnews.com/news/suspect-in-murders-headed-minuteman-group /article_3acf9cbf-1144-5739-8871-5250939570f8.html, and Daniel Newhauser, "Minutemen Regroup After Shootings," *Green Valley News and Sun*, June 20, 2009, www.gvnews.com/news/article_deaf7954-b631-5dbf-8c16-b97394cfaff1 .html.

271  **At least one of the new border-watch outfits:** See "J. T. Ready, Neo-Nazi and Anti-Immigrant Extremist," Anti-Defamation League profile, May 3, 2012, www.adl.org/main_Extremism/jason_t._ready_backgrounder.htm, and Nick R. Martin, "Border Vigilante Identified as Gunman in Arizona Massacre," *Talking Points Memo*, May 12, 2012, tpmmuckraker.talkingpointsmemo.com/2012/05 /jt_ready_arizona_massacre_border.php.

271  **Another splinter border-watch group:** See Tim Steller, "Group to Set Up Shop as a Paramilitary 'Company,'" *Arizona Daily Star*, April 21, 2010, azstarnet .com/news/local/border/article_e55b07ab-5bff-5a1e-a7c0-8aa36273a030.html, and Rick Anderson, "Minuteman Shawna Forde: Poster Girl for Arizona Immigration Law Battle," *Seattle Weekly*, April 27, 2010, blogs.seattleweekly.com/daily weekly/2010/04/minuteman_shawna_forde_poster.php.

272  **"The Forde killings":** See Burghart and Zeskind, *Beyond FAIR*.

272  **Glenn Spencer explained:** See David Holthouse, "Minuteman to Tea Party: A Grassroots Rebranding," Media Matters for America, May 24, 2011, mediamatters .org/blog/2011/05/24/minuteman-to-tea-party-a-grassroots-rebranding/179373.

273  **It was a mutual affair:** See Ed Pilkington, "America's Toughest Sheriff Rallies Tea Party Troops Against Illegal Immigrants," *Guardian* (London), Oct. 20, 2010, www.guardian.co.uk/world/2010/oct/20/tea-party-express-vegas-immigration.

273  **One of the movement's leading:** See Ellie-Xolo, "Understanding Anti-Immigrant America: Mobilizing the Tea Party," *Beyond the Choir*, April 28, 2011, www .beyondthechoir.org/diary/72/understanding-antiimmigrant-america-mobilizing -the-tea-party.

273  **Meanwhile, despite his years:** See Stephen Lemons, "Glenn Spencer, Nativist Anti-Semite, Lectures State Senate Border Security Committee," *Phoenix New Times*, March 1, 2012, blogs.phoenixnewtimes.com/bastard/2012/03/glenn _spencer_nativist_anti-se.php.

274  **Many Latinos were left wondering:** See Terry Greene Sterling, "The Minuteman Vigilante's Arizona Murder Trial," *Daily Beast*, Jan. 26, 2011, www.thedaily beast.com/articles/2011/01/26/minuteman-vigilantes-arizona-murder-trial -brisenia-flores-mother-testifies.html.

274  **When Bill O'Reilly:** See David Neiwert, "Finally! O'Reilly and Guests Tackle the Shawna Forde Case: Of Course, They Lie and Misinform from Beginning to

End," *Crooks and Liars*, Feb. 16, 2011, crooksandliars.com/david-neiwert/finally
-oreilly-and-guests-tackle-sh.

275  **When Shawna was convicted:** See Joe Coscarelli, "Justice for Brisenia Flores, Murdered Arizona Child: Shawna Forde Found Guilty," *Village Voice*, Feb. 14, 2011,
blogs.villagevoice.com/runninscared/2011/02/brisenia_flores_verdict.php.

276  **Carlos Galindo:** See Sterling, "The Minuteman Vigilante's."

276  **Kat Rodriguez:** See Tim Vanderpool, "Bloody Aftermath," *Tucson Weekly*, Aug.
25, 2011, www.tucsonweekly.com/tucson/bloody-aftermath/Content?oid=3140
878.

279  **Psychologists recognize:** See "Psychiatric Disorders: Personality Disorders," *Diagnostic and Statistical Manual of Mental Disorders*, 4th ed., allpsych.com/disorders
/personality/index.html.

280  **Dr. Robert Hare:** See "Hare Psychopathy Checklist," *Encyclopedia of Mental Disorders*, www.minddisorders.com/Flu-Inv/Hare-Psychopathy-Checklist.html, as
well as "Without Conscience" on Hare's own website (www.hare.org).

281  **As Dave Cullen explored:** See Dave Cullen, *Columbine* (New York: Twelve, 2009).

283  **As James Aho explored:** See James A. Aho, *This Thing of Darkness: A Sociology of
the Enemy* (Seattle: University of Washington Press, 1994), 26.

284  **Ervin Staub observed:** See Ervin Staub, *The Roots of Evil: The Origins of Genocide
and Other Group Violence* (Cambridge: Cambridge University Press, 1992), 25.

# INDEX